# SEA COMBAT

## FROM WORLD WAR I TO THE PRESENT DAY

ROBERT JACKSON

**amber**
BOOKS

First published as *Sea Warfare* in 2008

Copyright © 2008 Amber Books Ltd

This edition published in 2016

Published by
Amber Books Ltd
74–77 White Lion Street
London
N1 9PF
www.amberbooks.co.uk
Appstore: itunes.com/apps/amberbooksltd
Facebook: www.facebook.com/amberbooks
Twitter: @amberbooks

ISBN: 978-1-78274-335-4

Project Editor: Sarah Uttridge
Design: Anthony Cohen
Picture Research: Terry Forshaw

Printed in China

# Contents

# The Naval Arms Race
## 1900–1913

**In the last two decades of the nineteenth century, supremacy on the high seas rested with Great Britain. New ideas and inventions were emerging so quickly that a new vessel could be obsolete before it was launched. The problem was exacerbated by Britain's own naval policy, which was described as a 'two-power standard' and which kept the Royal Navy equal in numbers to any two foreign navies. In simple terms, warships were being built at too fast a rate to incorporate the latest technological advances.**

In 1889, the two-power standard was modified when the Naval Defence Act came into force, decreeing that the Royal Navy must be capable of matching the world's second and third largest navies. The result was a new phase of shipbuilding, and at its forefront was the 'Royal Sovereign' class of battleship. Apart from the *Royal Sovereign* herself, there were seven vessels in the class: the *Empress of India*, *Ramillies*, *Repulse*, *Resolution*, *Revenge*, *Royal Oak* and *Hood*. A highly successful design, the Royal Sovereigns were faster than contemporary battleships. Their main armament of four 343mm (13.5in) guns was mounted in twin barbettes; they also carried 10 152mm (6in) guns, 16 6-pounder guns and seven 457mm (18in) torpedo tubes. The exception was the *Hood*, whose main armament was mounted in turrets.

In the 1890s, the Royal Navy, closely followed by other major naval powers, developed a new standard type of battleship. Later known as the

The Russian pre-dreadnought battleship *Retvisan* was built in the United States and was similar to the Maine class. She was captured by the Japanese in 1905 and served under their flag as the *Hizen*.

The dreadnought HMS *Royal Sovereign*. Laid down in 1914, she had a long and distinguished career. In 1944 she was loaned to the Soviet Navy, serving for five years as the *Archangelsk*.

'pre-dreadnought', the first was the *Renown* of 1892, but it was the 'Majestic' class of 1893–94 that served as the pattern for battleship design for the next decade. Displacing 15,129 tonnes (14,890 tons), they were armed with four 305mm (12in) guns, 16 76mm (3in) guns and 12 47mm (1.85in) guns, as well as five 457mm (18in) torpedo tubes. In all, 42 pre-dreadnoughts were built for the Royal Navy up to 1904.

It was not these large warships that brought about the revolution in naval affairs in the nineteenth century, however. By the 1880s, all the major navies had invested in a much smaller instrument of war – the self-propelled torpedo. The most recent models had a range of about 500m (1640ft) at a speed of 18 knots, and the original compressed-air method of propulsion was gradually giving way to electric motors. Capital ships and specially designed torpedo boats both deployed torpedoes from tubes or launch cradles. These had to be launched from close range, meaning that torpedo boats were vulnerable to defensive fire, but an exercise conducted by the Royal Navy in 1885 showed that despite all the attacking craft being 'sunk', some of the practice torpedoes got through. The solution was to counter the torpedo boats with gun-armed 'catchers' that could be deployed from capital ships, and by the 1890s these had evolved into larger, independent vessels called

## DESTROYER PRODUCTION

By 1895, 36 destroyers had been launched. They were capable of 27 knots, but the torpedo boats then being built could reach 24, so the speed margin was slender. They were succeeded by an improved class, armed with two torpedo tubes mounted on the centreline, one 12-pounder and five 6-pounder guns; they were capable of 30 knots. Sixty-eight were built, their displacement gradually increasing from 285 tonnes (280 tons) to 365 tonnes (360 tons).

The pre-dreadnought battleship HMS *Formidable* pictured just before her launch in November 1898. She was torpedoed and sunk by the *U24* in November 1915.

HM Submarine No. 1 was built to the Irish-American J.P. Holland's design, but with the invaluable addition of a periscope designed by Captain R. Bacon, the Royal Navy's first Inspecting Captain of Submarines.

'torpedo boat destroyers', designed to accompany larger units. In 1892–93, the first six ships, now simply called 'destroyers', were ordered for service with the Royal Navy.

Torpedo boats and destroyers were not, however, to retain their pre-eminence as torpedo carriers. By the turn of the century, the French and American navies possessed small numbers of submarines, and the British Admiralty could no longer afford to ignore this new invention. Previously it had shown a complete lack of interest in the submarine, one admiral describing it as 'a despicable, un-English weapon of war'. The 1901–02 Naval Estimates made provision for the building of five improved boats of the 'Holland' type (an American design) for evaluation. The first five boats to be commissioned were built under licence by Vickers at Barrow-in-Furness.

collision with a passenger liner and sank with all hands. In all, 13 'A' class boats were built, with 11 of the 'B' class and 38 of the 'C' class. From now on, the submarine was to become a principal weapon of war, and its development would not be allowed to stagnate. In the Royal Navy, one of its principal advocates was Admiral Sir John Fisher, who was appointed First Sea Lord on 21 October 1904, the 99th anniversary of Lord Nelson's victory over the combined French and Spanish fleet at Trafalgar.

## THE 'SUPER-BATTLESHIP'

'Jackie' Fisher, as he was known throughout the service, was a comparative rarity in Queen Victoria's Navy: a senior officer with a firm grasp of scientific and technological principles. By the time he became First Sea Lord at the age of 58, Fisher had already put a lot of thought into the concept of a battleship armed with a maximum number of 254mm (10in) guns at the expense of secondary armament, and within weeks of his appointment in 1904 he convened a committee to design a battleship armed with the maximum number of 305mm (12in) guns, this calibre being preferred by the Admiralty. The committee was also to study a second type of warship, which would carry a battery of 305mm (12in) guns and have a speed of about 45km/h (28mph). This vessel was to be a hybrid, a cross between a heavy cruiser and a battleship – a battlecruiser, in other words.

One of the Royal Navy's 'A' class submarines seen here during construction. Twelve of these boats were in service at the outbreak of World War I.

In March 1904, all five boats of the 'A' class, as they were now called, took part in a simulated attack on the cruiser *Juno* off Portsmouth. It was successful, but *A1* was involved in a

Admiral 'Jackie' Fisher was a rare type of naval officer, having a sound grasp of science and technology. His thinking led to the development of the dreadnought.

The 'super-battleship' concept took shape rapidly, its development spurred on by the acceleration of the international naval arms race, and a prototype was laid down by Portsmouth Dockyard in October 1905. It was constructed in great secrecy and record time, the vessel being ready for initial sea trials a year and a day later. The name given to the formidable new ship was *Dreadnought*.

Some months earlier, on the other side of the world, events had dramatically demonstrated what could happen to a naval force encountering an opponent with superior tactics, training and equipment. Marking the start of the era of modern naval warfare, the episode began on 27 May 1905, when Vice-Admiral Rozhdestvensky led the 2nd Pacific Squadron of the Russian Baltic Fleet through the Straits of Tsushima, at the entrance to the Sea of Japan. The voyage from the home base had taken

> From now on, the submarine was to become a principal weapon of war, and its development would not be allowed to stagnate.

seven months and was mounted in response to a damaging Japanese attack on the Russian Naval Base at Port Arthur the previous year.

With eight battleships, three armoured cruisers, six light cruisers and 10 destroyers, the Russians appeared to have an advantage over the four battleships, seven armoured cruisers and seven light cruisers at the disposal of the Japanese commander, Admiral Heihachiro Togo. Togo's ships had a speed advantage over their adversaries of 3 knots, however, enabling them to manoeuvre and open fire at whatever range they chose, and whereas Russian tactics and training had been influenced by the French, the Japanese had been trained and equipped by the British. There was no comparison.

## NAVAL ACTION AT TSUSHIMA

The Russian fleet was steaming in line ahead, with its four most modern battleships – the *Kniaz Suvorov* (Admiral Rozhdestvensky's flagship), the *Imperator Alexander III*, the *Borodino* and the *Orel* – in the van. These were

followed by four older battleships, the *Oslyabya, Sisoi Velkiki, Navarin* and *Imperator Nikolai I,* the latter with two cruisers ahead and three coastal defence armour-clad vessels astern. The remaining cruisers brought up the rear.

Togo waited until the whole of the Baltic Fleet was in sight before making his move, turning his ships to port so that they were sailing almost parallel to the enemy. The Russians opened up with a fierce but inaccurate fire from a range of 5950m (6500yds), which did not prevent Togo's ships from concentrating their fire on the Russian flagship. The *Suvarov* was soon on fire and she gradually drifted out of line, shrouded in smoke. She continued to fight on, even after she had sustained a torpedo hit and Rozhdestvensky had been badly wounded; he was later taken prisoner by the Japanese after being evacuated

from the stricken battleship. The *Suvarov*'s end came at 1920, when Japanese torpedo boats scored two or three more hits on her. She capsized and sank with the loss of all remaining personnel on board, amounting to 928 officers and men.

HMS *Dreadnought,* seen here just after her launch in 1906, was the first battleship to feature a main armament of a single calibre. She served with the Grand Fleet throughout her career.

**The Battle of Tsushima proved a decisive victory for Japanese naval power, and reflected the training the Japanese Navy had received from Great Britain.**

Soon afterwards, it was the turn of the *Borodino*, whose captain had been trying to lead the warships out of the trap sprung by the Japanese. She was hit, set on fire and blew up, her magazine exploding. She sank with only one survivor from her 830-strong crew. By then, the *Alexander III* had capsized, after taking numerous hits from 305mm (12in) shells; there were no survivors from her crew of 823. Her demise left the *Orel* as the only modern Russian battleship still afloat. Accompanied by other survivors, and attacked constantly during the night, she surrendered the next morning.

In the second division, one of the older battleships, the *Oslabya*, had been heavily attacked by Japanese armoured cruisers, taking her first hits only 15 minutes after the start of the battle. She too sank, with the loss of 515 crew. Of the others, the *Navarin*

was damaged by gunfire, then sunk by torpedo attack with the loss of 619 lives; the *Sisoi Veliki* was scuttled by her own crew and went down with 50 dead; and the *Nikolai I* was captured after being damaged by gunfire. Taken into the Japanese Navy and renamed *Iki*, she was sunk as a target ship in 1915. The only ships to escape destruction or capture were those that sought refuge in neutral ports, where they were interned. The Japanese had gained a victory as great as Nelson's at Trafalgar, a century earlier. It would be more than half a century into the future before a Russian battle fleet once more ventured out of coastal waters into the world's oceans.

## SEA TRIALS

Back in Britain, HMS *Dreadnought* proceeded with her sea trials. Revolutionary, she was armed with 10 305mm (12in) guns, two on each of five turrets centrally placed on the ship. (In fact, only eight guns in the first of these ships could be fully brought to bear, but this was remedied

in its successors.) Once the concept of the dreadnought had been proven, construction of this revolutionary type of battleship proceeded rapidly, at the rate of three or four a year. By 1913, 31 were either in service or due to be commissioned.

Fisher's critics claimed that his introduction of the dreadnoughts made the great mass of British battleships obsolete and vulnerable, but his supporters realized that secondary armament was now of minor importance. The increasing range of torpedoes was making close-in actions dangerous. If a battleship could engage its adversary at extremely long range, its 152mm (6in) and 230mm (9in) guns were irrelevant. Gunnery experts realized that at the immense ranges now possible for 305mm (12in) guns – 12,810m (14,000yds) or more – only the biggest guns would count. Effective ranging depended on the firing of salvoes of shells and of a greater number in the salvo. A full salvo from a dreadnought meant that

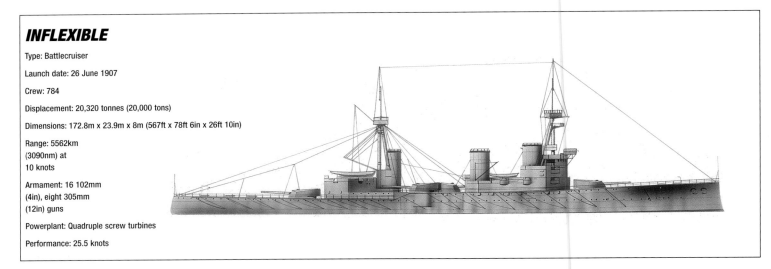

## INFLEXIBLE

Type: Battlecruiser

Launch date: 26 June 1907

Crew: 784

Displacement: 20,320 tonnes (20,000 tons)

Dimensions: 172.8m x 23.9m x 8m (567ft x 78ft 6in x 26ft 10in)

Range: 5562km (3090nm) at 10 knots

Armament: 16 102mm (4in), eight 305mm (12in) guns

Powerplant: Quadruple screw turbines

Performance: 25.5 knots

3.85 tonnes (3.79 tons) of high explosive was on its way to the enemy over 14km (8nm) away.

The other revolutionary warship concept, the battlecruiser, was nearly equal in armament to the new battleships but very much swifter. It was a ship that could cruise ahead and scout for the main battle fleet, and capable of overwhelming any conventional cruiser. The concept arose from the fact that existing armoured cruisers had evolved into ships so large and expensive that they had reached the end of their development potential.

The first ship of the new class was HMS *Inflexible*, completed in 1908. She carried eight 305mm (12in) guns and had a speed of 26 knots. Her firepower was four-fifths that of a dreadnought, but a lot had to be sacrificed in the cause of speed. While the indicated horsepower of the *Dreadnought* was 18,000, that of the *Inflexible* was 41,000, so that a large hull was needed to accommodate the necessary 31 boilers. With a reduced armament, and protection sacrificed for speed, the battlecruisers were inevitably more vulnerable, as later events were to show.

### THE RISE OF GERMANY

In continental Europe, the naval power of Germany was rising rapidly, and would soon become the main rival to Britain. Kaiser Wilhelm II, the German emperor, admired British naval technology, and under the energetic leadership of his naval Chief of Staff, Admiral von Tirpitz, several Navy Acts were passed with the intention of creating a modern naval force.

Between 1889 and 1904, Tirpitz ordered the construction of 20 battleships, the first being four ships of the 'Brandenburg' class. These displaced 10,174 tonnes (10,013 tons) and were armed with four 280mm (11in) guns mounted in centre-line turrets. They were followed by five each of the 'Kaiser Friedrich III', 'Mecklenburg', 'Braunschweig' and 'Deutschland' classes. Tirpitz's simple argument was that the possession of a powerful battle fleet was a matter of national prestige; Germany was becoming a major industrial nation, and needed a navy to match her economic capability. The fact that he was starting a naval arms race was of little consequence.

In 1908, the Germans passed yet another Navy Act, making provision for an increase in the number of heavy warships. The 'large cruisers' that were the outcome of the Navy Act of 1900 were now reclassified as battlecruisers, so that the combined

Admiral von Tirpitz, the Kaiser's naval Chief of Staff, was instrumental in developing a modern German navy and applying the latest technology to warship development.

battleship and battlecruiser strength envisaged for the Imperial German Navy over the coming years rose to 58 ships. The 'Helgoland' class of 1908 (*Helgoland, Oldenburg, Ostfriesland* and *Thüringen*) were enlarged 'Nassau' types with 305mm (12in) guns. The only German dreadnoughts with three funnels, they were marginally faster than the Nassau – 20 knots against 19

– and displaced 23,166 tonnes (22,800 tons). The complement was 1100. These were followed by the ships of the Kaiser class (*Friedrich der Grosse, Kaiser, Kaiserin, König Albert* and *Prinzregent Luitpold*), which were the first German battleships with a super-firing turret, mounted aft and turbine engines (built by Parsons of Tyneside!). The *Friedrich der Grosse*, launched in 1912, was designated flagship of the High Seas Fleet, and was to remain as such until 1917.

## RIVAL NAVIES

In 1909, the French government, shocked to realize that the French Navy had dropped to fifth place worldwide, began a belated attempt to rebuild the fleet. The Navy's already slender resources had suffered a blow in March 1907, when the pre-dreadnought battleship *Ièna* was destroyed by an internal explosion in the after magazine while the ship was in dry dock at Toulon, the result of cordite overheating. An even worse explosion was to destroy another pre-

---

### FIRST GERMAN DREADNOUGHTS

Germany's first dreadnought-type battleships were four vessels of the 'Nassau' class, initiated in 1906. Shorter and wider than the British dreadnought, and less heavily armed, they were nevertheless well protected and carried a main armament of 12 280mm (11in) guns, with a secondary armament of 12 150mm (5.9in). The disposition of the main armament, however, was poor, broadside fire being restricted by the positioning of two turrets on each side amidships and one each fore and aft. Ships in this class were the *Nassau, Posen, Rheinland* and *Westfalen*.

---

dreadnought, the *Liberté*, in September 1911. The two disasters together claimed 322 lives.

As a result of the reconstruction programme, France embarked on the building of its first four dreadnoughts, the *Courbet, France, Jean Bart* and *Paris*, in 1910–11. These vessels had six turrets, mounting 12 305mm (12in) guns, one turret being on each beam amidships. Only the first two were completed before the outbreak of World War I.

Italy's first dreadnought was the 19,813-tonne (19,500-ton) *Dante*

*Alighieri*, the first battleship to have its main armament – 12 305mm (12in) guns, in this case – positioned in triple turrets, all mounted on the centreline to achieve maximum broadside fire. Launched in 1910, the *Dante Alighieri* became the flagship of the Italian fleet in the Adriatic, although it did not see active service. It was followed by the 'Cavour' class (*Conte di Cavour, Giulio*

**The German cruiser *Emden* was a threat to British commerce in the Indian Ocean during the early months of World War I. She was sunk by the HMAS *Sydney* in November 1914.**

and new vessels, including five monitors, were surreptitiously built using funds provided for repairing old ones. It was not until 1883 that legislation was passed for the building of a 'New Navy', its first vessels to be based on foreign designs. What may best be described as the 'monitor mentality' was still strong, however, and the first of the new vessels, known as the 'Indiana' class, were completed as coast defence battleships with low freeboard.

In 1898, war broke out between the United States and Spain, the *casus belli* being an explosion that destroyed the US battleship *Maine* at Havana. The outdated nature of the Spanish Navy's equipment was brought home forcefully when the Pacific Squadron of old protected cruisers and gunboats was destroyed at the Battle of Manila Bay. A squadron of new armoured cruisers was sent to the Caribbean, only to be sunk by waiting US warships. The loss of the war, its fleet and its colonies ended Spain's interest in naval construction for several years until 1909, when construction of a new battleship, the *España*, was begun.

The US Navy, on the other hand, now included seven modern armoured warships, and the action at Manila Bay established the United States as a maritime power. The navy's

*Cesare* and *Leonardo da Vinci*), all displacing 23,485 tonnes (23,088 tons) and armed with 13 305mm (12in) guns. Two of these ships, the *Cavour* and *Cesare*, were to be totally reconstructed and uprated in the years between the two world wars. The last Italian dreadnoughts to be laid down before the outbreak of war were the *Andrea Doria* and *Caio Duilio*, which were modified 'Cavours' with a 152mm (6in) secondary armament. These, too, were to be completely reconstructed in the 1930s.

**American dreadnought-type battleships were easily identified by their bulky cage masts, which proved to be susceptible to damage in heavy weather and which were soon replaced.**

In the United States, support for the building of new, modern warships had been slow in gathering. Despite the success of the Union's ironclad warships in the Civil War, interest in the navy waned after the conflict ended, and monitors for coastal defence were thought to be the only necessary warships. No money was made available for building new ships,

The outdated nature of the Spanish Navy's equipment was brought home forcefully when the Pacific Squadron of old protected cruisers and gunboats was destroyed.

SEA WARFARE

prestige soared and a succession of new vessels was authorized. Under the presidency of Theodore Roosevelt, who had been Assistant Secretary of the Navy at the time of the Spanish-American war, the Panama Canal was begun, and in 1907 the 'Great White

**Dramatic photograph of an American battleship firing its main armament. US warships were the first to be designed with super-firing turrets, a feature that was copied by all other navies.**

Fleet' of 16 American battleships was sent around the world as a statement of American sea power. Despite the fact that these vessels were already obsolescent as a result of the appearance of the dreadnought two years earlier, the cruise was a success.

## PROPULSION SYSTEM
The first dreadnoughts built in the United States were the *Michigan* and *South Carolina*. Although laid down

after HMS *Dreadnought*, they were, in fact, the first battleships to be designed with an armament made up exclusively of big guns (eight 305mm/12in) and super-firing turrets, features that were subsequently copied by all other nations. Their propulsion system of two-screw vertical triple-expansion engines left a lot to be desired, producing a maximum speed of barely 17 knots. The next class, the 'Delaware' and 'Dakota', suffered similarly,

although they were generally a more successful class with a secondary armament of larger calibre. Other US dreadnoughts laid down before the outbreak of war in Europe were the *Florida, Utah, Arkansas, Wyoming, New York, Texas, Nevada, Oklahoma, Arizona* and *Pennsylvania,* all recognizable by their bulky cage masts.

All the American dreadnoughts mounted a main armament of 10 or 12 355mm (14in) guns, endowing

them with a degree of firepower that the Japanese, on the other side of the Pacific, felt compelled to match. Victory over the Russian fleet at Tsushima had given the Japanese naval ascendancy in the Pacific and they were determined to retain it. The Imperial Japanese Navy's first true dreadnoughts were the *Kawachi* and *Settsu,* laid down in 1910; they carried a main armament of 12 305mm (12in) guns in six twin turrets, one each fore and aft and two on each beam. They were strongly armoured and could make 21 knots. But it was in the design of the 'Kongo' class battle-cruisers of 1910–11, the *Haruna, Hiei, Kirishima* and *Kongo,* that Japan excelled herself.

Designed by Sir G.R. Thurston, *Kongo,* the class leader, was built by Vickers in England (the last capital ship to be built outside Japan). An improved version of the British 'Lion'

**The Japanese battlecruiser *Kongo* pictured at her launch in 1912. She was built by Vickers in the United Kingdom.**

class battlecruiser, it was the first of its kind to surpass a battleship in size. The 'Kongo' class, displacing 27,940 tonnes (27,500 tons) mounted eight 355mm (14in) and 16 152mm (6in) guns and could make 30 knots. This class could carry a complement of 1437 and outclassed all other contemporary ships.

In the years before the outbreak of World War I, the mighty dreadnoughts and battlecruisers were visible manifestations of sea power. And yet behind the scenes, virtually unnoticed, events had been unfolding that would make all of them obsolete within 50 years.

## SEAPLANE TENDERS
On 4 May 1912, Commander C.R. Samson, a pilot with the newly formed Naval Wing of the Royal Flying Corps – later to become the Royal Naval Air Service – provided one of the highlights of the Fleet Review at Weymouth, by flying a Short S27 biplane from the foredeck of the pre-dreadnought battleship HMS *Hibernia*

as she steamed into wind at 10 knots. It was the first time a British aircraft had taken off from a moving ship.

A year later, the old cruiser HMS *Hermes* was commissioned as the headquarters ship for the Naval Wing. She was fitted with a track-way on her forecastle, from which a Caudron amphibian made several trial flights during 1913, and was later equipped with three Short S41 floatplanes. In July 1913, aircraft were used for the first time by the Royal Navy in conjunction with surface vessels during a series of fleet manoeuvres,

As the war clouds gathered in 1914, it was the submarine that was seen, rightly, as the principal threat to domination of the seas.

and aircraft from the *Hermes* experimented with wireless telegraphy. In the summer of 1913, the Admiralty purchased a second seaplane tender, a 7518-tonne (7400-ton) merchant vessel then

under construction at Blyth, Northumberland. She was commissioned in 1914 and honoured with a very famous name: *Ark Royal*. Three more seaplane tenders, the *Empress, Engadine* and *Riviera* – all

## GERMANY'S SUBMARINES

**Although the Germans got off to a slow start in their submarine construction programme before World War I, the vessels were well engineered and used double hulls and twin screws from the start. German engineers refused to employ petrol engines in the early boats, preferring to use smellier but safer kerosene fuel. In 1908, suitable diesel engines were designed, and these were installed in the four boats of the U19 class and used exclusively thereafter.**

The *E.20* was laid down in November 1914 and commissioned on 30 August the following year. She was torpedoed in the Sea of Marmara by the German U-boat *UB-14* on 6 November 1915.

cross-Channel packets – were requisitioned and converted in the summer of 1914, in order to develop this new form of conducting naval warfare. No one could have envisaged, then, that naval aviation would one day become a potent striking force that would decide the outcome of battles, and hound capital ships to their destruction.

As the war clouds gathered in 1914 it was the submarine that was seen, rightly, as the principal threat to domination of the seas. The Royal Navy's submarine fleet had come a long way in the decade since Admiral Fisher's appointment as First Sea Lord. One of his first acts had been to launch a massive submarine construction programme, and by 1910 the Royal Navy's submarine flotillas had a total of 12 'A' class boats, 11 'Bs', and 37 'Cs', all progressive developments of the original Holland design. A new class, the 'D', was also laid down. Designed for overseas service, the 'D' class boats were 50.2m (164ft 6in) long and displaced 503 tonnes (495 tons) on the surface. They were the first British twin-screw submarines and, for surface running, petrol engines were abandoned in favour of heavy oil (diesel) engines. Although beset by teething problems, they were safer than petrol engines and gave off fewer noxious fumes, significantly improving the crew's working environment. During exercises in 1910, the crew of the submarine D.1 proved a point when, despite trouble with one engine, they took their boat from Portsmouth to the west coast of Scotland and remained on station off an 'enemy' anchorage for three days, claiming 39 successful dummy torpedo attacks on two cruisers.

The 'E' class, a straightforward development of the 'D', was just beginning to enter service at the outbreak of World War I. Displacing 677 tonnes (667 tons) surfaced, the 'E' class boats carried a crew of 30 and were armed with five torpedo tubes, two in the bow, one in the stern and two amidships – an arrangement which meant that the boat had to turn through no more than 45° to engage any target. In all, 55 'E' class submarines were built between 1913 and 1916; they were to become the mainstay of the Royal Navy's submarine fleet throughout World War I, operating in every theatre of the war, and their exploits were to become legendary.

It was Germany's submarines, however, that would strike the first blow in the conflict, proving how deadly submarines could be to unprotected surface shipping. Strangely enough, the German Naval Staff at the turn of the century had failed to appreciate the potential of the submarine, and the first submarines built in Germany were three 'Karp' class vessels ordered by the Imperial Russian Navy in 1904. Germany's first practical submarine, *U1*, was not completed until 1906. She was, however, one of the most successful and reliable of the period. Her two kerosene engines developed 400hp, as did her electric motors. She had an underwater range of 80km (43nm). Commissioned in December 1906, she was used for experimental and training purposes.

# World War I
## The North Sea and Atlantic 1914–1918

**Although the hostilities of World War I were eventually to encompass virtually the entire globe, the naval war was decided by the fleets of Great Britain and Germany. From the outset, the task facing the Royal Navy was prodigious: to protect the shores of Britain from the threat of invasion; to guard the maritime convoys that were vital to the country's survival; and to secure the English Channel area, thereby ensuring that the flow of supplies and personnel to the Western Front was not interrupted.**

For their part, the Germans, whose fleet was greatly outnumbered, feared a major attack on their principal naval base at Wilhelmshaven by the British Grand Fleet, based at Scapa Flow in the Orkneys. They were soon left in no doubt that the Royal Navy intended to follow an aggressive policy: on 28 August 1914, a force of British warships from Harwich swept into the Heligoland Bight, achieving complete surprise. Destroyers of the 1st and 2nd Flotillas, led by the cruisers *Arethusa* and *Fearless*, engaged in a furious battle with German destroyers and cruisers. The *Arethusa* was disabled in the action, but the German cruiser SMS (*Sein Majestäts Schiff*) *Mainz* and the destroyer leader *V.187* were sunk. Later, five British battlecruisers under Admiral Sir David Beatty came up in support, sinking the cruisers *Köln* and *Ariadne*. Two other German light cruisers and three destroyers were damaged.

**HMS *Canopus* was a pre-dreadnought battleship of the Royal Navy, built at Portsmouth Dockyard and laid down on 4 January 1897, launched 21 June 1898 and completed in December 1899.**

The German light cruiser SMS *Leipzig* was a victim of the Falklands battle. She was sunk by gunfire from the British cruisers *Cornwall* and *Glasgow* on 8 December 1914.

Any elation at this British victory soon dissipated. On 22 September 1914, the British armoured cruisers *Aboukir*, *Crecy* and *Hogue*, each of 12,192 tonnes (12,000 tons), were sunk in rapid succession some 48km (30 miles) southwest of Ijmuiden, Holland, by the German submarine *U-9*, under Lt Cdr Otto Weddigen. Some 60 officers and 1400 men were lost. A few weeks later came news of a major British defeat in the South Atlantic.

## BATTLE AT CORONEL

On the outbreak of war, a German naval squadron under Vice-Admiral Graf von Spee, which had been deployed to Tsingtao in China, set out on the voyage home. It comprised the armoured cruisers *Scharnhorst* and *Gneisenau* and the light cruisers *Leipzig*, *Dresden* and *Nürnberg*. By the end of October 1914, having eluded a Japanese battlecruiser squadron, it was off the west coast of South America, ready to enter the Atlantic. All that stood in its path was a hastily assembled British naval squadron comprising the armoured cruisers *Good Hope* and *Monmouth*, the light cruiser *Glasgow*, the auxiliary vessel *Otranto* and the old pre-dreadnought battleship *Canopus*.

On 1 November 1914, *Good Hope*, *Monmouth*, *Glasgow* and *Otranto* sighted Admiral von Spee's squadron off Coronel, on the coast of Chile. Hopelessly outgunned and outranged, *Good Hope* and *Monmouth* were soon on fire, and in the evening *Good Hope* exploded and sank. *Monmouth* went down soon afterwards, whereupon *Glasgow* broke off her own attack and

steamed away to join *Canopus*. Both ships headed for the Falkland Islands, where they were ordered to defend the wireless station, coal and oil stores.

In London, Admiral Sir John Fisher, anticipating von Spee's plan, despatched his Chief of Staff, Vice-Admiral Sir Frederick Doveton Sturdee, southwards with the battlecruisers *Invincible* and *Inflexible*. At the same time, orders were issued to the British warships on station off the central and southern American coasts – the cruisers *Cornwall*, *Kent*, *Caernarvon* and *Bristol* – to make for the Falklands with all speed and join the *Glasgow* and *Canopus*. Making contact with the enemy early in December, Sturdee used the same tactics against von Spee that the latter had used against Admiral Cradock, using his superior speed and gunnery

## DANGEROUS SITUATION

**The destruction of Admiral Cradock's squadron created a dangerous situation in the South Atlantic. Von Spee was now in a position to paralyze shipping in South American waters; he might even cross the Atlantic to attack the South African mercantile routes. Instead, after his ships had been replenished and his crews rested off Chile, he made plans to attack the Falklands and seize the facilities there. The islands, with their precious stocks of coal and oil, could then be used as a base for further operations.**

to good effect. At 1617, after a running fight lasting some three hours, the *Scharnhorst* went down by the stern. The two British battlecruisers now turned their joint fire on the *Gneisenau*, which continued to fight on, battered into a blazing wreck, until she too sank at about 1800. About 200 survivors were rescued from her 800-strong crew; all

860 of the crew aboard the ill-fated *Scharnhorst* perished.

The British cruisers, meanwhile, had caught up with the fleeing enemy ships. In the ensuing battle, the

Launched in 1901, HMS *Good Hope* was a 'Drake' class armoured cruiser. Badly hit and set on fire during the naval engagement off Coronel on 1 November 1914, she exploded and sank.

Battle damage: holes punched in the side of the British cruiser HMS *Kent* by German gunfire during the battle of the Falkland Islands, 1914.

*Leipzig* was sunk by *Glasgow* and *Cornwall*, while *Nürnburg* was sunk by HMS *Kent* after a five-hour pursuit. Captain Allen of the *Kent* had exhorted his engineers and stokers to achieve the impossible; the *Kent* was sister ship to the *Monmouth*, which *Nürnberg* had sunk, leaving her survivors to drown. The men of the *Kent* were eager for revenge, and they achieved it by feeding their ship's fires with anything that would burn. For a time, they pushed the old cruiser to go a knot or two faster than she had ever done in the days of her prime, until their efforts brought her guns within range of the enemy. Of von Spee's Pacific Squadron, only the *Dresden* escaped, but her days were also numbered. On 14 March 1915,

the cruisers *Kent* and *Glasgow* caught up with her off Juan Fernandez, and she was scuttled by her crew after receiving crippling damage.

## HIT-AND-RUN

The news of Sturdee's victory off the Falklands was soon tempered by the shock of an event that occurred only a week later. The Germans, hoping to lure part of the British fleet into an ambush, decided to carry out a series of hit-and-run attacks on British east coast towns. The British Admiralty was aware of these plans, because its experts were in possession of the German naval codes. Nevertheless, it came as a surprise when, in the early morning of 16 December 1914, the German battlecruisers *Seydlitz*, *Moltke* and *Blücher* bombarded West Hartlepool, while the *Derfflinger* and *von der Tann* shelled Scarborough and Whitby, killing 127 civilians and injuring 567. The *Moltke* and *Blücher* were hit by shore batteries, but all the raiders escaped in the mist.

The Royal Navy's 1st Battlecruiser Squadron under Admiral Beatty and the 2nd Battle Squadron under Admiral Warrender were already at sea to intercept the attackers, who were sighted on their approach to the coast by British destroyers. At 0445, the latter were engaged by the German cruiser *Hamburg* and escorting light forces, which disabled the destroyer HMS *Hardy* and damaged *Ambuscade* and *Lynx*. During the forenoon, the German battlecruisers were returning

from their attack. They passed some miles astern of the 2nd Battle Squadron, which sighted the German ships and turned to close with them, only to be thwarted by bad weather and ambiguous signals from Beatty, which led to the light cruisers breaking off the chase.

> The Germans, hoping to lure part of the British fleet into an ambush, decided to carry out a series of hit-and-run attacks on British east coast towns.

A golden opportunity was therefore lost, and another was squandered on 24 January 1915, when the Germans set out on an offensive sweep of the southeastern Dogger Bank. Beatty's 1st Battlecruiser Squadron, comprising his flagship HMS *Lion*, together with the *Princess Royal, Tiger,* *New Zealand* and *Invincible,* sighted the German battlecruisers *Seydlitz, Moltke* and *Derfflinger,* together with the armoured cruiser *Blücher,* six light cruisers and a number of destroyers, steering westward. On sighting the British, the German warships turned and made for home, but were

The cruiser HMS *Kent* was on the China Station from 1906 to 1913. In 1914, after a refit, she took part in the Falklands battle, sinking the German light cruiser *Nürnberg* on 8 December.

pursued at 28 knots and brought to battle at 0900, east of the Dogger Bank. HMS *Lion* led the British line, but dropped out after she was hit, Beatty transferring his flag to the *Princess Royal*. During the action, the *Blücher* was sunk and the *Derfflinger* and *Seydlitz* seriously damaged. Great punishment might have been inflicted on the Germans had Beatty, thinking he had spotted a submarine's periscope,

**The north-east coastal town of Hartlepool under attack by German battlecruisers in December 1914. The shelling of towns on the east coast came as a profound shock to the British people.**

not altered course, enabling the enemy to escape.

## JUTLAND

It was not until 31 May 1916 that the British and German main battle fleets met in combat, in the sea area to the west of Denmark. The British forces comprised the Battlecruiser Fleet (1st and 2nd Squadrons), with HMS *Lion* (commanded by Admiral Beatty), *Princess Royal* (Admiral Brock), *Tiger, Queen Mary, New Zealand* (Admiral Pakenham) and *Indefatigable,*

supported by the 5th Battle Squadron with the battleships HMS *Barham* (Admiral Evan-Thomas), *Warspite, Valiant* and *Malaya,* in advance of the main battle fleet under the command of Admiral Lord Jellicoe.

At 1420, British light forces scouting ahead of the Battlecruiser Fleet sighted German ships to the east-southeast and signalled the information to Admiral Beatty, who turned his ships south-southeast to intercept. Fifteen minutes later, Beatty altered course again, making for heavy

smoke that could be seen to the east-northeast. The seaplane carrier *Engadine* launched a scouting aircraft – the first time that such a reconnaissance mission was flown in action.

At 1531, Beatty sighted the German Battlecruiser Squadron, comprising SMS *Lützow* (under Admiral Hipper), *Derfflinger, Seydlitz, Moltke* and *von der Tann*, steering east-northeast. The British battlescruisers closed in on the German squadron from 21,000m (23,000yds) at 25 knots, with the 5th

Battle Squadron, 9150m (10,000yds) astern, coming up fast. At 1548, both battlecruiser forces opened fire almost simultaneously at about 17,000m (18,500yds), the range being reduced to 14,600m (16,000yds) over the next 10 minutes.

At 1606, HMS *Indefatigable* was hit by a salvo from the *von der Tann*. The battlecruiser's magazine exploded and a second salvo tore into the wreck, completing her destruction. She sank in minutes, with the loss of 1017 lives.

At 1608, the British 5th Battle Squadron joined the action at a range of 17,380–18,300m (19,000–20,000yds), opening accurate fire on the German Light Cruiser Squadron and driving the enemy away to the east. Some 20 minutes later, there was a repeat of the earlier disaster when the 'Lion' class battlecruiser *Queen Mary* took a direct hit from the German battlecruiser *Derfflinger* and blew up. There were only nine survivors from her crew of 1266.

At 1642, Admirable Beatty sighted the German High Seas Fleet under Admiral Scheer (whose flagship was the *Friedrich der Grosse*). Led by the 3rd

Squadron, it was steering northwards. In succession, the British ships turned 16 points to starboard and the German battlecruisers followed suit, taking station ahead to cover the High Seas Fleet. At the time of this manoeuvre, Admiral Beatty's ships and Admiral Jellicoe's Main Battle Fleet were over 80km (43nm) apart and closing at about 20 knots. By 1645, the 5th Battle Squadron's 'Queen Elizabeth' class battleships were in a position to engage the enemy, the *Barham* and *Valiant* supporting the Battlecruiser Fleet while the *Warspite* and *Malaya* engaged the German 1st and 3rd High Seas Squadrons at 17,380m (19,000yds). *Barham* was soon scoring hits on the *Seydlitz*, which was further damaged in a torpedo attack by British destroyers, while the *Valiant* was finding the range of the German *Moltke*.

At 1800, the Main Fleet under Admiral Jellicoe (flagship *Iron Duke*) arrived, the main force having

**Map showing the extent of incursions into the North Sea by German battlecruiser forces in 1914–15. Inset: The general area of the Battle of Jutland, 1916.**

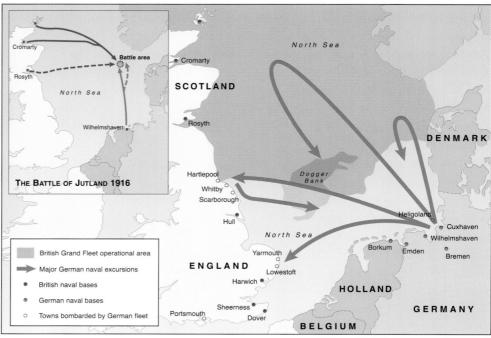

Admiral Sir David Beatty commanded the British battlecruiser forces at the Battle of Jutland. His ships suffered serious losses, accounting for most of the British casualties during the engagement.

The German battlecruiser *Seydlitz* suffered more damage than any other surviving capital ship at Jutland, but managed to limp back to harbour with her forecastle awash.

maintained a 'fleet speed' of 20 knots since 1600 on a southeasterly course, with the Battle Fleet in division lines ahead. Having received Admiral Beatty's report giving the position of the High Seas Fleet, Admiral Jellicoe signalled the Battle Fleet to form lines of battle. At this point, the Germans inflicted more casualties, the battleship *Friedrich der Grosse* sinking the armoured cruiser *Defence* (Rear-Admiral Sir Robert Arbuthnot) with the loss of 893 lives and damaging another armoured cruiser, HMS *Warrior*, which shortly after 1805 had crossed *Lion*'s bows from port to starboard in order to finish off *Wiesbaden*, one of the German light cruisers under their fire. The disabled *Warrior* passed astern of the 5th Battle Squadron (turning to port to form astern of the 6th Division) just as Warspite's helm jammed. This mishap compelled the latter to continue her turn and brought her under heavy fire, but enabled *Warrior* to draw clear. Unfortunately, *Warrior* foundered

under tow the next day. Meanwhile, the 3rd Battlecruiser Squadron, comprising HMS *Invincible* (Rear-Admiral Hood), HMS *Inflexible* and HMS *Indomitable*, was detached by Admiral Jellicoe at 1600 in support of Beatty. It came up from the eastward, where with *Canterbury* and *Chester* it had already engaged the German light cruiser screen in a sharp encounter in which the destroyer *Shark* was sunk. At 1600, and upon sighting *Lion*, Admiral Hood took station ahead of the Battlecruiser *Fleet* and engaged the German battlecruisers at 7870m (8600yds). Soon after 1830, *Invincible*, battered by repeated salvoes, notably from *Derfflinger*, blew up and sank, killing her crew of 1026 officers and men. Even so, Admiral Hood's arrival in a commanding position in relation to the German fleet caused the latter to make a large turn to starboard, his squadron probably being mistaken for the British Battle Fleet.

At 1831, HMS *Iron Duke* engaged the leading ship of the *König* squadron at 11,000m (12,000yds). On the starboard wing, HMS *Marlborough* (Adm Burney) had

opened fire earlier, at 1817, on a ship of the 'Kaiser' class from 11,900m (13,000yds). Within two minutes, the Battle Fleet, having increased speed to 17 knots, was fully committed to the battle, although its gunner was impeded by mist and smoke. At the head of the German battlecruiser line, *Lützow* hauled away badly damaged, and *Derfflinger* ceased firing. A few minutes later, the British fleet altered course to the south by divisions, in order to close the German fleet. The *Lützow* was now well ablaze and listing

**HMS *Indefatigable* was hit by a salvo from the *von der Tann*. The battlecruiser's magazine exploded and a second salvo tore into the wreck, completing her destruction.**

heavily. She was later abandoned and sunk by a German destroyer.

At 1900, Admiral Jellicoe ordered the 2nd Battle Squadron to take station ahead of *Iron Duke*, and the

1st Battle Squadron to form up astern. During the next 30 minutes, the British ships held their targets under intermittent but effective fire at ranges varying from 13,700m

## STRATEGIC VICTORY

The Germans had meted out far more punishment than they had taken. They had lost one battleship (the *Pommern*, sunk during the night in a torpedo attack), a battlecruiser, four cruisers and five destroyers, but the British had lost three battlecruisers, three cruisers and eight destroyers. British fatal casualties numbered 6097, against the German total of 2551. Even so, the Royal Navy had won a strategic victory at Jutland: the next time the German High Seas Fleet left Wilhelmshaven in full strength would be in November 1918, after the German surrender, when it sailed into internment at Scapa Flow.

Admiral Sir John Jellicoe commanded the British naval forces at Jutland. Although it proved decisive in favour of the British, it was technically a German victory, as they suffered fewer losses.

(15,000yds) in the van to 7800m (8500yds) in the rear. Some 15 minutes later, Admiral Scheer, drawing off his main force, ordered his already battered battlecruisers to 'close the enemy', but to all intents and purposes the main Battle of Jutland was over. At 1937, the German battlecruisers broke off the action.

As dawn broke over the North Sea on 1 June, following sporadic night actions in which more ships were lost, the fleets dispersed. By noon, both were returning to their respective bases. Jellicoe had intended to pursue the High Seas Fleet to its destruction. That he failed to do so was due to a combination of circumstances: vague reports, the failure of some of his captains to exercise initiative, and the failure of the British Admiralty to relay certain vital intelligence on the movements of the enemy warships.

### U-BOAT MENACE

With the German surface fleet penned up in Wilhelmshaven, the principal threat to the security of Britain's maritime commerce was the U-boat. As World War I progressed, the German Navy's submarine service became increasingly competent and its boats technologically more advanced, until by the end of 1916 it had become the navy's main offensive arm. Germany's large, long-range 'cruiser' U-boats were a revelation to the Allies, and had they been available in large numbers before the end of hostilities they would have posed a

serious threat to the survival of Britain, dependent as she was on supplies from overseas.

Germany was quick to recognize the potential of large, cargo-carrying submarines as a means of beating the blockade imposed on her ports by the Royal Navy, and in 1917 they converted two 'U-151' class submarines, *U-151* and *U-155*, as long-

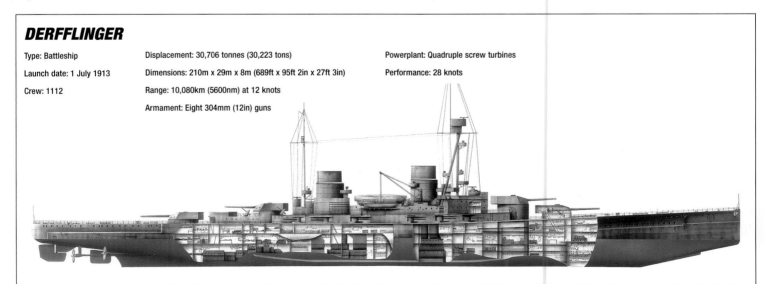

**DERFFLINGER**

Type: Battleship
Launch date: 1 July 1913
Crew: 1112

Displacement: 30,706 tonnes (30,223 tons)
Dimensions: 210m x 29m x 8m (689ft x 95ft 2in x 27ft 3in)
Range: 10,080km (5600nm) at 12 knots
Armament: Eight 304mm (12in) guns

Powerplant: Quadruple screw turbines
Performance: 28 knots

**Admiral Reinhard Scheer commanded the German High Seas Fleet from January 1916. The Battle of Jutland convinced him that the Royal Navy could not be defeated in a surface action.**

range cargo-carrying vessels. One, the *Deutschland,* made two commercial runs to the United States before that

country entered the war, bringing an end to the venture. It was then converted back to naval use along with her sister vessel, *Oldenburg.* The boats were reclassified as submarine cruisers and more were laid down, including *U-139, U-140* and *U-141.* The first two were among the very few German

submarines to be given names, probably because of their intended role as surface combatants; the *U-139* became the *Kapitänleutnant Schweiger,* and the *U-140 Kapitänleutnant Weddingen.* After their conversion, the two boats formed two of a class of seven (*U-151* to *U-157*).

In 1917, the threat to British commerce from the U-boats was dire, and in April that year they sank 907,000 tonnes (893,000 tons) of shipping, of which 564,019 tonnes (555,110 tons) were British vessels. The British developed counter-measures, attacking and neutralizing the main U-boat bases on the Channel coast at Ostend and Zeebrugge, and building the so-called Dover Barrage, consisting of heavily armed ships moored in lines across the Channel with minefields, nets and other obstacles between them. The barrage was a success; between 1 January and 18 August 1918, 30 German submarines were destroyed as they tried to pass it.

The principal weapon against the U-boat, however, was the convoy system. In 1917, following America's declaration of war on Germany, US warships began to share the task of convoy escort with their British counterparts. America's first act of war, on 13 April 1917, was to deploy six destroyers to European waters, and on the last day of the year four US battleships led by the USS *New York* (the flagship of Admiral Rodman), arrived in British waters and were incorporated in the Grand Fleet as the 6th Battle Squadron.

## NAVAL AIR POWER
By this time, aircraft and airships were playing an expanding role in the battle against the U-boats. The development of naval air power was an important step forward in 1917. At this time, the Royal Navy was a long

## FURIOUS

| | | |
|---|---|---|
| Type: Aircraft carrier | Displacement: 22,758 tonnes (22,400 tons) | Powerplant: Quadruple screw turbines |
| Launch date: 15 August 1915 | Dimensions: 239.6m x 27.4m x 7.3m (786ft 4in x 90ft x 24ft) | Performance: 30 knots |
| Crew: 1218 | Surface range: 5929km (3200nm) at 19 knots | |
| | Armament: Six 102mm (4in) guns, 36 aircraft | |

> At this time, the Royal Navy was a long way ahead of the rest of the world in the development of vessels that could truly be described as aircaft carriers.

way ahead of the rest of the world in the development of vessels that could truly be described as aircraft carriers – in other words, fitted with flight decks from which aircraft were able to operate. The first such ship was the light battlecruiser HMS *Furious*, laid down shortly after the outbreak of war. Launched on 15 August 1916, she was fitted initially with a flight deck forward of her superstructure, but was eventually completed with a continuous flight deck and hangar accommodation for 14 Sopwith One-and-a-Half Strutters and two Sopwith Pups (replaced in early 1918 by Sopwith Camels). She was also fitted with workshops, electrically operated lifts from her hangar to the flight deck and a primitive form of arrester gear, comprising strong rope nets suspended from cross pieces.

On 17 July 1918, two flights of Sopwith Camels led by Captain W.D. Jackson and Captain B.A. Smart, took off from the *Furious* to attack the Zeppelin sheds at Tondern. All six aircraft, each of which carried two 22kg (50lb) bombs, made successful attacks. Two sheds and an ammunition dump were hit and

**A Sopwith Pup being hoisted from the hangar of the aircraft carrier HMS *Furious*. On 2 August 1917, Squadron Commander Edwin Dunning successfully landed a Pup on HMS *Furious*.**

set on fire, and Zeppelins *L.54* and *L.60* were destroyed. Two British pilots regained the carrier; three more landed in Denmark in bad weather, and the other crashed in the sea and was drowned.

A similarly equipped vessel, HMS *Cavendish*, was commissioned in October 1918 and renamed HMS *Vindictive*, but her operational career was limited to a brief foray in support of the Allied Intervention Force in North Russia and the Baltic in 1918–20. The most important development was centred on three new carriers, all fitted with unbroken flight decks: the 11,025-tonne (10,850-ton) HMS *Hermes*, HMS *Argus* and HMS *Eagle*. Of the three, only HMS *Argus* joined the fleet before the end of hostilities.

When war broke out in August 1914, two powerful German warships, the battlecruiser *Goeben* and the cruiser *Breslau*, were operating in the Mediterranean. *Goeben* was one of two ships of the 'Moltke' class, which

formed the second group of battlecruiser built for the rapidly expanding Imperial German Navy. With the outbreak of war, the two warships were pursued across the Mediterranean by the British battlecruisers *Indomitable* and *Idefatigable*. They succeeded in out-running their pursuers and put into the Turkish port of Constantinople (Istanbul), and both ships were transferred to the Turkish Navy. *Goeben* was renamed *Yavuz Sultan Selim* on 16 August 1914.

In this theatre, the principal area of operations was the Dardanelles. Turkey had come out on the side of the Central Powers (Germany and Austria) and her troops were pressing the Russians hard in the Caucasus. In an attempt to relieve the pressure, an Anglo-French combined operation was mounted. Its aims were to force a passage of the Dardanelles – the winding, treacherous 64km (40-mile) stretch of water leading from the Aegean to the Sea of Marmara – and

> **Without military support ashore, it was clear that further attempts to force a passage of the Dardanelles would meet with failure.**

to land an expeditionary force before Constantinople, the assumption being that such a show of strength would quickly force Turkey out of the war.

The Turks, however, were ready to confront such a plan. With German help, they mined the waters and installed powerful shore batteries to cover the minefields, so that any attempt to sweep them could be met with devastating gunfire. Before the mines could be swept, the forts therefore had to be neutralized, and this could be achieved only by naval gunfire. A powerful Anglo-French naval force was assembled, comprising 14 pre-dreadnought battleships (four of them French), the battlecruiser *Inflexible* and the new dreadnought *Queen Elizabeth*.

The bombardment of the forts at the entrance to the Dardanelles began on 19 February 1915, with aircraft from the seaplane carrier *Ark Royal* acting as spotters. The forts

were shattered, enabling trawlers to sweep the first 6.4km (4 miles) of the straits, and on 26 February the pre-dreadnoughts *Albion*, *Majestic* and *Vengeance* proceeded to the limit of the swept area to bombard fort Dardanus. The bombardment continued throughout March, all the battleships being committed, including the *Queen Elizabeth*, whose 380mm (15in) guns were powerful enough to hit the vulnerable reverse faces of the fortifications by shooting right across the peninsula with the help of spotting from the air.

Despite the weight of firepower progress was slow, and minesweeping operations were thwarted by powerful searchlights and accurate enemy gunfire. In an attempt to break the deadlock, a maximum effort involving three squadrons of warships was mounted on 18 March 1915. It ended in disaster, the *Irresistible*, *Ocean* and the French *Bouvet* being mined and

sunk while *Inflexible* and the French *Gaulois* were damaged. The British losses were made good by the deployment to the theatre of the pre-dreadnoughts *Queen* and *Implacable*.

Without military support ashore, it was clear that further attempts to force a passage of the Dardanelles would meet with failure. Consequently April 1915 saw the beginning of the disastrous Gallipoli campaign, with Allied forces landing on the peninsula in what was then the largest opposed amphibious invasion in history. Poorly planned and badly executed, the venture was doomed from the start. Allied warships continued to support the ground forces until the latter were evacuated in January 1916, having suffered appalling attrition through enemy action and disease. The Royal Navy lost three more pre-dreadnoughts in the course of the campaign: the battleship *Goliath* was torpedoed by the Turkish destroyer *Muavenet* in May 1915, at a cost of 750 lives, and the *Triumph* and *Majestic* were torpedoed by the German submarine *U-21* in the same month, at a cost of 73 and 40 lives respectively.

### BEN-MY-CHREE

One Royal Navy vessel that made an everlasting name for herself in the

## QUEEN ELIZABETH

| | | |
|---|---|---|
| **Type:** Battleship | **Displacement:** 33,548 tonnes (33,020 tons) | **Armament:** Eight 380mm (15in), 16 (152mm) guns |
| **Launch date:** 16 October 1913 | **Dimensions:** 196.8m x 27.6m x 10m (646ft x 90ft 6in x 30ft) | **Powerplant:** Quadruple screw turbines |
| **Crew:** 951 | **Surface range:** 8100km (4500nm) at 10 knots | **Performance:** 23 knots |

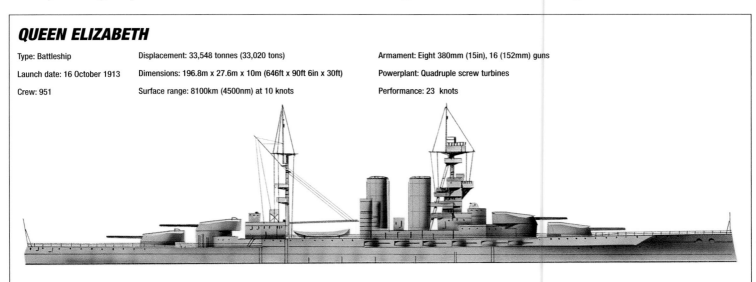

Above: The landings in the Dardanelles were poorly planned and badly executed. Allied intelligence had seriously underestimated the extent of the enemy minefields in the area.

The Allied landings at Gallipoli, 1915. One reason for this failing was that the Allies did not see the need to get their forces off the beaches quickly once the initial landings had been made.

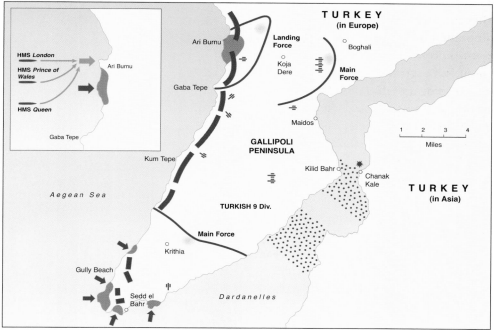

Dardanelles was the seaplane carrier *Ben-my-Chree*. Arriving on 12 June 1915, she carried two Short seaplanes, modified to carry torpedoes, and these scored some successes against enemy transports. On 12 August, Flight Commander C.H.K. Edmonds took off from the Gulf of Xeros and flew over the Bulair Peninsula into the straits, where he sighted an enemy transport. Descending to within 6m (20ft) of the water, he launched his torpedo from 100m (328ft) and scored a direct hit. Five days later, he torpedoed another transport and left her in flames.

On the same day, the pilot of another Short had just landed on the water with a misfiring engine when he saw an enemy tug a few hundred yards away. He launched his torpedo while taxiing and had the satisfaction of seeing the vessel blow up and sink. The *Ben-my-Chree* subsequently operated in the Eastern Mediterranean, the Red Sea and the Indian Ocean, until she was sunk by enemy gunfire off Castellorizo in Asia Minor.

Apart from the Dardanelles campaign, observation aircraft of the Royal Naval Air Service also served in Africa. In July 1915, three Short Type 827 seaplanes arrived in Mombasa aboard the armed liner *Laconia* to assist the British monitors *Severn* and *Mersey* in their efforts to force the German cruiser *Königsberg* out of her refuge 11km (7 miles) up the Rufiji

River in Tanganyika. One of the seaplanes, flown by Flight Lieutenant J.T. Cull, spotted for the monitors' guns during the final action. The aircraft was hit and crashed in the river, but Cull and his observer were picked up safely by the *Mersey*.

## ADRIATIC, BLACK SEA AND BALTIC OPERATIONS

In contrast to other theatres, naval operations in the Adriatic were desultory. When Italy entered the war in 1915, her fleet included six dreadnoughts, with four more under construction. Despite the possession of this fairly potent force, the Italian battle fleet achieved little during the war, its commanders failing to use their warships in an offensive fashion. Instead, they were preoccupied with defensive measures, moving the main operating base to Taranto, where it was safe from Austrian air attack.

As for Austria, its navy was undergoing a period of transformation at the outbreak of war. New ships were being built at an accelerated rate, but development was constantly hindered by lack of funds. During this period, the navy had two main supporters: the Archduke Franz Ferdinand, and the navy commander Admiral Montecuccoli, who took it upon himself to authorize the construction of new warships before government approval had been obtained. Apart from some large-scale fleet manoeuvres at the beginning, the war in the Adriatic involved some action by destroyers and patrol craft, although extensive use of aircraft was made by the Austro-Hungarians.

In the Black Sea, the former *Goeben* – which, despite her new Turkish name, retained her German crew and remained under German control throughout the war – was very active. On 29 October 1914, she bombarded Sevastopol, sinking a Russian

minelayer, and in November she was badly damaged by Russian warships off the Crimea, with 115 of her crew killed. In the course of her career, she fought several actions with Russian battleships, notably with the *Imperatritsa Ekaterina II* in January 1916. On 20 January 1920, she sank

The German light cruiser *Magdeburg* ran aground in fog in the Baltic in August 1914. She was boarded and destroyed by the Russians.

the British monitors *Raglan* and *M28* in Mudros harbour. She bore a charmed life, surviving shell hits and mine damage, and was formally

handed over to the Turkish Navy in November 1918. She was not decommissioned until 1954. Her consort, *Breslau*, was less fortunate. Incorporated into the Turkish Navy as the *Midilli*, she sank after striking five mines during a sortie against Imbros Island.

From the outset, the Russians placed much reliance on mining operations. On paper, their Order of Battle in the Baltic comprised four battleships, four cruisers, six submarines, and more than 60 destroyers and torpedo boats, but the shadow of the defeat at Tsushima 10 years earlier still hung over them and they never attempted to seize any initiative. They rarely showed any tactical skill even on the few occasions when they caught German warships at a disadvantage, and their attempts to interfere with essential iron-ore traffic from Sweden were ineffectual. Observers noted that the conning-tower of a Russian submarine would

A former Isle of Man steam packet, the seaplane carrier *Ben-my-Chree* became a familiar sight throughout the Mediterranean. She was set on fire by Turkish artillery in 1916, blew up and sank.

often break surface after a torpedo attack, a sure sign that the commander had inadequate control over the trim of his boat.

In the summer of 1915, at the request of the Russian government, a few British submarines were sent to the Baltic. The *E.9* in particular, under Lt Cdr Max Horton, achieved huge success, sinking a destroyer and the armoured cruiser *Prinz Adalbert* as well as a number of merchant vessels.

## SPIRITED OPERATIONS

Oddly enough, some of the most spirited naval operations in the Baltic

Naval operations in the Adriatic were desultory. When Italy entered the war in 1915, her fleet included six dreadnoughts, with four more under construction.

## BREAKING THE GERMAN CODE

**In the Baltic, naval affairs were dominated by the Germans, although there were occasions when the Russians made considerable contributions to the Allied war effort. One such occurred in September 1914, when the cruiser *Magdeburg*, operating at the entrance to the Gulf of Finland, was wrecked off the island of Odensholm. The body of one of her officers was picked up by the Russians, and on it were found signal books, ciphers and minutely squared maps of the North Sea and Heligoland Bight. The Russians set about breaking the code and passed on the resulting information to their naval allies, to whom it was of inestimable value.**

were conducted after the Armistice of November 1918. In the summer of 1919, a Royal Navy task force entered the Baltic to operate in defence of the state of Estonia. The primary task of the British naval force was to keep the Russian Baltic Fleet penned up in its base at Kronstadt, at the eastern end of the Gulf of Finland. A Royal Air

*The British submarine E.11 returning from a war patrol in the Aegean. The 'E' class submarines were excellent boats, and saw considerable action in the Mediterranean and Baltic.*

Force contingent commanded by Squadron Leader D.G. Donald and equipped with a miscellany of aircraft that included Sopwith Camels and Short Seaplanes, was transported to the area by the aircraft carriers *Vindictive* and *Argus* and placed ashore in rudimentary airstrips.

During their early operations, the RAF aircraft were employed mainly on reconnaissance and anti-submarine patrols from their principal base at Biorko. However, on 30 July 1919, the force commander, Admiral Cowan,

decided to mount an attack on Kronstadt to pre-empt a possible Russian naval sortie against his ships. A mixed force of 11 aircraft carried out the raid, dropping 10 112lb (50kg) and six 65lb (29kg) bombs on the depot ship *Pamyat Azova* and a neighbouring dry dock. The crews reported five hits and two large fires started. All the aircraft returned safely.

During August 1919, eight daylight and two night bombing raids were carried out in addition to routine patrols. Then, on the night of 17/18 August, all available aircraft – now reduced to eight – mounted a diversionary raid in conjunction with a daring and successful torpedo attack by Royal Navy coastal motor boats (CMBs) on the Russian Fleet in Kronstadt. There was, at that time, a detachment of two 12m (40ft) Coastal Motor Boats (CMBs) based at Terrioki, a village near the Finnish border about 48km (30 miles) east of Biorko. Under the command of Lieutenant Augustus Agar, its task was

to run British agents across Petrograd Bay. The CMBs were admirably suited to the job; quite apart from their small size, which enabled them to slip past the Bolshevik forts under cover of darkness without much fear of detection, their shallow draught permitted them to cross the enemy minefields in complete safety.

Admiral Cowan realized that the CMBs could be used for more than intelligence work. Each could carry two torpedoes, and he now had a stock of torpedoes sent up from Reval, just in case the chance of action presented itself. It did, on 13 June 1919, by which time Agar's boats had made two courier trips across the bay, the Bolshevik garrison of one of the forts defending the Petrograd approaches, Krasnaya Gorka, mutinied and turned their guns on the Red troops, who were trying to stem an advance by an Estonian force. Three days later, the Commander-in-Chief Soviet Baltic Fleet, Admiral A.P. Zelenoy, ordered the battleships *Petropavlovsk* and *Andrei Pervozvanni* to bombard the fort into submission.

The chance of neutralizing both great warships in one surprise attack

was too good to miss. On the night of 16 June, CMBs 4 and 7, armed with torpedoes, set out from Terrioki to attack. Unfortunately, the venture had to be abandoned when CMB 7 struck an underwater obstacle and damaged her propeller shaft. Preparations were made for another attempt the next day, but early in the morning the two battleships returned to Kronstadt. A few hours later, however, they were replaced by the *Oleg*, which continued to shell the fort. Despite the fact that the damage to CMB 7 had not been repaired, Agar decided to attack the cruiser that night.

At 2300, CMB 4 slipped out of Terrioki, manned by Agar, Sub-Lieutenant J. Hampsheir and Chief Motor Mechanic M. Beeley. The boat slipped through the minefield and past an enemy destroyer screen without incident; the dark bulk of the Oleg was sighted and Agar moved into position, firing his torpedo – in his own words – 'as if it were an ordinary practice run'. As the CMB turned away, the *Oleg* was shaken by an explosion and a thick column of smoke rose from her. With a gaping hole torn in her side, the cruiser went

A Coastal Motor Boat at speed. These craft proved themselves in the British naval expedition to the Baltic in 1918–20, carrying out a successful attack on Russian warships at Kronstadt.

down in just 12 minutes; amazingly, all but five of her crew were saved. The CMB, after running the gauntlet of heavy fire from the now thoroughly awakened destroyers and forts, regained Terrioki in safety at about 0300. For this exploit, Agar was subsequently awarded the Victoria Cross, while Hampsheir received the Distinguished Service Order and Beeley the Conspicuous Gallantry Medal.

**BRITISH WITHDRAWN**
Air operations against Kronstadt ceased in December 1919, when the naval base became icebound. During their five months of active service in the Baltic, the RAF aircraft had flown a total of 837 operational hours. Of the original 55 aircraft deployed, 33 had been lost, although only three were shot down. The British presence in the Baltic was withdrawn on 2 February 1920, when Estonia signed a peace treaty with the Bolshevik government.

# Naval Expansion 1919–1939

**When World War I ended in November 1918, the German High Seas Fleet remained substantially intact. This was due mainly to the outcome of the Battle of Jutland, fought on 31 May 1916. After Jutland, the High Seas Fleet played no further part in the war, remaining penned up in its base at Wilhelmshaven.**

Under the terms of the Armistice, the German Fleet was speedily disbanded. The newest and most powerful units of the Fleet – 11 battleships, five battlecruisers, eight cruisers and 50 destroyers – were seized and sailed to Scapa Flow in the Orkneys, where they were subsequently scuttled by their crews in a last gesture of defiance. All the Imperial Navy's submarines were handed over at Harwich. Of the remaining units of the Fleet, seven cruisers were handed over to the French and Italian Navies; a number of destroyers and submarines were also taken over and commissioned. Almost all the other vessels were scrapped.

Under the terms of the Peace Treaty, Germany was forbidden to have a submarine fleet or a naval air arm. The ships allowed to remain in German service were relegated to a coastal defence role and were already obsolete, comprising eight old pre-war battleships, eight light cruisers, 32 destroyers and torpedo boats, some minesweepers and auxiliary craft. The Allies, determined to ensure that Germany never again had warships comparable to those of other navies,

**The German battleship *Bayern* sinking at Scapa Flow after being scuttled by her crew. She was raised in 1934 and scrapped the following year.**

**The German light cruiser *Emden* was the first of her kind to be built after the end of World War I. She served throughout World War II, mostly in a training role, until being damaged in May 1945.**

stipulated that the size of new-build German ships should not exceed a displacement of 10,160 tonnes (10,000 tons) for capital ships and 6096 tonnes (6000 tons) for cruisers.

It was at this juncture that the Washington Naval Treaty was signed, on 6 February 1922. Engineered by the United States and, in effect, the first disarmament treaty in history, the Washington Treaty aimed to limit the size of the navies of the five principal maritime powers – Britain, the United States, France, Italy and Japan. For Britain, this meant a reduction in capital ship assets to 20 by scrapping existing warships and dropping new projects. However, because her capital ships were older and less heavily armed than those of the United States, she was permitted to build two new vessels as replacements for existing ones. The other nations were also allowed to build new capital ships to replace vessels that were 20 years old.

### TREATY RESTRICTIONS

This arrangement would allow France and Italy to lay down new warships in 1927, while Britain, the United States and Japan would not need to do so until 1931. No new capital ship was to exceed 35,561 tonnes (35,000 tons), nor mount guns larger than 41cm (16in). No existing capital ship was to

> One predictable result of the Washington Treaty was that all five major maritime powers built cruisers right up to the agreed limit of 10,160 tonnes (10,000 tons).

permitted 60,963 tonnes (60,000 tons) each. None of the carriers was allowed an armament in excess of eight 20cm (8in) guns, nor were these to be replaced until they were 20 years old. No other warships were to be built in excess of 10,160 tonnes (10,000 tons), nor have guns larger than 20cm (8in).

One predictable result of the Washington Treaty was that all five major maritime powers built cruisers right up to the agreed limit of 10,160 tonnes (10,000 tons) and with the heaviest armament allowed. Britain, for example, laid down seven 'Kent' class ships of 10,038 tonnes (9880 tons), mounting eight 20cm (8in) guns, and six similar 'London' class ships. A destroyer replacement programme of nine vessels a year, each displacing 1372 tonnes (1350 tons) and mounting four 119mm (4.7in) guns and eight torpedo tubes, was also begun in 1929. In addition, the decision was taken to give Britain's ageing submarine force a shot in the arm by building nine 'O' class and six 'P' class boats.

Meanwhile, outside the orbit of the Washington Treaty, a new German Fleet was being born. The first medium-sized German warship built after World War I was the light cruiser

be rebuilt, although an increase in deck armour against air attack was allowed, as were the addition of anti-torpedo bulges, provided these modifications did not exceed a total of 3048 tonnes (3000 tons).

The Washington Treaty also limited the tonnage of aircraft carriers. Each signatory nation was allowed to build two vessels of up to 33,530 tonnes (33,000 tons); the remainder were limited to 27,433 tonnes (27,000 tons). The total aircraft carrier tonnage in the case of Britain and the United States was not to exceed

137,167 tonnes (135,000 tons). Japan was allowed 82,300 tonnes (81,000 tons), while France and Italy were

**German torpedo boats in the English Channel. The vessel nearest the camera is an early Schnellboot. Furthest away is an early T-boat, with a 'Wolf' class ship in the centre.**

*Emden*, completed in January 1925 at the Wilhelmshaven Dockyard. Originally coal-fired, she converted to oil in 1934. Designed primarily for foreign service, she made nine foreign cruises as a training ship from 1926 and went on to see active service in World War II, carrying out mine-laying operations in September 1939 and during the Norwegian campaign of April 1940. She subsequently served with the Fleet Training Squadron in the Baltic and operated

**The armoured cruisers *Deutschland*, *Admiral Scheer* and *Admiral Graf Spee* were clever designs, making use of welding techniques instead of riveting to save weight.**

in support of the German offensive against Russia. One of her more unusual operations, in January 1945, was to evacuate the coffin of Field Marshal von Hindenburg from Konigsberg, East Prussia, after it had been removed from the Tannenberg Memorial during the Russian advance into Germany. In April 1945, she was damaged in a bombing raid on Kiel, and was later scuttled. She was broken up in 1949.

## TORPEDO BOATS

In 1924, the Wilhelmshaven Dockyard began the construction of 12 new torpedo boats, six of the 'Wolf' class and six of the 'Möwe' (Seagull) class.

With a displacement of around 945 tonnes (930 tons), these vessels were powered by two-shaft geared turbines and were capable of 61km/h (33 knots). All were armed with six 53cm (21in) torpedo tubes, three 10.4cm (4.1in) guns and four 20mm (0.79in) AA guns. They carried a complement of 129, and all were completed by 1929.

In that year, a significant step forward was taken with the commencement at the Deutsche Werke, Kiel, of the first of a new class of warship. Designated Panzerschiffe (Armoured Ships) by the Germans, they were to become popularly known as 'Pocket Battleships'. The 11,888-

tonne (11,700-ton) *Deutschland* (later renamed *Lützow*) was the first, the others being the *Admiral Scheer* and the *Admiral Graf Spee*. These were designed from the outset as commerce raiders with a large and economical radius of action – 16,677km (9000nm) at 35km/h (19 knots) – and were electrically welded to save weight and equipped with diesel engines. They had enough speed – 48km/h (26 knots) – to enable them to escape from any vessel that could not be overwhelmed by their guns. Their armament comprised six 28cm (11in), eight 15cm (5.9in), six 10.4cm (4.1in) AA, eight 37mm (1.44in) AA, 10 (later 28)

20mm (0.79in) AA and eight 53cm (21in) torpedo tubes. They carried a complement of 1150.

Of enormous significance, too, was the appointment in 1929 of Admiral Erich Raeder to command the Reichsmarine. Raeder had served as a staff officer to Admiral Franz von Hipper in World War I, and had later been assigned the task of writing the official German history of the war at sea. In doing so, he had become aware, for the first time, of the achievements of the handful of German commerce raiders in distant waters. Not only had they sunk a large tonnage of merchant shipping, they had also tied down many Allied capital ships and cruisers, which were diverted to search for them. It was Raeder who authorized the construction of the *Deutschland*'s two sister ships, the *Scheer* and *Graf Spee*. He would almost certainly have ordered more, had it not been for Adolf Hitler's rise to power in 1933 and a subsequent change of naval policy dictated by the new political climate.

Meanwhile, in defiance of the Versailles Treaty and under conditions of strict secrecy, Germany had been

Admiral Erich Raeder was Chief of Naval Staff from 1928 to 1935, and Commander-in-Chief of the Kriegsmarine until 1943. He opposed a war on two fronts, but remained loyal to Hitler.

taking steps to re-create a submarine arm. As early as 1922, a submarine design office was established at The Hague, under cover of a Dutch firm. It was under the guise of constructing submarines for foreign navies that the German designers and constructors – who had remained in close touch

## ECONOMIC CONSTRAINTS

**By 1930, all the construction programmes of the maritime powers had been severely affected by economic constraints, the world being in the grip of a savage depression. With the exception of Japan, all the maritime nations were eager to escape the cost of building replacement capital ships, as permitted by the Washington Treaty. On 22 April 1930 a new treaty, signed in London by the five principal powers, made fresh provisions. Britain, Japan and the United States agreed that they would lay down no new capital ships before 1936, while France and Italy decided to lay down only the two they were already allowed. Furthermore, the first three countries agreed to make further reductions in existing assets: Britain would reduce her force of capital ships to 15 by scrapping HMS *Tiger* and three 'Iron Duke'-class vessels, and relegating the *Iron Duke* to the role of training and depot ship. The United States and Japan also agreed to reduce their capital ship assets to 15 and nine respectively.**

An early-model German U-boat on the surface. Early German boats were built in Finland and Spain because of treaty restrictions forbidding the production of such craft in Germany.

since the end of World War I – set about producing craft that would actually serve as prototypes for a new German submarine service. In 1928–30, they set to work on one submarine for Turkey and five for Finland.

The Turkish craft, the *Gur*, was laid down in Spain in 1932 and furnished with machinery made principally in Holland. In fact, she was the prototype for two 876-tonne (862-ton) Type IA U-boats built in 1936, both of which were relegated to training duties at the outbreak of war in 1939. The Finnish submarines were a good deal more interesting; the last of them, the 258-tonne (254-ton) *Vessiko*, was built by the German firm Chrichton-Vulcan AB at Turku on the southwestern tip of Finland. Given the designation Submarine 707, she was actually the prototype for the Type IIA U-boat. To add to her cover story, a rumour was put about that she was destined for Estonia.

A German Officer, Commander Barttenburg, and an Engineer Assistant were appointed to the Finnish Naval Staff, and in the spring of 1931 a German crew arrived to take Submarine 707 through her trials. With the exception of four engine room ratings, the entire crew consisted of young German officers. Every year thereafter, a fresh crew was

sent to Finland, and in this way a score of potential U-boat commanders received six months' training in the latest attack techniques at the expense

of the Finns and without any complaint from the outside world. In the meantime, a 498-tonne (490-ton) ocean-going boat was being tested under the auspices of the Finns; she was the *Vetehinen*, and served as the prototype for the main operational U-boat class, the Type VII.

### THE MARCH OF EVENTS
Within three years, the Treaties of Washington and London had been torn to shreds. First of all, in 1933,

The Nazi Party was now in power in Germany, and one of the first acts of the new Chancellor, Adolf Hitler, was to initiate a massive rearmament programme.

Japan invaded Manchuria, giving notice to the world that she intended to dominate the Far East, and then withdrew from the League of Nations. She then announced her intention to end her adherence to the Washington and London Treaties, and to establish naval parity with Britain and the United States. France, increasingly alarmed by the growing hostility of fascist Italy, followed suit early in 1935. Also in 1935, and in defiance of the League of Nations, Italy embarked upon a campaign of aggression in Abyssinia; and in 1936 Germany repudiated the Treaty of Versailles and seized the Rhineland.

The Nazi Party was now in power in Germany, and one of the first acts of the new Chancellor, Adolf Hitler, was to initiate a massive rearmament programme. As far as the German Navy was concerned, the immediate result was the construction of a new class of Schlachtkreuzer (Battlecruiser). Five ships were projected, but only two were actually started. The first of these, the 32,514-tonne (32,000-ton) *Scharnhorst*, was laid down at Wilhelmshaven in April 1934; she was followed a year later by the *Gneisenau*.

## POWERFUL WARSHIPS

The design of these powerful warships was based on that of the uncompleted 'Mackensen' class battlecruisers of World War I, which in turn were based on the *Derfflinger* of 1912 – arguably

The *Scharnhorst* displaying the straight stem and bow emblem. She presented a tremendous threat to Allied Atlantic convoys.

The design of these powerful warships was based on that of the uncompleted 'Mackensen' class battlecruisers of World War I, which in turn were based on the *Derfflinger* of 1912.

the best battlecruiser of its day. The new ships were fitted with three-shaft geared turbines and their radius of action was 18,530km (10,000nm) at 19 knots. Their armament comprised nine 28cm (11in), 12 15cm (5.9in), 14 10.5cm (4.1in), 16 37mm (1.44in) AA, and 10 (later 38) 20mm (0.78in) AA guns, as well as six 53cm (21in) torpedo tubes. Each carried four 'spotter' aircraft and had a complement of 1800. They were capable of a speed of 57km/h (31 knots). *Scharnhorst* was launched in October 1936 and *Gneisenau* in December that year.

In the mid-1930s, a new class of Schwerer Kreuzer (heavy cruiser) was also laid down. There were five ships in all, named *Lützow*, *Seydlitz*, *Prinz Eugen*, *Blücher* and *Admiral Hipper*. The first of these, launched in July 1939,

was sold in 1940 to the Soviet Navy, in whose service she was successively named *Petropavlovsk* and *Tallinn*. The others were all launched in 1937–39. Capable of 59km/h (32 knots), they had an armament of eight 20cm (5in), 12 10.5cm (4.1in) AA, 12 37mm (1.44in) AA, and eight (later 28) 20mm (0.78in) AA guns, in addition to 12 53cm (21in) torpedo tubes. Each carried three spotter aircraft. The complement was 1600.

Completing the line-up of Germany's major surface vessels of the period between between World War I

and World War II were the light cruisers. The *Emden* of 1925 has already been mentioned; she was followed in 1927 by the *Karlsruhe*, launched in 1927, the *Köln* of 1928 and the *Leipzig* of 1929. Next came the *Nürnberg*, launched in 1934, and the *Königsberg* of 1937. The *Nürnberg* and *Leipzig*, at 6700 tonnes (6590 tons), were the largest, with a complement

The battlecruiser *Gneisenau* passing through the Kiel Canal. She was decommissioned in July 1942 and her turrets removed for coastal defence. An intended refit was abandoned.

The German heavy cruiser *Lützow*. The 'splinter' camouflage of green and grey was applied to German warships operating in Arctic waters.

of 850. Their armament comprised nine 15cm (5.9in), eight 8.9cm (3.5in), and eight 37mm (1.44in) AA, as well as 12 53cm (21in) torpedo tubes, and they had a top speed of 59km/h (32 knots). The others were smaller, displacing 5690 tonnes (5600 tons) and with a complement of 630. They carried an armament of eight 15cm (5.9in), three 8.9cm (3.5in) AA and four 37mm (1.44in) AA guns, in addition to four 53cm (21in) torpedo tubes. Three other light cruisers, which remained unnamed, were never finished and were broken up on their stocks in 1943. Three more remained projects only.

## MASSIVE INCREASE

On 20 June 1935, an Anglo-German Agreement was signed. Under its terms, German warship tonnage was restricted to 35 per cent of British equivalents of all classes except submarines, which could be built up to 45 per cent. In effect, this meant that Germany could legitimately build U-boats up to a total of 24,385 tonnes (24,000 tons). At this time, the Royal Navy had 59 submarines in commission, of which 20 ranged between 1372 tonnes (1350 tons) to 1834 tonnes (1805 tons); the rest were between 416 and 680 tonnes (410 and 670 tons), which was about the size

fleet, because 12 254-tonne (250-ton) U-boats had already been laid down before the Agreement was signed and 12 more were to be added during the year.

In July 1935, less than a month after the Anglo-German Agreement was concluded, a certain Captain Karl Dönitz was summoned to Admiral Raeder's office and ordered to assume command of the embryo U-boat service. Dönitz had served in U-boats during World War I, and although his career had not been very distinguished he showed exceptional qualities of leadership and organization. He did not initially relish the task in hand, but applied himself to it energetically, lobbying for 300 submarines to wage an unrelenting war on maritime commerce should it become

**The light cruiser *Nürnberg* seen passing through the Kiel Canal. Ceded to the USSR after World War II, she was incorporated into the Soviet Navy as the *Admiral Makarov* and broken up in 1959.**

necessary. In fact, by September 1939, the German Navy had only 56 submarines, of which 46 were in commission, although only 22 were ocean-going craft and suitable for service in the Atlantic. They were Type VIIs, with an endurance of 16,000km (8,850nm) at 10 knots but capable of 17 knots. With a conning tower only 5.2m (17ft) above the waterline, they were hard to detect even in daylight, and under night conditions they were practically invisible. They could dive in less than half a minute; they could go down to 100m (328ft) without strain and to 200m (656ft) if hard-pressed. They

the Germans were planning. The Agreement was concluded without consultation with the Dominions, France or the United States, and it is not clear why it was signed at all, unless the British Admiralty believed that it would lead to the Germans building 45 per cent of the British total in numbers rather than in tonnage, which would have resulted in only 26 U-boats. What it actually did was to open the door for a massive increase in Germany's submarine

The Agreement was concluded without consultation with the Dominions, France or the United States, and it was not clear why it was signed at all.

could maintain a submerged speed of 7.6 knots for two hours, 4 knots for 80 hours and 2 knots for 130 hours. In fact, their depth and endurance performance at high speed was twice as good as in any other submarines. It was with these boats that Dönitz, soon to be promoted to Admiral, would principally fight his underwater battle.

## TECHNOLOGICAL SUPERIORITY

While Dönitz was plotting the expansion of his U-boat fleet, Admiral Raeder and his naval staff were putting the finishing touches to a scheme designed to give Germany technological superiority on the high seas. It was based on two super-powerful battleships, the *Bismarck* and *Tirpitz*. Displacing 42,370 tonnes (41,700 tons) in the case of *Bismarck* and 43,589 tonnes (42,900 tons) in the case of *Tirpitz*, they would have a speed of 29 knots and a combat radius of 16,677km (9,000nm) at 19 knots.

Admiral Karl Dönitz confers with members of his naval staff. He became head of state for a few days after the suicide of Adolf Hitler in 1945, and served a lengthy prison sentence for war crimes.

They would carry a formidable armament of eight 38cm (15in), 12 15cm (5.9in), 16 10.5cm (4.1in) AA, 16 37mm (1.44in) AA and 16 (later 58) 20mm (0.78in) AA guns, together with eight 53cm (21in) torpedo tubes. Their complement would be 2400 officers and men. Both were laid down in 1936, but only the *Bismarck* was launched before the outbreak of World War II.

Six even larger battleships (57,100 tonnes/56,200 tons) were planned, known simply by the letters H, J, K, L, M and N. Only H and J were laid down, in 1938, and these were broken up on the stocks in the summer of 1940, at a time when Germany believed she had won the war. It has

The German aircraft carrier *Graf Zeppelin*. She was to have formed the core of a powerful battle group, but was never completed. Her wreck was located in the southern Baltic in 2006.

been speculated that the first two of these battleships were to be named *Friedrich der Grosse* and *Gross Deutschland*, although there is no concrete evidence for this.

Finally, there were plans to build a small number of aircraft carriers. In the event, there was only one, the 23,370-tonne (23,200-ton) *Graf Zeppelin*, laid down in 1936 and launched in December 1938. Her four-shaft geared turbines would have given her a maximum speed of 33 knots and a combat radius of

## GERMAN SEA POWER

When Germany went to war in September 1939, she was at a distinct numerical disadvantage in every respect. Yet during the long years that followed, she came close to starving Britain into submission. Her principal weapon in the murderous conflict that became known as the Battle of the Atlantic was the U-boat; but in the early months it was the German Navy's surface vessels that were to take the greatest toll of Allied shipping.

**The battleship HMS *King George V* served in all theatres of war. She took part in the hunt for the *Bismarck* in May 1941, the bombardment of Okinawa and the Japanese Home Islands in 1945.**

14,824km (8,000nm) at 19 knots. It was originally planned that she should carry an air group comprising 12 Junkers Ju87D dive bombers and 30 Messerschmitt Bf l09F fighters, later amended to 28 Ju87Ds and 12 Bf l09Gs. She was never completed. Construction was suspended in May 1940, when she was 85 per cent complete; she was afterwards towed to Gdynia and then to Stettin. In 1942 she went to Kiel, where work on her was restarted; it was again suspended in 1943, after which she was towed to

the Oder River and scuttled near Stettin in April 1945. In March 1946, she was raised by the Soviets and towed to Swinemünde. She was subsequently used as a target vessel and sunk by Soviet forces. The location of her wreck remained a mystery for many years until it was located in 2006, in the southern Baltic. The hull of a sister vessel was

completed up to the armoured deck but she was never launched, being broken up on the stocks in 1940. It was speculated that this ship was to have been named *Peter Strasser*, after the commander of the German Naval Airship Division in World War I.

In 1942, work was also started to convert the heavy cruiser *Seydlitz* as an aircraft carrier, but very little was

By 1930, the strength of the Royal Navy stood at 16 battleships, four battlecruisers, six aircraft carriers, 20 cruisers, 40 other cruisers and 146 destroyers.

carried out and the ship was scuttled at Konigsberg in April 1945, later being raised by the Soviets. Plans were also laid to convert the liners *Europa*, *Gneisenau* and *Potsdam* as an emergency measure, but these came to nothing.

## ROYAL NAVY

At the end of World War I, the Royal Navy had 44 capital ships, plus one more being built. By 1920, this total had been reduced to 29, a figure generally accepted as being the minimum number needed to defend Britain's worldwide interests and to maintain parity with the rapidly growing naval forces of the United States and Japan. However, on

6 February 1922 the number of capital ships available to the Royal Navy was reduced still further with the signing of the Washington Naval Treaty. By 1930, the strength of the Royal Navy stood at 16 battleships, four battlecruisers, six aircraft carriers, 20 cruisers with 190mm (7.5in) or 203mm (8in) armament (with three more building), 40 other cruisers, and 146 destroyers (with 10 more building).

In the mid-1930s, faced not only with a potential threat to her positions in the Far East, but also with threats much closer to home from a revitalized and increasingly aggressive Germany and an ambitious Italy, Britain began to rearm. Five 'King George V' class fast battleships of 35,560 tonnes (35,000 tons) were laid down, each armed with 10 356mm (14in) guns and 16 133mm (5.25in) dual-purpose (DP) guns. They were followed, after Japan had abandoned the Treaty limits, by four 'Lion' class battleships of 40,642 tonnes (40,000 tons) mounting nine 406mm (16in) guns, although this class was later cancelled. At the same time, existing British capital ships were modernized with the provision of extra armour and improved armament. The cruiser

HMS *Tartar* was one of the Royal Navy's powerful 'Tribal' class destroyers, which performed valiant service on convoy escort duties during the darkest days of World War II.

force also underwent substantial upgrading. Eight 'Leander' class vessels of 7112 tonnes (7000 tons), armed with eight 152mm (6in) guns, were built, followed by four 5303-tonne (5220-ton) 'Arethusas' with six. This kept the cruiser tonnage within the limits imposed by the London Treaty, but the subsequent crash rearmament programme produced eight 'Southamptons' of 9246 tonnes (9100 tons), each mounting 12 152mm (6in) guns, followed by two slightly larger 'Edinburghs' and 11 'Fiji' class of 8941 tonnes (8800 tons), with the same armament. Eleven 'Dido' class vessels were also laid down; these were 5862 tonnes (5770 tons) with an armament of 10 133mm (5.2in) DP guns, their primary role being to counter air attack.

As well as these new warships, the older 203mm (8in) cruisers of post-war vintage were retained in service, as were 23 'C', 'D' and 'E' class vessels. Six of these were armed with eight 102mm (4in) AA guns as anti-aircraft cruisers. There were also three surviving 'Hawkins' class cruisers, one of which, HMS *Effingham*, was rearmed with nine 152mm (6in) guns.

Destroyers, too, were key participants in the maritime arms race. In order to keep pace with destroyer developments in other countries, Britain laid down 16 big 'Tribal' class vessels of 1899 tonnes (1870 tons), armed with eight 119mm (4.7in) guns and four torpedo tubes, followed by the 1717-tonne (1690-ton) 'J' and 'K' classes, with six 119mm (4.7in) guns and eight torpedo tubes. An entirely new design of small, fast destroyer (915 tonnes/900 tons and 32 knots) was also introduced; this was the 'Hunt' class, 20 of which were on the stocks at the outbreak of war. Although of limited endurance, they were to perform excellent service in home waters.

To bolster trade protection, the Admiralty ordered more vessels of the type known as sloops, which displaced between 1016 tonnes (1000 tons) and 1270 tonnes (1250 tons) and which, although slow, had a good endurance. By 1939, 53 were in service. Finally, a completely new type of small long-endurance vessel, designed on the lines of a whale-catcher and called a corvette, began to be introduced from 1939.

## NAVAL AVIATION

Naval aviation, in which the Royal Navy had established a commanding lead by the end of World War I, had stagnated in the years since: by 1930,

HMS *Ark Royal* under air attack. The Germans claimed to have sunk the carrier several times in the early months of the war; it was not until November 1941 that she fell victim to a torpedo.

the nation's fluctuating fortunes meant that all three services were fighting for survival, and with politicians committed to disarmament, nothing at all had been done to authorize even the modest expansion of the Fleet Air Arm that the Admiralty wanted. The upshot was that, of the six aircraft carriers in service at the beginning of 1939, only one, the *Ark Royal* – laid down in 1935 and in the process of completing her trials – was a modern, purpose-built ship. Four of the others were conversions from battleship or battlecruiser hulls and the fifth, HMS *Furious*, was too small to be of much use. Five new 23,368-tonne (23,000-ton) fleet carriers were either under construction or planned; again, it would be 18 months before the first of these was ready for commissioning. As for the first-line aircraft at the Fleet Air Arm's disposal at the beginning of 1939 – the Fairey Swordfish torpedo-bomber, the Blackburn Skua fighter/dive-bomber and the Gloster Sea Gladiator fighter – all of these were obsolescent.

When war came, it was the Royal Navy that would bear the main responsibility for maritime operations in the North Sea and the Atlantic. It was also envisaged that the French Navy would have an important part to play in convoy protection on the more

southerly Atlantic routes and in hunting down enemy commerce raiders. Although the French Navy had emerged from World War I in a badly weakened state, it had managed – thanks to the efforts of a succession of excellent commanders – to overcome the indifference of politicians and regain its strength during the next two decades. In 1939, it had 175 warships at its disposal, including five old battleships, three of which – the *Bretagne*, *Provence* and *Lorraine* – had been extensively refitted. In addition, there were two new fast battleships, the *Dunkerque* and *Strasbourg*, two old aircraft carriers, the *Béarn* and *Commandant Teste*, seven heavy cruisers, 12 light cruisers and 70 destroyers of various types. There were also 77 submarines, including the massive *Surcouf*. The

> In the Mediterranean, operations would be divided between Britain and France, the French being responsible for the western part and the British for the eastern.

*Surcouf* was, in effect, an experimental, one-off boat, described by the French Navy as a 'Corsair submarine'. She was fitted with the largest calibre of guns allowed on submarines under the terms of the Washington Treaty, and in 1939 she was the largest, heaviest submarine in the world.

She would remain so until the Japanese 400 series entered service in World War II. Several formidable new warships were either under construction or on order, including four new 35,560-tonne (35,000-ton) fast battleships: the *Richelieu, Jean Bart, Clemenceau* and *Gascogne.*

In the Mediterranean, operations would be divided between Britain and France, the French being responsible for the western part and the British for the eastern, although there were plans for some French warships to operate under the command of the British Mediterranean Fleet. The

## IJN HOSHO

Country: Japan

Type: Light Carrier

Launch date: 13 November 1932

Crew: 550

Displacement: 7470 tons standard; 10,000 tons full load

Dimensions: 168.1m x 18m x 6.2m (551ft x 59ft x 20ft 4in)

Range: 13,300km (7169nm) at 10 knots

Armament: 4 x 140mm (5.5in) 2 x 80mm (3.2in) AA (1941), eight

twin 25-mm (0.985-in) AA guns; aircraft: 11 'Kate' torpedo bombers

Powerplant: Two-shaft geared steam turbines delivering 22,370kW (30,000shp)

Performance: 25 knots

## US CARRIERS

**The first US carrier built as such from the keel up was the USS *Ranger* of 1930, which proved too slow to be effective as a first-line unit. She was, however, developed into the successful 'Yorktown' class of 1933 (*Enterprise*, *Hornet* and *Yorktown*), followed by the Wasp of 1934. At the same time, battleship development was not neglected, and in the late 1930s three new classes of fast battleship emerged: the 'North Carolina' of 1937, the 'South Dakota' of 1938 and the 'Iowa' class of 1939. The basis was being laid for the task forces that would one day dominate the Pacific.**

Italian Navy, the Regia Marina, was seen as a formidable threat; it possessed modern battleships, cruisers and destroyers, a force of over 100 submarines, and was backed up by large numbers of bombers belonging to the Regia Aeronautica, the Italian Air Force. In the face of this threat, the British and French Admiralties took the joint decision that in the event of war the Mediterranean would be closed to all mercantile traffic bound for the Middle East. This would be diverted round the Cape of Good Hope, a 17,700km (11,000-mile) haul necessitating the rapid establishment of shore bases on the east and west coasts of Africa. The British and French naval planners had little doubt that their combined navies would be more than a match

for the Regia Marina, even though its fighting ability remained an unknown quantity; neither the British nor the French had ever fought against it.

### JAPAN'S STRATEGY

What was also unknown was the true state of the Japanese Navy and its associated maritime air strength. Great Britain had played a considerable part in assisting Japan to build a modern fleet in the early years of the century, but that association had come to an end with the rise of Japanese militarism. By the 1930s, Japan's naval and military activities had become effectively hidden from the outside world. Naval air power was at the core of Japan's strategy. She had completed her first aircraft

carrier, the *Hosho*, in 1922, and this vessel had soon been followed by larger and more powerful vessels like the 38,812-tonne (38,200-ton) *Kaga*. Launched on 17 November 1920, *Kaga* was originally laid down as an improved Nagato-type dreadnought, with increased armour protection and an enlarged main battery. She was cancelled in February 1922 to comply with the terms of the Washington Naval Treaty. However, instead of scrapping her, the Japanese Naval Staff decided to complete her as an aircraft carrier to replace another carrier, the *Amagi*, which had been destroyed in an earthquake while under construction. *Kaga* was completed in March 1928 and joined the Combined Fleet in 1930. In 1934–35 she was reconstructed, a full-length flight deck and island being added. Recommissioned in June 1935, she was assigned to the First Carrier Division with the *Akagi*, her air group seeing action during the Sino-Japanese war. Japanese fast-attack carrier construction up to 1939 culminated in the 39,800-tonne (25,675-ton) *Shokaku* and *Zuikaku*. The emphasis in Japanese naval construction during the inter-war years was therefore on aircraft carriers,

---

### *LEXINGTON*

| | | |
|---|---|---|
| Type: Aircraft carrier | Displacement: 48,463 tonnes (47,700 tons) | Armament: Eight 203mm (8in), 12 127mm (5in) guns, 80 aircraft |
| Launch date: 3 October 1925 | Dimensions: 270.6m x 32.2m x 9.9m (88ft x 105ft 8in x 32ft 6in) | Powerplant: Quadruple screw turbo electric drive |
| Crew: 2327 | Range: 18,900km (10,500nm) at 10 knots | Performance: 33.2 knots |

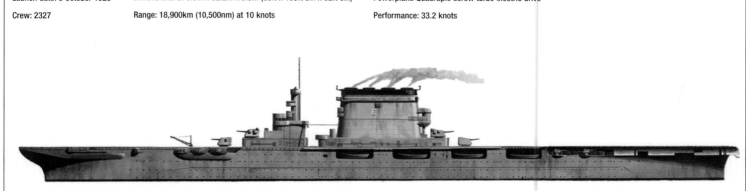

although the navy retained a powerful
fleet of reconstructed battleships
and battlecruisers. In addition, two
new battleships, the *Yamato* and
*Musashi*, were laid down in 1937;
displacing 71,695 tonnes (67,123
tons), they were the largest and
most powerful battleships ever
built, and they were constructed
in great secrecy.

## AGGRESSIVE THREAT
In the United States, the tempo of
naval construction was dictated by
the need to keep abreast of the
growing and increasingly aggressive
threat from Japan. The US Navy's
first aircraft carrier was the USS
*Langley*. She was converted from
the fleet collier *Jupiter*, which was
launched in 1912 and subsequently
used as a test bed for turbo-electric
propulsion. The collier's
superstructure was removed and a
flight deck erected the full length of

the hull; the cranes were also removed
and the coal bunkers converted to
accommodate disassembled aircraft.
The carrier had no island, and smoke
was vented by means of a hinged
funnel on the port side. A second
funnel was fitted later. Conversion was
completed in March 1922 and *Langley*
joined the Pacific Fleet in 1924.

In 1916–17, the US Naval Staff
had ordered a class of six new
battlecruisers, as a counter to the
powerful Japanese 'Kongo' class.
These were named *Constellation*,
*Constitution*, *Lexington*, *Ranger*, *Saratoga*
and *United States*. To comply with
the terms of the 1922 Washington
Naval Treaty, construction of these
warships was suspended when they
were partially complete, and the
contract was cancelled. However,
it was decided to complete two of
them, *Constitution* (rather confusingly
renamed *Lexington*) and *Saratoga*, as
aircraft carriers. *Lexington* was re-

In late 1942, the USS *Enterprise* was the only
Allied carrier in the Pacific. *Enterprise* survived
the war and was scrapped in 1958.

ordered as a carrier in July 1922
and given the designation CV-2;
*Sarotoga* was designated CV-3,
although in fact she was the first to be
launched, on 7 April 1925. *Lexington*
was launched on 3 October that year
and appeared in US Pacific Fleet
exercises for the first time in January
1929, together with her sister ship.
As finally completed, both ships were
armed with 8in (203mm) rather than
6in (152mm) guns, these weapons
being designed to match the new
generation of cruisers, which were
similarly armed. As a defensive
measure, there were also plans to
incorporate torpedo tubes, but
these were not implemented. At the
time of their completion, they were
the two biggest aircraft carriers in
the world.

# World War II
## The Opening Battles
## 1939–1941

**World War II began on the shores of the Baltic Sea at dawn on the first day of September 1939, when the old German battleship *Schleswig-Holstein* fired her opening salvo at the Polish fortress of Westerplatte, commanding the entrance to Danzig Bay. The first day saw air and naval action in the Baltic as the *Luftwaffe* sought to render the Polish Navy ineffective. Bad visibility and generally poor weather conditions hampered air activity on 1 September, but Junkers Ju 87 Stuka dive-bombers of *IV Gruppe, Lehrgeschwader 1* (IV/LG1) under Hauptmann Kogl sank the Polish torpedo boat *Mazur* in Oksywie harbour at about 1400.**

In fact, Rear-Admiral Unrug, the Commander-in-Chief of the Polish Navy, had already ordered the main units of his fleet out of the danger zone, conscious of its vulnerability under the threat of massive German air attack, and with the knowledge that seaborne operations would play little part in the forthcoming invasion. On 30 August, the destroyers *Blyskawica*, *Burza* and *Grom* sailed for Britain. One destroyer, the *Wicher*, remained, together with one minelayer, five submarines, two old torpedo boats, two gunboats, six small minesweepers and some auxiliary and training vessels.

Early in the morning of 3 September, the Officer Commanding Torpedo Boats, Rear-Admiral Gunter Lütjens, made a sortie towards the Hela peninsula in

The mighty German battleship *Bismarck*, pictured just before her launch in February 1939. She was completed in the summer of 1940.

the Vistula delta with a force of destroyers. In an engagement with the Polish minelayer *Gryf*, the destroyer *Wicher* and a shore battery, the latter's 150mm shells obtained hits on the destroyer *Leberecht Maas*, killing four German sailors.

The Germans were soon to have their revenge. Later in the day, the destroyer *Wicher*, the minelayer *Gryf*, the gunboat *General Haller* and some smaller vessels were surprised at anchor off Hela by the Ju 87 Stukas of *4/Trägergruppe 186* (a unit formed for

operation from the German aircraft carrier *Graf Zeppelin*, then under construction) and Heinkel He 115 floatplanes of Küstenfliegergruppen 506 and 706. All the Polish vessels were sunk.

Then came a new development. In the afternoon of 3 September, Admiral Lütjens was ordered to proceed with the destroyer force to Wilhelmshaven, from where the warships were to undertake minelaying operations in the North Sea. Germany was now at war with

**The German pre-dreadnought battleship *Schleswig-Holstein* fired the opening shots of World War II against the Polish fortress of Westerplatte.**

Britain and France. The move from the Baltic to the new operational area began early the next day.

### OCEAN-GOING SUBMARINES

The departure of the destroyers made it possible for the Polish Navy's submarines to operate with a greater degree of latitude. From its very beginnings in the early 1920s, the Polish Navy had made its submarine force the cornerstone of its defensive doctrine, and an approach to France in 1924 resulted, two years later, in the Polish government making the decision to place an order for three minelaying submarines of the Normand-Fenaux type. In Polish

> As officers and ratings gained experience in the techniques of underwater warfare, it was decided to acquire two more large ocean-going submarines.

service, the boats were designated the *Wilk* (Wolf) class, the *Wilk*'s sister craft being the *Rys* (Lynx) and *Zbik* (Wildcat).

As officers and ratings gained experience in the techniques of underwater warfare, it was decided to acquire two more large ocean-going submarines. The contract went to Holland, and the first boat, the *Orzel* (Eagle), was built with the help of funds raised by public subscription. Launched on 15 January 1938 and commissioned on 2 February 1939, the *Orzel* was constructed at the De Schelde Navy Yard, Vlissingen (Flushing); her sister boat, *Sep* (Vulture) was built at the Rotterdam Dockyard. She was launched on 17 October 1938, but progress in completing her was slow, partly because of pro-German sympathies among the Dutch shipyard workers. Following the German occupation of Czechoslovakia in March 1939, there were fears that she might be sabotaged. On 2 April, she put to sea for trials, but instead of returning to Rotterdam she sailed for the Baltic, with some very surprised and indignant Dutch workers still on board. With 160km (100 miles) still to go, she ran out of fuel, and had to be towed into Gdynia, arriving on 18 April.

On 4 and 5 September, while the *Schleswig-Holstein* and other warships continued to batter the Westerplatte defences, the *Rys*, *Wilk* and *Zbik* laid 50 mines north of the Vistula estuary, east of Hela and northeast of Heisternest. *Rys*, *Wilk* and a third submarine, *Sep*, were depth-charged and damaged by ships of the 1st Minesweeping Flotilla and most of the mines were soon cleared, although one claimed a German victim, the minesweeper M85, on 1 October, with the loss of 24 lives. Late on 5 September, all five of these

boats were ordered to journey to the northern Baltic to obtain some respite from the German attacks and to repair the damage they had sustained.

On 11 September, with the Polish armies in a state of collapse and the Germans breaking through on all fronts, the Polish submarines were ordered to escape to Britain or, alternatively, to allow themselves to be interned in neutral Baltic ports.

German naval cadets receiving instruction in anti-aircraft gunnery with the Baltic Fleet Training Squadron. With the Soviet fleet immobilized in Kronstadt, the Baltic was a safe training area.

*Wilk* set out immediately, arriving at Rosyth on 20 September; *Sep* and *Rys*, which had sustained battle damage, sailed for Sweden with the undamaged *Zbik* and were interned there. *Orzel* (under Lt-Cdr Grudzinski) reached Britain on

14 October via Reval, after an adventurous voyage without charts.

## WAR STATIONS

In August 1939, with the invasion of Poland imminent, the German Naval Staff lost no time in deploying units of the *Kriegsmarine* to their war stations in the Atlantic, ready to begin an immediate offensive against Allied shipping. On 19 August, 14 U-boats were despatched from Wilhelmshaven and Kiel, and two days later the 13,208-tonne (13,000-ton) pocket battleship *Admiral Graf Spee* also sailed from Wilhelmshaven, under cover of darkness and unobserved, to make rendezvous with her supply ship, the fleet tanker *Altmark*, in the South Atlantic. She was followed on 24 August by a second pocket battleship, the *Deutschland*, which sailed for her war station south of Greenland, to be joined later by her own replenishment vessel, the fleet tanker *Westerwald*. Within the next 24 hours, signals had been despatched to all German merchant vessels, ordering them to make for home, friendly or neutral ports with all possible speed.

On 3 September, following the declaration of war by Britain and France, the light cruiser HMS *Ajax* drew first blood – not in northern waters but in the South Atlantic, where she intercepted two German freighters. Their captains ordered the ships to be scuttled in order to avoid capture. Also on this day, the U-boats struck their first blow when the *U-30*, commanded by Leutnant Lemp, torpedoed and sank the British passenger liner *Athenia* south of the Rockall Bank. About 1300 survivors

**Close-up of the *Admiral Graf Spee*'s heavily armoured conning tower, taken by a US Navy photographer while the ship lay in Montevideo harbour.**

were rescued by the destroyers *Electra* and *Escort*, assisted by some foreign vessels, but 112 people lost their lives. Although the story was put out that Lemp had mistaken the liner for an armed merchant cruiser, it seems more likely that he had misconstrued his orders and believed such attacks to be permitted by the German government. Whatever the truth, the British Admiralty took the sinking as evidence that unrestricted submarine warfare was in force, a belief that was to lead to the early establishment of a full convoy system for the protection of mercantile trade. In fact, the first convoy sailed on 6 September, from the Firth of Forth to the Thames Estuary, and the next day three escorted Atlantic convoys were also despatched, to Gibraltar, Halifax and Sierra Leone.

Although the liner *Bremen* escaped the attentions of the Home Fleet on her homeward run from New York (by taking refuge in Murmansk), the British naval blockade enjoyed considerable success during September, the warships intercepting 108 merchant vessels and escorting 28 of them to Kirkwall, Orkney, for inspection. British submarines deployed in a screen between the

## HUNTING THE GERMAN MERCHANT FLEET

If the German Naval Staff was determined to bring home the bulk of its merchant fleet, many of whose vessels were carrying raw materials vital to the German war effort, the British Admiralty was equally determined to seize them – in particular the German mercantile flagship, the fast Atlantic liner *Bremen*. From 31 August, Admiral Sir Charles Forbes, C-in-C Home Fleet, deployed the battleships *Nelson*, *Ramillies*, *Rodney*, *Royal Oak* and *Royal Sovereign*, the battlecruisers *Hood* and *Repulse*, the aircraft carrier *Ark Royal*, 12 cruisers and 16 destroyers in a blocking screen across the Iceland–Faeroes–UK gap, combing and searching those high-latitude waters for the elusive merchantmen.

Shetlands and Norway, and off the north German coast, were less successful, the only damage being done to their own side. On 10 September, the submarine *Triton* sank another British submarine, HMS *Oxley*, on the surface in a tragic case of misidentification that left only two survivors; four days later, HMS *Swordfish* almost suffered the same fate in a torpedo attack by HMS *Sturgeon*; and on 17 September, HMS *Seahorse* survived a bombing attack by an Avro Anson of RAF Coastal Command.

### HUNTING GROUPS

The Home Fleet continued its northern patrol, moving its main operating base from Scapa Flow to

Loch Ewe on the Clyde during September for fear of air attack, the Orkney base being very poorly defended at this time. However, two hunting groups, each consisting of an aircraft carrier and four destroyers, had been formed to operate against U-boats in the Western Approaches and the Channel area. Minelaying accounted for a good deal of U-boat activity, and mines were responsible for the sinking of a high proportion of the 25 merchant vessels lost in this area during September. Operations to

**The battleship HMS *Royal Oak* was sunk in a torpedo attack by the German submarine *U-47* as she lay at anchor in the supposedly secure confines of the naval anchorage of Scapa Flow.**

the west of the British Isles were undertaken by 11 submarines of the 2nd U-boat Flotilla. During the same period, 11 more submarines of the 6th and 7th U-boat Flotillas, operating in the Atlantic west of the Bay of Biscay and off the Iberian Peninsula, sank seven merchant ships and captured two more.

On 14 September, the U-boats missed their chance to deal a telling blow at the Royal Navy when the *U-39* fired a salvo of torpedoes at the fleet carrier *Ark Royal* west of the Hebrides. Luckily for the carrier, the torpedoes – a new type fitted with magnetic pistols – detonated prematurely and the submarine was sunk by the escorting destroyers *Faulknor*, *Foxhound* and *Firedrake*, her crew being

**An early victim of the war at sea, the aircraft carrier HMS *Courageous* was sunk in the Western Approaches by the German submarine *U-29* on 17 September 1939.**

> # On 14 September the U-boats missed their chance to deal a telling blow at the Royal Navy when the *U-39* fired a salvo of torpedoes at the fleet carrier *Ark Royal*.

taken prisoner. Three days later, the Royal Navy's luck ran out. On 17 September, the fleet carrier *Courageous* was hit by three torpedoes from the *U-29* west of the English Channel. She went down with the loss of 515 crew, and an immediate result was the withdrawal of aircraft carriers from anti-submarine operations. On 22 September, the Navy's destroyers enjoyed a revenge of sorts when the *U-27*, commanded by Kapitänleutnant Franz, was sunk off the west coast of Scotland by the *Fortuna* and *Forester*.

On 25 September, the Royal Navy fought its first air action of the war

when a Dornier Do 18 maritime reconnaissance aircraft was shot down by Blackburn Skuas of No. 803 Squadron, Fleet Air Arm, from HMS *Ark Royal*, led by Lieutenant C.L.G. Evans. The next day, the *Ark Royal* formed part of a Home Fleet force that had been despatched to cover ships of the 2nd Cruiser Squadron engaged in recovering the submarine *Spearfish*, which had been badly damaged in the central North Sea. She was attacked by Junkers Ju 88s of I/KG 30, which missed. One bomb hit the battlecruiser *Hood* but bounced off. Nine Heinkel He 111s of I/KG 26

were also despatched to attack the 2nd Cruiser Squadron, but failed to locate the warships.

By 21 September, British Naval Intelligence was aware that two powerful German commerce raiders, the *Graf Spee* and *Deutschland*, were at sea. The Admiralty was now compelled to deploy substantial numbers of ships – including some detached from the Mediterranean – to search for them. On 7 October, the German Naval Staff, concerned about the mounting pressure on the pocket battleships, ordered units of the German Fleet to make a sortie towards the southern coast of Norway. The force comprised the battlecruiser *Scharnhorst*, the light cruiser *Köln* and nine destroyers, and the intention was to draw the Home Fleet across a concentration of four U-boats and within range of the Luftwaffe.

As soon as Admiral Forbes learned that the enemy was out, he stationed

A youthful and rather diminutive figure, Kapitanleutnant Gunther Prien, the man who sank the *Royal Oak*, was the hero of the hour in Germany. He lost his own life later in the war.

his main units north-east of the Shetlands, where they could cover the exit to the Atlantic. These were the battleships *Nelson* and *Rodney*, the battlecruisers *Hood* and *Repulse*, the cruisers *Aurora*, *Sheffield* and *Newcastle* and the carrier *Furious*, accompanied by 12 destroyers. At the same time, he despatched the Humber Force, comprising the light cruisers *Edinburgh*, *Glasgow* and *Southampton*, to search for the German ships.

The operation was fruitless, and bombers despatched by both sides failed to find their targets. On 9 October, after dark, the German force reversed its course and returned to Kiel, and by 11 October the main units of the Home Fleet were back in Loch Ewe and the light cruisers were back in the Humber.

## ROYAL OAK

There was an exception to this. One of Forbes' battleships had been detached from the main force in order to guard the Fair Isle Channel, between the Shetland and Orkney Islands, and when the threat receded she made her way to the anchorage at Scapa Flow. She was the *Royal Oak*. On the night of 13/14 October, the German submarine *U-47*, commanded by Kapitänleutnant Gunther Prien, penetrated the defences of Scapa Flow and sank the *Royal Oak* with three torpedo hits. The attack, in which 833 lives were lost, was carried out with great coolness, skill and daring, and came as a severe shock to Britain.

Two days after this tragedy, Junkers Ju 88 bombers of KG 30 carried out an attack on warships of the Home Fleet in the Firth of Forth, HMS *Hood* being the main target. The attack was unsuccessful, the bombers inflicting only light damage on the cruisers *Southampton* and *Edinburgh* and the destroyer *Mohawk*. Two Ju 88s were shot down by Spitfires. The next day, KG 30 also attacked Scapa Flow, but apart from the depot ship *Iron Duke*, which was damaged by a near miss, the nest was empty.

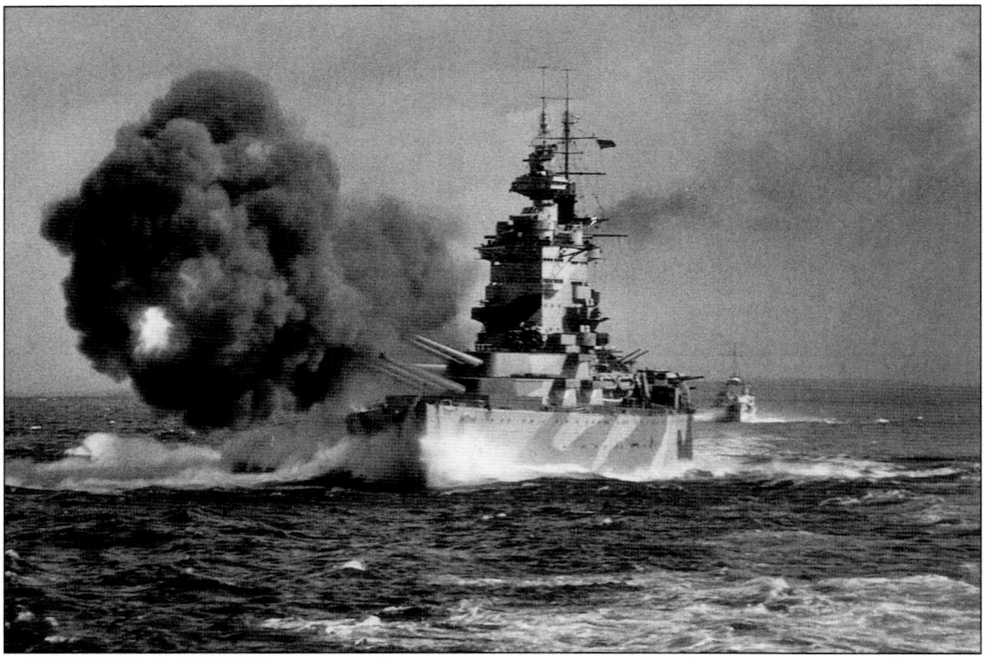

The power of the battleship is shown in this shot of HMS *Nelson* firing her main armament. In a long battle, the vibration from the heavy guns could damage the ship's structure.

Enemy mines continued to be the main threat to British shipping in home waters, and for a time the Germans enjoyed a definite advantage through the use of the magnetic mine, which was detonated by the magnetic field of a vessel passing over it. Such mines accounted for 59,974 tonnes (59,027 tons) of British coastal shipping in September and October 1939, and to compound the problem the entire British minesweeping service was equipped to deal only with moored contact mines that detonated on impact. Minelaying operations by U-boats and destroyers intensified during November, the submarines being active in the Straits of Dover, the Firth of Forth, off Cromarty and in the Home Fleet's new refuge of Loch Ewe. On 21 November the cruiser *Belfast* was damaged by a mine in the Firth of Forth, and on 4 December the battleship *Nelson* was also damaged by a mine laid by the *U-31* in Loch Ewe.

Meanwhile, on 21 November, the battlecruisers *Scharnhorst* and *Gneisenau* had sailed from Wilhelmshaven for the North Atlantic, the purpose of their sortie being to divert attention away from the operations of the pocket battleship *Admiral Graf Spee* in the South Atlantic. Passing undetected to the north of the Shetlands and Faeroes, the warships were sighted on the 23rd by the Armed Merchant Cruiser *Rawalpindi* (Captain E.C. Kennedy), which engaged them in a gallant but one-

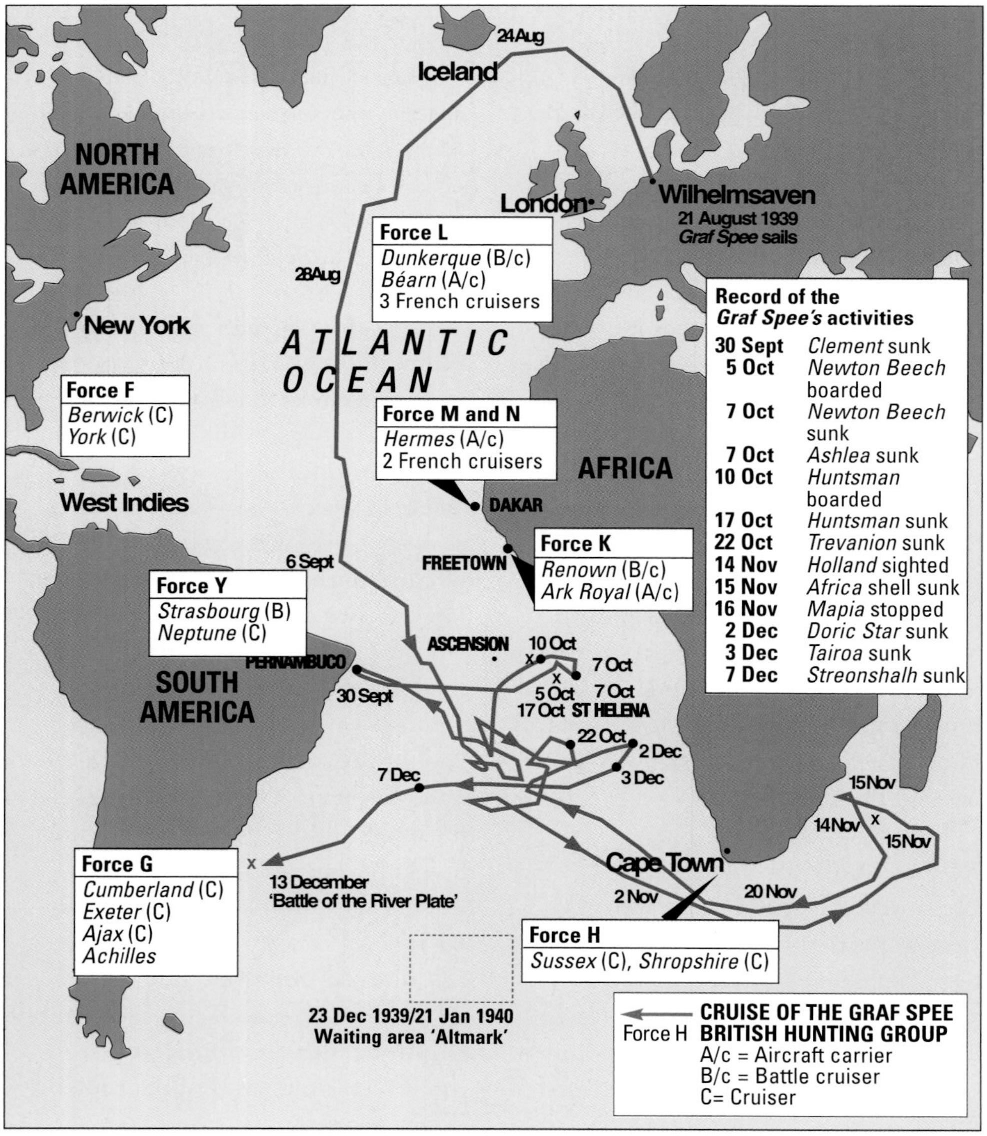

24Aug
Iceland
NORTH AMERICA
London
Wilhelmsaven
21 August 1939
Graf Spee sails
Force L
Dunkerque (B/c)
Béarn (A/c)
3 French cruisers
28Aug
Record of the Graf Spee's activities
30 Sept Clement sunk
5 Oct Newton Beech boarded
7 Oct Newton Beech sunk
7 Oct Ashlea sunk
10 Oct Huntsman boarded
17 Oct Huntsman sunk
22 Oct Trevanion sunk
14 Nov Holland sighted
15 Nov Africa shell sunk
16 Nov Mapia stopped
2 Dec Doric Star sunk
3 Dec Tairoa sunk
7 Dec Streonshalh sunk
New York
ATLANTIC OCEAN
Force F
Berwick (C)
York (C)
Force M and N
Hermes (A/c)
2 French cruisers
AFRICA
West Indies
DAKAR
Force K
Renown (B/c)
Ark Royal (A/c)
FREETOWN
6 Sept
Force Y
Strasbourg (B)
Neptune (C)
ASCENSION
10 Oct
7 Oct
PERNAMBUCO
SOUTH AMERICA
30 Sept
5 Oct
7 Oct
17 Oct
ST HELENA
22 Oct
2 Dec
3 Dec
7 Dec
15Nov
14Nov
15Nov
Force G
Cumberland (C)
Exeter (C)
Ajax (C)
Achilles
13 December
'Battle of the River Plate'
Cape Town
2 Nov
20 Nov
Force H
Sussex (C), Shropshire (C)
23 Dec 1939/21 Jan 1940
Waiting area 'Altmark'
CRUISE OF THE GRAF SPEE
Force H BRITISH HUNTING GROUP
A/c = Aircraft carrier
B/c = Battle cruiser
C= Cruiser


Map showing the commerce-raiding cruise of the *Admiral Graf Spee*, and the locations of the merchant ships she sank before making for the port of Montevideo, where she met her end.

> The search for the enemy battlecruisers, abortive though it was, illustrated the close co-operation that existed at the time between the Royal and French navies.

sided duel and had time to radio their presence to Scapa Flow before she was sunk by the *Scharnhorst*. Admiral Sir Charles Forbes at once ordered the entire Home Fleet to sea in a bid to intercept the battlecruisers. In fact, they were sighted by the cruiser *Newcastle*, which had been patrolling in the vicinity, as they picked up survivors from the *Rawalpindi*, but they avoided her in a rain squall and withdrew to a waiting position inside the Arctic Circle.

## ABORTIVE SEARCH

On the 26th, the battlecruisers came south once more, passed through the cruiser and destroyer patrol lines that Admiral Forbes had established off Norway, and regained Wilhelmshaven the next day. No fewer than 60 warships – six battleships (three French), two battlecruisers, 20 cruisers (two French), 28 destroyers (eight French), three submarines and an aircraft carrier – had been redeployed to various positions in the North Atlantic and North Sea to hunt the *Scharnhorst* and *Gneisenau*, and the Germans had eluded the lot.

The search for the enemy battlecruisers, abortive though it was, illustrated the close co-operation that existed at this time between the Royal and French Navies. On 5 October, the Admiralty, in conjunction with the French Navy, had formed eight Atlantic 'hunting groups' of aircraft carriers and cruisers for the defence of the trade routes against surface raiders. Three were under the orders of the Commander-in-Chief, South Atlantic, whose headquarters were at Freetown, Sierra Leone. Group G, comprising the heavy cruisers *Exeter* and *Cumberland* and reinforced later

by the light cruisers *Ajax* and *Achilles*, the latter belonging to the Royal New Zealand Navy, was responsible for the waters off the east coast of South America – and it was there that the *Admiral Graf Spee*'s rampage at last came to an end.

The pocket battleship sank her first merchantman off Pernambuco on 30 September. Between 5 and 12 October, she sank four more before breaking off to replenish from her supply ship, the *Altmark*. She turned up again on 15 November, when she sank a small tanker in the Mozambique Channel. There was no further news of her until 2 December, when she sank the freighters *Doric Star* and *Tairoa* between St Helena and South Africa. On receiving intelligence of these sinkings, the C-in-C South Atlantic, Vice-Admiral d'Oyly Lyon, ordered Force H, with the cruisers *Shropshire* and *Sussex*, to proceed to the area between Cape Town and St Helena. Meanwhile

**HMS *Ajax* pictured during the Battle of the River Plate. *Ajax* spent most of the war serving with the Mediterranean Fleet. She underwent a refit in the United States in 1943 and was scrapped in 1949.**

**Famous for her part in the Battle of the River Plate, the Leander-class cruiser HMNZS *Achilles* served with the Royal New Zealand Navy in World War II. She saw action in the Pacific later.**

Force K, comprising the battlecruiser *Renown*, the aircraft carrier *Ark Royal* and the cruiser *Neptune*, was despatched to search along a line from Freetown to the Central South Atlantic.

Force G (as Group G was now designated) meanwhile assembled off the River Plate with the cruisers *Achilles*, *Ajax* and *Exeter*, *Cumberland* having been detached to cover the Falkland Islands. There was plenty of mercantile traffic around the estuary of the River Plate, and Force G's senior officer, Commodore H. Harwood, reasoned that Langsdorff would be attracted there sooner or later. He was right. After sinking two more ships in mid-ocean, Captain Langsdorff elected to steer directly

for the Plate estuary, where his ship was sighted at 0608 on 13 December.

The three British cruisers were soon in action against her, opening fire from different directions. Langsdorff at first divided his armament, but then concentrated his fire on the *Exeter*, his 27.9cm (11in) shells inflicting heavy damage on the cruiser. Despite this, Captain F.S. Bell continued to engage the enemy throughout the night, at the end of which the *Exeter* was ablaze, with only one turret left in action. Langdorff could easily have finished her off; instead, he made smoke and turned west, allowing *Exeter* to pull away to the south-east to make repairs, with 61 of her crew dead and 23 wounded.

## UNDER FIRE
The pocket battleship now steered for the coast of Uruguay, under fire all the while from the light cruisers *Ajax* and *Achilles*. At 0725, a 27.9cm (11in)

shell hit *Ajax* and put both her after turrets out of action, but again Langsdorff failed to take the opportunity to finish off one of his adversaries, whose remaining guns were now barely superior to his own secondary armament. The two cruisers continued to shadow the *Graf Spee*, which fired salvoes at them from time to time, until the battleship entered the estuary. Commodore Harwood then called off the pursuit and set up a patrol line, aware that he was in a very parlous position if Langsdorff chose to fight his way out to the open sea.

The *Graf Spee* was damaged, however, having taken some 70 hits, while 36 of her crew were dead and another 60 wounded. Langsdorff now decided to make for a neutral port, where he could effect temporary repairs before attempting a breakout into the North Atlantic and a run back to Germany. He was also short of ammunition. He reached Montevideo on the evening of 14 December, and a prolonged diplomatic effort now began to remain in port beyond the legal limit of 72 hours, since the necessary repairs would take an estimated two weeks to complete. British propaganda, meanwhile, went all out to create the impression that a large British fleet was lying in wait to ambush the *Graf Spee* as soon as she re-emerged from La Plata estuary.

The aircraft carrier *Ark Royal* and the battlecruiser *Renown* were reported to be at Rio de Janeiro. In fact, they were 4020km (2500 miles) away, and the cruiser force had been reinforced by only one more ship, another cruiser, HMS *Cumberland*. Langsdorff fell for it. On 16 December, he sent the following signal to Berlin:

1. Strategic position off Montevideo: Besides the cruisers and destroyers, *Ark Royal* and *Renown*. Close blockade at night.

**A Vickers Wellington fitted with a 'de-gaussing' ring, designed to detonate magnetic mines. The aircraft had to fly low, and there was always a risk of damage when the mine detonated.**

## MINE COUNTERMEASURES

**In November 1939, enemy minelaying became so intensive that only a single channel into the Thames remained open, and in that month mines accounted for 27 ships totalling 122,899 tonnes (120,958 tons). As the official naval historian Captain S.W. Roskill later wrote:**

> **While awaiting the arrival of the new sweep many extemporised measures were adopted, and together they just succeeded in keeping the east coast traffic moving. Though losses continued on a considerable scale in the New Year, and in the first seven months of war no less than 128 ships totalling 429,899 tons [436,797 tonnes] fell victims to mines, we never again had to face as serious a crisis as that of the first autumn.**

Escape into open sea and breakthrough to home waters hopeless.

2. Propose putting out as far as neutral boundary. If it is possible to fight our way through to Buenos Aires, using remaining ammunition, this will be attempted.

3. If a breakthrough would result in certain destruction of *Graf Spee* without opportunity of damaging enemy, request decision on whether the ship should be scuttled in spite of insufficient depth in the estuary of the La

Plata, or whether internment is to be preferred.

The reply that came back from Berlin was unequivocal. There was to be no question of internment. The authority was given to scuttle the ship, should the German envoy in Montevideo fail to gain an extension of the time limit in neutral waters. By nightfall on 17 December, it was plain that no such extension was to be permitted by the Uruguayan authorities.

On the following morning, watched by a vast crowd of sightseers, *Graf Spee* put to sea. The British warships cleared for action, but before

they could engage the enemy, their spotter aircraft reported that the *Graf Spee* had been scuttled and blown up by her own crew. Within a short time, it was learned that Captain Langsdorff had committed suicide. The *Graf Spee*'s crew were later transferred to Argentina, where they were interned. They remained there until February 1946, when 900 were repatriated to Germany on the liner *Highland Monarch* – escorted, in a nice touch of irony, by HMS *Ajax*.

### MAGNETIC MINE

The destruction of the *Graf Spee* was a major coup for the Royal Navy.

Another was the recovery, on 23 November 1939, of two German magnetic mines from the mud flats at Shoeburyness. Defused and made safe by a gallant Royal Navy team – Lt Cdrs Ouvry and Lewis, CPO Baldwin and AB Vearncombe – they were transported to Portsmouth for detailed examination. Once the magnetic mine's secrets were unlocked, the Admiralty initiated all technical measures to combat it. Before long, a research team under Rear-Admiral W.F. Wake-Walker had devised effective countermeasures in the form of a so-called degaussing girdle, an electric cable fitted to

The German supply ship *Altmark* captured in a Norwegian fjord by an RAF reconnaissance aircraft. The prisoners she carried, mainly merchant seamen from ships sunk by the *Admiral Graf Spee*, were released by the Royal Navy.

the hulls of ships to de-magnetize them. Degaussing girdles were also fitted to the modified Vickers Wellingtons of No. 1 General Reconnaissance Unit, RAF Coastal Command, whose task it was to fly low over the sea and detonate the mines by triggering their detonators through the generation of an electromagnetic field.

### NOTABLE SUCCESSES

In December 1939, the Royal Navy, in co-operation with RAF Coastal Command, steadily tightened its blockade of German maritime traffic in the North Atlantic and North Sea. During this period, British submarines scored some notable successes. In the Heligoland Bight, HMS *Salmon*, under

> Rear-Admiral W.F. Wake-Walker had devised effective countermeasures in the form of a deguassing girdle, an electric cable fitted to the hulls of ships to de-magnetize them.

Lt Cdr Bickford, sank the *U-36*, and on 12 December Bickford almost succeeded in intercepting the passenger liner *Bremen*, homeward bound from the Kola Inlet. However, he was thwarted by the appearance overhead of a Dornier Do 18 patrol aircraft. The next day, Bickford sighted a force of three light cruisers, escorting five destroyers that had been out on a minelaying sortie, and launched a salvo of torpedoes; the *Leipzig* took a severe hit amidships and the *Nürnberg* was hit in the bow. The enemy force was then attacked by HMS *Ursula* (Lt Cdr Phillips), which sank the escort vessel *F9*.

These successes were tempered, in January 1940, by the loss of three British submarines in rapid succession. The *Undine* and *Starfish* were both forced to the surface by depth-charge attacks and had to scuttle themselves, while the *Seahorse* was sunk. These losses brought an abrupt halt to Home Fleet submarine operations in the inner Heligoland Bight.

In the early weeks of 1940, the Baltic remained icebound for an unusually long period, so the Germans made increasing use of the alternative route via the north Norwegian port of Narvik to ship Swedish iron ore, a commodity that was vital to Germany's war industries. The British Admiralty laid plans to extend its blockade to enemy merchant shipping passing along Norway's coastline, but this was difficult to implement. For most of the route, the cargo vessels were able to remain inside Norwegian territorial waters by using the narrow passages between the mainland and the offshore islands known as the Inner Leads. The use of Norwegian ports by enemy blockade runners was also a sore point. Matters came to a head on 14 February 1940, when the tanker

*Altmark* – the *Graf Spee*'s supply ship, carrying some 300 merchant seamen from vessels sunk by the pocket battleship – sought refuge in Trondheim under Norwegian protection. The *Altmark*'s Captain Dau had ignored Captain Langsdorff's order to land his captives at a neutral port, and had instead remained in the South Atlantic until a signal from Berlin advised him that it was safe to run for home. Passing through the Denmark Strait and entering Norwegian territorial waters, the

*Altmark* had been intercepted by a Norwegian torpedo boat, but Dau had refused to allow his ship to be searched.

On 15 February, Admiral Sir Charles Forbes, C-in-C Home Fleet, learned that the *Altmark* was off Bergen, and instructed Captain Q.D.

**How the *Daily Express* announced the German success in Norway. The Allied campaign in Norway, poorly led, lacking adequate air support and vital combat equipment, was always doomed to fail.**

Graham of the cruiser *Arethusa*, returning with five destroyers from a sortie into the Skagerrak, to intercept her. She was sighted the next day, steaming down the Leads, but attempts by the British destroyers to close with her were frustrated by Norwegian torpedo boats steaming close alongside. Darkness found the enemy tanker in Josing fjord, where she was followed by Captain P.L. Vian in the destroyer *Cossack*. Informing the senior Norwegian officer that there were British prisoners on the *Altmark*, Vian demanded the right to

search for them; the Norwegian replied that his orders were to resist, and trained his torpedo tubes on the destroyer.

Faced with this delicate situation, Vian withdrew and sought the Admiralty's instructions. Three hours later, they came through, and the signal was penned by the resolute hand of Winston Churchill, then First Lord of the Admiralty:

Unless Norwegian torpedo-boat undertakes to convoy *Altmark* to Bergen with a joint Anglo-Norwegian guard on board, and a joint escort, you should board *Altmark*, liberate the prisoners, and take possession of the ship pending further instructions. If Norwegian torpedo-boat interferes, you should warn her

to stand off. If she fires upon you, you should not reply unless attack is serious, in which case you should defend yourself, using no more force than is necessary, and ceasing fire when she desists.

For the equally resolute Vian, it was enough. Persuading the Norwegian vessels to withdraw, he took the Cossack into Josing fjord and went alongside the *Altmark*, evading an attempt by Dau to ram him, and sent over an armed boarding party. Six German guards were killed and six wounded before they escaped ashore, leaving the British sailors free to break open the *Altmark*'s hatches. Someone asked if there were any British below, and a tremendous yell assured him that the prisoners were all British. The words that followed

**A German destroyer of the 'Leberecht Maass' class beached and on fire after being attacked by British destroyers in Narvikfjord, April 1940. Of the 16 destroyers in this class, six were lost in the Norwegian campaign.**

were to become enshrined in British naval tradition: 'Come on up, then – the Navy's here!'

## NORWAY AND THE CHANNEL PORTS, 1940

On 9 April 1940, the period that had become known as the 'Phoney War' came to a violent end when German forces invaded Norway and Denmark. The decision to occupy Norway was not simply prompted by the need to secure the vital iron ore route; the German naval C-in-C, Grossadmiral Erich Raeder, had learned an important lesson from history, or rather from a book published in 1929 entitled *Maritime Strategy of the Great*

*War.* In it, Vizeadmiral Wegener argued that Germany should have occupied Norway in 1914, giving the High Seas Fleet the use of Norwegian harbours, enabling it to operate against Britain's North Atlantic convoys instead of remaining blockaded in the North German ports by the Royal Navy's Home Fleet based at Scapa Flow.

In the spring of 1940, there was plenty of warning of Germany's intention to invade Norway. For several days early in April, the British Government had been receiving intelligence reports of unusual German activity in the Baltic ports, and had interpreted this as a

**The British battleship HMS *Rodney* spent most of her operational career in service with the Home Fleet. She was named after Admiral Lord Rodney, a celebrated British naval commander of the eighteenth century.**

sign that heavy units of the German Fleet were preparing to break out into the Atlantic. The interpretation was wrong. The bulk of the enemy invasion force was already at sea on 7 April, steaming northwards through savage weather. This part of the invasion force was divided into three Task Groups. Group One, with Narvik as its objective, had the farthest distance to travel – roughly 1600km (1000 miles) – and was heavily escorted by the battlecruisers *Scharnhorst* and *Gneisenau*, together with 10 destroyers. Group Two, bound for Trondheim, was guarded by the heavy cruiser *Admiral Hipper* and four destroyers, while Group Three, heading for Bergen, was protected by the cruisers *Köln* and *Königsberg*, screened by torpedo boats.

On 9 April 1940, the period that had become known as the 'Phoney War' came to a violent end when German forces invaded Norway and Denmark.

The battlecruiser *Renown* pictured after she was reconstructed just before the outbreak of war. She was very active, serving in home waters, the Mediterranean and the Indian Ocean.

Groups Four and Five, assigned to Kristiansand and Oslo, did not have to sail so early. The plan was that all five groups would reach their objectives at more or less the same time.

Meanwhile, the British War Cabinet, responding at last to pressure from the First Lord of the Admiralty, Winston Churchill, had agreed that minelaying operations in the Leads would begin on 8 April. Mines (some of them dummies) would be laid at three key points off the Norwegian coast, and on 5 April two minelaying forces set sail to carry out the operation, codenamed Wilfred. One force was recalled, but the other, consisting of the minelaying destroyers *Esk, Icarus, Impulsive* and *Ivanhoe*, escorted by the destroyers *Hardy, Havock, Hotspur* and *Hunter*, laid a mine barrage off Bodo on 8 April.

## LOST OPPORTUNITY

What might have proved a damaging blow to the enemy, a plan by Admiral Forbes to attack enemy forces at Bergen with four cruisers and seven destroyers early on 9 April, was frustrated when it was cancelled by the Admiralty following the receipt of an air reconnaissance report that two German cruisers were in the harbour. In the afternoon of 9 April, units of the Home Fleet were attacked almost without pause for three hours by 41 Heinkel 111s of KG26 and 47 Junkers 88s of KG30. The battleship *Rodney* received a direct hit from a 500 kg (1100lb) bomb, which splintered her armoured deck but failed to explode; the cruisers *Devonshire, Southampton* and *Glasgow* were damaged by near misses, and the destroyer *Gurkha* was sunk west of Stavanger. The Germans lost four Ju 88s. During this first encounter, the Royal Navy had learned to its cost what it meant to operate within range of enemy land-based bombers without fighter cover.

The covering force comprised the battlecruiser *Renown* and the destroyers *Hyperion, Hero, Greyhound* and *Glowworm*, and it was the latter that made the first contact with the German ships.

### FIRST CONTACT

Detached to make a vain search for a seaman swept overboard from *Renown* in the murky dawn of 8 April, she sighted the warships of Task Group Two, bound for Trondheim. *Glowworm* fired two salvoes at an enemy destroyer before the latter was lost to sight in heavy seas and fog; a few minutes later, a second destroyer came into view and *Glowworm* gave chase, the two warships exchanging shot for shot. The larger German vessel increased speed in an attempt to shake off her adversary, but her bow ploughed under, forcing her to slow down. *Glowworm* closed in,

The German invasion of Norway, in contrast to the haphazard Allied response, was a masterpiece of planning. It involved the use of airborne as well as seaborne forces.

her captain, Lt Cdr G.B. Roope, trying to get into position for a shot with torpedoes.

Some distance ahead, a great, dark shape burst from a fog bank. For a few seconds, the men on *Glowworm*'s bridge were elated, believing the ship to be HMS *Renown*. Then a salvo of heavy shells struck the British destroyer, setting her on fire. The newcomer was the *Admiral Hipper*. Roope sheered off for long enough to radio a report, then turned back towards the German cruiser in the hope of torpedoing her. When this proved impossible, he headed his burning ship straight for the *Hipper*, ramming her starboard bow, tearing off 40m (130ft) of her armour belt and wrenching away her starboard torpedo tubes. The cruiser's captain, H. Heye, ordered his guns to hold their fire as the *Glowworm* fell away, ablaze and doomed. A few minutes later, at 0900, she blew up. Kapitän Heye ordered his ship's crew to search for survivors. They plucked 38 from the sea. Lt Cdr Roope himself reached the cruiser's side, but was too exhausted to hold on to the rope German sailors threw to him, and was drowned. His matchless courage earned him a posthumous Victoria Cross, the first to be won by the Royal Navy in World War II.

Meanwhile, in consultation with its French and Polish allies, the British Government had made plans to transport 18,000 British, French and Polish troops to reinforce the Norwegian garrisons of Stavanger, Bergen, Trondheim and Narvik as soon as there was clear evidence that the Germans intended to invade Norway. On 6 April, the cruisers

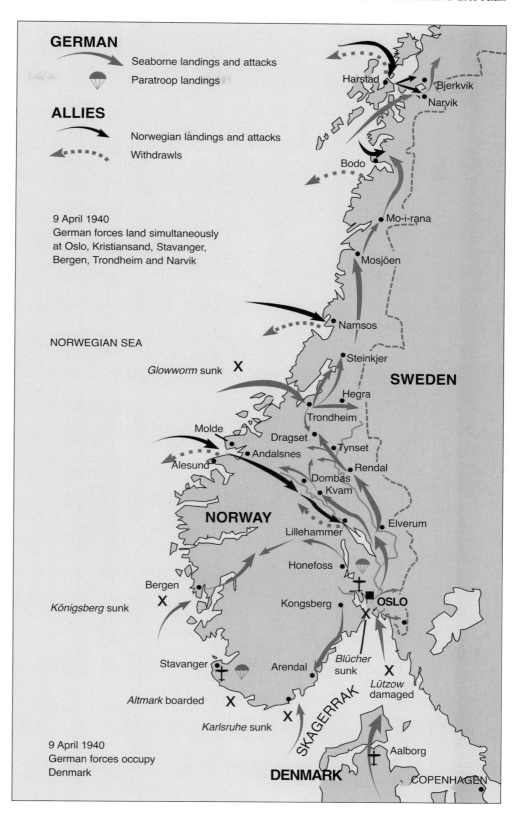

**GERMAN**

→ Seaborne landings and attacks

⛱ Paratroop landings

**ALLIES**

→ Norwegian landings and attacks

⤙ Withdrawls

9 April 1940
German forces land simultaneously at Oslo, Kristiansand, Stavanger, Bergen, Trondheim and Narvik

NORWEGIAN SEA

*Glowworm* sunk ✕

*Königsberg* sunk ✕

*Altmark* boarded ✕

*Karlsruhe* sunk ✕

9 April 1940
German forces occupy Denmark

Harstad • Bjerkvik
Narvik

Bodo

Mo-i-rana

Mosjöen

Namsos

Steinkjer

SWEDEN

Hegra

Trondheim

Molde
Dragset
Andalsnes • Tynset
Alesund
Rendal
Dombas
Kvam
Elverum

NORWAY

Lillehammer

Honefoss

Bergen

Kongsberg • OSLO

Stavanger • Arendal
*Blücher* sunk
*Lützow* damaged ✕

SKAGERRAK

Aalborg

DENMARK COPENHAGEN

*Devonshire*, *Berwick*, *York* and *Glasgow*, together with six destroyers, were despatched to Rosyth to embark garrison troops. Admiral Forbes had available to him the battleships *Rodney* and *Valiant*, the battlecruiser *Repulse*, the cruisers *Penelope* and *Sheffield* and 10 destroyers, plus the French cruiser *Emile Bertin* and two destroyers. On 7 April, he instructed them to leave Scapa Flow and head north, while the cruisers *Arethusa* and *Galatea* with

eight destroyers headed for Stavanger. A troop convoy bound for Bergen was recalled, and its escorts – the cruisers *Manchester*, *Southampton* and four destroyers – ordered north to join the main body of the Home Fleet, as were the destroyers that had been covering the minelayers. As an additional measure, Vice-Admiral Sir Max Horton deployed 26 of his submarines to the operational area.

## PRIMARY OBJECTIVE

On 8 April, having received *Glowworm's* enemy sighting report and distress signal, Admiral Forbes ordered the warships at Rosyth to disembark their troops and put to sea, at the same time detaching the *Repulse*, *Penelope* and four destroyers to join *Renown* and her destroyers. That evening, the Admiralty, which still believed that a major breakout into the Atlantic was in the offing, instructed Forbes that his primary objective was the interception of the *Scharnhorst* and *Gneisenau*. Further evidence that this

The port of Narvik, seen here under air attack, soon became choked with wrecked ships. British First Lord of the Admiralty Winston Churchill saw the possession of Narvik as vital to the success or failure of the Norwegian campaign.

was the Germans' intention had seemed to come in the afternoon, when an RAF reconnaissance aircraft reported an enemy battlecruiser and two cruisers off Trondheim, steaming west. In fact, the ships were the *Hipper* and her accompanying destroyers, covering the Group Two invasion force. Yet the Germans' true intention had already been laid bare on that afternoon of 8 April, when the Polish submarine *Orzel* – part of Sir Max Horton's screen – torpedoed and sank the troop transport *Rio de Janeiro* off Lillesand, on the south coast of Norway. Norwegian fishermen rescued about 100 survivors, some of whom, interrogated by the military authorities, revealed that they had been on their way to Bergen 'to protect Norway against English invaders'. The military authorities at once called for the full mobilization of Norway's small armed forces, and the mining of the approaches to Norwegian harbours. However, the pacifist Norwegian Government, fearful of provoking Nazi Germany even at this late hour, did nothing.

It was not until 1900 on 8 April that the Admiralty decided that an invasion was underway, following an assessment of further intelligence

The destroyer HMS *Hardy*, seen here leading a flotilla, was lost at the Battle of Narvik in April 1940.

reports on the movements of German vessels (including one from the submarine HMS *Trident*, which had made an unsuccessful torpedo attack on the battleship *Lützow* as the latter headed for Oslo Fjord). Even so, the possibility of a simultaneous breakout into the Atlantic was not discounted. A signal was flashed to the commander of the northernmost group of British warships, Vice-Admiral William Whitworth, in HMS *Renown*:

> Most immediate. The force under your orders is to concentrate on preventing any German force proceeding to Narvik.

It was too late. Before midnight, the German invasion forces were already entering the fjords that led to their objectives. At 0337 on 9 April, however, *Renown*, positioned 80km (50 miles) off the entrance to Vestfjord, sighted the *Scharnhorst* and *Gneisenau*, heading northwest to prevent any British interference with the Narvik assault group. Mistaking one of the enemy ships for the cruiser *Hipper*, the British battlecruiser opened fire at 17,366m (19,000yds)

81

The British destroyer HMS *Hotspur*, one of the heroines of the Battle of Narvik, survived the war and was later sold to the Dominican Navy, in whose service she became the *Trujillo*.

and got three heavy hits on the *Gneisenau*. The German warships returned fire with their 18 280mm (11in) guns, hitting *Renown* twice but causing little damage, and then turned away to the northeast; the German commander, Admiral Lütjens, had decided not to take unnecessary risks against what he believed to be the battleship *Repulse*.

### RANGING RADAR

It was perhaps lucky for the *Renown* that one of her shells put the *Gneisenau's* Seetakt ranging radar and its associated gunnery control system

out of action. *Renown* herself, at this stage, was not radar-equipped. In fact, only seven Royal Navy warships – the *Rodney, Valiant, Sheffield, Suffolk, Curlew, Carlisle* and *Curacao* – were fitted with radar at the start of the Norwegian campaign, and this was mainly anti-aircraft equipment, which proved to have severe limitations when operating close inshore in the vicinity of high cliffs. The aircraft from the carrier *Furious* had, in fact,

been ordered from the Clyde to join the Fleet, but she had left in such a hurry that there had been no time to embark them. Realizing that she could contribute nothing to the safety of his ships, Admiral Forbes ordered her to stay out of range until she had flown on her air group, and in the late afternoon of the 9th he took his main force westward to meet the carrier and the battleship *Warspite* north of the Shetlands. By nightfall on 9 April, the

> The destroyers ought to have made the return passage to Germany at high speed once their troops were ashore, but before they could do so they needed fuel.

German invasion forces had secured their main objectives, but the operation had not been accomplished without loss. On the approach to Oslo, the new heavy cruiser *Blücher* was crippled by gunfire from a Norwegian fort and finished off with torpedoes, taking more than 1000 men to the bottom with her, while the light cruiser *Karlsruhe* was torpedoed by HM submarine *Truant* and so badly damaged that she had to be sunk in the Kattegat by a German torpedo boat. Other warships, including the *Lützow* and the light cruiser *Königsberg*, were damaged by shellfire from Norwegian coastal defences.

## BATTLE OF NARVIK
Meanwhile, Group One of the German invasion force – 10 destroyers

under Kommodore Friedrich Bonte, carrying 2000 men of General Dietl's 3rd Mountain Division – had made an unopposed passage through the narrow waterway between the Lofoten Islands and the Norwegian mainland. As they entered Ofotfjord on the approach to Narvik, Bonte detached seven destroyers: three to deal with Norwegian forts said to be defending the Ramnes Narrows (there were none, in fact), and four to occupy the township of Elvegaard in Herjangsfjord. The remaining three – Bonte's flagship the *Wilhelm Heidkamp*, followed by the *Berndt von Arnim* and *Georg Thiele* – pressed on to Narvik, sinking the Norwegian defence vessels *Eidsvold* and *Norge* as they entered the harbour. The small Norwegian garrison was quickly overwhelmed

and Bonte redeployed his destroyers, bringing the *Anton Schmitt, Diether von Roeder* and *Hans Ludemann* into Narvik after they had disembarked their troops.

The destroyers ought to have made the return passage to Germany at high speed once their troops were ashore, but before they could do so they needed fuel, and only one of the expected tankers had turned up. Bonte therefore decided to delay the voyage home until the next day, while his destroyers took it in turns to take on fuel. He was not expecting any trouble; the submarine *U-51* had reported sighting five British destroyers in Vestfjord at 2022, but had signalled that they were steering southwest, away from the entrance of Ofotfjord. In fact, the British

83

destroyers were already making for Narvik, with orders to 'make certain that no enemy troops land', or if they had already landed 'to sink or capture enemy ships and land forces if you think you can recapture Narvik from number of enemy present.'

The destroyers, under the command of Captain B.A. Warburton-Lee, were the *Hardy, Hunter, Havock, Hotspur* and *Hostile* of the 2nd Destroyer Flotilla. Signalling his intention to attack at dawn high water, which would give him the advantage of surprise and enable his ships to pass safely over any mines, Warburton-Lee led his ships slowly in line ahead through Ofotfjord. In visibility reduced by falling snow, he reached the entrance to Narvik harbour without being detected by the enemy. Detaching *Hotspur* and *Hostile* to watch for and neutralize any shore batteries, he took *Hardy* into the harbour at 0430 and launched seven torpedoes at shipping in the anchorage. One torpedo ripped through the *Heidkamp*'s plating and exploded in her after magazine, killing Bonte and most of his sleeping crew. Two more torpedoes destroyed the *Anton Schmitt*; the other four struck merchant vessels, or missed their targets to explode on the rocky shore. *Hardy* swung round in a tight circle, her 119mm (4.7in) guns firing, as the *Hunter* and *Havock* entered the anchorage in turn. Their torpedoes set the *Hans Ludemann* ablaze and then they turned on the *Diether von Roeder*, assisted by the *Hotspur* and *Hostile*, and reduced her to a burning

wreck that just managed to reach the shore, where her captain beached her. Only one German destroyer, the *Hermann Kunne*, escaped the attack, but was disabled even so, her engines damaged by the explosions of the torpedoes which sank the *Schmitt*.

## MORTALLY WOUNDED

The British destroyers withdrew from the harbour and made their way down Ofotfjord at 15 knots, still with plenty of ammunition left. As they passed Herangsfjord to starboard, the German destroyers *Wolfgang Zenker, Erich Giese* and *Erich Koellner* were seen emerging from it, and both sides opened fire, the British ships increasing speed to 30 knots. Ahead of them, two more German destroyers, the *Georg Thiele* and *Berndt von Arnim*, crept out of Ballangenfjord into the British warships' path, trapping them between two forces. In the savage fight that ensued, HMS *Hardy* received the full weight of fire from the *Thiele* and *Arnim*. With her captain mortally wounded and her steering gear shattered, she grounded on some rocks 274m (300yds) from shore. About 170 of her crew struggled ashore, taking Warburton-Lee with them, lashed to a Carley Float. He died just as they pulled him from the water.

Lt-Cdr L. de Villiers in HMS *Hunter* now led the British line. Raked by shells and burning, *Hunter* rapidly lost way, wallowing to a stop. Close behind her, Lt Cdr H.F. Layman in HMS *Hotspur* gave urgent orders to take

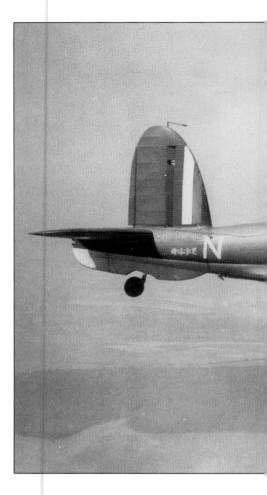

The Blackburn Skua was a fine dive-bomber and registered some success in that role during the Norwegian campaign. It was also used as a fighter, a task to which it was not well suited.

avoiding action, but at that moment a German shell cut the steering controls and *Hotspur*'s bow ripped into the helpless destroyer in front. Both ships now came under heavy fire. With shells bursting all around, Layman managed to make his way from the bridge to the after steering position, and after much effort succeeded in extricating his badly damaged ship from the sinking Hunter. The other two British destroyers, *Havock* and *Hostile*, came to *Hotspur*'s rescue, engaging the *Thiele* and *Arnim* as the latter ran down the fjord in the opposite direction, both seriously damaged. The German vessels vanished in the murk, leaving the British warships free to continue their

> It had left the Germans with two destroyers sunk, three so badly damaged as to be unseaworthy, one with a flooded magazine and another with her engines out of action.

dash for the open sea. Of the *Hunter's* crew of nearly 200, 50 men were rescued from the freezing waters by the Germans.

The encounter was not quite over. As the British destroyers headed seawards, they sighted a large German merchant ship, the *Rauenfels*, entering the fjord. Two shells compelled her crew to abandon ship; two more

caused her to blow up. The Germans might still be in possession of Narvik, but their surviving destroyers could no longer depend on fresh supplies of ammunition with which to replenish their dwindling stocks. So ended the action that came to be known as the first Battle of Narvik. It had left the Germans with two destroyers sunk, three so badly damaged as to be

0unseaworthy, one with a flooded magazine and another with her engines out of action. Set against the loss of two British destroyers, it was a notable victory, and one that earned Captain Warburton-Lee the award of a posthumous Victoria Cross.

The exploit of Warburton-Lee's destroyers was not the only British success of 10 April. Early that

## *WARSPITE*

| | | |
|---|---|---|
| **Type:** Battleship | **Dimensions:** 197m x 28m x 9m (646ft x 90ft 6in x 29ft 10in) | **Powerplant:** Quadruple screw turbines |
| **Launch date:** 26 November 1913 | **Range:** 8100km (4500nm) at 10 knots | **Performance:** 23 knots |
| **Crew:** 951 | **Armament:** Eight 380mm (15in) and 16 152mm (6in) guns | |
| **Displacement:** 33,548 tonnes (33,020 tons) | | |

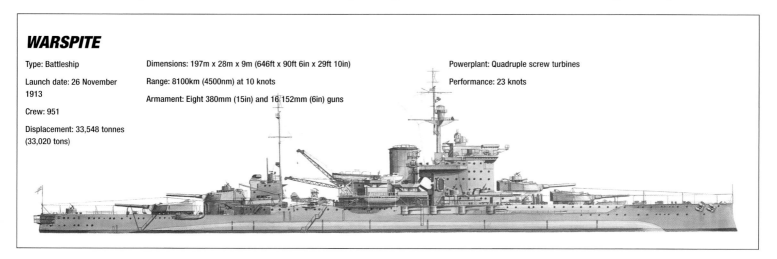

The aircraft carrier HMS *Furious* preparing to recover one of her Fairey Swordfish torpedo-bombers. *Furious* was the Royal Navy's first true aircraft carrier.

morning, 16 Blackburn Skua dive-bombers of the Fleet Air Arm – seven of No. 800 Squadron led by Lt W.P. Lucy, RN and nine of No. 803 led by Capt R.T. Partridge, Royal Marines – took off from Hatston, north of Kirkwall in the Orkneys, each aircraft carrying a 225kg (500lb) bomb. Their target was the German naval force at Bergen, which included the light

cruisers *Königsberg* and *Köln* and the gunnery training ship *Bremse*. The ships had already been attacked by Hampdens of RAF Bomber Command during the night, but without success.

## DIVE-BOMBING ATTACK

After a gruelling 480km (300-mile) flight in darkness, the Skuas – their number reduced to 15 after one aircraft returned with engine trouble – made landfall on the Norwegian coast just as the sun was rising. Climbing to 2440m (8000ft), they made their dive-bombing attack on

the *Königsberg* in line astern. The bombing was highly accurate and the cruiser, having suffered three direct hits and a dozen near misses, exploded and sank. She was the first major warship to be sunk by air attack in war. One Skua was shot down by AA fire, which was quite heavy once the Germans had got over their initial surprise, and two more were damaged. It was unfortunate that the *Köln* was no longer in Bergen harbour when the Skuas made their attack; together with the *Bremse* and some smaller craft, she had put to sea earlier on the orders of Konteradmiral Schmundt, commanding the Bergen task group.

Admiral Sir Max Horton's submarine screen, meanwhile, had been enjoying mixed success. HMS *Truant* had sunk the *Karlsruhe* (as already mentioned), and in the early days of the campaign the submarines also sank a dozen enemy transports, the U-boat *U-1* and a tanker. The success was tempered, however, by the loss of three of their own number: *Thistle* (11 April, by *U-4*); and *Tarpon* (14 April) and *Sterlet* (18 April), both by depth-charge attack. One major success was registered by HMS *Spearfish* (Lt Cdr J.G. Forbes). Early on 11 April, she was on the surface and recharging her batteries after running the gauntlet of enemy warships. Then the heavy cruiser *Lützow* was sighted, returning to Germany at high speed. Forbes fired a salvo of torpedoes at her and one struck her right aft, wrecking her propellers and rudder and leaving her helpless. Unaware that the battleship had no anti-submarine escort, and with his batteries still not replenished, Forbes broke off the attack, leaving the *Lützow* wallowing in the water. She summoned help and was towed to Kiel in a near-sinking condition, and it was to be a year before she was ready for sea again – a year in which she might

> The cruiser, having suffered three direct hits and a dozen near misses, exploded and sank. She was the first major warship to be sunk by air attack in war.

otherwise have been free to prey on Britain's convoys.

Also on 11 April, Admiral Forbes authorized a sortie towards Trondheim with the battleships *Rodney*, *Valiant* and *Warspite*, the carrier *Furious* and the heavy cruisers *Berwick*, *Devonshire* and *York*. The carrier launched a strike of 18 Fairey Swordfish of Nos. 816 and 818 Squadrons against the *Hipper*, reported to be at Trondheim, but the German cruiser had departed for Germany with the destroyer *Friedrich Eckoldt*. Three other destroyers, the

*Paul Jacobi*, *Theodor Riedel* and *Bruno Heidemann*, were still at Trondheim, awaiting the arrival of their tanker. These were attacked, but the water was too shallow for the air-dropped torpedoes to function properly and they exploded harmlessly on the bottom.

The Admiralty, meanwhile, was anxious to finish the job begun by Captain Warburton-Lee's destroyers at Narvik on 10 April. On the 13th, the destroyers *Bedouin*, *Cossack*, *Eskimo*, *Forester*, *Foxhound*, *Hero*, *Icarus*, *Kimberley* and *Punjabi*, covered by the

**Like *Furious*, HMS *Glorious* was a light cruiser before her conversion to an aircraft carrier. She fell easy prey to the heavy armament of the German battlecruisers off Norway.**

*Warspite*, were sent to comb the surrounding fjords for the eight surviving German vessels. The *Warspite*'s Swordfish floatplane, spotting for her guns, sighted the submarine *U-64* and sank her, while the destroyer force fell on the enemy ships, starved of fuel and ammunition. The Germans fought bravely to the end, but they were no match for the

**The destroyer *Acasta* was sunk by the *Scharnhorst* as she was trying to defend the doomed aircraft carrier HMS *Glorious*, but she torpedoed the enemy battlecruiser beforehand.**

British destroyers and the battleship's guns, and all were destroyed or scuttled. Three British destroyers were damaged, two seriously. Swordfish from the *Furious* also took part in this second Battle of Narvik, but scored no successes and lost two of their number. After this, the carrier remained at Tromso for several days to provide air-reconnaissance facilities after the fleet returned to Scapa Flow for replenishment, suffering damage from a near miss during an air attack. In all, she was in action for 14 days, during which she lost nine Swordfish, with three aircrew killed and nine wounded. All the remaining aircraft of her air group were damaged to some extent.

Between 14 April and 2 May, 11,000 Allied troops were landed at Aandalsnes and Molde (Sickle Force) and Namsos (Maurice Force), air support being provided by a squadron (No. 263) of Gloster Gladiator fighters, flown off HMS *Glorious*. Both

ports of disembarkation, however, were soon rendered unusable by the *Luftwaffe*, whose bombers were operating primarily from Stavanger airfield. In an ill-conceived scheme to deny the use of this base to the Germans, the cruiser HMS *Suffolk* (Captain J. Durnford) was despatched to bombard it on 17 April. Predictably, she was dive-bombed, and damaged so severely that she only just managed to limp home with her quarterdeck awash.

## UNTENABLE POSITION

Before the end of April, it became clear that the position of the Allied forces facing Trondheim was untenable, and on the 28th Admiral Forbes was ordered to re-embark the troops with all possible speed. This was achieved by 3 May, nearly all the men being lifted off by eight cruisers, seven destroyers, one sloop and two troop transports. The King of Norway and the Crown Prince were also evacuated to Tromso by the cruiser *Glasgow*. The British destroyer *Afridi*, the French destroyer *Bison* and the sloop *Bittern* were sunk by air attack during these operations.

Other naval forces, meanwhile, had been operating in support of landings further north, the objective being to capture Narvik. The naval side of

## SEIZURE OF THE CHANNEL PORTS

**On 10 May 1940, German forces invaded France and the Low Countries, and within 10 days were menacing the Channel ports of Calais and Boulogne. Despite gallant resistance by French troops and British reinforcements, the Allied position quickly became untenable and orders were issued for evacuation. This was carried out in the main by eight British and three French destroyers, HMS *Wessex* being lost to air attack during the Calais evacuation on 24 May.**

these operations was under the command of Admiral of the Fleet Lord Cork and Orrery, who was later placed in command of the whole expedition. Air support was again provided by the Gladiators of No. 263 Squadron, joined this time by the Hawker Hurricanes of No. 46, flown off the carriers *Furious* and *Glorious* and operating from airstrips at Bardufoss and Skaanland. During the landing operations on 21 May, the

cruiser *Effingham* grounded on a shoal off Bodo while taking avoiding action during an air attack and capsized.

On 26 May, the anti-aircraft cruiser HMS *Curlew*, intended to be the flagship of Lord Cork, was bombed and sunk by Junkers 88s of KG30 off Skaanland. Cork transferred his flag to the AA cruiser *Cairo*, and on the night of 27/28 May this ship, together with the cruisers *Coventry*, *Southampton*, five destroyers and a sloop, gave fire

support to French Foreign Legion and Polish troops advancing on Narvik, which was captured on the 28th. Once again, the action came too late.

By this time, the focus of Allied operations had switched to France and the Low Countries, invaded by the Germans a fortnight earlier. The need for every available man to stem the enemy invasion left the Allied governments with no alternative but to evacuate Narvik as soon as its port facilities had been destroyed, and orders were issued for the evacuation of the 25,000-strong Allied force almost as soon as the town was captured. This was accomplished by 15 large troopships, with air cover

**A convoy in the North Atlantic during the early months of the war. The British had used the convoy system successfully in World War I, and lost no time in adopting it again.**

provided by the few surviving fighters on shore and by aircraft from the *Ark Royal* and *Glorious*, and naval escort by the cruisers *Southampton* and *Coventry*, plus five destroyers.

Two major warships proceeded independently on 7 June. One was the cruiser *Devonshire*, sailing for

**Exhausted British troops arrive back in England. Contrary to what is often claimed, the British Expeditionary Force in France was extremely well equipped, but lacked adequate air support.**

Scapa Flow with King Haakon of Norway and members of his government; the other was the carrier *Glorious*, homeward bound at reduced speed because she was short of fuel. She carried the surviving Gladiators and Hurricanes, together with the personnel of the two fighter squadrons, and was escorted only by the destroyers *Ardent* and *Acasta*.

In the afternoon of 8 June, *Glorious* and her escorts were intercepted by the *Scharnhorst* and *Gneisenau*, out on

a sortie against the Allied troop transports west of Harstad. The carrier was caught completely unaware; for reasons that were never explained, none of her reconnaissance Swordfish was airborne. Desperate attempts were made to arm and launch them as the enemy battlecruisers came in sight, but she was overwhelmed and sunk before this could be accomplished. Her escorting destroyers were also sunk, but not before the *Acasta*, already doomed, had hit the

*Scharnhorst* with a torpedo. The warship limped into Trondheim, and on 13 June the *Ark Royal* flew off a strike of 15 Skuas of Nos. 800 and 803 Squadrons against her. One 225kg (500lb) bomb hit the battlecruiser and failed to explode; eight Skuas failed to return.

On 21 June, a reconnaissance Sunderland reported that the *Scharnhorst* had left Trondheim and was steaming slowly south escorted by eight destroyers and torpedo boats.

> As the destroyer went down, her survivors saw Commodore Charles Glasfurd standing along on her shattered bridge, smoking a cigarette, waving to them and wishing them good luck.

Attacks by RAF Beaufort torpedo-bombers and by Fleet Air Arm Swordfish were beaten off, the attackers suffering heavy losses, and the *Scharnhorst* reached Kiel on 23 June without further damage. The important fact, though, was that *Acasta*'s torpedo hit had almost certainly averted the destruction of the Allied convoys, which were the German warships' main objectives. Just before making the attack, the *Acasta*'s captain addressed his crew with these words:

You may think we are running

Craft of all kinds were pressed into service to lift the British and French troops off the beaches at Dunkirk. Small boats were used to ferry men from the beach to larger craft waiting offshore.

away from the enemy. We are not. Our chummy ship [*Ardent*] has sunk, the *Glorious* is sinking; the least we can do is make a show. Make a show he and his crew did. And as the destroyer went down, her survivors saw Commodore Charles Glasfurd standing alone on her shattered bridge, smoking a cigarette, waving to them and wishing them good luck. He was never seen again.

## CALAIS AND BOULOGNE

Meanwhile, by 19 May, the prospect of mass evacuation as the only means of saving the British Expeditionary Force had already become reality. On that day, the task of operational planning for such an eventuality was assigned to Admiral Sir Bertram Ramsay, the Flag

Officer Commanding Dover. Together with Admiral Sir Reginald Drax, the C-in-C Nore, Ramsay had hitherto been responsible for the naval units – mainly destroyers detached from Scapa Flow – which had been providing a shuttle service for naval and military personnel to Ijmuiden, the Hook of Holland, Flushing and Antwerp. Following the Dutch collapse, these craft had been involved in evacuating servicemen and VIPs, including the Dutch royal family; clearing useful shipping from the harbours; and transferring the substantial Dutch reserves of gold and diamonds to England. Attention was then switched to the Belgian ports, and naval parties successfully removed large numbers of merchantmen, barges and tugs from Antwerp. The relatively small destroyer force worked tirelessly, embarking and landing troops, bringing out Allied missions and foreign nationals, and bombarding shore targets as well as providing additional anti-aircraft capability against the *Luftwaffe*'s increasingly furious attacks.

## DUNKIRK

Even at a time when Boulogne and Calais were still in Allied hands, it was clear that any major evacuation would have to be from Dunkirk, or more precisely from the adjoining beaches. There was no possibility of using the main harbour, with its seven dock basins; this had already been blocked by air attack on 20 May. Indeed, were it not for the action of Admiral Jean

Abrial, C-in-C French Naval Forces (North), who had ordered several merchantmen and French naval craft out to sea as soon as the attacks began, the blockage would certainly have been much worse.

Destroyers were vital to Ramsay's plans; although far from ideal as troopships, they could take their quota of men, and their speed and manoeuvrability would make them difficult targets to hit. Moreover, their

firepower would prove an invaluable asset, particularly in the anti-aircraft role. The problem was that in May 1940 destroyers were fast becoming worth more than their weight in gold; of the 220 on the Royal Navy's inventory at that time, the majority were in the Mediterranean or the Far East, and many of those serving with the Home Fleet were heavily committed to the Norwegian campaign. The withdrawal of destroyers and, to a lesser extent, cruisers from the Home Fleet for service with the Nore and Dover Commands was a serious step, at a time when the protection of the Atlantic shipping routes was becoming vital to the survival of Britain. It was a risk that had to be taken. Fortunately, although the British did not know it at

> The withdrawal of destroyers and, to a lesser extent, cruisers from the Home Fleet for service with the Nore and Dover Command, was a serious step.

The Junkers Ju 87 Stuka dive-bomber was feared by the Allied ground forces during the Battle of France, but it was vulnerable to fighter attack, as was shown later in the Battle of Britain.

closed, which meant using the longer routes – and then, with the armada of ships exposed for hours on the long haul, it would be the *Luftwaffe's* turn. For the bulk of the BEF, still fighting its way back to the perimeter, the chances of survival now seemed slender indeed.

## EXTREMELY HAZARDOUS

The naval forces committed to Dynamo by Ramsay on this, the first major day of the evacuation, consisted of one anti-aircraft cruiser (HMS *Calcutta*), nine destroyers and four minesweepers, all of which had been ordered to close the beaches and use their small boats to supplement the lifts being carried out by the cross-Channel steamers and drifters. But at low tide the destroyers could approach no closer than a mile inshore, which meant that the crews of their whalers faced a 20-minute pull to the beaches, at the end of which they could take on a maximum of 25 men. By this method, loading a destroyer to its maximum capacity of 1000 men could take six hours or more, and there was also the weather to be considered. The approaches to the beaches were tricky in ideal conditions, and if the wind, which was at present blowing from the east, veered to the north, small-boat operations in the shallows would become extremely hazardous.

The only alternative was to use the East Mole, although whether ships would be able to berth alongside it safely was by no means certain. Nevertheless, it was a risk that had to be taken. At 2230 on the 27th, Tennant ordered the personnel vessel *Queen of the Channel* (under Captain

the time, the losses suffered by the German Navy off Norway had been extensive enough to prevent any forays into the Atlantic for some time to come.

Every hour's delay would mean the sacrifice of men as the jaws of the German vise tightened. At 1857 hours on 26 May, the signal went out: 'Operation Dynamo is to commence.' It was a singularly appropriate codename, thought up by someone on Ramsay's staff because the operations room at Dover Castle had once housed electrical plant.

The ships that were to spearhead Dynamo – the elderly Isle of Man steam packets *Mona's Isle* and *King Orry* – were already at sea. They berthed at Dunkirk shortly after dark and at once began taking on troops.

The *Mona's Isle* was the first to leave, at dawn on the 27th, carrying 1420 soldiers. As she retraced her path along Route Z, she was straddled by enemy shellfire, and a few minutes later low-flying Messerschmitts raked her decks. By the time she reached Dover, 23 of her passengers were dead and 60 wounded.

Meanwhile, five more transports had made an abortive attempt to reach Dunkirk early that morning. They ran into heavy fire from the Gravelines batteries. The motor vessel *Sequacity* was hit and sank within minutes; the remainder, unable to break through the fearsome curtain of water hurled up by the shells, turned away and came back to Dover empty. It was clearly only a matter of time before Route Z would have to be

**One of the Royal Navy's older destroyers, HMS *Verity* was built in 1919. She and her sister vessels all served in home waters and were relegated to training duties in 1943.**

W.J. Odell) to come alongside the mole; the ship berthed successfully, which gave Tennant a glimmer of hope. Where one ship had gone, others could follow, and the mole was long enough to accommodate 16 vessels at a time. During the early hours of 28 May, five destroyers – the *Wakeful, McKay, Harvester, Codrington* and *Sabre* – bore the brunt of the evacuation. Dispatched hurriedly from Dover and other ports along England's south coast, their captains had not had time to receive any briefing other than to proceed to Dunkirk to pick up troops.

It was not the German Air Force that struck the first serious blow against the Royal Navy during Dynamo. In the early hours of 29 May, the destroyer *Wakeful*, homeward bound with 640 troops, was torpedoed and sunk by the German MTB *S30*, one of three *Schnellboote* (or E-boats)

that had sailed from Wilhelmshaven the previous afternoon and entered the operational area after dark. Torn in two, *Wakeful* went down in less than a minute, taking more than 700 men with her. Some time later, the destroyer *Grafton*, searching for *Wakeful's* survivors, was torpedoed by the German submarine *U62* and disabled. Her guns, and those of the minesweeper *Lydd*, opened fire on what looked like the silhouette of a torpedo boat, which was then rammed and sunk by the *Lydd*. The 'enemy intruder' was, however, the drifter *Comfort*, laden with men from the *Wakeful*. There were only five survivors, among them the *Wakeful's* captain, Commander Ralph Fisher. As for the stricken *Grafton*, she was sunk by the destroyer *Ivanhoe* after her survivors had been taken off.

## STUKA ATTACK

This was only the beginning of a terrible toll that was to be exacted from the British ships on 29 May. In the afternoon, Dunkirk came under

attack by 180 Stukas, and the destroyer *Grenade*, taking on troops at the East Mole, was an early casualty. Hit by three bombs, ablaze from stem to stern, she was towed clear by a trawler minutes before she exploded. Next to suffer was the destroyer *Jaguar*, which had just got underway when she took a direct hit and had to be abandoned, although she remained afloat and was rescued later. Another destroyer, HMS *Verity*, succeeded in getting clear, with near misses exploding all around, only to run aground beyond the harbour mouth and suffer damage. The armed boarding vessel *King Orry*, the trawler *Calvi*, the paddle minesweeper *Gracie Fields* and the personnel ship *Fenella* were also sunk in the Stuka attack, the *King Orry* colliding with the mole after being hit and putting it temporarily out of action.

**British and French troops embarking in France for the passage to England. The defence of the Dunkirk perimeter by French soldiers in the final stages of the evacuation was vital to the success of Operation Dynamo.**

After the Stukas came the horizontal bombers, the Heinkels and Dorniers, together with more dive-bombers, this time twin-engined Junkers 88s. The latter attacked the biggest merchant vessel used in the Dunkirk evacuation – the 7010-tonne (6900-ton) Glasgow freighter *Clan MacAlister* – and set her on fire, killing a third of her crew as well as many of the soldiers who had recently boarded her. Her survivors were taken off by the minesweeper *Pangbourne*, which was already laden with those from the *Gracie Fields*. Some 10km (6 miles) west of Dunkirk, Heinkels caught the

**Those who were left behind. Some of the thousands of Allied troops captured at Dunkirk after the last evacuation boats had sailed away.**

Southern Railway ship *Normannia* in the open sea off Mardyck and sent her to the bottom. Her sister ship, the *Lorina*, suffered a similar fate minutes later, while the minesweeper *Waverley*, with 800 troops on board, went down in that same cauldron. Hard by the beaches, the old Thames river paddle steamer *Crested Eagle*, filled to capacity with troops and the survivors of the *Fenella*, was hit by a single bomb and

burst into flames. A red-hot furnace, with burning men leaping overboard into the oily water, she slowly approached the beach under the direction of her skipper, Lt Cdr Booth. At last, she grounded and the survivors were able to struggle ashore through the shallows.

**AWFUL TOLL**

Such was the awful toll of 29 May. And, in addition to the ships sunk,

> On the morning of 30 May, fog descended on the beaches, enabling the small craft to go about their evacuation task without interference from the *Luftwaffe*.

many others had been seriously damaged. As dusk fell on the 29th, the scene off the beaches at Dunkirk was one of utter carnage. Nevertheless, 47,310 men had been lifted off during the day, 33,558 of them from the East Mole before it was put out of action. But the day's losses had persuaded the First Sea Lord, Admiral Sir Dudley Pound, to withdraw the Navy's eight most modern destroyers from Dynamo. This meant that the burden

of the evacuation would now fall on the 15 elderly destroyers still at Ramsay's disposal, and these would be capable of lifting not more than 17,000 men in the next 24 hours.

On the morning of 30 May, fog descended on the beaches, enabling the small craft to go about their evacuation task without interference from the *Luftwaffe*. And as the fog persisted, the evacuation received an unexpected boost when the First Sea

**The RAF pressed all kinds of aircraft into use to fly what became known as the 'sands patrol' during the Dunkirk evacuation. Here, a Lockheed Hudson of RAF Coastal Command flies over ships of the evacuation fleet.**

Lord decided to lift his restriction on the use of the modern 'G', 'H', 'I' and 'J' class destroyers. The lifting of the ban was supposed to be temporary, but in the event the demands of Operation Dynamo were

to become so pressing over the next 24 hours that the destroyers remained committed to the end.

The activities of the rescue ships were now co-ordinated by Rear-Admiral Frederick Wake-Walker, controlling a staff of 80 officers and ratings. His primary concern was to get the East Mole operational once more. By 2030 on 30 May, following hasty repairs, he judged that it was once again fit for use by destroyers and minesweepers (the latter being particularly hard-worked during the evacuation), and he sent a signal to that effect to Admiral Ramsay in Dover. With ships once again working from the mole, the number of troops lifted off increased substantially, and by midnight the

Top: HMS *Skipjack*, seen here in 1940, was a 'Halcyon' class minesweeper. She was bombed and sunk off Dunkirk in June 1940.

Right: By the end of the evacuation, Dunkirk harbour was choked with sunken ships. It took the Royal Navy a long time to recover from the loss of some of its most modern destroyers.

day's total had reached 53,823, of whom some 30,000 had been taken from the beaches.

On Friday 31 May, the task of the evacuation personnel doubled, for now the decision had been taken to lift off French troops in equal numbers – and the evacuation fleet had already suffered badly, from collisions, groundings and mechanical troubles as much as from enemy

## OTHER EVACUATION OPERATIONS

It should not be forgotten that the Royal Navy participated in other evacuation operations after Dunkirk. Between 4 and 25 June 1940, British ships carried out a whole series of evacuations beginning at Le Havre, moving west to the Gulf of St Malo, the Channel Islands and Cherbourg, round Ushant to Brest, along the French Biscay coast to St Nazaire and La Pallice, and finally from Bayonne and St Jean de Luz near the Spanish frontier. These operations, collectively known by the codename of Aerial, resulted in the rescue of an additional 191,870 fighting troops and 35,000 civilians. The biggest loss incurred during this phase occurred at St Nazaire, when the troopship *Lancastria* was sunk with 9000 on board; 5000 men were killed or reported missing.

action. Moreover, navigation on the approaches to Dunkirk was becoming extremely hazardous because of sunken wrecks; and to make matters worse the wind had risen to Force 3, seriously complicating the task of the small craft in the shallows. The crisis seemed grave; and then, in the afternoon, both enemy activity and the swell decreased. By the time the

The British liner *Lancastria* sinking after being bombed by Ju 88s off St Nazaire. The loss of life was enormous – nearly 2000 – and the story of the sinking was suppressed for a long time.

day ended, no fewer than 68,104 men had been taken off – the highest daily total of the whole operation.

## FULL SALVO
The morning of 1 June dawned bright and clear, and the *Luftwaffe* was over the beaches from first light. It was a terrible day, and it began with the destruction of the fleet minesweeper HMS *Skipjack*. She was lying at anchor, still taking on troops, when she took a full delivery from a dive-bomber and exploded. She sank quickly with 275 men on board, and there were few

survivors. The massacre went on unchecked. Some vessels, in the act of taking on troops, were powerless to take evasive action; other captains, like Lt Cdr Kirkpatrick of the minesweeper HMS *Dundalk,* suspended operations and kept their ships on the move, zig-zagging along the coast amid a hail of bombs. The fleet destroyer HMS *Havant* headed out into the channel with so many troops on board that her entire superstructure seemed to be covered in khaki. The next instant, a full salvo of bombs hit her, killing all her engine-room staff. Immediately,

She was lying at anchor, still taking on troops, when she took a full delivery from a dive-bomber and exploded. She sank quickly with 275 men on board. Few survived.

two minesweepers closed alongside her and the troops poured from the stricken ship on to their decks. The *Havant* had taken two bombs through her engine room and a third exploded as she passed over it. The

minesweeper HMS *Saltash* tried to take her in tow, but it was hopeless. At 1015, after further air attacks, she sank with the loss of 34 hands.

Other ships were more fortunate. The destroyer *Ivanhoe* had a bomb rip through her forward funnel and explode in the boiler room; terror-stricken soldiers scrambled from her lower decks and on to the minesweeper HMS *Speedwell*, which came alongside. Despite her damage,

the destroyer remained afloat and was taken in tow by the tug *Persia*. The air attacks continued throughout the day, and claimed other victims. The French destroyer *Foudroyant* took three direct hits and went down in minutes, her survivors defiantly singing 'La Marseillaise' as they drifted with the tide amid islands of debris and pools of oil. Nor was it only the warships that suffered, although they were the bombers' primary targets. The old *Brighton Queen*, a paddleboat converted for minesweeping, had just set out for Dover with 700 French troops on

The destroyers *Worcester* and *Walpole* in line astern. Although old ships, they rendered excellent service on convoy-protection duties in home waters throughout World War II.

Some troops arrived back in England with hardly any clothing, having lost everything swimming out to rescue craft that waited to evacuate them.

board when the Stukas pounced and hit her afterdeck with a 225kg (550lb) bomb, causing fearful casualties. The survivors were taken off by the minesweeper *Saltash* before the *Brighton Queen* sank. There were casualties, too, on the personnel vessel *Prague*, which was steaming away from Dunkirk with 3000 French troops on board when she was hit and damaged; another merchant ship, the

*Scotia*, was also hit while carrying 2000 French troops, many of whom were drowned when they panicked and rushed the boats. The destroyer HMS *Esk* took off most of the survivors. The *Scotia*, of 3500 tonnes (3454 tons), was the largest ship to be lost that day.

## HEAVILY SHELLED

On some ships that managed to limp back to Dover, the casualty toll was frightening. The old destroyer HMS *Worcester* was relentlessly attacked for 30 minutes by dive-bombers, sustaining damage that reduced her speed to a mere 10 knots. Even so,

she limped across the Channel with her pitiful cargo of 350 dead and 400 wounded. In all, the evacuation fleet lost 31 vessels sunk and 11 damaged on 1 June, a day in which the seaborne units nevertheless managed to lift off 64,429 British and French troops. Since the last stretches of beach still in Allied hands, and the ships offshore, were now being heavily shelled, Admiral Ramsay planned to lift as many men as possible in a single operation on the night of 1/2 June, concentrating all available ships after dark in the Dunkirk and St Malo areas. For this purpose, he had at his

disposal some 60 ships, together with the many small craft still involved in the operation; the French could provide 10 ships and about 120 fishing craft. By midnight on 2 June, a further 26,256 soldiers had been evacuated.

There remained the French, some 30,000 of them, who continued to defend the Dunkirk perimeter throughout 3 June. The last great effort of Ramsay's evacuation fleet therefore had to be made during the night of 3/4 June, and the resources

available to accomplish the task were seriously depleted. Of the 41 destroyers originally allocated to Dynamo, only nine remained, and only five of the 45 personnel vessels. Nevertheless, they performed a magnificent task on this last night, and when the last ship – the elderly destroyer *Shikari* – left the East Mole just before dawn on 4 June, her load brought the total for the night to 26,209, all but seven of them French troops. At 0900, the Dunkirk garrison

**A convoy in the English Channel. With the French coast dominated by the Germans, it was no longer possible to send unescorted merchant vessels through the Channel with impunity.**

capitulated. Later that day, at 1423 to be precise, the Admiralty announced the completion of Operation Dynamo. In nine days of incredible achievement 198,284 British troops had been brought away. Including the 26,042 'useless mouths' taken off before the start of the evacuation proper, this

**The crew of a British warship keeps a watchful eye for enemy aircraft and S-boats as a convoy is shepherded through the narrow seas of the English Channel.**

made a grand total of 224,686 men of the British Expeditionary Force, of whom 13,053 were wounded. The number of Allied troops evacuated eventually rose to 141,445, making a combined total of 366,131.

The cost of Operation Dynamo had been terribly high for the seaborne forces engaged. Of the 693 British ships committed, 226 had been sunk, 56 of them destroyers, minesweepers and personnel vessels. For the small ships of the Royal Navy, Dunkirk was a chapter of gallantry and achievement that was not to be surpassed in the grim years to come.

## PROTECTING THE CONVOYS, 1940–41

There was to be no respite for the Royal Navy in the months following Dunkirk. While the British Army strove to make good the attrition it had suffered in France, and to fortify England's coastal defences against an expected invasion, the Royal Navy also strove to organize a strong defence force of four destroyer flotillas – 32

With the capture of the Channel and North Sea ports in France and the Low Countries, German *Schnellboote* – known as E-boats to the British – were a principal threat to coastal convoys.

ships in all – based on Harwich, Dover, Portsmouth and Plymouth. It was a desperately difficult task, for most of the destroyers that had survived the Dunkirk evacuation had been dispersed for repairs and others were still engaged in evacuating British personnel from the Biscay ports and the Channel Islands. Fortunately, because of the attrition suffered in the Norwegian campaign,

the German Navy was as yet in no position to offer a serious challenge. In June 1940, the Germans had only one flotilla of large destroyers, two flotillas of smaller destroyers and many fast motor torpedo craft – the S-boats, referred to erroneously as E-boats by the British. It was these *Schnellboote* that would prove to be the biggest thorn in the Royal Navy's side, especially now that they were able to operate from newly captured French harbours.

On 19 June, they struck their first blow against mercantile traffic in the Channel when *S19* and *S26* sank the freighter *Roseburn* off Dungeness. On the night of 24/25 June, *S36* and *S19* sank the tanker *Albuera* and the coaster *Kingfisher* in the same area. By this time, a flotilla of five British MTBs was operating from Dover with the task of countering the S-boat threat,

but it was to be some time before these craft became available in sufficient numbers to make any impression on the enemy. In any case, the S-boats were faster, bigger and better armed than the British craft, and it needed skill and judgement – which would come only with operational experience – to get the better of them.

### INTENSIVE AIR ATTACKS

Early in July, the *Luftwaffe* began a series of intensive air attacks on British East coast convoys, and in the course of the month these operations accounted for 40 Allied merchant ships totalling 76,912 tonnes (75,698

For the small ships of the Royal Navy, Dunkirk was a chapter of gallantry and achievement that was not to be surpassed in the grim years to come.

The sea shall not have them. Fortuately a timely rescue comes along for the survivors of a sunken merchant ship in the Western Approaches.

tons), together with the destroyers *Brazen* (20 July), *Codrington* (27 July), *Delight* (29 July) and *Wren* (27 July). Mines, too, remained a constant threat. In mid-July enemy aircraft laid mines in the Thames Estuary and off Harwich, while surface craft sowed two new mine barrages in the English Channel. Two more barrages were laid in August, in the south-west part of the North Sea. Also in August,

German minelaying aircraft extended their activities to the harbour entrances of Belfast, Falmouth, Liverpool, Penzance, Plymouth and Southampton. On 31 August, a German minefield off Texel brought about the loss of the destroyers *Esk* and *Ivanhoe*, with a third destroyer, HMS *Express*, being severely damaged. Minesweeping operations assumed high priority; the Royal Navy now had some 700 minesweepers at its disposal, the majority auxiliary craft such as converted trawlers and drifters. Quite apart from the dangers inherent in

their task, they were constantly attacked from the air and by enemy surface craft and U-boats, and their losses were not light. Theirs is an often forgotten page of quiet heroism in the story of Britain's fight for survival.

While the fighter pilots of the Royal Air Force fought their own grim battle in British skies, the Royal Navy took every available opportunity to strike at shipping movements off the enemy coast, even though operating conditions in the Channel had become very difficult because of air attack. On 8 September 1940, for example, three motor torpedo boats (MTB 14, MTB 15 and MTB 17) set out from Dover to attack a German convoy of about 30 small vessels approaching Ostend. Two of the boats, MTBs 15 and 17, entered Ostend harbour under cover of darkness and an RAF air raid, and launched their torpedoes, hitting two unidentified vessels. It was the first successful British MTB torpedo attack of the war.

On the night of 10/11 September, a striking force comprising the destroyers *Malcolm*, *Veteran* and *Wild Swan* set out to patrol the Channel off Ostend, which was again under air attack, when radar contact was made with an enemy convoy by *Malcolm*, the destroyer leader. Soon afterwards, the destroyers made visual contact with the enemy, aided by the light of flares dropped by RAF aircraft. They opened fire, sinking an escort vessel, two trawlers that were towing barges, and a large barge. Offensive sweeps of this kind were a regular feature during September 1940, when the threat of invasion was at its height, the naval forces usually operating from Harwich or Portsmouth; the Dover destroyer flotilla had been dispersed, having suffered severely in air attacks. At the same time, aircraft of the Fleet Air

WORLD WAR II: THE OPENING BATTLES

Arm, operating from shore bases, joined the RAF in attacks on enemy-held Channel ports, where an invasion fleet of barges was being assembled.

The biggest guns the Navy could bring to bear on enemy coastal targets were mounted in two warships of World War I vintage, the battleship *Revenge* and the monitor *Erebus*. Both mounted 381mm (15in) guns, the *Erebus* being fitted with a twin turret bearing her main armament and also with four twin 102mm (4in) and two single 76mm (3in) AA guns. She carried a crew of 300. On 20 September, she set out from Sheerness to bombard the German gun battery at Cap Gris Nez, but the sortie had to be abandoned because of bad weather. On 30 September, however, she fired 17 rounds into a concentration of invasion craft in the Calais docks area, the fire being directed by a Swordfish spotter aircraft. On the following day, the German battery at Ushant fired precisely the same number of rounds at Dover by way of retaliation.

On 10 October, it was the turn of HMS *Revenge*, the old battleship sailing from Plymouth with a screen of 5th Flotilla destroyers: the *Jackal*,

Two members of the gun crew of a British destroyer take a deserved break after night exercises.

*Kipling, Jupiter, Jaguar, Kashmir* and *Kelvin*. The cruisers *Newcastle* and *Emerald* were also at sea, protecting the western flank, while a flotilla of six MTBs sailed from Portland to provide a screen against S-boats.

## TARGET CHERBOURG

*Revenge*'s target was Cherbourg, and for 18 minutes, beginning at 0333 on 11 October, she laid a barrage of 120 381mm (15in) shells across the

**The battleship HMS *Revenge* served in home waters and on Atlantic convoy duty before joining the Eastern Fleet in 1942. She became a training ship later, and was scrapped in 1948.**

crowded harbour, to which was added a total of 801 119mm (4.7in) shells from the seven escorting destroyers. The resulting conflagration could be seen 65km (40 miles) out to sea. The British force reached Spithead at 0800 without damage, despite being shelled for almost 16km (10 miles) by a German heavy battery. On 16 October, HMS *Erebus*, escorted by the destroyers *Garth* and *Walpole*, again bombarded the French coast in the vicinity of Calais with the aid of spotter aircraft. Forty-five salvoes were fired, beginning at 0100, before the British force withdrew. Neither the *Erebus* nor the *Revenge* made any further sorties of this kind, even though the British heavy gun defences on the Channel coast in October were still pitifully weak.

While the British strove to disrupt German invasion plans, German destroyers were extremely active in the Channel area during September and October 1940, laying more minefields to protect the flanks of their projected cross-Channel invasion routes and also making hit-and-run sorties against British shipping. One particularly successful sortie was undertaken on the night of 11/12 October by the German 5th Flotilla from Cherbourg, comprising the torpedo boats *Greif*,

action was fought between British destroyers of the 5th Flotilla, supported by the light cruisers *Newcastle* and *Emerald*, and the enemy destroyers *Karl Galster*, *Hans Lody*, *Friedrich Ihn* and *Erich Steinbrinck* off Brest on 17 October, with no damage suffered by either side.

The destroyers of the British 5th Flotilla were again in action on the night of 27/28 November 1940, when they intercepted the four German warships named above as the latter made a sortie towards Plymouth. In the ensuing engagement, HMS *Javelin* was hit by two torpedoes, which blew off her bow and stern and detonated the ammunition in her magazine, destroying her superstructure as well as killing three officers and 43 ratings. Remarkably, she remained afloat and

The destroyer HMS *Javelin* in rough seas. *Javelin* later deployed to the Mediterranean, where her class suffered heavy casualties. She was lucky to survive the war, and was scrapped in 1949.

was towed into harbour, to spend 13 months in dock being virtually rebuilt. She eventually returned to operations and went on to survive the war. Notwithstanding actions such as these, it was enemy mines that accounted for the highest proportion of British shipping losses in the closing months of 1940. Of the 42 Royal Navy vessels lost in the Channel area between 1 September and the end of the year, 28 were sunk by mines.

## BRITISH VICTORY
By the end of October 1940, the threat of invasion had receded, and

*Kondor*, *Falke*, *Seeadler* and *Wolf*. They sank the armed trawlers *Listrac* and *Warwick Deeping* with gunfire and torpedoes, and shortly afterwards destroyed the Free French submarine chasers *CH6* and *CH7*, manned by mixed French and Polish crews. The German ships withdrew safely; although they were engaged by the British destroyers *Jackal*, *Jaguar*, *Jupiter*, *Kelvin* and *Kipling*, the latter achieved nothing more spectacular than several near misses. Another inconclusive

### OPERATION SEALION: A NAVAL HISTORIAN'S VIEW

We who lived through those anxious days may reasonably regret that the expedition never sailed; for, had it done so, it is virtually certain that it would have resulted in a British victory comparable for its decisiveness to Barfleur or Quiberon Bay; and it can hardly be doubted that such a victory would have altered the entire course of the war. It is indeed plain today that, of all the factors which have contributed to the failure of Hitler's grandiose invasion plans, none was greater than the lack of adequate instruments of sea power and of a proper understanding of their use on the German side.

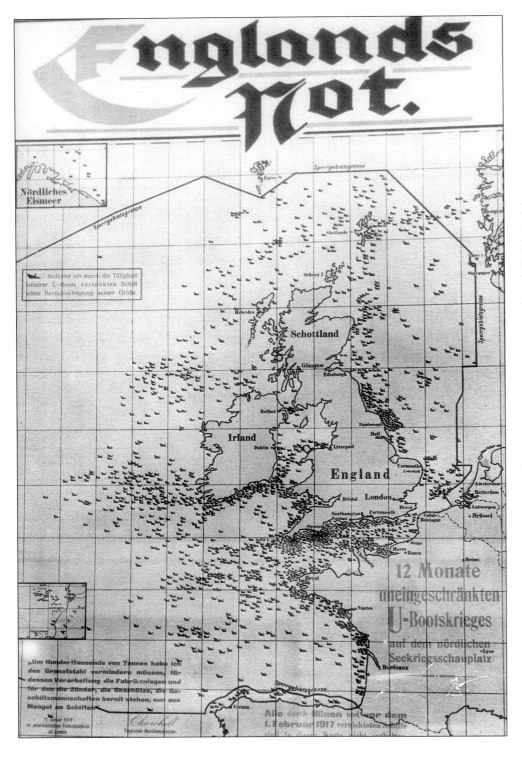

England's peril: A German propaganda illustration shows the British Isles surrounded by sunken ships after a year of submarine warfare. Britain's situation at the end of 1940 was dire.

Hitler's eyes were already turning towards the east. But the question must be asked whether the planned invasion might have succeeded, had it gone ahead. In the opinion of Captain Stephen Roskill, the official Royal Navy historian, it would not have done:

Fine words, and it has to be admitted that the Germans never properly understood how to put their available sea power to its best use. But the principal factor that contributed to the frustration of Germany's invasion plan was the gallantry and determination of a dwindling band of RAF fighter pilots; and the Royal Navy, despite its foretaste off Norway and Dunkirk, had yet to assimilate fully the lesson of what enemy air power could achieve against warships stripped of their own air cover.

In the closing months of 1940, the maritime convoys that were Britain's life-blood faced a threat from several directions. Firstly there were the U-boats, covering the North Sea and the Atlantic approaches. Then there were the surface raiders, ranging from pocket battleships and heavy cruisers to fast merchantmen converted to the armed raider role. Finally, with the capture by the Germans of air bases in the North Sea/English Channel area and on the French Atlantic coast, there was the *Luftwaffe*. The East Coast convoys, which operated on a two-day cycle between the Thames and the Firth of Forth, could be assured of reasonable protection from enemy air attack by RAF Fighter Command, although they were always vulnerable to hit-and-run attacks by S-boats, particularly at night, when air cover was not available. The Channel convoys, on the other hand, were so hard hit from the air in July 1940 that the Admiralty stopped them altogether for a time. Only once the crisis of the Battle of Britain had passed was the RAF able to provide more adequate fighter protection, enabling these convoys to resume under strong air and surface escort. From that point, mines and S-boat attacks were the principal dangers they faced.

## ATLANTIC CONVOYS

The Atlantic convoys fell into several categories. First there were the convoys from Halifax, Nova Scotia, proceeding at 9–10 knots, and the slower convoys sailing at 7–8 knots from Sydney, Cape Breton Island, some distance to the northwest. Then there were the even slower convoys, UK-bound from Freetown, Sierra Leone, and vice versa; and also the convoys sailing to and from Gibraltar. With U-boats and anti-shipping aircraft now established on the French Atlantic coast, all these convoys had to be re-routed. The Admiralty considered the passage south-west of Ireland to be too dangerous, and diverted the bulk of shipping to the

The North Atlantic was an unforgiving place, as this photograph shows. Merchant seamen had to contend with frequent Atlantic storms as well as U-boats.

> The Germans had used similar tactics in World War I, and during the inter-war years had made no secret of the fact that they would use them again.

northwest approaches and the North Channel leading to the Irish Sea.

Because of the need to concentrate warships in UK waters to meet the invasion threat, few escort vessels were available at this time, and the enemy submarines consequently enjoyed considerable success. In June 1940, they sank 58 ships, amounting to nearly 304,814 tonnes (300,000 tons),

their biggest triumph so far. The boats were now operating in packs of four or more craft, making their attacks at night and on the surface – tactics that rendered useless the ASDIC submarine underwater detection equipment carried by the British escort vessels. The Germans had used similar tactics in World War I, and during the inter-war years had made

Triumphant German submariners being welcomed ashore at their base in France. Their triumph was short-lived. Three out of four U-boat crews did not survive the war.

no secret of the fact that they would use them again; the commander of the German U-boat arm, Admiral Karl Dönitz, had even described the surface night-attack method in a book published in 1939. Yet the Royal Navy's anti-submarine crews were trained only to deal with submerged submarines, and were consequently caught unprepared. The result was that for a period of some months, the German submariners enjoyed a complete tactical advantage and were able to inflict heavy losses on the North Atlantic convoys – and this with never more than 15 U-boats at sea at any one time.

Not every factor, however, was in the enemy's favour. At the beginning of September, an agreement was concluded between the British and American Governments whereby 50 surplus US destroyers would be transferred to the Royal Navy in exchange for the lease of bases on British territory in the western hemisphere. Old and ill-equipped though these destroyers undoubtedly were, for the hard-pressed British they were a godsend, and they were quickly brought into service on the Atlantic routes. In addition, new destroyers, sloops and corvettes were being commissioned in growing numbers, enabling the size of the escort groups to be increased; anti-submarine warfare training was gradually becoming more proficient; and co-operation between the Royal Navy and Royal Air Force Coastal Command was steadily improving.

Despite its continuing successes, the German submarine service was hampered by a lack of operational U-boats throughout 1940. Indeed, the

There was also the German training system, which required a U-boat crew to undergo nine months of training in the Baltic and carry out 66 simulated attacks before it was considered operational.

The German commerce raider *Orion* (Schiff 36) and her skipper, Cdr Weyher. *Orion* was sometimes known as the 'Ship without harbour', referring to her wanderings on the high seas.

training system, which required a U-boat crew to undergo nine months of training in the Baltic and carry out 66 simulated attacks before it was considered operational. The overall result was that by the end of 1940, their operational strength stood at only 22 submarines.

## ATLANTIC LIFELINE

It was fortunate for Britain that this was so, because even with the depleted U-boat resources at their disposal, the Germans came close to severing the Atlantic lifeline in the autumn of 1940. To give just one example, between 18 and 20 October convoys SC7 and HX71 lost 31 ships between them to U-boat attacks. And German

Another German commerce radar, the *Thor*, sank 22 merchant ships in two cruises.

low priority accorded to submarine construction in the early part of the war – partly because the German

Naval planners had not expected war before 1944 – meant that the Germans did not have enough craft coming off the slipways to replace the 31 boats lost in the first 15 months of hostilities. There was also the German

submarines were not the only ones with which the Royal Navy had to contend. After some experimental forays through the Straits of Gibraltar in July and August 1940, the Italian Admiralty, the *Supermarina*, began to deploy submarines in considerable numbers to Bordeaux, from where they operated against the Atlantic convoys. By the end of October, 17 Italian boats were operating west of the Bay of Biscay – more submarines than the Germans had in the operational area at this particular time. Under the tactical command of the German Navy, they scored their first successes in the North Atlantic during November.

Although Germany's major warships were mostly inactive during the closing months of 1940, this was far from true of her armed raiders – fast merchantmen heavily armed with six to eight guns and torpedo tubes, and usually carrying a reconnaissance floatplane. The first of them, the *Atlantis*, put to sea on 31 March 1940, and in 622 days of operations she sank 22 ships of 148,034 tonnes

(145,697 tons). By the end of 1940, six more were deployed: the *Orion, Widder, Thor, Pinguin, Komet* and *Kormoran*. Replenishing from supply ships at secret ocean rendezvous points, they were carefully disguised and preyed only on solitary unescorted vessels sailing the world's oceans. Some of their voyages were quite remarkable; the *Kormoran*, for example, left Bergen on 9 July 1940 and reached her operational area in the Pacific by way of the Siberian sea route, her passage assisted by Soviet icebreakers.

The Admiralty's answer to these commerce raiders was to launch a major search for them using Armed Merchant Cruisers, 50 of which had been converted from fast liners. They were unarmoured and underarmed, and no match for their adversaries. A few actions were fought between these vessels towards the end of 1940; all resulted in the British ships suffering severe damage, while inflicting none on the enemy. They fared even worse when they encountered major German warships, as was

The Focke-Wulf Fw 200 Kondor long-range maritime patrol aircraft sank more Allied shipping than U-boats and warships combined in the early months of 1941.

demonstrated on 5 November 1940, when the *Admiral Scheer* attacked Convoy HX84, homeward bound from Halifax with 37 merchantmen and escorted only by the Armed Merchant Cruiser *Jervis Bay*. The latter's captain, E.S.F. Fegen, at once ordered the convoy to scatter under cover of a smokescreen and engaged the *Scheer*. The *Jervis Bay* was sunk with the loss of 191 crew, but Fegen's action (which earned him a posthumous Victoria Cross) bought vital time for the convoy, which lost five ships to the *Scheer*'s guns. Three more were damaged, one of which was the tanker *San Demetrio*. Sixteen men of her crew, who had abandoned the burning vessel, sighted her again 20 hours later and brought their lifeboat alongside; they boarded her, extinguished the fires after a struggle lasting two days, and brought her to harbour in Northern Ireland. Their exploit was

The Admiralty's answer to these commerce raiders was to launch a major search for them using Armed Merchant Cruisers, 50 of which had been converted from fast liners.

made into a propaganda film. However, there is a sad end to the *San Demetrio* story. On 17 March 1942, she was torpedoed by *U-404* east of Chesapeake Bay, and this time she did not survive.

## AIR POWER CAUSES LOSSES

In the first half of 1941, German aircraft presented the main threat to Atlantic and North Sea traffic, causing the heaviest losses. In April alone, they sank 116 ships totalling 328,183 tonnes (323,000 tons), their highest

figure of the whole war. The unit principally responsible for the losses was KG40, whose four-engined Focke Wulf Fw 200 Kondor aircraft, operating from Bordeaux and Stavanger, ranged far to the west of Ireland, seeking targets of opportunity and providing reconnaissance facilities for the U-boat packs. KG40 had already enjoyed substantial success, claiming 368,825 tonnes (363,000 tons) of Allied shipping between August 1940 and February 1941. From 1 January 1941, KG40 came under the

direct control of the *Fliegerführer Atlantik*, a naval command. The Fw 200 threat began to diminish somewhat with the establishment of No. 252 Squadron at Aldergrove, in Northern Ireland, in the spring of 1941. Equipped with long-range, heavily armed Bristol Beaufighters, the squadron and its successors formed a barrier of sorts between the German bombers and the convoys they were threatening, but their effectiveness was hampered in the early days by the reluctance of the RAF to allow the convoy escorts to communicate directly with the aircraft, so that many interception chances were missed. It was not until

**Adolf Hitler, on a visit to the *Bismarck* during her completion. He was fascinated by battleships, and memorized vast amounts of technical information about them.**

## BISMARCK

**Type:** Battleship

**Launch date:** 14 February 1939

**Crew:** 2039

**Displacement:** 50,955 tonnes (50,153 tons)

**Dimensions:** 250m x 36m x 9m (823ft 6in x 118ft x 29ft 6in)

**Range:** 15,000km (8100nm) at 18 knots

**Armament:** Eight 380mm (15in) and 12 152mm (6in) guns and six aircraft

**Powerplant:** Three shaft, geared turbines

**Performance:** 29 knots

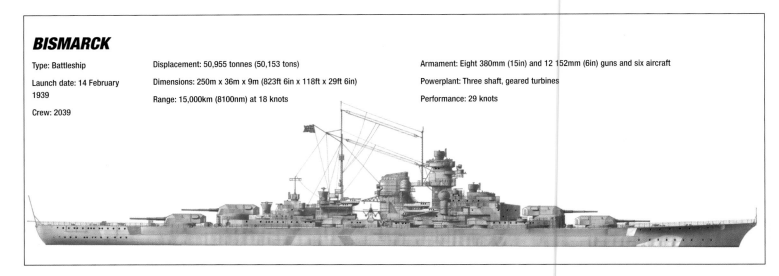

**The battleship *Bismarck* represented a massive threat to the Atlantic convoys that were vital to Britain's survival. She was to have formed part of a powerful battle group.**

the middle of 1941 that a form of fighter direction procedure was instituted.

### DEFENSIVE AIRCRAFT

Another solution to the problem of long-range enemy bombers, as envisaged by the Admiralty, was for the convoys to take their own defensive aircraft with them. For this purpose, and lacking proper escort carriers, a makeshift system was devised whereby merchant ships were fitted with catapults from which a single fighter – either a Fulmar or a Hurricane – could be launched with rocket assistance; the pilot either ditched or bailed out after making his interception. Thirty-five merchant vessels were so equipped, each carrying an aircraft of the Speke-

based Merchant Service Fighter Unit. The vessels were designated either Fighter Catapult (FC) ships, which were naval-manned and flew the White Ensign, or Catapult Aircraft Merchantmen (MAC) ships, which carried normal cargoes and flew the Red Ensign. The ships were fitted with either RAF Ground Controlled Interception (GCI) or type 286P naval radar equipment to give warning of approaching aircraft. The first success was achieved on 3 August 1941, when a Hurricane flown by Lt Everett RN (No. 804 Sqn) from the RN-manned *Maplin* – a converted banana boat – destroyed a Fw200 400 miles from land. Only five Kondors were destroyed by the catapult fighters, but the knowledge that they were accompanying the convoys had an important effect on the morale of both sides.

In the winter of 1940–41, attacks by enemy *Schnellboote* on British coastal convoys were also presenting a serious threat to British coastal convoys, and in December 1940, as a countermeasure, the 6th Motor Gunboat (MGB) Flotilla was formed. It consisted of three previously converted boats, armed with four Lewis guns and one Oerlikon, and five boats originally built for the French Navy; these were armed with four Lewis guns and four .303 Browning machine guns in a Boulton Paul power-operated turret. In March 1941, the 6th MGB Flotilla deployed to Felixstowe and was soon in action

**The battleship HMS *Ramillies* at anchor. A warship of the Royal Sovereign class, *Ramillies* was completed in 1916. She served in the Atlantic, Mediterranean and Indian Ocean.**

## ATLANTIC MARAUDERS

**On 22 January 1941, the *Scharnhorst* and *Gneisenau* left Kiel and broke out into the North Sea, heading for the commerce routes of the North Atlantic. They were sighted in passage on the following day, and the British Home Fleet, commanded by Admiral Sir John Tovey, set out to intercept them south of Iceland. Patrolling cruisers sighted them as they tried to break through, but contact was broken and the German warships withdrew into the Arctic for replenishment. On the night of 3–4 February, they passed through the Denmark Strait undetected, their murderous spree in the Atlantic about to begin.**

against the enemy, joining the existing MTB flotillas in patrolling lines from the Humber to the Hook of Holland and from Texel to the Thames. The Coastal Forces, as these light craft flotillas were collectively known, were to be greatly expanded before the end of 1941.

Meanwhile, Britain was about to face the most serious threat so far to her transatlantic convoy routes. In March 1941, the mighty German battleship *Bismarck* was completing her sea trials in the Baltic. While these were in progress, she was joined by the new 14,224-tonne (14,000-ton) heavy cruiser *Prinz Eugen*, whose captain, Helmuth Brinkmann from Lübeck, had been a classmate of

*Bismarck*'s captain, Rhinelander Ernst Lindemann, at Naval College. The *Prinz Eugen* was a formidable warship in her own right.

On 2 April 1941, the German Naval Staff issued preparatory orders for the deployment of *Bismarck* and other surface units to the Atlantic. In the next new moon period at the end of the month, the *Bismarck*, *Prinz Eugen* and the battlecruiser *Gneisenau* were to rendezvous in the Atlantic to launch a combined attack on Allied shipping.

The *Gneisenau* was then in the French Atlantic port of Brest together with her sister ship, the *Scharnhorst*, which was unable to join the others because her boilers were being

repaired. Even without her, however, it was a formidable battle squadron that was making ready to put to sea. Had it done so in its entirety, the result might have been disastrous for Britain, for *Bismarck* was capable of engaging escorting warships single-handed while her two consorts attacked the merchant convoys themselves. The carnage would have been terrible, as the British were well aware, having already had a taste of the destruction that could be meted out by major German surface units.

## MURDEROUS SPREE

On 8 February, in the North Atlantic, they sighted the British convoy HX106 east of Newfoundland, but the Fleet

The most powerful British battleship to see service in World War II, the *King George V* was deployed to the Pacific in the closing months of the war as flagship of the British Pacific Fleet.

Commander, Admiral Günther Lutjens, thought it prudent not to attack since the merchantmen were escorted by the battleship HMS *Ramillies*. On 22 February, however, still about 500nm east of Newfoundland, they fell upon a westbound convoy that had dispersed and sank five ships, totalling 26,198 tonnes (25,784 tons).

On Saturday 15 March 1941, the two warships were operating in the central North Atlantic when they encountered the scattered ships of another dispersed convoy. The result

The battleship HMS *Nelson. Nelson* served with the Home Fleet and in the Mediterranean and was deployed to the East Indies in 1945 after a refit in the USA.

was a massacre. The *Gneisenau* sank seven freighters totalling 27,121 tonnes (26,693 tons) and captured three tankers of 20,462 tonnes (20,139 tons), while the *Scharnhorst* sank six ships totalling 35,642 tonnes (35,080 tons). The *Gneisenau* had a narrow escape: as she was picking up survivors from her last victim, she was surprised by the battleship HMS *Rodney*, whose

> The carnage would have been terrible, as the British were well aware, having already had a taste of the destruction that could be meted out by major German surface units.

captain, alerted by a distress call, had detached his ship from convoy XH114 and rushed to the scene. The *Gneisenau*'s skipper, Captain Fein, making good use of his ship's superior speed and manoeuvrability, managed to avoid an engagement with his more heavily armed opponent, and got away.

The British Admiralty immediately launched a major operation to trap the German warships, sending the battleships HMS *Rodney* and *King George V* north, to join a third battleship, HMS *Nelson*, a cruiser and two destroyers in covering the Iceland passages. Meanwhile, Force H, with the battlecruiser *Renown*, the aircraft carrier *Ark Royal*, the cruiser *Sheffield* and some destroyers, set out from Gibraltar to cover the approaches to the French Atlantic ports. On 20 March, a Swordfish reconnaissance aircraft from the carrier sighted the tankers captured by the *Gneisenau*. With Force H coming up fast, the prize crews were forced to scuttle two of the vessels, but the third managed to evade the British warships and reached the Gironde estuary. The two German battlecruisers were also sighted by a Swordfish later in the day, but the aircraft had radio trouble and by the time its sighting report was

transmitted the warships had slipped away. On 22 March, they were met by the torpedo boats *Iltis* and *Jaguar* and some minesweepers and escorted into Brest. Their sortie had cost the Allies 22 ships totalling 117,474 tonnes (115,622 tons).

Photographic reconnaissance by RAF Spitfires did not detect the presence of the German warships at Brest until 28 March. As soon as he learned of it, Prime Minister Winston Churchill issued a directive that the battlecruisers were to become a primary target for RAF Bomber Command. The air offensive against them began on the night of 30/31 March, when 109 aircraft were despatched to attack Brest Harbour without result. There was a further abortive attack on 4/5 April by 54 aircraft; their bombs caused considerable damage to the town and one fell in the dry dock alongside the *Gneisenau* without exploding. Her captain thought it advisable to move the ship to the outer harbour, where she would be safer if the bomb detonated while it was being disarmed.

## GALLANT ACTION

She was located there by a photo-reconnaissance Spitfire, and a strike by Coastal Command aircraft was

arranged. The sortie was flown at dawn on 6 April 1941 by six Bristol Beaufort torpedo-bombers of No. 22 Squadron from St Eval, Cornwall, but only one succeeded in locating the target in bad visibility. Its pilot, Flying Officer Kenneth Campbell, made his torpedo run at mast height through intense flak put up by more than 250 guns around the anchorage, as well as three flak ships and the *Gneisenau*'s own armament. The Beaufort was shot down with the loss of all its crew, but not before Campbell had released his torpedo at a range of 457m (500yds). The torpedo exploded on the *Gneisenau*'s stern below the waterline, putting the battlecruiser out of action for months. For his gallant action, Campbell was posthumously awarded the Victoria Cross. The other members of his crew were Sergeants J.P. Scott, W. Mullis and R.W. Hillman. It was one of the bravest, and in retrospect the most important, deeds of the war.

The Commander-in-Chief of the German Navy, Admiral Raeder, was now faced with a dilemma. He could postpone the planned Atlantic sortie until the *Bismarck*'s sister ship, the *Tirpitz*, was ready to join her, but she was only just about to begin her trials, and the longer the mission was

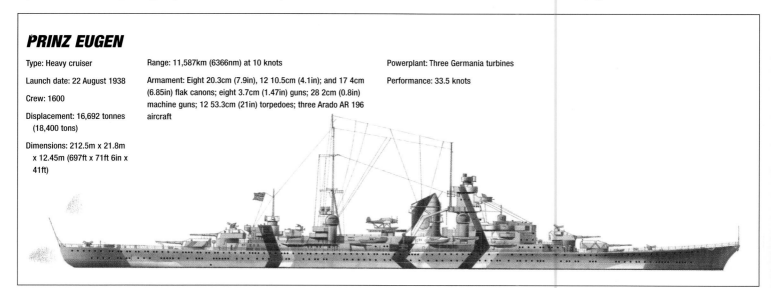

### PRINZ EUGEN

**Type:** Heavy cruiser

**Launch date:** 22 August 1938

**Crew:** 1600

**Displacement:** 16,692 tonnes (18,400 tons)

**Dimensions:** 212.5m x 21.8m x 12.45m (697ft x 71ft 6in x 41ft)

**Range:** 11,587km (6366nm) at 10 knots

**Armament:** Eight 20.3cm (7.9in), 12 10.5cm (4.1in); and 17 4cm (6.85in) flak canons; eight 3.7cm (1.47in) guns; 28 2cm (0.8in) machine guns; 12 53.3cm (21in) torpedoes; three Arado AR 196 aircraft

**Powerplant:** Three Germania turbines

**Performance:** 33.5 knots

## PRINCE OF WALES

Type: Battleship

Launch date: 3 May 1939

Crew: 1422

Displacement: 43,786 tonnes (43,094 tons)

Dimensions: 227.1m x 31.4m x 9.9m (745ft x 103ft x 32ft 7in)

Range: 25,942km (14,000nm) at 10 knots

Armament: 10 356mm (14in) and 16 131mm (5.25in) guns

Powerplant: Four shaft, geared turbines

Performance: 28 knots

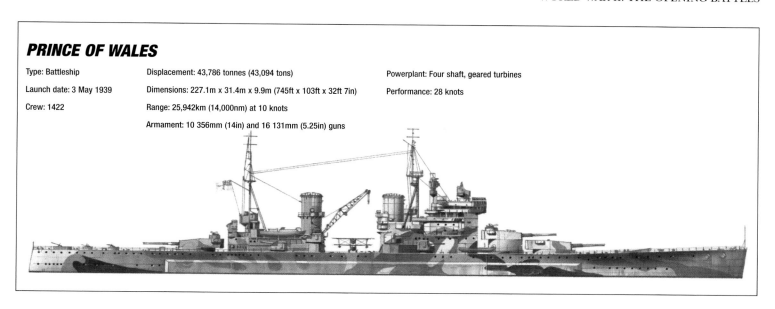

delayed, the less chance there would be of the ships breaking out into the Atlantic undetected, for the northern nights would be short. On the other hand, an immediate sortie would divert the Royal Navy's attention from the Mediterranean, where German forces had just invaded Greece.

On 8 April 1941, Fleet Commander Admiral Günther Lütjens, fresh from his Atlantic raiding experiences with the battlecruisers, flew to Paris to confer with Admiral Karl Dönitz about co-operation between *Bismarck* and U-boats. Then, on 24 April, came a further setback; the *Prinz Eugen* was

damaged by a magnetic mine, and a fortnight was needed to make repairs. Once again, Raeder was forced to

**Aircraft carrier *Ark Royal* played a key part in the destruction of the *Bismarck*. Note the Swordfish aircraft on deck, with wings folded. *Ark Royal* was sunk by a U-boat a few months later.**

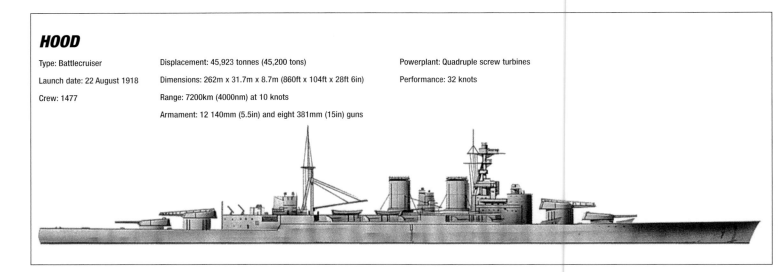

## HOOD

Type: Battlecruiser

Launch date: 22 August 1918

Crew: 1477

Displacement: 45,923 tonnes (45,200 tons)

Dimensions: 262m x 31.7m x 8.7m (860ft x 104ft x 28ft 6in)

Range: 7200km (4000nm) at 10 knots

Armament: 12 140mm (5.5in) and eight 381mm (15in) guns

Powerplant: Quadruple screw turbines

Performance: 32 knots

consider postponement, but despite the fact that Lütjens was in favour of it – at least until the *Scharnhorst* or *Tirpitz* was ready for deployment – he decided to go ahead with the sortie at the earliest opportunity. At the beginning of May, Lütjens flew to Gotenhafen and embarked on the *Bismarck* with the officers of his staff. The forthcoming operation was allocated a codename – *Rheinübung* (Rhine Exercise) – and was to start on 18 May 1941.

As the day of the *Bismarck's* departure approached, the small fleet of escort vessels that would accompany her on the first leg of her voyage began to assemble. Foremost among them were three of Germany's latest destroyers: Z10 *Hans Lody*, Z16 *Friedrich Eckoldt*, and Z23. The 5th Minesweeping Flotilla would be responsible for clearing a path ahead of the warships, while three small flak ships guarded their flanks. Already at sea, in the *Bismarck's* operational area, were 16 U-boats deployed to intercept any British warships, while a fleet of 20 tankers, supply vessels and weather

ships were strung out along the warships' route, from the Arctic to the mid-Atlantic.

On the morning of Sunday, 18 May, Admiral Lütjens held a final conference in his cabin, attended by his staff officers and the captains of the *Bismarck* and *Prinz Eugen*. His operational brief came from Admiral Carls of Naval Group Command

**The *Bismarck* pictured during trials in the Baltic from the deck of the *Prinz Eugen*. The two made a formidable combination, and would have been virtually unbeatable.**

North in Wilhelmshaven, who had authority over the sortie until the ships crossed the line between southern Greenland and the Hebrides, when it was to come under the control of Group Command West in Paris. Carls recommended sailing direct to Korsfjord near Bergen and remaining there for a day while the *Prinz Eugen*, whose radius of action was limited, replenished her tanks. The ships were then to sail direct for the Atlantic through the Iceland-Faeroes gap. Lütjens' intention, however, was to bypass Korsfjord and proceed directly to the Arctic Ocean, refuel from the tanker *Weissenburg* near Jan Mayen Island, and then make a high-speed dash for the Atlantic through the

## The 5th Minesweeping Flotilla would be responsible for clearing a path ahead of the warships, while three small flak ships guarded their flanks.

Denmark Straits. After the conference, Lütjens went over to the *Prinz Eugen* to carry out an inspection.

The two warships left harbour shortly after 1100 and dropped anchor in the Roads, and at 1130 the crews of both warships were told that *Rheinübung* was about to begin. In the afternoon, *Bismarck* and *Prinz Eugen* carried out exercises with the *Tirpitz*, the *Prinz Eugen* testing her degaussing

equipment, and dropped anchor again in the Roads. The next few hours were spent in taking on fuel oil.

At about 0200 on Monday, 19 May 1941, both warships weighed anchor and proceeded westwards independently. At 1100, they made rendezvous off Arkona, the northernmost cape of Prussia, and continued with their escort of minesweepers and destroyers. All

that day, and through the night, the squadron sailed in formation westward and northward. Skirting the eastern edge of Kiel Bay, the ships passed through the Great Belt, the seaway that divides the two parts of Denmark, at about 0200 on Tuesday morning.

## NORTHWARD MOVEMENT

On 20 May, the warships were reported in the Kattegat by the Swedish cruiser *Gotland*, and intelligence of the enemy force's northward movement reached the British Admiralty early the next day. Admiral Sir John Tovey, who was now C-in-C Home Fleet, at once strengthened surveillance of the northern passages into the Atlantic, ordering the battleship *Prince of Wales*, the battlecruiser *Hood* and six destroyers to sail from Scapa Flow under Vice-Admiral L.E. Holland (in the flagship *Hood*) while reconnaissance aircraft were despatched to search for the enemy warships. That same afternoon, the *Bismarck* and her consort were photographed by a PRU Spitfire as they refuelled in Korsfjord, near Bergen. The Spitfire pilot, Fg Off Michael Suckling, landed at Wick in northeast Scotland, where his film was developed; he then made a high-speed dash south with the precious prints, being forced to land at an airfield in the Midlands because of dense cloud. At 0100 on 22 May, having completed his journey in a fast

## THE DESTRUCTION OF THE *HOOD*

**At 0537, the opposing forces sighted each other at a range of 27km (17 miles), and opened fire at 0553. Both German ships concentrated their fire on the *Hood* and, thanks to their stereoscopic rangefinders, straddled her immediately; the *Bismarck*'s second and third salvoes struck the battlecruiser amidships, and those from the *Prinz Eugen* started a fire among her ready-to-use AA ammunition. At 0600, as the British warships were altering course in order to bring all their guns to bear, the *Hood* was hit again by a salvo that pierced her lightly armoured decks and detonated in her after magazines. She blew up with a tremendous explosion and disappeared with a speed that stunned all who witnessed the event. Only three of her crew of 1419 officers and ratings survived.**

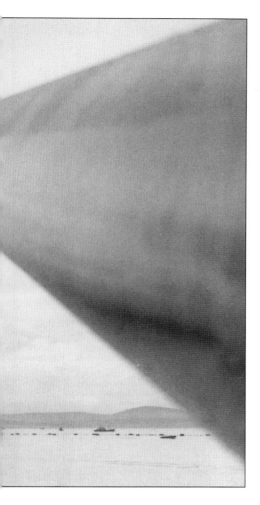

The battlecruiser HMS *Hood* at her moorings in Scapa Flow. In her heydey the *Hood* was the largest, most powerful warship in the world, she was synonymous with Great Britain's naval power.

car, Suckling – unshaven and still wearing his flying kit – arrived at the Air Ministry in London, where he handed over the package of photographs to Air Chief Marshal Sir Frederick Bowhill, AOC-in-C Coastal Command.

Less than two hours after Suckling had walked into Bowhill's office, aircraft of Coastal Command were on their way to attack the German warships, but their operations were frustrated by bad weather. Then, shortly before nightfall on the 22nd, a Martin Maryland reconnaissance aircraft of No. 771 Naval Air Squadron from Hatston in the Orkneys penetrated Korsfjord. Its crew, Lt N.E. Goddard RNVR (pilot) and Commander G.A. Rotherham (observer) returned with the news that the *Bismarck* and *Prinz Eugen* were gone.

At 2245, Admiral Tovey left Scapa Flow with the main body of the Home Fleet, heading for Icelandic waters to reinforce the heavy cruisers *Norfolk* and *Suffolk* that were patrolling the Denmark Strait. Three more cruisers were guarding Lütjens' alternative breakout route, between Iceland and the Faeroes. First to arrive were the Home Fleet's two fastest ships, the *Prince of Wales* and the *Hood*, which had set out in advance of the main force; behind them came Tovey's Fleet

Flagship, the new battleship *King George V*, the aircraft carrier *Victorious*, four cruisers and six destroyers. The carrier was not yet fully worked up, and her air group comprised only nine Swordfish and six Fulmars. She had been earmarked to escort Convoy WS.8B, bound for the Middle East with troops, but had been released on Admiralty orders to take part in the hunt for the *Bismarck*. So had the battlecruiser *Repulse*, which also sailed north accompanied by three destroyers withdrawn from the Western Approaches.

## SIGHTING REPORT
At 1922 on 23 May the *Bismarck* and *Prinz Eugen* were sighted emerging from a snow squall in the Denmark Strait by the cruiser *Suffolk*, under Capt R.M. Ellis. About an hour later, *Suffolk* was joined by *Norfolk*, under Capt A.J.L. Phillips and flying the flag of Rear-Admiral W.F. Wake-Walker, in command of the 1st Cruiser Squadron. HMS *Norfolk* came under enemy fire at a range of 11,882m (13,000yds) and was straddled by

Hit by a shell from the *Prince of Wales*, the *Bismarck's* bows are noticeably lower in the water after the Denmark Strait battle, which the Germans called the Battle of the Iceland Sea.

three 381mm (15in) salvoes before retiring under cover of smoke, miraculously undamaged, to radio her enemy sighting report to Admiral Tovey, whose main fleet was still some 965km (600 miles) to the southwest. The two cruisers continued to shadow Lütjens' ships at high speed throughout the night, *Suffolk* maintaining contact with her Type 284 radar.

The *Prince of Wales* and *Hood*, meanwhile, were coming up quickly; Vice-Admiral Holland's ships had been about 354km (220 miles) away at the time of the first sighting report,

The battleship HMS *Renown*. In March 1942, *Renown* formed part of a huge fleet of battleships, cruisers and destroyers hunting for the latest German ocean menace, the *Tirpitz*.

and Holland was anticipating a night action. His plan was to concentrate the fire of his heavy ships on the *Bismarck*, leaving Wake-Walker's cruisers to deal with the *Prinz Eugen*. What he did not know was that the *Bismarck* was no longer in the lead; the blast from her guns had put her own forward radar out of action, so Lütjens had ordered the *Prinz Eugen* to change position.

As his heavy ships approached, Admiral Holland, conscious of the need for surprise, imposed strict radio and radar silence, relying on *Suffolk*'s reports to keep him informed of the enemy's position. Soon after midnight, however, *Suffolk* lost contact, and did not regain it until 0247. In the meantime, Holland had turned his ships south to await full

daylight, but when information once again began to come through from *Suffolk* he increased speed to 28 knots and turned on an interception course. It was now 0340, and visibility was 19km (12 miles).

As the *Prince of Wales* altered course sharply to avoid the wreckage, she herself came under heavy fire. Within moments, she sustained hits by four 381mm (15in) and three 203mm (8in) shells, one of which exploded on the bridge and killed or wounded almost everyone there except her captain, J.C. Leach, who ordered the battleship to turn away under cover of smoke. The *Prince of Wales* was so newly completed that she had not yet finished working-up; the contractors were still working on her 356mm (14in) turrets when she sailed, and

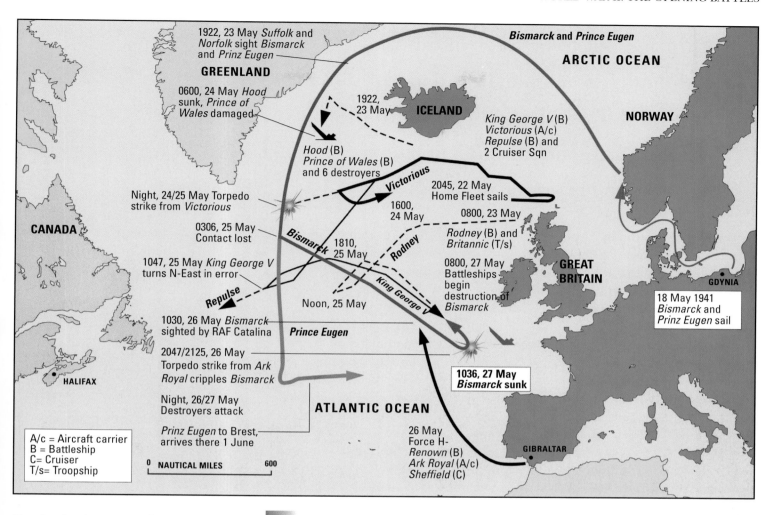

**Map showing the progress of the hunt for the battleship *Bismarck* and her consort, the heavy cruiser *Prinz Eugen*. The doomed *Bismarck* was to have formed the core of a powerful battle group.**

Admiral Holland, conscious of the need for surprise, imposed strict radio and radar silence, relying on *Suffolk*'s reports to keep him informed of the enemy's position.

she was therefore not fully battleworthy, a fact of which Captain Leach was obviously conscious. The additional damage had made her even more vulnerable, and Leach's intention now was to use his damaged ship to assist Wake-Walker's cruisers in maintaining contact with the enemy until Admiral Tovey's main force could reach the scene.

## IN FOR THE KILL

What Leach had no means of knowing was that his gunners had obtained three hits on the *Bismarck*, causing two of her fuel tanks to leak oil and contaminating others. Because of this, Lütjens decided to abandon the sortie

and steer southwest for St Nazaire, the only port on the Atlantic coast of France with a dry dock large enough to accommodate his flagship while repairs were carried out. Tovey's ships were still 530km (330 miles) to the southeast and could not expect to make contact until 0700 on 25 May at the earliest. However, other ships were also heading for the scene. Admiral Somerville's Force H had been ordered north from Gibraltar by the Admiralty to intercept the German squadron, and the battleships *Rodney*,

*Revenge* and *Ramillies* and the cruiser *Edinburgh* were also released from escort duties to take part in the chase. The main concern now was to reduce the *Bismarck*'s speed, giving the hunters a chance to close in for the kill. At 1440 on 24 May, Admiral Tovey ordered the carrier *Victorious* to race ahead to a flying-off point 160km (100 miles) from the enemy ships and launch a Swordfish strike against them.

At 2210, the carrier flew off nine Swordfish of No. 825 Squadron, led by

It turned out to be a fortuitous move. Although Tovey's warships had lost valuable ground during their false quest to the northeast, the net around *Bismarck* was gradually closing.

Lt Cdr Eugene Esmonde. Flying through rain and sleet, they obtained radar contact with the enemy at 2337 and briefly sighted the *Bismarck*, only to lose her again. Twenty minutes later, the shadowing British cruisers re-directed the Swordfish on to their target and they made their attack through heavy defensive fire. One torpedo hit the *Bismarck* amidships without causing significant damage; the other eight missed. All the attacking Swordfish recovered safely to the carrier, although two reconnaissance Fulmars out of six

**The German battlecruiser *Scharnhorst* remained a threat to the Allied Arctic convoys until she was sunk by the British battleship *Duke of York* at the Battle of North Cape in December 1943.**

despatched failed to return. The returning crews reported no sign of the *Prinz Eugen*, which had been detached by Admiral Lütjens to continue on her way alone.

At 0300 on 25 May, Lütjens altered course to the southeast, and at this critical juncture the shadowing cruisers, which had been following at extreme radar range, lost contact. The problems facing *Bismarck*'s pursuers were compounded by the receipt of some bearings transmitted by the Admiralty which, through a combination of errors, led Admiral Tovey to believe that the battleship was heading northeast, into the Atlantic. As a result, Tovey's flagship and many other pursuing vessels followed this false trail throughout

most of the 25th, until, at about 1800, Tovey decided that the *Bismarck* was probably heading for Brest and changed course accordingly. A signal received at 1924 indicated that the Admiralty also thought that this was the case; in fact, the Admiralty, much earlier in the day, had already instructed Admiral Somerville's Force

H to position itself on a line from which its ships and aircraft could intercept the *Bismarck* should she head for the Bay of Biscay.

**OPERATIONAL EXPERIENCE**

It turned out to be a fortuitous move. Although Tovey's warships had lost valuable ground during their false quest to the northeast, the net around *Bismarck* was gradually closing, and it was now that the experience and tactical awareness of one man came into play. Air Chief Marshal Bowhill, who had served in the Royal Navy as a young man, persuaded his colleagues in the Admiralty that Admiral Lütjens would not steer directly for Brest, but

An Allied convoy forming off the east coast of Canada. Once air power had closed the mid-Atlantic gap, the German submarine wolfpacks began to suffer heavy losses.

would instead make his landfall at Cape Finisterre. Coastal Command's search aircraft were accordingly instructed to patrol well to the south,

129

A German Enigma code machine. The breaking of the German naval codes and ciphers was a vital factor in the Allied victory in the Atlantic and elsewhere.

conditions of high winds, driving rain and rough seas, and some time later their radar revealed a target, which their crews assumed to be the *Bismarck*. In fact, it was the *Sheffield*, whose presence in the area had not been signalled to *Ark Royal*. The Swordfish came down through low cloud and attacked from different directions; several of them released their torpedoes before the mistake was recognized, but fortunately – thanks to a combination of effective evasive manoeuvring by the cruiser and faulty magnetic pistols fitted to the torpedoes – no damage was caused.

This first (and somewhat penitent) strike force returned to the carrier, which at 1910 launched a second wave of 15 Swordfish. The aircraft, led by Lt Cdr T.P. Coode, were directed to the target by the *Sheffield*, but in the prevailing weather conditions, coupled with fading light and heavy defensive fire, they had little chance of making a co-ordinated attack. Nevertheless, two torpedoes found their mark; one struck the *Bismarck*'s armoured belt and did little damage, but the other struck her extreme stern, damaging her propellers and jamming her rudders 15° to port. At 2140, Admiral Lütjens signalled Berlin:

Ship no longer manoeuvrable. We fight to the last shell. Long live the Führer.

Shortly afterwards, five destroyers, led by Captain Philip Vian in the *Cossack*, arrived on the scene, having been detached from convoy duty. They made contact with the *Bismarck* and shadowed her throughout the night,

and at 1030 on the 26th *Bismarck* was sighted nearly 1126km (700 miles) west of Brest by a Catalina of No. 209 Squadron from Castle Archdale (Lough Erne) in Northern Ireland. The aircraft's captain was Flying Officer Dennis Briggs, but the warship was actually sighted by his co-pilot, US Navy Ensign Leonard B. Smith, one of several US Navy pilots gaining

**Some of the *Bismarck*'s survivors are rescued. All but 119 of her crew of over 2000 lost their lives. The wreck of the *Bismarck* lay undisturbed on the ocean floor for nearly half a century.**

operational experience with Coastal Command. As the United States was still neutral, Smith's presence on the aircraft was kept a strict secret.

Soon after the Catalina crew sighted the *Bismarck*, contact was also made by two Swordfish reconnaissance aircraft from the *Ark Royal*, Force H's aircraft carrier. Admiral Somerville sent the cruiser *Sheffield* to shadow the battleship with her Type 79Y radar and, when the opportunity arose, to direct a strike by the carrier's Swordfish torpedo-bombers. Fourteen of the latter were flown off at 1450 in transmitting regular position reports and closing in to make a series of determined torpedo attacks, but these were disrupted by heavy and accurate radar-controlled gunfire. During the night, the battleships *King George V* and *Rodney* came within striking distance of their crippled enemy. However, Admiral Tovey, aware of the accuracy of her radar-directed gunnery, decided to wait until daylight before engaging her; she had no means of escaping him now.

## BLAZING WRECK

Soon after dawn on 27 May, he closed in from the northwest, his two battleships opening fire at about 0845 from a range of 14,600m (16,000yds). By 1020, the *Bismarck* had been reduced to a blazing wreck, with all her armament out of action, but she was still afloat despite the fact that the two British battleships had fired more than 700 shells at her. Only a small proportion had found their target, prompting Admiral Tovey to tell his fleet gunnery officer that he would stand a better chance of hitting her if he threw his binoculars at her. In the end, the battleships, undamaged but seriously short of fuel, were compelled to break off the action, and it was left to the cruisers *Norfolk* and *Dorsetshire* to close in and finish the *Bismarck* off with torpedoes. (Some of the ship's survivors later claimed, however, that she had been scuttled by her crew.) She sank at 1036, her colours still flying, in position 48 10'N, 16 12'W, taking all but 119 of her crew of more than 2000 officers and men with her. Her wreck was to lie undisturbed on the ocean floor for nearly half a century, when it was located and photographed by an underwater archaeology expedition, the swastika painted on the warship's bow still clearly visible.

The *Prinz Eugen*, meanwhile, had headed south to refuel in mid-Atlantic after parting company with the *Bismarck* on 24 May, but continuing engine defects persuaded Kapitän Brinkmann to abort his sortie and make for Brest. Although she was sighted by a Coastal Command patrol, she reached harbour unmolested on 1 June, aided by the fact that many British warships were in port refuelling and rearming after the pursuit of the *Bismarck*. For the rest of the year, the *Prinz Eugen*, together with the battlecruisers *Scharnhorst* and *Gneisenau*, were immobilized in the Biscay ports, where they were subjected to heavy and costly attacks by RAF Bomber Command, in which all three suffered damage. As a further insurance against future sorties by the enemy surface raiders,

**The crew of a crippled merchantman prepares to abandon ship. Number one lifeboat has already been filled and swung outboard ready to be lowered.**

the Royal Navy began a systematic hunt for their tankers and supply ships following the sinking of the *Bismarck*. In June 1941, five tankers and three supply ships, plus a couple of weather observation vessels, were destroyed or scuttled after being intercepted.

## TORPEDO HIT

On 12 June, the German heavy cruiser *Lützow* (Kapt Kreisch) attempted to break out into the North Atlantic, escorted by five destroyers, to attack merchant shipping. She was sighted by an RAF reconnaissance aircraft off Lindesnes shortly before midnight,

The men in the lifeboat pull hard to put as much distance as possible between themselves and the stricken ship, fearful that the U-boat might be about to launch a second torpedo.

and 14 Beaufort torpedo-bombers of Nos. 22 and 42 Squadrons were despatched to search for her. She was located by Flt Sgt R.H. Loveitt of No 42 Squadron, who secured a torpedo hit amidships. The *Lützow* struggled back to Kiel with partially disabled engines and a heavy list, reaching harbour in the afternoon of 14 June. She was to remain in dock for six months, and Loveitt was awarded a well-deserved DFM. It was the last

attempt by a surface raider to interfere with the Atlantic convoys; when the German Navy's heavy warships once more joined battle in 1942, their focus of operations, dictated by the German invasion of Russia, would be the Arctic. In the Atlantic, with the RAF's long-range fighters making life difficult for the Focke-Wulf Kondors, there remained the threat posed by the German and Italian submarines.

## THE CODE-BREAKERS

**The decrease in the numbers of Allied ships being sunk in the summer of 1941 was due in the main to the implementation of an increasingly efficient convoy system. The real key to what seemed to be a growing Allied success, however, was Intelligence. The story of Ultra and the code-breaking operation at Bletchley Park is now well known, although it was kept a closely guarded secret for more than 30 years after the war. Without the efforts of this dedicated band of experts, the outcome of the Battle of the Atlantic might have been very different.**

In the summer of 1941, there was a welcome decrease in the tonnage of shipping sunk by these boats, and several factors contributed to it. From late May, for example, continuous escort was provided for UK-bound North Atlantic convoys by groups of Canadian and British warships, something that had not previously been possible because of a shortage of escort vessels. The month of May also saw the genesis of the Atlantic 'support groups', whereby the escorts of other convoys could be diverted to strengthen the defences of one under threat. This system was first tested from 23–28 June 1941, when Convoy HX133 was attacked by 10 U-boats south of Greenland. For five days and nights, a fierce battle raged between the U-boats and 13 escort vessels; five merchantmen were lost, but the escorts sank *U-556* and *U-651*.

### WINDFALL

On 8 May 1941, the experts at Bletchley Park had a real windfall when the destroyer *Bulldog*, escorting Convoy OB318, drove a German submarine to the surface. She was the *U-110* (commanded by Kapt Lt Julius Lemp). The Germans set explosive charges and abandoned ship, but the detonators failed. A party from *Bulldog* went aboard the U-boat, at no small risk to themselves, and removed her code books and Enigma code machine. In the words of the official history, these captures

… yielded the short-range code books, which enabled GC&CS (Government Code and Cypher School) to read from May onwards the *Kurzsignale*, the short signals in which the U-boats transmitted

their sighting reports and weather information. Captures enabled GC&CS to read all the traffic for June and July, including 'officer-only' signals, currently. By the beginning of August it had finally established its mastery over the Home Waters settings [the code used by the German naval Enigma machine], a mastery which enabled it to read the whole of the traffic for the rest of the war except for occasional days in the second half of 1941 with little delay. The maximum delay was 72 hours and the normal delay was much less, often only a few hours.

The Home Waters setting of the Enigma cypher, which was changed daily, carried 95 per cent of the German Navy's radio message traffic. Its yield, and that of other enemy high-grade cyphers, became known as Ultra. The breakthrough of May 1941 moved the whole war against the U-boats into a new dimension. The codebreakers and the Admiralty Submarine Tracking Room staff now had an insight into the whole operational cycle of a U-boat, and although many months were to pass before the Tracking Room could claim to know more about the U-boats' deployment than Admiral Dönitz's own staff, the summer of 1941 was the point at which Bletchley moved the process out of the realms of guesswork. It was this knowledge of U-boat movements and positions, derived from Ultra, that enabled the

A German U-boat on the surface. Many U-boat actions took place with the boat surfaced, especially at night, when the submarines were extremely difficult to spot.

Admiralty to re-route convoys to avoid the U-boat packs, and it was this knowledge which enabled it to reinforce the escort of HX133, with results we have seen.

### SUBMARINE TRACKING ROOM

The decryption of enemy naval signals traffic was by no means new. The monitoring and decryption of enemy radio signals dated from the earliest days of August 1914. Indeed, in the anti-submarine war of World War I, it was perhaps the most significant contribution to British and Allied victory. During the latter half of 1941, by a very cautious estimate, the Admiralty Submarine Tracking Room, using Ultra decrypts, re-routed the convoys so cleverly around the German 'wolf-packs' that as many as 300 ships may have been saved from destruction – surely a decisive factor in the outcome of the Battle of the

The decryptions of enemy naval signals traffic was by no means new. The monitoring and decryption of enemy radio signals dated from the earliest days of 1914.

Atlantic. Admiral Dönitz's U-boat offensive in the spring of 1941 had been launched in the expectation that the previously high rate of merchant ship sinkings could not simply be maintained but also decisively increased as more submarines were deployed. In this way, the German Naval Command hoped to neutralize Britain before help arrived from the United States in significant proportions, avoiding a two-front war and leaving the German armies free to deal with the Soviet Union. In Whitehall, as the offensive got underway, the outlook was bleak. At the beginning of 1941, food stocks in Britain were dangerously low: there was enough wheat for 15 weeks; meat (rationed to one shilling's-worth per person per week) for only two weeks; butter for eight weeks on ration; margarine for three weeks on ration; and bacon for 27 weeks on ration. There were no longer any stocks of imported fruit. All this added up to the grim fact that, unless merchant ship sinkings could be reduced, Britain would starve before new merchant vessels could be built fast enough to maintain imports at the level needed for her survival.

At this point, mercifully, there came the Ultra breakthrough. The intelligence it yielded came in two categories, the first and most important being that for immediate operational use. The wolf-pack tactics employed by the U-boats called for the transmission of sighting reports and homing signals between boats so that they could concentrate and attack on the surface at night in areas out of range of shore-based aircraft. Convoys were, at this time, virtually defenceless against these tactics, but their success depended on tightly centralized control by U-boat Command and the transmission of a stream of tactical orders, patrol instructions, situation reports, and so on. This made them vulnerable to Ultra and to high-frequency direction finding (HF/DF). Secondly, Ultra provided huge quantities of valuable background information that included such details as the exit and approach routes from and to the U-boat bases, frequency of patrols and the rate of commissioning of new boats. It also revealed operational characteristics such as the speed, diving depths, endurance, armament, signals and radar equipment of the various types of U-boat, and the current operational state of boats at sea.

## CLEAR OF DANGER

Despite Ultra, merchant-ship sinkings remained high in June 1941, partly because of difficulties in interpreting the disguised grid references for U-boat positions in the decrypts, and partly because of an increase in enemy submarine operations in West African waters, where the defences were ill-prepared and many ships were still sailing independently. The submarines involved in these operations had to return to their bases at the end of June since they had no refuelling facilities at sea, the tankers sent out to supply them (and the *Bismarck*) all having been sunk. When they resumed operations in this area in

This U-boat had been depth-charged to the surface and is being abandoned by its crew. An American escort vessel is standing by to pick up survivors.

September, they achieved comparatively little, since the convoy and escort group system was now established and the Allied ships could be routed clear of danger thanks to Ultra.

The North Atlantic saw an even more important, if not dramatic, decline in sinkings from the end of June. This was partly because steps had been taken to reduce the number of ships sailing independently, but mainly because Ultra-directed evasive routing could now be practised on a large scale. By the summer of 1941, Coastal Command had driven the U-boats westward, beyond the range of air patrols, which gave more scope for evasive routing and at once brought about a sharp fall in the number of

convoy attacks. Sinkings dropped from 304,814 tonnes (300,000 tons) in May and June to 101,604 tonnes (100,000 tons) in July and August.

Mystified, Dönitz switched his boats back and forth in a mostly vain effort to find the elusive convoys. Although the German authorities knew that the British were obtaining valuable intelligence information, they never suspected that their naval codes had been compromised. They knew, too, that the British had captured an Enigma machine, but not that their enemies had access to the daily settings, without which the machine was useless. They therefore concluded that the information must be coming from leaks in other communications.

With a Catalina flying boat circling watchfully overhead, a tug stands by to take the surrendered *U-570* under tow. The submarine was towed to Iceland and was later impressed into Royal Navy service as HMS *Graph*.

Dönitz was so enraged by the fact that the British frequently transmitted accurate plots of U-boats (information ironically gained from German decrypts of British codes, broken before the war) that he took drastic steps to stem the leaks, even to the extent of having himself investigated as a possible source.

## U-BOAT DISPOSITIONS

The great mistake made by the Germans, however, was to place the

## U-47

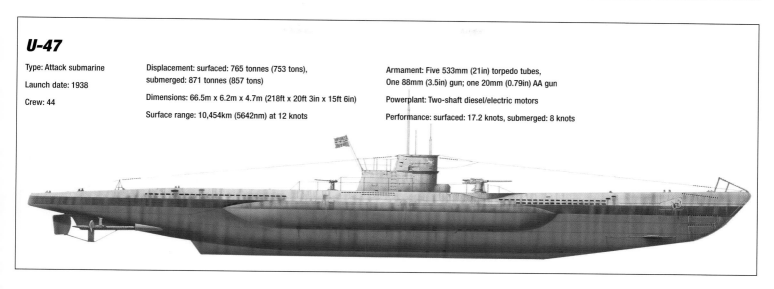

**Type:** Attack submarine
**Launch date:** 1938
**Crew:** 44

**Displacement:** surfaced: 765 tonnes (753 tons), submerged: 871 tonnes (857 tons)
**Dimensions:** 66.5m x 6.2m x 4.7m (218ft x 20ft 3in x 15ft 6in)
**Surface range:** 10,454km (5642nm) at 12 knots

**Armament:** Five 533mm (21in) torpedo tubes, One 88mm (3.5in) gun; one 20mm (0.79in) AA gun
**Powerplant:** Two-shaft diesel/electric motors
**Performance:** surfaced: 17.2 knots, submerged: 8 knots

> Although the German authorities knew that the British were obtaining valuable intelligence information, they never suspected that their naval codes had been compromised.

investigation in the hands of their cryptanalysts. Because these men and women had such unshakeable faith in Enigma, and considered its code to be unbreakable in a timescale that would produce useful intelligence, they wasted their time in following one false trail after another. They were also unaware of the importance of HF/DF in determining U-boat dispositions, and of the fact that knowledge of their weather codes also assisted the British analysts.

In September 1941, sinkings rose again, mainly because of renewed grid reference difficulties, but by October these had been overcome. Evasive routing could be practised once more and sinkings again declined, despite the fact that the number of U-boats known to be at sea – now 80 – was double that at the start of the offensive. In November, sinkings dropped to 62,994 tonnes (62,000

tons), the lowest for 18 months. At this point, many boats were diverted to the Arctic and Mediterranean while the rest were mostly concentrated off Gibraltar, to which area Coastal Command's patrols were at once directed. For the time being, the offensive against the trans-Atlantic routes was virtually abandoned.

Some weeks earlier, in August, the British intelligence effort against the U-boats had been assisted by the capture of one intact. She was the *U-570*, one of a group operating southwest of Iceland against Convoy HX145, which had been located by the German 'B' Signals Intelligence Service. The submarine was attacked in bad weather by a Hudson of No. 269 Squadron flown by Sqn Ldr J. H. Thompson, and was damaged. Her commander, Lt Hans Rahmlow, raised the flag of surrender and the Hudson

continued to circle the boat until relieved by a Catalina of No. 209 Squadron. The first of a succession of armed trawlers reached the scene on 27 August; the submarine's crew was taken off and she was towed to Iceland, where she was beached. Although her crew had destroyed most of the secret material on board, the capture of an intact U-boat was an important achievement. After Royal Navy service as HMS *Graph*, she was decommissioned and used in depth charge trials, yielding important information about the effects of explosions on her pressure hull.

Despite the carnage that was to come, some German historians see the end of 1941 as the turning point in the Battle of the Atlantic: the ships saved by evasive routing not only defeated Dönitz's offensive but also provided a cushion against future heavy losses. The second half of 1941 also provided something of a breathing space, in which the Allies could forge ahead with the development of anti-submarine weapons and tactics, and lay the foundations for the later surge in merchant ship building, which was to ensure victory. The triumph of 1941 was Ultra's, and it was a triumph that also extended to the Royal Navy's operations in the calmer waters of the Mediterranean.

# World War II
## The Mediterranean Theatre
## 1940–1941

**The last troops had barely been lifted from the beaches when Britain found herself facing a new enemy. On 10 June 1940, Italy – anxious for her share of the spoils of a war that her leader, Benito Mussolini, clearly believed had already been won – declared war on Britain and France. At this time, Italy had at her disposal six battleships (only two of which were ready for operations), seven heavy cruisers, 12 light cruisers, 59 destroyers, 67 torpedo boats and 116 submarines. Against this, the British in the Eastern Mediterranean had four battleships, nine light cruisers, 21 destroyers and six submarines, to which could be added one French battleship, three heavy cruisers, one light cruiser, a destroyer and six submarines. Six more British submarines and a destroyer were at Malta.**

In the western Mediterranean, the combined Anglo-French naval assets were five battleships (four of them French), one aircraft carrier, four heavy cruisers, seven light cruisers (six of them French), 46 destroyers (37 French) and 36 submarines (all French). By 10 June, the Italian Navy had laid extensive mine barrages on

**Contact with the enemy. A British destroyer makes smoke to protect a supply convoy bound from Alexandria for Malta. Italian warships have been sighted.**

The heavy shells hit the magazine of the battleship *Bretagne* and she blew up; the *Dunkerque* and *Provence* were badly damaged, and two destroyers were sunk.

the Italian Mediterranean coasts and also in the Adriatic. In addition, 54 submarines were deployed to their war stations, and on 12 June one of these, the *Bagnolini*, achieved an early success by sinking the British light cruiser *Calypso*. The British also lost three submarines in quick succession, *Odin* being sunk by the destroyer *Strale* in the Gulf of Taranto on 13 June, *Grampus* by torpedo boats off Syracuse three days later, and *Orpheus* by the destroyer *Turbine* off Tobruk.

Shortly before Italy's declaration of war Admiral Sir Andrew Cunningham, C-in-C British Mediterranean Fleet, had decided to move a strong proportion of his forces into a

**Admiral Sir Andrew Cunningham, commander of the British Mediterranean Fleet during the crucial battles of 1940–42. He had momentous decisions to make, some of them unpalatable.**

position where they could challenge the Italians in the central Mediterranean. On 11 June, the Fleet mounted its first offensive sortie against Italian shipping heading for Libya, a force of cruisers and destroyers being detached to shell Tobruk. The sortie was abortive, resulting in the sinking of one small Italian minesweeper and, on the debit side, the *Calypso*. On the 14th, four French heavy cruisers and 11 destroyers made a sortie from Toulon to bombard targets on the Italian coast, including Genoa harbour.

Towards the end of June 1940, a powerful Royal Navy squadron assembled at Gibraltar under the command of Vice-Admiral Sir James Somerville. Known as Force H, it consisted of the aircraft carrier *Ark Royal*, newly arrived from Britain, the battleships *Valiant* and *Resolution*, two cruisers and 11 destroyers, together with the battlecruiser *Hood*. Force H was only a week old when it was called upon to carry out one of the most tragic and melancholy operations in the history of the Royal Navy: Operation Catapult, the attempted destruction of the French Fleet at Oran and Mers-el-Kebir. Admiral Somerville was ordered to sail with his squadron to Oran and to offer an ultimatum to the French commander, Admiral Gensoul: join forces with the British; sail to the French West Indies with reduced crews; scuttle his ships – or face destruction. On 3 July, Captain C.S. Holland, in command of the *Ark Royal*, was sent to Oran to parley with

Gensoul, but the French admiral refused even to consider any of the options. Shortly before 1800, the *Valiant, Resolution* and *Hood* opened fire, their guns directed by Swordfish spotter aircraft from the *Ark Royal*, while another flight of Swordfish laid mines in the entrance of the nearby port of Mers-el-Kebir. The heavy

shells hit the magazine of the battleship *Bretagne* and she blew up; the *Dunkerque* and *Provence* were badly damaged, and two destroyers were sunk.

As the sun went down, the battleship *Strasbourg* and five destroyers made a dash for safety. They were attacked by the *Ark Royal*'s

Swordfish, but in the face of heavy anti-aircraft fire and the gathering darkness the pilots' aim was poor and the French warships got away to Toulon. The following morning, the *Ark Royal* launched another strike of torpedo-carrying Swordfish to finish off Gensoul's flagship, the *Dunkerque*, which was aground in Oran harbour.

The destruction of the French fleet at Mers-el-Kebir. The *Provence* is in the foreground, her guns trained seawards, with *Bretagne* on fire in the background.

Four torpedoes hit the auxiliary vessel *Terre Neuve*, which was lying alongside *Dunkerque* with a cargo of depth charges; these exploded and ripped

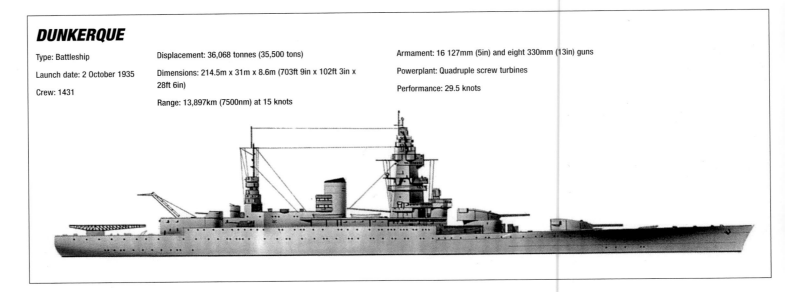

## DUNKERQUE

**Type:** Battleship

**Launch date:** 2 October 1935

**Crew:** 1431

**Displacement:** 36,068 tonnes (35,500 tons)

**Dimensions:** 214.5m x 31m x 8.6m (703ft 9in x 102ft 3in x 28ft 6in)

**Range:** 13,897km (7500nm) at 15 knots

**Armament:** 16 127mm (5in) and eight 330mm (13in) guns

**Powerplant:** Quadruple screw turbines

**Performance:** 29.5 knots

open the battleship's side, putting her out of action.

Another French squadron, comprising the battleship *Lorraine*, four cruisers and number of smaller warships, was at Alexandria, where it had been operating under Admiral Cunningham, commanding the British Eastern Mediterranean Fleet, before France's collapse. Here Cunningham managed to arrive at a peaceful settlement with his French opposite number, Admiral Godfroy, and the French warships were deactivated. That still left the new battleships *Jean Bart* and *Richelieu*: having escaped from Brest before the

port was captured by the Germans, they were now in the West African ports of Casablanca and Dakar. On 8 July, a fast motorboat from the carrier *Hermes* entered the harbour of Dakar and dropped depth charges under the *Richelieu*'s stern in an attempt to put her rudder and propellers out of action. But the depth charges failed to explode, and although the battleship was later attacked by Swordfish from the *Hermes*, their torpedoes inflicted only light damage. She was attacked again two months later, this time by the *Ark Royal*'s aircraft, during an abortive British attempted landing in Senegal. Once again, however, the air

strikes proved ineffective, and this time nine Swordfish and Skuas were shot down.

## UNFORTUNATE AFFAIR

On 7 July, Admiral Cunningham sailed from Alexandria, with the twofold intention of providing protection for two convoys carrying supplies from Malta to Alexandria, and of throwing down a challenge to the Italian Navy by operating within sight of the southern coast of Italy. Cunningham's force was split into three: the leading unit (Force A) consisted of five cruisers; the centre (Force B) of the battleship *Warspite* and her destroyer screen; Force C brought up the rear, and comprised the aircraft carrier *Eagle*, 10 destroyers and the veteran battleships *Malaya* and *Royal Sovereign*. The British Fleet's air cover consisted of 15 Swordfish and three Sea Gladiators, forming *Eagle*'s air group. Two days earlier, the Swordfish had scored a resounding success when, operating from an RAF airfield in Egypt, they had sunk the Italian destroyer *Zeffiro* and the 4064-tonne (4000-ton) freighter *Manzoni*, as well as badly damaging the destroyer *Euro* and the 15,240-tonne (15,000-ton) troopship *Liguria*, in a torpedo attack on Tobruk harbour.

## BRITAIN'S RUTHLESS DETERMINATION

The controversy over this unfortunate affair, which cost the French Navy 1297 dead, has raged ever since. The three senior British naval officers involved – Admiral Sir Dudley North at Gibraltar, Admiral Cunningham and Admiral Somerville – were all opposed to it, believing that a solution without the use of force would have been reached in time. But time, in the summer of 1940, was something Britain did not have. The British Government did not know which way the wind would blow under Marshal Petain's post-armistice regime. And there was only one certainty: if the French warships ceased to be neutral, their power would tilt the balance in the Mediterranean towards the enemy. Under the circumstances, the British Government's decision was the only one possible; and it showed the world that Britain, alone now, was prepared to act ruthlessly if the occasion demanded.

Early on 8 July, a patrolling submarine reported that a strong enemy force, including two battleships, was steaming southwards between Taranto and Benghazi. Reconnaissance Swordfish were launched, and they in turn reported that the enemy warships were following an easterly course, which led Cunningham to believe that they were covering a convoy en route to Benghazi. Postponing the departure of the British convoy from Malta, he altered course to position himself between the enemy and their base at Taranto. In the afternoon of that same day, the British Fleet was subjected to a series of high-level attacks by 126 Italian bombers. The *Eagle* was singled out as a special target, but despite several near misses she emerged unscathed. Only one ship, the cruiser *Gloucester*, was hit and damaged. Even so, the Italian bombing was accurate, and at the bombers' operating height of over 3048m (10,000ft) most of the British warships' anti-aircraft armament was ineffective.

At dawn on 9 July, Cunningham was 96km (60 miles) off the southwest

tip of Greece, with the enemy force – two battleships, 16 cruisers and 32 destroyers – about 240km (150 miles) ahead of him, in the Ionian Sea. By 1145, only 145km (90 miles) separated the two forces, and the *Eagle* launched a strike force of nine Swordfish in an attempt to slow down the enemy force. They failed to find the main force, which had altered course, but launched their torpedoes through a heavy barrage of fire at an Italian cruiser that was bringing up the rear, missed, and returned to the *Eagle* to refuel and rearm.

At 1515, Cunningham's advance force of cruisers sighted the enemy, who immediately opened fire on them. Ten minutes later, the *Warspite* arrived on the scene and engaged the Italian cruisers with her 381mm (15in) guns until they were forced to withdraw under cover of a smoke screen. At 1545, a second Swordfish strike was flown off, and three minutes after the aircraft had gone the *Warspite* made contact with the Italian flagship *Giulio Cesare* and opened fire on her from a range of 23,764m

**The *Richelieu* was the latest of France's battleships to be commissioned. Having escaped to Dakar, she was attacked by British forces but sustained only light damage.**

(26,000yds), severely damaging her and reducing her speed to 18 knots. The Italian commander, Admiral Campioni, at once broke off the action and headed for the Italian coast, accompanied by the *Cesare's* sister ship *Conte di Cavour*. He also ordered his destroyer flotillas to attack and lay down smoke.

## PALL OF SMOKE

At 1615, the nine Swordfish, led by Lt Cdr Debenham, arrived in the vicinity of the Italian warships, the pilots striving to identify targets in the dense pall of smoke that now hung over the sea. After a few minutes, Debenham spotted two large warships emerging from the smoke and led his aircraft in to the attack. In fact, the two ships were the cruisers *Trento* and *Bolzano*; they immediately turned away into the smoke once more, throwing down a heavy barrage in the path of the attacking Swordfish as they did so.

The torpedoes failed to find their mark, and all the aircraft returned safely to the carrier. They landed at 1705 in the middle of yet another high-level attack by Italian bombers; fortunately none of the British warships was hit, although both *Eagle* and *Warspite* were shaken by near misses.

At 1730, Cunningham abandoned the chase and set course for Malta. Without adequate fighter cover, it would have been suicidal to sail any closer to the Italian coast. Late in the following day, however, *Eagle*'s Swordfish flew off on one more strike, this time against a concentration of enemy cruisers and destroyers that had been reported in the Sicilian harbour of Augusta. The aircraft arrived over the harbour at dusk to find only one destroyer and an oil tanker still there; both were torpedoed, and the destroyer – the *Leone Pancaldo* – capsized and sank within minutes.

Having refuelled and rearmed his force in Malta, Cunningham now turned to his main task of escorting the convoy to Alexandria. The ships were repeatedly attacked by the *Regia Aeronautica* during the next three days, but they reached Alexandria without loss on 14 July. The 'Action off Calabria', as Cunningham's brush

# *EAGLE*

Type: Aircraft carrier

Launch date: 8 June 1918

Crew: 950

Displacement: 27,664 tonnes (27,229 tons)

Dimensions: 203.4m x 32m x 8m (667ft 6in x 105ft x 26ft 3in)

Range: 5559km (3000nm) at 15 knots

Armament: Five 102mm (4in) and nine 152mm (6in) guns

Powerplant: Quadruple screw turbines

Performance: 22.5 knots

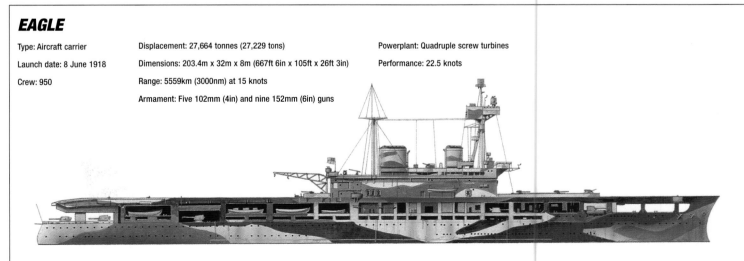

with the Italians came to be known, was the first fleet action in which carrier aircraft took part. Presumably due to lack of experience on the part of the Swordfish crews, the Fleet Air Arm made little material contribution other than to help convince the enemy that, in the face of repeated if ineffective torpedo attacks, withdrawal was the best policy. If the Italians had possessed an aircraft carrier (even one as outdated as the *Eagle*) with a complement of fighter aircraft, the outcome might have been very

different, and prohibitive losses inflicted on the Swordfish.

## HIGH-LEVEL BOMBING

As far as the *Regia Aeronautica* was concerned, the precision and concentration of its high-level bombing had been little short of poetic, but totally ineffective against the elusive moving targets presented by the warships. The Italian Air Force's lack of success against Cunningham's force did, however, have one damaging effect. It bred a

**The battleship HMS *Warspite* firing a salvo from her main armament. Severely damaged by radio-controlled glider bombs off Salerno in 1943, she was only partially repaired.**

sense of complacency, a belief that bombing could not seriously interfere with the Royal Navy's freedom of movement in the Mediterranean. This belief was strengthened on 17 August. Following a bombardment of Bardia and Fort Capuzzo in Cyrenaica by the battleships *Warspite*, *Malaya* and *Ramillies*, the heavy cruiser *Kent* and

145

Originally built as a dreadnought, the battleship *Giulio Cesare* was reconstructed in the 1930s. She missed the crippling air attack on the Italian Fleet at Taranto and remained a formidable opponent.

During September, Swordfish aircraft operating from *Illustrious* and *Eagle* made several night dive-bombing attacks on Italian airfields in the Dodecanese.

12 destroyers, the British force was attacked by Italian aircraft and suffered no damage. Moreover, 12 enemy bombers were destroyed by shore-based fighters of the *Eagle*'s air group. The complacency, however, was to be shattered before many months had passed, with the arrival of the first German dive-bomber squadrons in Sicily and Italy.

Towards the end of the month, the Royal Navy's striking force in the Mediterranean received a powerful new addition in the shape of the 23,369 tonne (23,000-ton) armoured fleet carrier HMS *Illustrious*. In addition to her two Swordfish squadrons, Nos. 815 and 819, she carried No. 806 Squadron, the first to equip with the Fairey Fulmar monoplane fighter. Powered by a Rolls-Royce Merlin engine, the Fulmar was armed with eight Browning .303 machine guns. It had a maximum speed of 435km/h

(270 mph), a limit partly imposed by the addition of a second crew member, and was thus a good deal slower than contemporary land-based fighters such as the Hawker Hurricane, but it was nonetheless a distinct improvement on the Sea Gladiator and Skua. Fourteen Fleet Air Arm squadrons were eventually equipped with it. For the first time, thanks to the Fulmars, Admiral Cunningham now had an effective means of countering the Italian high-level bombers and the reconnaissance aircraft that shadowed his warships. After some two months of operations, the pilots of No. 806 Squadron had claimed the destruction of over 20 enemy aircraft.

During September, Swordfish aircraft operating from *Illustrious* and *Eagle* made several night dive-

bombing attacks on Italian airfields in the Dodecanese. On one occasion, during a raid on Maritza airfield on the Island of Rhodes, the Swordfish failed to get clear of enemy territory before sunrise and were attacked by Italian CR.42 fighters. Four of the 13 Swordfish, all from the *Eagle*, were shot down. The Fleet Air Arm had its revenge on the night of 17 September, however, when 15 Swordfish from the *Illustrious* sank two Italian destroyers and damaged several other vessels in Benghazi harbour. The *Ark Royal*'s Swordfish were also in action during this period, carrying out a series of bombing raids on airfields in Sicily to

The carrier HMS *Illustrious* with her complement of Fairey Albacore torpedo bombers. She suffered terrible damage while escorting supply convoys to Malta and was repaired in the USA.

divert attention from the carriers *Furious* and *Argus*, which had just arrived from Britain with reinforcement Hurricane fighters for Malta. The island had been under attack by the *Regia Aeronautica* ever since Italy's entry into the war in June, and for nearly three weeks the sole air defence had been provided by three Sea Gladiators, a fourth being retained for spares.

The worst of Malta's ordeal was yet to come, but in the meantime events in the Mediterranean were moving towards the action that was to form the very basis of the Fleet Air Arm's tradition in the years to come: the attack on the Italian Fleet at Taranto.

### STRIKE AT TARANTO

Plans for an attack on Taranto by carrier-borne aircraft had been laid as long ago as 1935, when Italian forces invaded Abyssinia. There were actually two main Italian naval bases, one at Naples and the other at Taranto; and it was at the latter, in the autumn of 1940, that the Italians began to concentrate their heavy naval units to counter the threat from the British Mediterranean Fleet. With only the old *Eagle* at Admiral Cunningham's disposal, an attack on the big Italian base had been regarded as impracticable, but the arrival of the *Illustrious* changed the picture. The plans were revised, and it was decided to mount a strike from the *Illustrious* and *Eagle* on the night of 21 October, the anniversary of the Battle of Trafalgar. Before that date, however, a serious fire swept through *Illustrious*'s hangar. Some of her aircraft were destroyed and others put temporarily out of action, and the strike had to be postponed by three weeks.

> Because of defects caused by the many near-misses she had suffered, the *Eagle* had to be withdrawn from the operation at the last moment.

Italian battleship *Conte di Cavour* in Valletta, Malta, during a pre-war visit. Seized by the Germans after Italy's surrender, she was sunk by aircraft bombs at Trieste in February 1945.

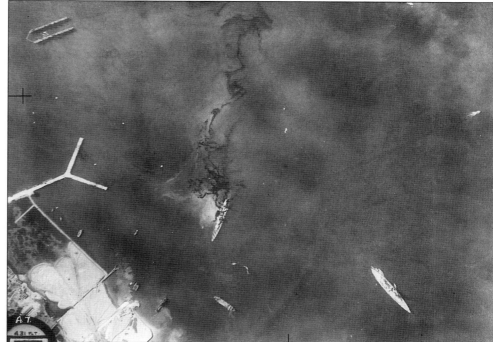

Oil pours from stricken Italian warships after the Fleet Air Arm attack on Taranto in November 1940. The Japanese used the lesson of Taranto as a blueprint for the strike on Pearl Harbor.

Air reconnaissance had revealed that five of the six battleships of the Italian battle fleet were at Taranto, as well as a large force of cruisers and destroyers. The battleships and some of the cruisers were moored in the outer harbour (the Mar Grande, a horseshoe-shaped expanse of fairly shallow water), while the other cruisers and destroyers lay in the inner harbour, the Mar Piccolo. The ships in the outer harbour were protected by torpedo nets and lines of barrage balloons. It was the balloons, perhaps even more than the anti-aircraft batteries, that would present the greatest hazard to the low-flying Swordfish. The date of the attack, codenamed Operation Judgment, was fixed for the night of 11 November. Because of defects caused by the many near-misses she had suffered, the *Eagle* had to be withdrawn from the operation at the last moment; five of her aircraft were transferred to the other carrier. The *Illustrious* and the fleet sailed from Alexandria on 6 November, and two days later the warships made rendezvous with several military convoys in the Ionian Sea, on their way from Malta to Alexandria and Greece. The concentration of ships was located and attacked by the *Regia Aeronautica* during the next two days, but the attacks were broken up by the Fulmars of No. 806 Squadron, which claimed the destruction of 10 enemy aircraft for no loss.

At 1800 on the 11th, with the convoys safely on their way under escort, the *Illustrious* detached herself from the main force and headed for her flying-off position 274km (170 miles) from Taranto, screened by four cruisers and four destroyers. Some 21 aircraft were available for the strike: 12 from No. 815 Squadron, led by Lt Cdr K. Williamson, and nine from No. 819 under Lt Cdr J.W. Hale. Because of the restricted space available over the target, only six aircraft from each wave were to carry torpedoes; the others were to drop flares to the east of the Mar Grande, silhouetting the warships anchored there, or to dive-bomb the vessels in the Mar Piccolo.

The first wave of Swordfish began taking off at 2040 and set course in clear weather, climbing to 2438m (8000ft) and reaching the enemy coast at 2220. The Swordfish formation now split in two, the torpedo-carriers turning away to make their approach from the west while the flare-droppers headed for a point east of the Mar Grande. At 2300, the torpedo aircraft were in position and began their attack, diving in line astern with engines throttled well back. Williamson, descending to 10m (30ft), passed over the stern of the battleship *Diga di Tarantola* and

released his torpedo at the destroyer *Fulmine*; it missed and ran on to explode against the side of a bigger target, the battleship *Conte di Cavour*. Then the Swordfish was hit by AA fire and had to ditch; Williamson and his observer, Lieutenant N.J. Scarlett, were taken prisoner. Two torpedoes from the remaining Swordfish hit the brand-new battleship *Littorio*; the aircraft all got clear of the target area and set course for the carrier. So did the other six Swordfish, whose bombs had damaged some oil tanks and started a big fire in the seaplane base beside the Mar Piccolo.

## GLARE OF FIRES

The second wave took off some 50 minutes after the first, and had no

difficulty in locating Taranto: the whole target area was lit up by searchlights and the glare of fires. There were only eight aircraft in this wave; the ninth had been forced to turn back to the carrier with mechanical trouble. This time, the five torpedo-carriers came in from the north. Two of their torpedoes hit the *Littorio* and another the *Caio Duilio*; a fourth narrowly missed the *Vittorio Veneto*. The fifth Swordfish (Lt G.W. Bayley and Lt H.G. Slaughter) was hit and exploded, killing both crew members. By 0300, all the surviving Swordfish had been recovered safely, although some had suffered substantial battle damage. Some of the crews who bombed the vessels in the Mar Piccolo reported that some

The battleship *Vittorio Veneto* in action. Repaired after Taranto, she saw active service until the Italian surrender, when she was interned at Lake Amaro in the Suez Canal.

bombs had failed to explode; one hit the cruiser *Trento* amidships, only to bounce off into the water, and the same happened with a hit on the destroyer *Libeccio*.

The following day, RAF reconnaissance photographs told the full story of the damage inflicted on the Italian Fleet. The mighty *Littorio*, with great gaps torn in her side by three torpedoes, was badly down by the bow and leaking huge quantities of oil; it would take four months to effect repairs. The *Caio Duilio* and the *Conte di Cavour* had taken one hit

HMS *Illustrious* on fire after being attacked by Stukas on 10 January 1941. The appearance of the German dive-bombers in the Mediterranean came as an unpleasant surprise to the British.

each; the former had been beached and the latter had sunk on the bottom. The *Duilio* was repaired and returned to service after six months; the *Cavour* was later salvaged and moved to Trieste, and she was still there when RAF bombers sank her on 17 February 1945.

It is no exaggeration to say that the Fleet Air Arm's exploit sent a ripple of alarm through naval commanders around the world, but one in particular regarded it as a blueprint for the possible solution to a dilemma. This was the commander of the Combined Fleet of the Imperial Japanese Navy – Admiral Isoroku Yamamoto.

On 9 January 1941, a convoy of four big supply ships, escorted by HMS *Ark Royal* and the other warships of Force H, entered the narrows between Sicily and Tunis on its way to Malta and Piraeus. The passage of the ships through the troubled waters of the central Mediterranean – known as Operation Excess – at first followed the pattern of earlier convoys. In the afternoon of the 9th, the usual formation of Savoia SM79s appeared and bombed from high altitude without scoring any hits; two of the SM79s were intercepted by *Ark Royal*'s Fulmars and shot down.

## TROUBLED WATERS

As darkness fell, Force H turned back towards Gibraltar, leaving the cruiser *Bonaventure* and the destroyers *Jaguar*, *Hereward*, *Hasty* and *Hero* to shepherd the convoy through the narrows under cover of night. At dawn on the 10th, 96km (60 miles) west of Malta, the transports were met by the ships of the Eastern Mediterranean Fleet

The naval base at Taranto, scene of the famous attack by Fleet Air Arm Swordfish in November 1940.

**2300, 11 Nov 1940**
**Main direction of Swordfish torpedo attacks**

**Mar Piccolo**

Cruiser    Cruiser

**Second wave**

**Mar Grande**

**Torpedo nets**

**TARANTO**

Fiume

Zara

Duilio

Littorio    Cesare

Gorizia

**First waves**

Vittorio Veneto

**Balloon barrage**

Doria

**San Paulo**

Cavour

**Diga di Tarantola**

**Diga di San Vito**

SHIPS CRIPPLED

0          1 MILE

## *ILLUSTRIOUS* OUT OF ACTION

**With the *Illustrious* out of action, Admiral Cunningham was forced to restrict the operations of the Eastern Mediterranean Fleet for several weeks because of the lack of air cover. Until March, with the arrival of *Illustrious*'s sister carrier *Formidable*, the full burden of naval air operations in the Mediterranean rested on the *Ark Royal*. The carrier had recently taken on two new Fulmar squadrons, Nos. 807 and 808, and with the air defence of Force H assured by these aircraft Admiral Somerville now made plans to use his *Swordfish* in a more offensive role, by striking at targets on the Italian mainland and in Sardinia.**

(Force A), which comprised the carrier *Illustrious,* the battleships *Warspite* and *Valiant* and seven destroyers. Admiral Cunningham's ships had already suffered; shortly before first light, the destroyer *Gallant* had been badly damaged by a mine and had to be taken in tow by HMS *Mohawk.*

Torpedo attacks by 10 SM79s were beaten off in the course of the morning, and the Italian MTB *Vega* was sunk by the *Bonaventure.* Then *Illustrious*'s radar detected another incoming formation of enemy aircraft, which soon afterwards was sighted approaching the warships at 3658m (12,000ft). Sailors who had fought in the waters off Norway and Dunkirk recognized the enemy aircraft at once; they were Junkers Ju 87 dive-bombers.

The Stukas were the aircraft of StG1 and StG2, led by Hauptmann Werner Hozzel and Major Walter Enneccerus. They formed the mainstay of the *Luftwaffe*'s special anti-shipping formation, *Fliegerkorps X,* and they had arrived at Trapani in Sicily less than a week earlier. Their presence should not have come as a surprise; Air Ministry Intelligence,

thanks to Ultra intercepts, had been aware since 4 January of *Fliegerkorps X*'s move south from Norway, and it was also aware of the unit's specialized role. The threat to the Mediterranean Fleet was clear; unfortunately, at this point there appears to have been a breakdown in communication between the Air Ministry and the Admiralty, and the Stukas came as an unpleasant shock.

Now, as they began their attack dive, it was clear that they had singled out *Illustrious* as their principal target.

The first bomb tore through S1 pompom on the carrier's port side, reducing the weapon to twisted wreckage and killing two of its crew before passing through the platform and exploding in the sea. Another bomb exploded on S2 pompom and obliterated it, together with its crew. A third hit the after-well lift, on its way to the flight deck with a Fulmar on it; debris and burning fuel poured into the hangar below, which quickly became an inferno of blazing aircraft and exploding fuel tanks. Splinters struck the eight 11.4cm (4.5in) gun turrets aft, putting them all out of action. A fourth bomb crashed through the flight deck and ripped through the ship's side, exploding in the water; splinters punched holes through the hull and the shock of the detonation caused more damage in the hangar. The fifth bomb punched through the flight deck and hangar deck and exploded in the wardroom flat, killing everyone there and sending a storm of fire raging through

**The Germans switched the full ferocity of their air attacks to Malta. Here, HMS *Illustrious* and the cruiser HMAS *Perth* come under air attack in the island's Grand Harbour on 16 January 1941.**

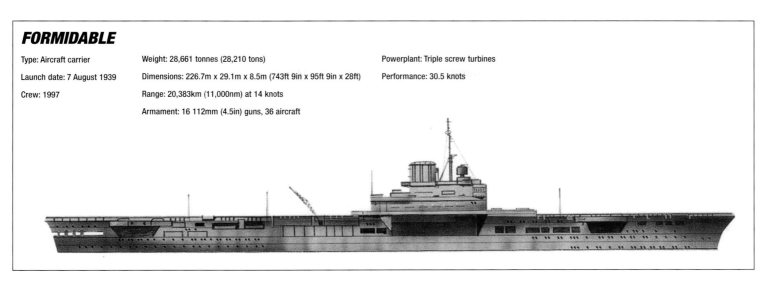

**FORMIDABLE**

Type: Aircraft carrier

Launch date: 7 August 1939

Crew: 1997

Weight: 28,661 tonnes (28,210 tons)

Dimensions: 226.7m x 29.1m x 8.5m (743ft 9in x 95ft 9in x 28ft)

Range: 20,383km (11,000nm) at 14 knots

Armament: 16 112mm (4.5in) guns, 36 aircraft

Powerplant: Triple screw turbines

Performance: 30.5 knots

the neighbouring passages. A sixth plunged down the after-lift well and exploded in the compartment below, putting the steering-gear out of action.

**SAVED BY HEAVY ARMOUR**

*Illustrious* was terribly hurt, but her heavy armour had saved her. Slowly the crew gained a measure of control and she turned towards Malta, shrouded in a pall of smoke from the

fires that still raged, steering on her main engines as the stokers worked in dense, choking fumes and temperatures reaching 60°C (140°F) while they strove to maintain steam. Two hours later, the Stukas attacked again and the carrier was hit by yet another bomb; she was now listing badly, but she remained afloat. As darkness fell, she limped into Valletta's Grand Harbour and stopped alongside the dockyard wall.

During the weeks that followed, *Illustrious* sustained several more bomb hits as she underwent repairs, but she escaped crippling damage and by 23 January she had been made seaworthy enough to sail for Alexandria. From there, she later sailed for the US Navy shipyards at Norfolk, Virginia, where she underwent more permanent repairs before returning to active service.

Accordingly, on 2 February, eight Swordfish took off from the *Ark Royal* and set course for Sardinia. Their target was the dam on the Tirso, the river that fed Lake Omodeo, the site of the island's only major hydro-electric plant. The mission was ill-starred from the beginning; the Swordfish pilots had a hard time flying down the twisting Tirso Valley, blinded by rain, and when they reached the lake they were met by heavy fire from fully alerted AA defences. Only four Swordfish managed to make a torpedo run, but the dam was unscathed and one aircraft was shot down. While this abortive attack was in progress, other Swordfish bombed an oil refinery at Livorno (Leghorn).

Between 6 and 11 February, Somerville's Force H executed a carefully planned attack on Genoa, where the damaged battleship *Caio Duilio* lay in dock. Somerville split his

153

force into three groups, Group One comprising the *Ark Royal*, the battleship *Malaya*, the battlecruiser *Renown* and the light cruiser *Sheffield*, and the other two groups consisting of six and four destroyers respectively.

On 6 February, Groups One and Two sailed from Gibraltar on a westerly heading, ostensibly to escort the UK-bound convoy HG53. During the night, however, they reversed course and slipped back through the straits to join Group Three, which had been carrying out a submarine search to the east of the Rock. On 8 February, the Italian *Supermarina,* having received reports of British naval aircraft operating to the south of the Balearics, despatched a strong naval force. Under Admiral Iachino, it comprised the battleships *Vittorio*

**Italian destroyers about to engage a British convoy en route from Alexandria to Malta. The Italian Navy fought bravely, but was hopelessly outclassed after the Taranto disaster.**

*Veneto, Andrea Doria* and *Giulio Cesare,* with 10 destroyers and three heavy cruisers, and made rendezvous southwest of Sardinia in order to intercept what was believed to be a Malta convoy – which was exactly what Somerville wanted the Italians to think. Meanwhile, Force H sailed north-eastwards, approached the Italian coast and bombarded Genoa harbour, sinking four freighters and damaging 18 more, as well as causing severe damage to the city. Belatedly, Iachino's force headed north to intercept the British, but, without the benefit of radar, failed to make

contact in thick mist. By 11 February, Force H was back in Gibraltar.

On 9 March, the carrier gap was filled when HMS *Formidable* joined the Mediterranean Fleet. She carried only four Swordfish; the rest of her aircraft complement was made up of the 13 Fulmars of No. 803 Squadron, transferred from the *Ark Royal*; and from No. 826 Squadron, 10 Fairey Albacores – these were biplanes, like the Swordfish, but bigger and faster, with a longer range and an enclosed cockpit. The fighter complement would be brought up to full strength in the following month, when No. 806 Squadron joined the carrier from Malta. Before that, however, *Formidable* and her aircraft were to play a decisive part in another large-scale action against the Italian Fleet.

At dawn on 28 March, while the Mediterranean Fleet was engaged in covering the passage of convoys of British Commonwealth troops from Alexandria to Greece to counter an imminent German invasion of that country, a reconnaissance Albacore from the *Formidable* reported a force of enemy cruisers and destroyers to the south of Crete. This force, which comprised the battleship *Vittorio Veneto* (Admiral Iachino's flagship), six heavy cruisers, two light cruisers and 13 destroyers, had put to sea from Taranto, Naples, Brindisi and Messina, and had made rendezvous south of the Straits of Messina on 27 March with the object of intercepting the British troop convoys. Iachino had agreed to the operation only when the *Luftwaffe* promised him extensive fighter cover and reconnaissance facilities, and after the crews of two He 111 torpedo bombers had erroneously reported hits on two large warships – 'possibly battleships' – during an armed reconnaissance flight 55.5km (30nm) west of Crete on 16 March. It was a mistake that was to

> ## The Fleet Air Arm pilots attacked in two waves at 1125, but the Italian battleship took evasive action and all of the torpedoes missed.

have serious consequences for the Italian admiral.

## TORPEDO STRIKE

At 0815 on 28 March, the Mediterranean Fleet's cruisers, which were about 160km (100 miles) ahead of the main force, came under fire from the Italian warships and were in danger of being cut off by the enemy, who was steaming in a large pincer formation. With no hope of Admiral Cunningham's heavy brigade arriving in time to ease the situation, it was apparent that only a torpedo strike by *Formidable*'s aircraft could ease the pressure on the outgunned British cruisers. At 1000, six Albacores – the only ones available, as the other four were earmarked for reconnaissance duties – took off with an escort of two Fulmars and headed for the Italian squadrons. Their orders were to attack the enemy cruisers, but the first ship

**Fleet Air Arm aircrews boarding their Fairey Albacore torpedo bombers on HMS *Indomitable*. The Albacore was an improved version of the Swordfish, with a fully enclosed cockpit.**

they sighted was the *Vittorio Veneto*, whose 381mm (15in) guns were pounding the British cruiser squadron. The Fleet Air Arm pilots attacked in two waves at 1125, but the Italian battleship took evasive action and all the torpedoes missed. The two

SEA WARFARE
Fulmars, meanwhile, had engaged two
Ju 88s high overhead and destroyed
one of them, driving the other off.

Admiral Iachino, seeing his air
cover melt away, now turned away
and headed west at speed, reducing
Cunningham's hopes of bringing him
to action. The British commander
ordered a second air strike, this time
with the object of slowing down the
Vittorio Veneto, and the Formidable
accordingly flew off three Albacores
and two Swordfish, again escorted by
a pair of Fulmars. They sighted their
target – which had meanwhile been
unsuccessfully attacked by RAF
Blenheim bombers from bases in
Greece – an hour later. This time,
mainly because they were on the alert
for more RAF aircraft approaching
from a different direction, the Italian
gunners failed to see the Fleet Air
Arm aircraft until the latter began
their attack. The Albacores came in
first, led by Lt Cdr Dalyell-Stead, who
released his torpedo seconds before
his aircraft was hit and blew up. The
torpedo ran true and exploded on
the battleship's stern, jamming her
steering gear and flooding the
compartment with 4064 tonnes (4000
tons) of water. No further torpedo
hits were registered, but the Vittorio
Veneto was forced to slow down and
stop while her engineers made
temporary repairs, spurred by the
knowledge that Cunningham's
battleships were now only three
hours' steaming time away. They
succeeded in repairing the propeller
shaft, and gradually the battleship's
speed was worked up until she was
able to proceed at between 15 and 18
knots, with the cruisers and destroyers
forming a tight screen around her.

**The British 5th Battle Squadron with HMS Valiant
in the foreground. The battleships HMS Malaya
and Barham are beyond. All were assigned to
convoy protection work in the Mediterranean.**

The Formidable's third and last
attack was launched at dusk. Led by Lt
Cdr W.H.G. Saunt, six Albacores and
four Swordfish, two of the latter from
Maleme airfield on Crete, caught up
with the damaged battleship and her
escort and attacked through heavy
AA fire. The Vittorio Veneto escaped
further harm, but one torpedo
heading for the battleship was
blocked by the cruiser Pola, which
was badly damaged. Admiral Iachino
detached the cruisers Zara and
Fiume and four destroyers to escort
her, while the rest of the Italian
force accompanied the Vittorio Veneto
to safety.

## DETECTED BY RADAR
At 2210, the three cruisers and the
destroyers were detected by radar on
board the battleship HMS Valiant and
the cruiser Orion. Fifteen minutes
later, the Italian ships were engaged
by Valiant and Warspite and the Zara
and Fiume were quickly reduced to
blazing hulks; two destroyers were
sent in to finish them off with
torpedoes. The crippled Pola was also
sunk before morning, as well as two
of the Italian destroyers. The enemy
warships, which were not equipped
with radar, had no idea that they were

156

steaming across the bows of the British force until the battleships opened fire on them. The Italians had lost five warships and nearly 2500 officers and men; the British had lost just one Albacore. So ended the action that was to become known as the Battle of Cape Matapan. It represented an overwhelming victory for the British Mediterranean Fleet, and it had been made possible by two factors: naval air power and the priceless gift of Ultra, which had alerted the Admiralty to the movements and dispositions of Iachino's fleet.

The jubilation, however, was to be short-lived. On 6 April, German forces attacked Yugoslavia and Greece. Two days later, the Yugoslav armies crumbled and the *Wehrmacht* smashed its way into Greek territory through the thinly defended Aliakhmon Line, forcing an Allied withdrawal. The German Army, with powerful air support, poured southwards through Greece, and the Greek forces rapidly disintegrated before its onslaught. The burden of defence now rested on the New Zealand Division, the 6th Australian Division, the 1st Armoured Brigade and a handful of depleted

**Ships burning in Suda Bay, Crete, after an enemy air attack. The Royal Navy suffered heavy losses off Crete, mainly because vital air cover was not available.**

RAF squadrons. By 2 May, the position in Greece was untenable and 43,000 Allied troops were evacuated from Greek soil, 11,000 being withdrawn to Crete.

On 20 May, in the wake of a massive air bombardment, German airborne forces landed on Crete as part of Operation *Merkur*. The next morning, the *Luftwaffe* launched the first of a series of heavy attacks on

The destroyer HMS *Sikh* escorting a damaged merchant vessel to safety in Malta during the siege. Many merchant seamen gave their lives to keep Malta's vital supply lines open.

British warships in the area, sinking the destroyer *Juno* and damaging the cruiser *Ajax*. During the night of 21/22 May, the Germans attempted to send in reinforcements by sea, but the convoy, comprising 20 motor sailing vessels, was attacked 33km (18nm) north of Canea by the British Force D under Rear-Admiral Glennie (the cruisers *Ajax*, *Dido* and *Orion*, supported by four destroyers) and scattered. Ten enemy vessels were sunk, and 297 of the 2331 troops on board lost their lives. The toll would almost certainly have been greater had it not been for a determined defence put up by an escorting Italian torpedo boat, the *Lupo* (Cdr Mimbelli), whose sister craft, the *Sagittario* (Cdr Cigala) also fought a gallant action after daybreak while escorting a second troop convoy. This convoy was attacked by Rear-Admiral King's Force C (the cruisers *Naiad*, *Perth*, *Calcutta* and *Carlisle*, with three destroyers), but the British warships came under constant air attack and

succeeded in destroying only two transports. The *Carlisle* and *Naiad* were both damaged by bomb hits.

## HEAVY AIR ATTACK

The Royal Navy suffered heavily in the afternoon, when the fleet came under heavy air attack. The battleship *Warspite* was hit several times, the cruiser *Gloucester* and the destroyer *Greyhound* sunk – the former with the loss of 45 officers and 648 ratings – and the cruiser *Fiji* was so badly hit that she had to be abandoned. The *Carlisle* and *Naiad* suffered further damage, and the battleship *Valiant* was also damaged to a lesser extent. On 23 May, the destroyers *Kashmir* and *Kelly* were both sunk by air attack, while attacks on Suda Bay destroyed five MTBs of the 10th MTB Flotilla.

On 25 May, Vice-Admiral H.D. Pridham-Wippell put to sea from Alexandria with the battleships *Barham* and *Queen Elizabeth*, the aircraft carrier *Formidable* and nine destroyers to attack the enemy airfield at Scarpanto. Returning from this sortie on the 26th, the *Formidable* and the destroyer *Nubian* were both badly damaged by Ju 87s, and the next day the *Barham* was also damaged by Ju 88s. By this time, it was clear that

> Orion suffered fearsome casualties among the troops she was carrying; of the 1100 soldiers in board, 260 were killed and 280 wounded.

The Australian destroyer HMAS *Nizam* laden with troops during the evacuation of Crete. Commonwealth troops would have held on to the island, had not the Germans captured the key airfield at Maleme, letting reinforcements fly in.

Crete could no longer be held. Suda Bay was being so heavily bombed that it was no longer possible to run in supplies and reinforcements. And without air cover Admiral Cunningham's forces were certain to suffer unacceptable losses in their efforts to prevent seaborne landings on the island – a task that, in any case, could not be guaranteed. In the afternoon of 27 May, therefore, the War Cabinet decided to evacuate the garrison of some 32,000 troops, and on the night of 28/29 May some 4700 were embarked at Heraklion and Sphakia. During this operation, the destroyer *Imperial*, part of the evacuation force, was damaged by enemy aircraft and had to be abandoned and sunk by the *Hotspur* off Malea Bay. Another 6000 troops were evacuated on the next night, but during the day Stukas sank the destroyer *Hereward* and damaged the cruisers *Ajax*, *Dido* and *Orion*, as well as the destroyer *Decoy*. *Orion* suffered fearsome casualties among the troops she was carrying; of the 1100 soldiers on board, 260 were killed and 280 wounded.

## ARK ROYAL

Type: Aircraft carrier

Launch date: 13 April 1937

Crew: 1580

Displacement: 28,164 tonnes (27,720 tons)

Dimensions: 243.8m x 28.9m x 8.5m (800ft x 94ft 9in x 27ft 9in)

Range: 14,119km (7620nm) at 20 knots

Armament: 16 114mm (4.5in) guns, 60 aircraft

Powerplant: Triple shaft geared turbines

Performance: 31 knots

On the night of 31 May/1 June, Rear-Admiral King sent in the destroyers *Abdiel, Hotspur, Jackal, Kimberley* and *Phoebe* in a last attempt to evacuate at least some of the 6000 troops assembled at Sphakia. By Herculean efforts, the destroyers lifted off 4000 men before the onset of dawn brought an end to the operation; the destroyers then headed for Alexandria, and the AA cruisers *Calcutta* and *Coventry* were despatched to meet them. These two warships, however, were located about 185km (100nm) north of Alexandria by two Ju 88s, which dive-bombed and sank the *Calcutta*; 255 survivors were rescued by the other cruiser.

The Royal Navy had succeeded in evacuating 17,000 troops from Crete, but 15,743 had been killed or captured. In addition, the Royal Navy had lost 2011 personnel. German casualties had not been light, either; the enemy had suffered 6580 dead, wounded or missing. The battle for Crete had cost the Royal Navy three cruisers and six destroyers. In addition, two battleships, an aircraft carrier, six cruisers and seven destroyers had sustained varying degrees of damage. It was exactly a year since the Royal Navy had suffered terrible losses at Dunkirk.

Hard on the heels of the evacuation of Crete came more crises, this time in the Middle East. An insurrection in Iraq, begun in April, was put down after several weeks by troops ferried from India, supported by warships of Vice-Admiral G.S. Arbuthnot's East Indies Squadron deployed to Basra, and by the RAF, which assisted loyal Iraqis in containing the rebellion until the ground forces arrived. And from 7 June to 14 July, Vice-Admiral King's 15th Cruiser Squadron was in action in the Eastern Mediterranean in support of the occupation of Vichy French Syria by Commonwealth and Free French forces. Several British warships sustained damage during this short but bitterly contested campaign, either by air attack or in engagements with Vichy French destroyers. These operations – followed by others aimed at preventing a seizure of power by pro-Axis factions in Iran during August – secured the passage of Allied shipping through the Red Sea and also forestalled a potentially dangerous threat to Britain's oil supplies.

The Admiralty's main preoccupation in the Mediterranean theatre in 1941 was to sustain the island of Malta, which was entirely dependent on supplies brought in by sea. Malta was kept supplied in late

### FIGHTERS FOR MALTA

**Admiral Somerville's Force H had scarcely returned to Gibraltar when, on 21 May, it was required to undertake Operation Splice, involving the flying-off of 48 more Malta-bound Hurricanes from the carriers *Ark Royal* and *Furious*. All these aircraft arrived safely, providing a much-needed boost for the island's air defences. This was followed, on 6 June, by Operation Rocket, in which the same two carriers flew off another 35 Hurricanes, and on 14 June by Operation Tracer, in which *Ark Royal* and *Victorious* launched 47 more Hurricanes from a point south of the Balearics. Four of this latter batch failed to reach Malta. Finally, on 26 June, came the week-long Operation Railway, in which *Ark Royal* flew off another 22 Hurricanes and returned to the flying-off position three days later to launch 26 more.**

1940 by convoys from Alexandria, heavily escorted by the Mediterranean Fleet, but providing adequate fighter reinforcements presented an ongoing problem, as these had to make the long and dangerous passage from Gibraltar.

## A CRITICAL SITUATION

The situation fast became critical, and was saved only by the transfer of *Luftwaffe* units from Sicily to support the German invasion of Russia in June 1941, leaving the Italians to conduct the Malta air offensive alone. On 2 April, in an operation codenamed Winch, the carrier *Ark Royal*, with a strong Force H escort, set out from Gibraltar carrying 12 Hurricanes and three Skuas; these were flown off at a distance of 740km (400nm) from Malta, and all arrived safely. In Operation Dunlop, on 28 April, 20 more Hurricanes, ferried from the UK by the *Argus* and transferred to

the *Ark Royal* at Gibraltar, were also flown off to Malta, together with three Fulmars.

The scene now briefly shifted to Egypt, where the Eighth Army, under heavy pressure from General Erwin Rommel's *Panzerarmee Afrika*, was in urgent need of reinforcements, particularly tanks and fighter aircraft. Between 5 and 12 May 1941, therefore, Force H and the Mediterranean Fleet mounted a joint operation, codenamed Tiger, to push a convoy of five fast merchantmen carrying the necessary equipment through the Mediterranean from Gibraltar to Alexandria. At the same time, the battleship *Queen Elizabeth* and two light cruisers from UK waters were being sent out to join Admiral Cunningham's fleet. The convoy passed Gibraltar on 6 May and was escorted by Force H to a point south of Malta, where it was covered by destroyers and cruisers from the

The Royal Navy had the monopoly on aircraft carriers in the Mediterranean. In the foreground is HMS *Eagle*, which was sunk by the *U73* south of the Balearic Islands on 11 August 1942.

island base until it could be met by a strong force sent out from Alexandria. Several German and Italian air attacks en route were broken up by Fulmars from the *Ark Royal* and *Formidable* and the ships suffered no loss from this quarter, although one of the transports, the *Empire Song*, was sunk by mines on 9 May. The remainder reached Alexandria, carrying the surviving 238 tanks and 43 Hurricanes.

In July, the Admiralty decided to take a considerable risk and run a convoy of six supply ships and one troop transport through to Malta from the west, covered by Force H and supported by warships detached from the Home Fleet. The operation was named Substance. The convoy left the Clyde on 11 July and reached

**Malta's Grand Harbour. In April 1942, King George VI awarded the George Cross to the island and its people, in recognition of their gallantry under sustained and ferocious attack.**

Gibraltar safely, but when the eastward movement started on the 21st the troopship *Leinster* – carrying replacement RAF ground crews for Malta – went aground and had to be left behind. On 23 July, Italian aircraft attacked the ships, securing hits on the cruiser *Manchester* and the destroyer *Fearless*, which had to be abandoned. The destroyer *Firedrake* also received a bomb hit and had to return to Gibraltar. Further losses were averted by the spirited action of *Ark Royal's* Fulmars, and the convoy reached Malta on the following day to discharge its precious supplies. The merchantmen made their way back independently to Gibraltar. One of them, the *Hoegh Hood*, was hit by a torpedo south of Sardinia, but survived.

On the night of 25/26 July, the Italian 10th MTB Flotilla made a gallant attempt to penetrate Grand Harbour and attack the merchantmen while they were still unloading. The frigate *Diana*, with eight explosive boats and two MTBs carrying human torpedo teams, reached Malta, but their approach had been detected by radar and the defences were alerted. One human torpedo team and two explosive boats wrecked the harbour boom, but this was to the defenders' advantage, because the explosion caused the St Elmo bridge to collapse and barred the way to the other six explosive boats, which were then

merchantmen, laden with the most urgently needed supplies and escorted by Force H, heavily reinforced by warships of the Home Fleet, while Admiral Cunningham staged a diversion in the eastern Mediterranean. The Italian main battle fleet put to sea, together with a strong force of submarines, but air reconnaissance had greatly underestimated the strength of the British force and the Italian surface vessels made no attempt to attack. On the evening of 27 September, when the convoy reached the narrows between Sicily and Tunisia, Force H turned back and the convoy sailed on to Malta, escorted by five cruisers and nine destroyers. It lost one transport to an aerial torpedo attack, but the remainder reached the island safely, bringing the total of merchantmen getting through to Malta since the beginning of the year to 39. The Royal Navy suffered one casualty in this operation; the battleship *Nelson* was torpedoed by an Italian aircraft south of Sardinia, but reached Gibraltar without further incident.

## TURNING IN BRITAIN'S FAVOUR

With the *Luftwaffe* still occupied in Russia, the naval war in the Mediterranean, despite strong opposition by the *Regia Aeronautica*, seemed to have turned firmly in Britain's favour. The Admiralty decided to exploit the situation by basing a small force of cruisers and destroyers (Force K) on Malta. They arrived on 21 October and were soon in action; on 9 November, in a brilliantly executed night attack, they sank all seven merchant ships in a heavily defended Italian convoy, and later in the month they sent two Africa-bound tankers to the bottom. Malta's striking force had been further augmented in October with the arrival

> With the *Luftwaffe* still occupied in Russia, the naval war in the Mediterranean, despite strong opposition by the *Regia Aeronautica*, seemed to have turned in Britain's favour.

destroyed by shore batteries. The two MTBs were also sunk the next morning by fighter-bombers.

Between 8 and 14 September, the *Ark Royal* and *Furious* flew off a further

55 Hurricanes to Malta (Operation Status), and on the 24th the Admiralty mounted a large resupply operation codenamed Halberd. This involved the passage to Malta of nine large

of 11 Albacore and two Swordfish torpedo-bombers, so that Axis convoy losses began to climb steadily.

On 13 November, however, Force H suffered a major setback. Three days earlier, the carriers *Ark Royal* and *Argus* had set out from Gibraltar to a flying-off point 724km (450 miles) from Malta, and on the 12th they launched 37 Hurricanes, of which 34 reached the island together with seven Blenheim bombers. As the carriers made their homeward run, the *Ark Royal* was hit by a torpedo, one of a salvo of four fired by the German submarine *U-81*. She was hit near her starboard boiler room.

Although only one crew member lost his life in the attack and valiant efforts were made to save the carrier, she sank under tow only 40km (25 miles) from Gibraltar.

By late November 1941, the supply situation of the Axis forces in North Africa was fast becoming critical, thanks to the attacks on their convoys by the Malta-based warships, submarines and strike aircraft. In an attempt to redress matters, the Germans heavily reinforced their U-boat fleet in the Mediterranean. At the same time, they also ordered the *Luftwaffe* back to Sicily: not *Fliegerkorps* X this time (it had been deployed to

**The battleship HMS *Barham* was substantially reconstructed in 1927–28, but further reconstruction plans were halted because of the outbreak of war.**

Norway for operations against the Arctic convoys), but *Fliegerkorps* II, mostly equipped with Ju 88s and with substantial fighter support. For Malta, 1942 would be the critical year.

Also occupying much of the Mediterranean Fleet's effort in 1941 was the need to supply the besieged garrison of Tobruk, isolated by the British retreat from Libya in April 1941. Night after night, when conditions were favourable, pairs of destroyers and other fast vessels made the dangerous 'Tobruk run', and by the time the siege was lifted on 8 December 1941 the Royal Navy had brought in 72 tanks, 92 guns, 34,545 tonnes (34,000 tons) of stores and 34,113 reinforcement troops. But the cost to the Navy was 25 warships, together with five merchant vessels.

> To cap it all, as the British warships returned to Alexandria, three Italian human torpedo teams penetrated the harbour through the open boom.

During the closing months of 1940, the British submarine offensive in the Mediterranean had been sustained mainly by the large P- and R-class boats of the 1st SM Flotilla, based on Alexandria. Then, in January 1941, the 10th SM Flotilla was formed, based on Malta and equipped with small 640-tonne (630-ton) U-class boats, which were better suited to operations in the shallow waters of the central basin. They began to make their mark in the summer, and between June and September 1941 they sank 49 troop transports and supply ships totalling 152,407 tonnes (150,000 tons). One particularly successful sortie was carried out by HMS *Upholder* (Lt Cdr M.D. Wanklyn), which on 18 September sank the Italian troop-carrying liners *Neptunia* and *Oceania*, both of 19,812 tonnes (19,500 tons).

It was the Axis powers, though, that had the last word in the Mediterranean battles of 1941. On 25 November, the battleship *Barham*, part of Admiral Cunningham's main fleet which had put to sea from Alexandria to search for an Italian convoy, was torpedoed by the *U-331*, and blew up with the loss of 861 men; there were 450 survivors. Then, on the night of 14/15 December, the *U-557* sank the cruiser *Galatea* off Alexandria, and four days later the cruiser *Neptune* and the destroyer *Kandahar* were sunk by mines, the former with the loss of all but one of her 550 crew. To cap it all, as the British warships returned to Alexandria, three Italian human torpedo teams penetrated the harbour through the open boom. Launched from the submarine *Scire* (under Cdr Prince Borghese), the teams were Lt Cdr Durand de la Penne and Sgt Maj Bianchi; Capt Marceglia and L/Cpl Schergat; and Capt Martellotta with Sgt Maj Marino. They succeeded in

**HMS *Barham* exploding after being torpedoed three times by the *U331* off Sollum, Egypt, on 25 November 1942. The Admiralty censored news of her sinking, and the loss of 862 crew.**

placing explosive charges under the battleships *Queen Elizabeth* and *Valiant* and the Norwegian tanker *Sagona*, all of which came to rest on the bottom, badly damaged. The destroyer *Jervis*, lying alongside the tanker, was also damaged. It was a most gallant action, and, with the loss of the *Barham*, it deprived Admiral Cunningham of the battle squadron that had kept the Italian fleet at bay for so long.

## GRIM OUTLOOK FOR BRITAIN

As 1941 drew to a close, the outlook for the survival of Britain seemed grim. But on the other side of the world, events were about to unfold that would alter the course of the war in a dramatic and unforeseen way.

# World War II

## From Pearl Harbor to Guadalcanal 1941–1942

**The fleet that assembled in Hitokappu Bay, in the remote Kurile Islands off the northern tip of Japan, was the most formidable assembled in Japanese waters since Tsushima, 36 years earlier. At its core were the aircraft carriers of the 1st Air Fleet, the *Akagi*, *Kaga*, *Hiryu*, *Soryu*, *Zuikaku* and *Shokaku*, under the command of Vice-Admiral Chuichi Nagumo. They were accompanied by the battleships *Hiei* and *Kirishima*, the heavy cruisers *Tone* and *Chikuma*, the light cruiser *Abukuma* and nine destroyers of the 1st Destroyer Squadron.**

This was the battle fleet assigned by the Imperial Japanese Navy to the Hawaiian Operation: the planned surprise attack on Pearl Harbor, the principal base of the US Pacific Fleet. Setting sail on 26 November 1941, the fleet was prepared to turn back if diplomatic negotiations between Japan and the United States reached a satisfactory conclusion. They did not, and the coded signal *Niitaka Yama Nobore* (Climb Mount Niitaka), signifying the go-ahead, was transmitted to Vice-Admiral Nagumo on 2 December.

**Personnel of the Imperial Japanese Navy's Fast Attack Carrier Force wave off a Nakajima B6N Tenzan torpedo-bomber on its way to Pearl Harbor, 7 December 1941.**

After replenishment at sea, the fleet proceeded to its flying-off position 370km (200nm) north of Oahu.

The first strike, launched at dawn on 7 December 1941, was made by 40 Nakajima B5N Kate torpedo-bombers led by Lt Cdr Shigeharu Murata; 49 B5Ns carrying armour-piercing bombs and led by Commander Mitsuo Fuchida; and 51 Aichi D3A1 Val dive-bombers under Lt Cdr Kakwichi Takahashi. It was escorted by 43 Mitsubishi A6M Zero fighters of the *Akagi* Fighter Squadron, the first wave covering force under Lt Cdr Shigeru Itaya.

Against this impressive force, the American garrison on Oahu, the main island of the Hawaiian group, nominally had a strength of 394 aircraft. However, only a small proportion of these could be classed as combat-ready. Many were obsolete, others were undergoing repair and servicing, and others had no pilots to fly them. After all, this was a peaceful Sunday morning, and despite the ongoing diplomatic wrangling with

The Japanese attack on Pearl Harbor. The illustration shows Ford Island early on in the attack, with water rising from a torpedo hit on the battleship *Oklahoma* (centre).

> Of the 94 warships in the harbour, 18 were sunk or suffered major damage; eight were battleships, the attackers' primary targets.

Japan over various issues in the Pacific, the United States was not at war. Most of the 94 vessels anchored in Pearl Harbor, too, were without steam and manned by skeleton crews. At the Army's radar station near Kahuku Point, only two men were on duty; and at the Shafter Information Center, the key point of the radar defences, one solitary officer remained on call while his staff went to breakfast. The boom defence of the harbour, vital protection against submarines and torpedoes, was left open for more than 75 minutes, because it was Sunday and no one could be bothered to close it.

**COMPLETE SURPRISE**

Commander Fuchida, leading the first wave, had devised two attack plans, one to be implemented in the event of complete surprise being achieved and the other if the surprise was lost.

In the first case, the B5N torpedo-bombers were to go in first, before smoke from the dive-bombing obscured their targets. If surprise were lost, the dive-bombers and horizontal bombers would go in first to obliterate the airfields and anti-aircraft defences, and the torpedo aircraft would follow when resistance had been crushed. The appropriate attack plan was to be signalled by Fuchida: one flare for 'surprise' and two for 'surprise lost'.

It was a simple enough code, but it went wrong. Fuchida fired one flare to indicate 'surprise'. Some of the aircrews recognized it, but others did not, so Fuchida fired a second flare. The result was confusion, with all the attack aircraft going in at once. It made little difference, however. The surprise was complete, and the Americans offered no defence at first, many believing that they were being subjected to manoeuvres.

The first attack lasted 30 minutes, striking the anchorage and outlying air bases. The second strike, just over an hour later, was made by 54 Kate bombers, 78 Val dive-bombers and 35 fighters; this lasted 65 minutes but was hampered by dense smoke from the burning anchorage and by heavy anti-aircraft fire, as well as by small numbers of American fighters. Of the 94 warships in the harbour, 18 were sunk or suffered major damage; eight were battleships, the attackers' primary targets.

Among the casualties was the battleship *Arizona*, pride of the Pacific Fleet and flagship of Rear-Admiral

The USS *Arizona* burning after the devastating Japanese attack. She was hit by a torpedo and eight bombs, and 1104 of her crew lost their lives. Her wreck is preserved at Pearl Harbor.

Isaac C. Kidd, which was hit by a torpedo and eight bombs. It exploded and sank with the loss of 1404 lives. Also hit was the *California*. Severely damaged by bombs and with 98 of her crew dead, she sank three days later. A similar fate befell the *Nevada*, *Oklahoma*, *West Virginia*, *Maryland*, *Pennsylvania* and *Tennessee*, all of which were sunk, beached, or, at the very least, heavily damaged, leaving the Pacific Fleet crippled in the space of just a few hours.

## DAY OF INFAMY

The three aircraft carriers of the US Pacific Fleet were not present at the time of the attack. The USS *Saratoga* (CV-3) was just out of overhaul and was moored at San Diego; the USS *Lexington* (CV-2) was at sea about

The Japanese attack on Pearl Harbor required meticulous planning and careful fleet movements in order to preserve secrecy. Various warnings of the strike were ignored by the Americans.

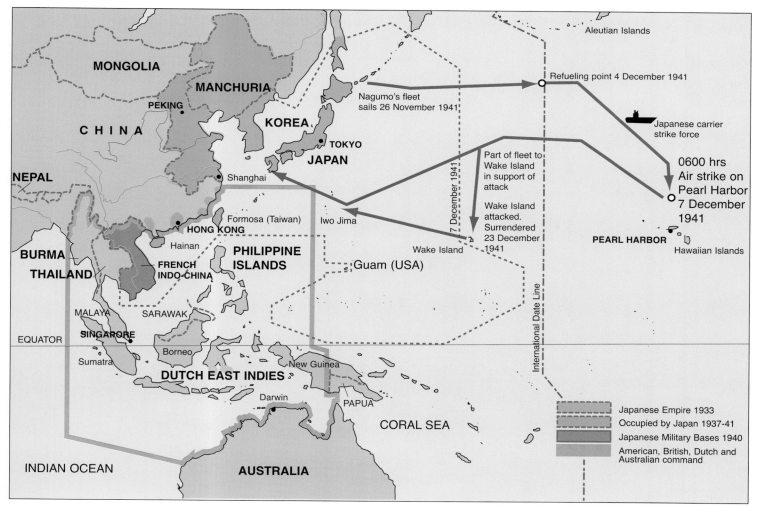

680km (425 miles) southeast of Midway Island, towards which she was heading to deliver a Marine scout bombing squadron; and the USS *Enterprise* (CV-6) was also at sea about 320km (200 miles) west of Pearl Harbor, returning from Wake Island after delivering a Marine fighter squadron. It was these carriers that, in the early months of 1942, would form the nucleus of a rebuilt Pacific Fleet.

The assault on Pearl Harbor, a 'day of infamy' in the words of President Franklin D. Roosevelt, was a masterstroke of planning and execution. Its architect was Admiral Isoroku Yamamoto, C-in-C of the Japanese Combined Fleet, one of the ablest naval commanders of all time – and a man on whom the lesson of the British air attack on the Italian fleet at Taranto just over a year earlier had not been lost. Born in 1884, Yamamoto was an adopted child, his original family name being Takano. He graduated from the Japanese Naval Academy in 1904, and in the following year he saw naval action at Tsushima, losing two fingers. He attended the Naval War College and then went to the United States to study at Harvard. Later, as a captain, he served as Naval Attaché to the United States from 1925 to 1927. Fluent in English, he knew the Americans well – well enough, indeed, never to underestimate their resolve and determination. He had never wanted war with the United Sates, but now that it had been thrust upon him,

The attack on Pearl Harbor effectively eliminated the US Pacific Fleet as a fighting force, all except for the vital aircraft carriers, which were absent at the time.

he was determined to conduct it to the best of his ability.

The destruction of the American capital ships left the way open for the Japanese conquest of key islands and island groups in the Pacific, surprise and a lack of support hindering any significant opposition to the Japanese advance. There remained, however, the Indian Ocean and the Java Sea, the respective preserves of Great Britain and the Netherlands.

The Admiralty's plan to reinforce the Indian Ocean theatre with warships drawn from the Mediterranean Fleet, leaving the French Navy to concentrate on the Mediterranean, was dislocated by the collapse of France in 1940. In August 1941, another Admiralty plan envisaged reinforcing the Far East with six capital ships, a modern aircraft carrier and supporting light forces by the spring of 1942. In the meantime, the best that could be done was to send out the new battleship *Prince of Wales*, supported by the old battlecruiser *Repulse* (she had been launched in 1916) and the

The *Prince of Wales* was a relatively new battleship at the time of Pearl Harbor, but she had already seen action, having engaged the German battleship *Bismarck* in May 1941.

## NAVAL SUPREMACY

**The key to British naval supremacy in eastern waters was Singapore. Britain's decision to build a strong naval base in the Far East was taken in the early 1920s in the hope of ensuring that an increasingly powerful Japan would be deterred from threatening important British political and economic interests in South East Asia, Australasia and India. The choice of Singapore was based on the assumption that naval power would be the key; in other words, that a battle fleet based at Singapore would be sufficient to deter and if necessary repel attack.**

aircraft carrier *Indomitable*, which was to provide the essential air component. Even this plan was disrupted when the *Indomitable* ran aground off Jamaica while she was working up; it was another fortnight before she was ready to sail.

The *Prince of Wales*, meanwhile, flagship of Rear-Admiral Sir Tom Phillips, had sailed from the Clyde on 25 October accompanied by the destroyers *Electra* and *Express*. Their orders were to proceed to Singapore via Freetown, Simonstown and Ceylon, where they were joined on 28 November by the *Repulse* from the Atlantic and the destroyers *Encounter* and *Jupiter* from the Mediterranean. The force reached Singapore on 2 December. The Admiralty had always been reluctant to concentrate its warships on Singapore, preferring to

base them further back on Ceylon. The fact that they were there at all was at the insistence of Winston Churchill, whose view – supported by the Foreign Office – was that their presence would be enough to deter the Japanese from taking aggressive action. In view of the *Indomitable*'s absence, the force was vulnerable to enemy air attack, for the RAF's air defences on Singapore and the Malay peninsula were woefully weak.

### EXPOSED POSITION

Anxiety over the exposed position of Phillips' ships led the Admiralty to urge him to take them away from Singapore, and on 5 December 1941 the *Repulse* (under Capt Tennant) sailed for Port Darwin in North Australia. The next day, however, a Japanese convoy was reported off

**The battlecruiser HMS *Repulse* served with the Grand Fleet during World War I and underwent a complete refit in the mid-1930s. She was active during the Norwegian campaign, and in the hunt for the *Bismarck*.**

Indo-China, and Tennant was ordered back to Singapore to rejoin the flagship. Only hours later came the news of the Japanese attack on the US Pacific Fleet at Pearl Harbor, with simultaneous amphibious assaults elsewhere, including Malaya and Siam. On the evening of 8 December, Admiral Phillips took the *Prince of Wales*, *Repulse* and four destroyers, collectively known as Force Z, to attack Japanese amphibious forces that had landed at Singora on the northeast coast of Malaya. Early the next morning, Singapore advised him that no fighter cover would be available and that strong Japanese bomber forces were reported to be assembling in Siam. This, together with the knowledge that his warships had been sighted by enemy reconnaissance aircraft, persuaded Phillips to abandon his sortie at 2015 on 9 December, reversing course for Singapore. Force Z had also been sighted by the submarine *I-65*, but the position it transmitted was inaccurate,

and other enemy submarines failed to detect the ships at this time.

Just before midnight, Phillips received a signal that the Japanese were landing at Kuantan and he turned towards the coast, intending to intercept this new invasion force. The report was false, but in the early hours of 10 December Force Z was sighted by the submarine *I-58* (Lt Cdr Kitamura). He made an unsuccessful torpedo attack, then shadowed the British ships for 5½ hours, sending regular position reports that enabled reconnaissance aircraft of the 22nd Naval Air Flotilla to sight them and maintain contact. Already airborne from airfields in Indo-China were 27 bombers and 61 torpedo aircraft, the flotilla's attack element, flying steadily south. They passed to the east of Force Z and flew on for a considerable distance before turning, and at about 1100 they sighted the ships.

The air attacks were executed with great skill and co-ordination. The high-level bombers – Mitsubishi G4M1 Bettys – ran in at 3658m (12,000ft) to distract the attention of the warships' AA gunners while the torpedo bombers, G3M2 Nells, initiated their torpedo runs from different directions. Two torpedo hits were quickly registered on the *Prince of Wales*, severely damaging her propellers and steering gear and putting many of her AA guns out of action. For some time the *Repulse*, by skilful evasive action, managed to avoid the attackers; but there were too many aircraft, and eventually she was hit by four torpedoes. At 1233, she rolled over and sank, and 50 minutes later the same fate overtook the flagship, which had meanwhile sustained two more torpedo hits. The accompanying destroyers picked up 2081 officers and men; 840 were lost,

Phillips received a signal that the Japanese were landing at Kuantan and he turned towards the coast, intending to intercept this new invasion force.

among them Admiral Phillips and Captain Leach of the *Prince of Wales*. Captain Tennant of the *Repulse* survived, having been literally pushed off the bridge by his officers at the last moment.

## NAVAL DISASTER

After the naval disaster off Malaya, with its incalculable consequences on the morale of the defenders of the peninsula and Singapore, came more bad news. On Christmas Day, Hong Kong fell, and Japanese forces were making rapid progress towards the capital of the Philippines, Manila, having made a two-pronged amphibious landing on the islands. Meanwhile, command of the British Eastern Fleet had been assumed by Admiral Sir Geoffrey Layton – or rather reassumed, for he had just handed it over to the unfortunate Admiral Phillips. It was a command with precious few ships, and scarcely

in better shape was a new Allied naval command, ABDA (American, British, Dutch, Australian), set up on Java in January 1942 under Admiral T.C. Hart, USN. For five weeks in January and early February, Hart's motley collection of warships – mostly British and Dutch – were employed in escorting troop convoys to Singapore, but by the end of January the Singapore naval base was so badly damaged that it could barely function. What had become the barest trickle of reinforcements was finally stopped after the Japanese gained a foothold on Singapore island on 9 February 1942, and on the 12th, three days before the Singapore garrison surrendered, there was a mass exodus of every seaworthy vessel from the base, laden with civilian and military personnel.

On 13 February, a Japanese invasion force was reported to be heading for Sumatra and the ABDA

Oil storage tanks at Singapore burning after a Japanese air attack. Singapore's air defences were weak, and the Allied fighter types based there were no match for the Japanese Zeros.

Command despatched a naval force of five cruisers and 10 destroyers (including the British cruiser *Exeter*) to intercept it. However, the Allied ships were heavily attacked from the air, and although none was lost to air attack the force commander, the Dutch Admiral Karel Doorman, decided to call off the operation and withdraw. The enemy blows now fell thick and fast. On 18 February, Japanese forces landed on the island of Bali, isolating Java from the east. The following day, aircraft of their main striking force, the 1st Carrier Air Fleet, launched a devastating attack on Port Darwin, sinking 11 transports and supply ships and causing severe damage to the port installations. As Darwin was the only base in North

The cruiser HMS *Exeter*, veteran of the River Plate battle, sinking after being engaged by Japanese naval forces in the South Java Sea on 1 March 1942.

Some 800 survivors from the three ships were picked up by the Japanese, many to die miserably in captivity. So ended the Battle of the Java Sea.

Australia from which Java could be reinforced and supplied, this attack effectively sealed the fate of the defenders.

On 27 February, Admiral Doorman, who had meanwhile been in action against the Japanese in the Bandoeng Strait with a mixed force of Dutch and American warships, sailed from Soerabaya with five cruisers and nine destroyers to intercept Japanese invasion forces in the Java Sea. The Japanese force was escorted by four cruisers and 14 destroyers, and at 1600 the opposing cruisers began an exchange of gunfire. Shortly afterwards, HMS *Exeter* was hit by a heavy shell and compelled to withdraw to Soerabaya, escorted by the Dutch destroyer *Witte de With;* another Dutch destroyer, the *Kortenaer*, had been sunk by a torpedo. Of the 120 torpedoes launched by enemy destroyers during this phase of the battle, it was the only one that found a target. To cover the *Exeter*'s withdrawal, the three British destroyers became engaged in a short-range action with eight enemy destroyers accompanying the cruiser *Naka*. In a confused battle in poor visibility, caused by dense smoke screens, HMS *Electra* was sunk.

## FURTHER LOSSES

Admiral Doorman then reformed his force with four cruisers and six destroyers and made a sortie to the northwest, where his ships fought a brief action in the dark with the cruisers *Haguro* and *Nachi*. Soon after this, the British destroyer *Jupiter* blew up – either as the result of striking a Dutch mine or because she was torpedoed in error by the American submarine *S-38*. The Allied force suffered further losses during the night when the Dutch cruisers *Java* and *De Ruyter* were sunk by torpedoes; the two remaining cruisers, the USS *Houston* and HMAS *Perth*, headed for Batavia in a bid to escape from the trap that was rapidly closing on them. The four American destroyers, meanwhile, had returned to Soerabaya to rearm and refuel, while the sole remaining British destroyer, the *Encounter*, had been despatched to pick up survivors from the *Kortenaer*.

Early in the morning of 28 February, the four US destroyers (the USS *Stewart, Parrott, John D. Edwards* and *Pillsbury*) passed through the Bali Strait bound for Australia, which they reached after a short and indecisive engagement with three Japanese warships. In the afternoon, the cruisers *Houston* and *Perth*, followed by the Dutch destroyer *Evertsen*, sailed from Batavia and headed into the Sunda Straits, making for Tjilatjap.

Doolittle's Tokyo raiders. North American B-25 Mitchell bombers on the deck of the carrier USS *Hornet*. The raid boosted American morale and shocked the Japanese.

attacked and sunk by TBDs and SBDs of the Lexington's air group, together with TBDs of VT-5; meanwhile, Japanese aircraft attacked the separately operating attack group, sinking the destroyer USS *Sims* and the fleet oiler USS *Neosho*. On 8 May, the fleet carrier *Shokaku* was attacked and heavily damaged by aircraft from both US carriers, but Japanese carrier aircraft, in a parallel attack, hit the *Lexington* with two torpedoes and damaged the *Yorktown* with a bomb hit below decks, although she remained operational. Later, fuel vapour in the *Lexington* exploded, causing uncontrollable fires; the carrier was abandoned and sunk by a US destroyer. Although a tactical victory for the Japanese, the Battle of the Coral Sea left them with no option but to call off the Port Moresby invasion, resulting in a clear strategic victory for the Allies.

Six months after Pearl Harbor, a crushing humiliation was about to descend on the Japanese. At the beginning of June 1942, the

Japanese launched a strong thrust in the central Pacific; its objective, as part of Yamamoto's eastward expansion plan, was to occupy Midway Island. The thrust was led by a four-carrier Mobile Force comprising the *Akagi*, *Kaga*, *Hiryu* and *Soryu*, supported by heavy units of the First Fleet and covered by a diversionary attack by carrier aircraft on Dutch Harbor in the Aleutians.

## MIDWAY

The thrust towards Midway was met by a greatly outnumbered US carrier force composed of Rear Admiral Fletcher's Task Force 17, with the USS *Yorktown*, and Rear Admiral R.A. Spruance's Task Force 16, with the

**Although the US Navy's carrier forces suffered heavily in the Battle of the Coral Sea, their aircraft inflicted sufficient damage on the enemy to compel the latter to call off their planned landing at Port Moresby.**

NEW IRELAND
Japanese Carrier Force
RABAUL
NEW BRITAIN
NEW GUINEA
BOUGAINVILLE
LAE
Solomon Sea
CHOISEUL
SOLOMON ISLANDS
PAPUA
NEW GEORGIA
SANTA ISABEL
BUNA
WOODLARK
Support Force
Milne Bay
GUADALCANAL
MISIMA
DEBOYNE IS.
PORT MORESBY
ROSSEL
TAGULA
Japanese landings at Port Moresby planned for 10 May
0630, 7 May Crace detaches to attack Invasion Group
TF 44
0900, 8 May air attack launched (*Shokaku* damaged)
Coral Sea
1118, 8 May *Yorktown* damaged, *Lexington* hit and sinks at 1956 hrs
Task Force 17

The Japanese fleet carrier *Hiryu* under heavy air attack during the Battle of Midway. The loss of four aircraft carriers, and most of its best naval aircrew, ultimately cost Japan the war.

USS *Hornet* and USS *Enterprise*, supported by Navy, Marine Corps and Army air units based on Midway.

The opening action of the battle took place on 3 June, when the Japanese fleet was sighted by a PBY Catalina; six Grumman TBF Avengers of Torpedo Squadron VT-8's shore-based detachment were launched to attack the Japanese, together with Army Air Force B-17s and Marine Vought SB2U Vindicators. None of the Avengers scored a hit and only one returned to Midway. At 0700 on 4 June, the *Enterprise* and *Hornet* launched their strike groups, comprising 14 TBDs of VT-6 and 15 of VT-8, with F4Fs of VF-6 flying top cover. VT-8 attacked first and all 15 aircraft were shot down by Zeros; only one crew member survived. VT-6, attacking the *Kaga* in turn, lost 10 aircraft before they reached their dropping points. The *Enterprise*'s air group, attacking the *Soryu* with 12 TBDs of VT-3 and 17 SBDs of VB-3, escorted by six F4Fs of VF-3, fared no better. Only five TBDs survived to make their torpedo attacks, and three of these were shot down on the way out. Of the 41 TBDs launched, only six returned to the task force, and one of these ran out of fuel and ditched.

The sacrifice of the three VT squadrons was not in vain. They had absorbed the bulk of the enemy fighter attacks, and the Zeros were

## YORKTOWN

Type: Aircraft carrier

Launch date: 4 April 1936

Crew: 2919

Displacement: 19,800 tonnes (17,679 tons)

Dimensions: 246.7m x 25.3m x 8.53m (809ft 6in x 83ft x 28ft)

Range: 23,200km (12,500nm) at 15 knots

Armament: 8 127mm (5in) anti-aircraft guns; 4 quadruple 28mm

(1.1in) anti-aircraft guns and 16 12.7mm (0.5in) machine guns;

Aircraft: 20 fighters, 38 dive-bombers and 13 torpedo-bombers

Powerplant: Four shaft geared steam turbines

Performance: 32.5 knots

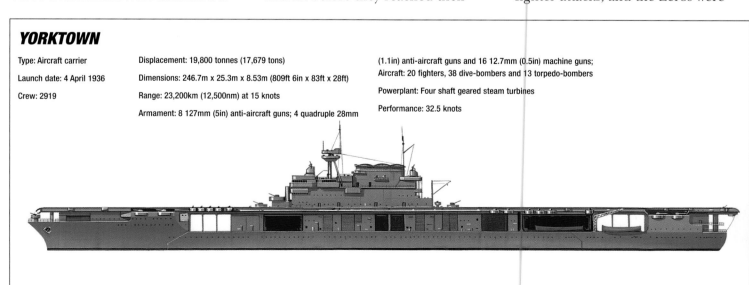

still scattered when 37 Dauntless dive-bombers from the *Enterprise*'s VB-5 and the 17 from *Yorktown*'s VB-3 made their attack, sinking the *Akagi*, *Kaga* and *Soryu*. The cost to the dive-bombers was 16 aircraft lost from *Enterprise*'s air group. A Japanese counterattack from the *Hiryu* damaged the *Yorktown*, but she returned to full operation after a short time. Then a second attack was made by six B5N Kate torpedo-bombers; two were shot down, but the other four launched their torpedoes and two hit the carrier, which had to be abandoned. She was later sunk by a submarine. At 1700, the *Hiryu* was crippled in an attack by 24 SBDs from

**Flying through a barrage of anti-aircraft fire, Japanese aircraft attack the carrier USS *Yorktown*. She was torpedoed and sunk by the submarine *I-168* on 7 June 1942.**

the *Enterprise*; her burned-out hulk was sunk by a Japanese destroyer the next day. For the cost of 92 aircraft and the *Yorktown*, the US Navy had destroyed four fleet carriers, three-quarters of the Imperial Japanese Navy's carrier striking force. With control of the air irretrievably lost, the Japanese withdrew on 5 June, under attack by Midway-based aircraft and carrier air; on 6 June, the cruiser *Mikuma* was sunk and her sister ship *Mogami* severely damaged in an air strike from the USS *Enterprise*.

Other US losses in the Midway battle were 40 shore-based aircraft and the destroyer *Hammann*, sunk by the same submarine that torpedoed the crippled *Yorktown*. In addition to the four carriers, the Japanese lost 258 aircraft and a large percentage of their most experienced carrier pilots. Midway was a decisive defeat that put

an end to Japan's offensive plans, and effectively turned the tide of the Pacific war.

## GUADALCANAL

On 7 August 1942, the US Marines carried out their first amphibious landing of World War II, its objective being the capture of Guadalcanal, in the Solomon Islands. Air support was provided by the aircraft carriers USS *Wasp*, USS *Enterprise* and USS *Saratoga* of the Air Support Force (under Rear Admiral L. Noyes) and by Navy, Army and Marine units of Aircraft, South Pacific (under Rear Admiral J.S. McCain) operating from bases on New Caledonia and in the New Hebrides. The carrier forces withdrew from direct support on 9 August, but remained in the area to give overall support to the campaign, during which they participated in several of

the naval engagements fought over the island. Land-based air support, based on the newly captured Henderson Field, initially comprised the F4F Wildcats of VMF-223 and VMF-224 and the SBD Dauntlesses of VMSB-231 and VMSB-232, the latter delivered by the escort carrier USS *Long Island* on 20 August.

On 23 August, land-based bombers from Henderson Field and strike aircraft from the USS *Saratoga* set out in search of Japanese surface units located by US scouting seaplanes. In bad weather, they failed to find the enemy. On 24 August, Japanese strike aircraft from the light carrier *Ryujo* were intercepted by Wildcats from Henderson Field and heavily

defeated; the *Ryujo* herself was sunk in an attack by 30 SBD dive-bombers and eight TBM Avengers. Strike aircraft from the main Japanese striking force, the carriers *Zuikaku* and *Shokaku*, attacked and damaged the USS *Enterprise*, forcing her to retire, although the attackers suffered heavy losses from American combat air patrols and AAA. The *Shokaku* was slightly damaged by SBDs from the *Enterprise* air group. The Japanese naval commander, Admiral Nagumo, had by now lost so many aircraft and crews in these encounters that he was forced to withdraw his forces, leaving a troop convoy bound for Guadalcanal without support. Attacked by aircraft from Henderson

Field and by AAF bombers, the convoy was also compelled to retire. This action, known as the Battle of the Eastern Solomons, marked the end of the first phase of the struggle for Guadalcanal.

In October 1942, the Japanese launched a determined campaign to capture and neutralize Henderson Field as a preliminary to the destruction of the remaining US naval air resources in the Solomons. At this point, the US Navy had only two carriers in the area, the USS *Enterprise* and the USS *Hornet*, the latter having replaced the USS *Saratoga*, which had been damaged by a submarine torpedo on 31 August and withdrawn to Pearl Harbor for repair. The Americans had also lost the USS *Wasp*, sunk by a submarine on 15 September while escorting a troop convoy to Guadalcanal.

### BATTLE OF SANTA CRUZ
To activate their plan, the Japanese naval forces put to sea from Truk on 11 October. They included the Carrier Striking Force with the *Shokaku* and *Zuikaku*, the light carrier *Zuiho* and seven destroyers; the Advance Striking Force with the new carriers *Junyo* and *Hiyo* supported by two battleships, five cruisers and 13 destroyers; and the Battleship Striking Force with two battleships, three cruisers and eight destroyers. The latter subjected Henderson Field to a very heavy bombardment on 13 October and on three successive nights; aircraft losses were partly made good by the deployment of 19 F4Fs from Espiritu Santo, together with seven SBDs. The total number of aircraft available to defend Henderson Field was now

> The Japanese naval commander, Admiral Nagumo, had by now lost so many aircraft and crews in these encounters that he was forced to withdraw his forces.

Dejected crewmen on the carrier USS *Yorktown*, listing and sinking after being attacked by the Japanese submarine *I-168*. She could not be saved, despite efforts on the part of her crew.

60, but on 15 October enemy forces were able to land.

On 26 October 1942, the opposing carrier task forces located one another almost simultaneously and launched their strike aircraft. The Japanese force, in two waves 45 minutes apart, comprised 42 Aichi D3A2 Val dive-bombers, 36 Mitsubishi B5N2 Kate torpedo-bombers and 55 Zero fighters from the *Shokaku*, *Zuikaku* and *Zuiho*; the *Hornet* and *Enterprise* launched

**The USS *Wasp*. Three torpedoes from the submarine *I-19* tore a gash in her hull and fractured fuel pipelines. A spark ignited the vapour and several explosions wrecked the ship.**

three waves comprising 30 SBD Dauntlesses, 20 TBM Avengers and 24 F4F Wildcats. While these forces were en route, two SBDs from the *Enterprise*, on an armed reconnaissance, encountered the *Zuiho* and bombed her, damaging her flight deck and rendering it unusable.

At 0940, purely by chance, the opposing air groups ran into each other and a brief air battle developed, in which the Zeros shot down three

**The defence of Guadalcanal by US Marines and other forces in the face of heavy Japanese attacks launched the 'island-hopping' campaign across the Pacific to the Japanese homeland.**

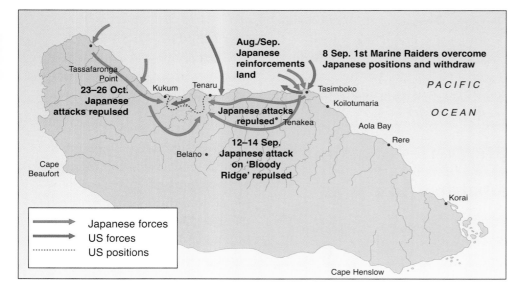

Tassafaronga Point

**23–26 Oct. Japanese attacks repulsed**

Kukum  Tenaru

**Aug./Sep. Japanese reinforcements land**

**8 Sep. 1st Marine Raiders overcome Japanese positions and withdraw**

Tasimboko

Koilotumaria

*PACIFIC*

*OCEAN*

**Japanese attacks repulsed**

Tenakea

**12–14 Sep. Japanese attack on 'Bloody Ridge' repulsed**

Aola Bay

Rere

Belano

Cape Beaufort

Korai

→ Japanese forces
→ US forces
····· US positions

Cape Henslow

The United States fleet pictured under a flak-filled sky during the Battle of Santa Cruz, October 1942. The aircraft carrier on the left of the picture is the USS *Enterprise*.

SBDs and four Wildcats for the loss of five of their own number. At 1010, the first Japanese wave located the *Hornet* and subjected her to a bomb and torpedo attack that left her burning and listing in the water. Thirty minutes later, the *Hornet*'s strike aircraft also found the *Shokaku* and

scored four hits with 450kg (1000lb) bombs, putting the carrier out of the battle. The other US strike aircraft located the enemy cruiser and destroyer forces and attacked with bombs and torpedoes, damaging one cruiser. Meanwhile, the second Japanese wave attacked the *Enterprise*, scoring three bomb hits; torpedo attacks were frustrated by the Wildcat combat air patrols. Further attacks in the afternoon, launched by the *Zuikaku* and *Junyo*, succeeded in

sinking the crippled *Hornet*. Fortunately for the Americans, the Japanese were unable to exploit their tactical successes. They had exhausted their fuel reserves and were compelled to withdraw to Truk to replenish.

## BATTLESHIP FIREPOWER

The first real test of battleship firepower in the Pacific conflict came during the battle for Guadalcanal. On the night of 11/12 November 1942, the fast battleships *Hiei* and *Kirishima* attempted to bombard Henderson Field, but were surprised by US cruisers and destroyers and forced to withdraw after sustaining damage. The next day, the *Hiei* was located and attacked off Savo Island by aircraft from the USS *Enterprise* and set on fire. With 300 of her crew

The battle opened with a series of actions between the Japanese battle group and US destroyers, three of which were sunk and a fourth damaged.

The USS *Hornet* under heavy air attack at the Battle of Santa Cruz. Damaged by torpedoes and bombs, the carrier was sunk by Japanese destroyers after being abandoned.

dead, she was abandoned and sunk by Japanese destroyers.

The *Kirishima* attempted another bombardment the following night, but this time the US battleships *Washington* and *South Dakota*, the former redeployed from duty in the Atlantic, were in support. The battle opened with a series of actions between the Japanese battle group and US destroyers, three of which were sunk and a fourth damaged. Shortly afterwards, the *South Dakota*, with her radar out of action and manoeuvring to avoid the burning destroyers, came up against the *Kirishima* and the heavy cruisers *Atago* and *Takao*, which opened fire, scoring 42 hits on her superstructure. Luckily for the *South Dakota*, the USS *Washington*, unseen by the Japanese, approached to within 7686m (8400yds) with radar assistance, and in seven minutes she hit the enemy battleship with nine 406mm (16in) shells. Abandoned and ablaze, the *Kirishima* was finished off by destroyers.

# World War II

## European Waters 1942: Holding On

Malta resupply operations during the early weeks of 1942 were carried out from Alexandria, using fast merchant vessels under heavy naval escort and also large minelaying submarines. By this time, however, Admiral Cunningham's forces were so overstretched because of the losses of 1941 that he could not hope to fulfil all his commitments in the Mediterranean, and the Italian Navy was once again in a position to push through supply convoys to the Axis forces in North Africa, enabling Rommel to take the offensive. And what lay in store for the British convoys bound for Malta was demonstrated in mid-February: German bombers attacked three transports heading for the island from Alexandria, sinking two and damaging the other so badly that she had to put into Tobruk, with the result that Malta obtained no relief at all.

Another attempt to run a supply convoy – this time of four transports – was made on 20 March, when the ships left Alexandria protected by four light cruisers and 16 destroyers under the command of Admiral

German sailors at work cleaning the gun barrels of the heavy cruiser *Admiral Hipper*. A successful commerce raider, the *Hipper* mostly served in northern waters and with the Baltic Fleet Training Squadron.

Vian. The convoy's passage was detected by two Italian submarines and a strong Italian surface force, comprising the battleship *Littorio*, three cruisers and 10 destroyers, sailed from Taranto and Messina on the 22nd to intercept it. The Italian warships were sighted at 1427 by the cruiser *Euryalus* and Vian ordered his ships to deploy in six divisions according to a pre-arranged plan, some to attack the enemy with torpedoes, others to lay a smokescreen to windward of the convoy, and others to protect the merchantmen from air attack.

> The destroyers *Havock* and *Kingston* were badly damaged, but the convoy remained unharmed thanks to Vian's skilful use of smoke and resumed its course for Malta.

### LONG-RANGE GUN DUEL

*Euryalus*, together with Vian's flagship, the *Cleopatra*, engaged in a long-range gun duel with the Italian cruisers, which turned away. Vian's ships now rejoined the convoy, which by this time was coming under heavy air attack. Soon afterwards, the *Littorio* put in an appearance, accompanied

The cruiser HMS *Euryalus* listing after sustaining battle damage in an engagement with Italian warships. She survived the war and was scrapped in 1959.

The battleship *Littorio* was one of Italy's newest capital ships, having been completed in 1940. She was renamed *Italia* in July 1943 and was interned after Italy's surrender, being broken up in 1960.

by the cruisers, but they were kept at bay by four destroyers, which made a series of gallant torpedo attacks until the *Cleopatra* and *Euryalus* came up to their assistance. In the confused, high-speed action that followed in heavy seas, the destroyers *Havock* and *Kingston* were badly damaged, but the convoy remained unharmed thanks to Vian's skilful use of smoke and resumed its course for Malta. The

Italians broke off their attacks at about 1900 as darkness began to fall, the weather now being stormy. On their passage home, almost all the ships, British and Italian alike, suffered varying degrees of storm damage and two Italian destroyers, the *Lanciere* and *Scirocco*, foundered during the night.

So ended the action that became known as the Second Battle of Sirte. There is a sad postscript to it. Because of the combined effects of the battle and the storm, the convoy did not reach Malta until after daybreak on 23 March – and the bombers of *Fliegerkorps II* pounced.

The transport *Clan Campbell* was sunk with 32km (20 miles) to run; the *Breconshire*, heroine of previous Malta runs, was so badly damaged that she had to be beached, a total loss; and the two merchantmen that did reach harbour, the *Pampas* and *Talabot*, were both sunk on 26 March. Of the 29,973 tonnes (29,500 tons) of cargo carried by the four vessels, only 5080 tonnes (5000 tons) were brought ashore.

At this time, the attentions of *Fliegerkorps II* were concentrated on

Malta's airfields, of which only Luqa remained serviceable, and the fighter defences themselves were suffering severely from attrition. On 7 March, by which time they had been reduced to 30 Hurricanes, they received a welcome boost with the arrival of 15 Spitfires, the first of their kind to reach the island, flown off the carriers *Eagle* and *Argus* south of the Balearics in an operation codenamed Spotter. On 21 and 29 March, in Operations Picket I and Picket II, the *Eagle* and *Argus* respectively flew off nine and seven more Spitfires, all of which arrived safely.

## THE *WASP* STINGS TWICE

The loss of the *Ark Royal*, with her greater capacity, was keenly felt, but on 20 April it was temporarily made good by the arrival in the Mediterranean of the American carrier USS *Wasp*, which launched 47 Spitfires to Malta. All but one arrived safely, but most were

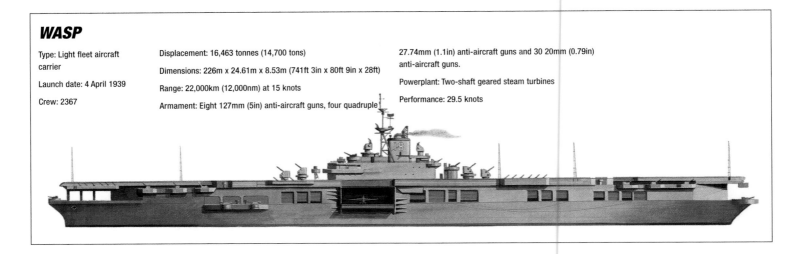

**WASP**

Type: Light fleet aircraft carrier

Launch date: 4 April 1939

Crew: 2367

Displacement: 16,463 tonnes (14,700 tons)

Dimensions: 226m x 24.61m x 8.53m (741ft 3in x 80ft 9in x 28ft)

Range: 22,000km (12,000nm) at 15 knots

Armament: Eight 127mm (5in) anti-aircraft guns, four quadruple

27.74mm (1.1in) anti-aircraft guns and 30 20mm (0.79in) anti-aircraft guns.

Powerplant: Two-shaft geared steam turbines

Performance: 29.5 knots

destroyed or made unserviceable by air attacks within the next 48 hours. This operation, codenamed Calendar, was followed on 9 May by Bowery, in which the *Wasp* and *Eagle* between them flew off another 64 Spitfires, 60 of which reached Malta.

In May, June and July, following the *Wasp*'s departure, it was the *Eagle* that bore the brunt of Malta's air reinforcement. Except for one occasion on 18 May, when she and *Argus* flew off 17 Spitfires in Operation L.B., she single-handedly launched 125 Spitfires to Malta in Operations Style (3 June), Salient (9 June), Pinpoint (16 July) and Insect (21 July.) Of these, 118 arrived.

The fighter reinforcements flown to Malta in June brought the island's air defences up to numerical strength, but the supply situation was desperate. In the middle of the month, therefore, two convoys sailed to Malta's relief: one from Alexandria, Port Said and Haifa, codenamed Vigorous and consisting of 11

transports, escorted by units of the Mediterranean Fleet; and Harpoon from Gibraltar, shepherded as usual by Force H, again strengthened by warships of the Home Fleet. Air cover for Harpoon was provided by the *Eagle* and *Argus*, the former with 16 Sea Hurricanes of No. 801 Squadron and the latter with half a dozen Fulmars. The Vigorous convoy, on the other hand, had no carrier and consequently no air support.

**EFFECTIVE DEFENCE**

Harpoon entered the Mediterranean on 12 June and was detected by enemy reconnaissance aircraft south of the Balearics later that day, but it was not until the 14th that it was located by Italian SM79 torpedo-bombers. They sank one transport, the *Tanimbar*, and scored a hit on the cruiser *Liverpool*, which had to be towed back to Gibraltar. Further air attacks were unsuccessful; the Sea Hurricanes and Fulmars put up an effective defence and claimed the

destruction of six Italian aircraft during the day. On 15 June, the western convoy was attacked by cruisers and destroyers of the Italian 7th Naval Division from Palermo, which sank the destroyer *Bedouin* and badly damaged the *Partridge*. The Italians were beaten off by the convoy's remaining seven escorting destroyers, but more heavy air attacks developed while these were engaged. The freighters *Burdwan* and *Chant* and the tanker *Kentucky* were so badly damaged that they had to be abandoned. The two surviving freighters reached Malta, but the escort suffered more casualties when it ran into a minefield, losing one destroyer (the Polish *Kujawiak*), with three more damaged.

The Vigorous convoy from Port Said and Haifa, which was the main one and was designated Convoy MW11, had also sailed on 12 June, to be joined by its escort and covering force of eight cruisers, 26 destroyers, four corvettes and two minesweepers under Admiral Vian. Thirteen British submarines were also stationed off Taranto and south of the Straits of Messina. The convoy was detected almost immediately by air reconnaissance and attacked south of Crete by the Ju 87s of I/KG54; the transport *City of Calcutta* was damaged and had to put into Tobruk. Another

> The two merchantmen of the western convoy that had got through to Malta carried enough supplies to give the island a breathing space, but it was short-lived.

Military vehicles being unloaded from supply ships at Valletta, Malta. The convoys kept Malta alive, but only just, and at a terrible cost in ships and men.

freighter, the *Aagterkerk*, also had to divert to Tobruk on 14 June because of engine trouble, but was sunk a few kilometres short of the harbour by enemy bombers; the escorting corvette *Primula* was damaged. In the afternoon, Ju 88s of LG1 from Crete attacked the main eastern convoy, sinking the freighter *Bhutan* and damaging another, the *Potaro;* and in attacks by the German 3rd S-boat flotilla from Derna that evening, the cruiser *Newcastle* was torpedoed by the *S56* and the destroyer *Hasty* sunk by the *S55*. Soon afterwards, Admiral

Vian learned that the main Italian Fleet had put to sea in strength from Taranto and was steaming south, its forces including the battleships *Littorio* and *Vittorio Veneto*, two heavy cruisers, two light cruisers and 12 destroyers. The fleet was attacked during the night by torpedo bombers from Malta; a Beaufort torpedoed the cruiser *Trento*, which was later sunk by the submarine *Umbra*.

In the afternoon of 15 June, the eastern convoy was heavily attacked by the Ju 87s of StG3, which sank the cruiser *Birmingham* and the destroyer *Airdale* and damaged another destroyer, the *Nestor*, so badly that she sank the next day. Faced with these losses, and with the Italian Fleet apparently still steering a

course to intercept, Admiral Vian decided to abandon the operation and make for Alexandria. The Italian Fleet also turned away, but as it was heading for Taranto, a Wellington from Malta got a torpedo hit on the *Littorio*, again without inflicting serious damage.

## OPERATION PEDESTAL

The two merchantmen of the western convoy that had got through to Malta carried enough supplies to give the island a breathing space, but it was short-lived. By the beginning of August, the situation on Malta was once again critical, and on the 10th the Admiralty mounted Operation Pedestal, which was virtually a desperate, do-or-die attempt to relieve

**Fairey Fulmar fighters. This two-seat carrier-borne fighter was the first eight-gun combat aircraft to serve with the Fleet Air Arm. It became operational on HMS *Illustrious* in September 1940.**

the island. On that day, 13 freighters and the tanker *Ohio* passed into the Mediterranean en route for Malta. To support the convoy, every available warship had been assembled; the

escort and covering force included the carriers *Victorious*, *Indomitable* and *Eagle*, the battleships *Nelson* and *Rodney*, seven cruisers (three anti-aircraft) and 25 destroyers. The

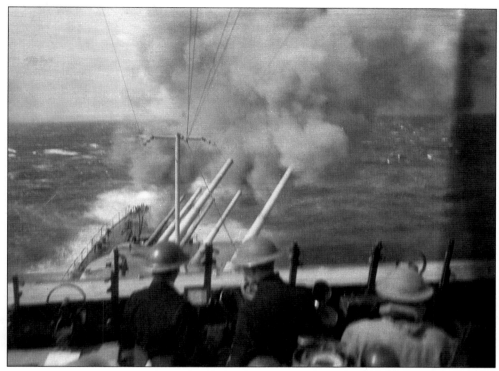

needed Spitfires. The convoy was sailing into the teeth of formidable odds. On airfields in Sardinia and Italy, the Germans and Italians had massed nearly 800 aircraft. Across the convoy's route, between Gibraltar and the Narrows, 19 enemy submarines were lying in wait. In the Sicilian Channel, a force of cruisers, destroyers and MTBs was lurking, ready to attack under cover of darkness after the main escort had turned away.

The first day passed fairly quietly. On the carriers, the fighter pilots remained at readiness and the crews of the torpedo aircraft helped to man the ships' guns. Early on 11 August, however, the first Junkers 88 reconnaissance aircraft appeared and circled the convoy at a respectful distance. The *Indomitable* sent up two flights of Sea Hurricanes of Nos. 800 and 880 Squadrons to try to intercept the shadowers, but the Ju 88s easily outpaced their pursuers. Then, at 1316, a series of explosions reverberated through the convoy. For a few moments, nobody knew quite

Naval anti-aircraft guns in action. The warships protecting the Mediterranean convoys could put up a formidable barrage, but enemy bombers and torpedo-bombers always broke through.

what had happened; then the *Eagle* was seen to be listing and shrouded in smoke. She had been hit by four torpedoes from the submarine *U-73*, commanded by Kapt Lt Rosenbaum. The other ships of the escort immediately increased speed and began to take evasive action, depth-charging at random. Just eight minutes later, the *Eagle* had gone, taking 160 of her crew to the bottom with her; 759 were rescued. The loss of the old carrier was a bitter blow. During her time in the Mediterranean, she had despatched 185 fighters to Malta, quietly and without the publicity that had attended some of the other carrier reinforcement operations. Indeed, she was a significant factor in the island's survival.

Minutes after the *Eagle* had sunk, the white track of a torpedo crossed the bow of the *Victorious*. As the

convoy also included the old carrier *Furious*, whose mission – Operation Bellows – was to accompany the main body to a point 240km (150 miles) west of Malta and fly off 38 badly

# The convoy was now coming well within range of enemy airfields, and the bombers that came that day would undoubtedly have fighter escorts.

convoy continued to take evasive action, a submarine was sighted and the escorts raced off to unload their depth charges on it, but without any visible result. In all, six submarine sightings were reported in the hours that followed. Shortly before sunset, the *Furious* flew off her Spitfires and turned back towards Gibraltar, her mission completed, escorted by five reserve destroyers. The Italian submarine *Dagabur* attempted to attack her, but was rammed and sunk by the destroyer *Wolverine*. Another submarine, the *Giada*, was bombed and damaged by a Gibraltar-based Sunderland. The *Furious* was to undertake two more fighter reinforcement missions before Malta was relieved: Baritone on 17 August, carrying 32 aircraft, and Train on 24 October, carrying 31 aircraft.

Soon after *Furious* had flown off her aircraft, as dusk was beginning to spread over the sea, the convoy was subjected to its first air attack by 36 Ju 88s and He 111s. They dropped their bombs and escaped before the defending fighters could engage them – except for three, which were shot down by AA fire. None of the ships was hit. First light on the 12th revealed a pair of SM79s shadowing the convoy; both were shot down by 809 Squadron's Fulmars. It was a good start to the day, but everyone knew

that the real test was still to come. The convoy was now coming well within range of enemy airfields, and the bombers that came that day would undoubtedly have fighter escorts. The first raid materialized at 0900, when a formation of 20 Ju 88s appeared at 2440m (8000ft). They were intercepted by the *Indomitable*'s Hurricanes, which shot down two on their first pass and forced several others to jettison their bombs. More Hurricanes and Fulmars from the *Victorious* arrived a couple of minutes later and joined the fray, destroying four more bombers and driving the others away.

After two more small and unsuccessful attacks that morning, a huge raid appeared at noon. Nearly 100 enemy bombers, with a strong fighter escort, were hotly engaged by every available Fleet Air Arm fighter as they approached the convoy. Harried by the fighters, the enemy formations became dislocated while still some distance from the target. The only real damage was caused by a formation of Ju 88s that broke through the fighter screen and dive-bombed the freighter *Deucalion*; badly damaged, the vessel began to lag behind the rest of the convoy and had to be left, escorted by the destroyer *Bramham*. She was attacked and sunk before dusk by two torpedo-bombers.

The *Victorious* had one narrow escape when a pair of Italian Reggiane Re 2000 fighter-bombers came down in a very fast dive on the carrier's port quarter. Levelling out just above the

The aircraft carrier HMS *Indomitable* photographed from her sister ship, HMS *Victorious*. The aircraft in the foreground are Fairey Fulmars and Sea Hurricanes.

## DAGABUR

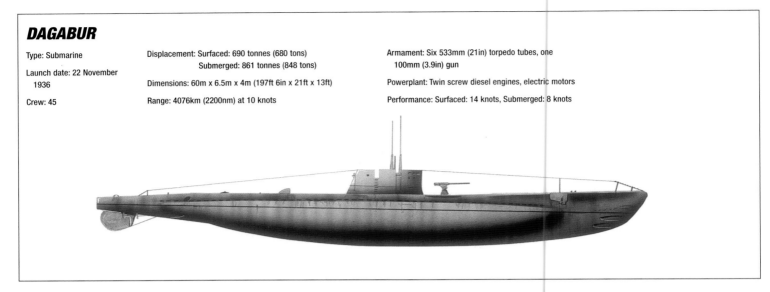

Type: Submarine

Launch date: 22 November 1936

Crew: 45

Displacement: Surfaced: 690 tonnes (680 tons)
Submerged: 861 tonnes (848 tons)

Dimensions: 60m x 6.5m x 4m (197ft 6in x 21ft x 13ft)

Range: 4076km (2200nm) at 10 knots

Armament: Six 533mm (21in) torpedo tubes, one 100mm (3.9in) gun

Powerplant: Twin screw diesel engines, electric motors

Performance: Surfaced: 14 knots, Submerged: 8 knots

**The aircraft carrier HMS *Victorious* served in all theatres of war. In 1945, with her sister carriers, she sailed to join the British Pacific Fleet, forming part of Task Force 57.**

sea, they pulled up over the flight deck, releasing two bombs. One was a dud; the other bounced off the armoured deck and exploded in the water. That afternoon, the convoy ran into a submarine ambush laid by the Italian Navy. One submarine, the *Cobalto*, was brought to the surface by depth charges and rammed by the destroyer *Ithuriel*, which was itself badly damaged. None of the torpedoes launched by the submarines scored hits.

The convoy was under continual air attack throughout the afternoon, but emerged relatively unharmed. By 1700, however, the ships were within range of *Fliegerkorps II*'s dive-bombers in Sicily, and from now on the attacks were pressed home with great determination. For two hours, the bombers came over without pause,

The battlecruiser *Scharnhorst* pictured in her final form in 1942, with a lengthened 'clipper' bow that gave her a rakish and graceful appearance.

allowing the exhausted Navy pilots no respite. Part of a formation of 29 Ju 87s of StG3, harried by Fulmars and Grumman Martlets (nine of which were operated by *Indomitable*'s No. 806 Squadron), broke through and dropped three bombs on the carrier; they failed to penetrate her flight deck, but for the time being she could not operate her aircraft, and those of her fighters still airborne had to land on the *Victorious*. An attack was also made by 14 SM79s, which torpedoed the destroyer *Foresight;* she had to be abandoned and sunk later.

By 1930, the last of the raiders had disappeared; the convoy was still more or less intact and was now only 210km (130 miles) from Malta, within range of the island's Beaufighters. The first of these arrived overhead as dusk was falling, and the two fleet carriers, their job done, now turned away towards the sunset. They had lost 13 aircraft, but their pilots had claimed 39 enemy aircraft definitely destroyed during the three days of air fighting, plus a further nine probably destroyed. It was a classic demonstration of the value of carrier-borne fighters: the Navy pilots had proved their ability to break up the most determined enemy attacks. That the convoy had travelled so far without suffering serious harm was due, in large measure, to them.

Now, however, the carriers turned for home, leaving the convoy to steam on through the night with only the scant air cover that could be provided by the RAF on Malta. And the story of 13 August was to be tragically different from that of the three preceding days. During the night, the convoy was repeatedly attacked by enemy MTBs and submarines, followed up by a savage air onslaught that lasted until the surviving ships reached Malta. Only four of the merchantmen – including the vital and severely damaged tanker *Ohio* – got through, and the escort suffered the loss of the cruisers *Cairo* and *Manchester*. Nevertheless, the supplies that did get through enabled the island to keep going until November,

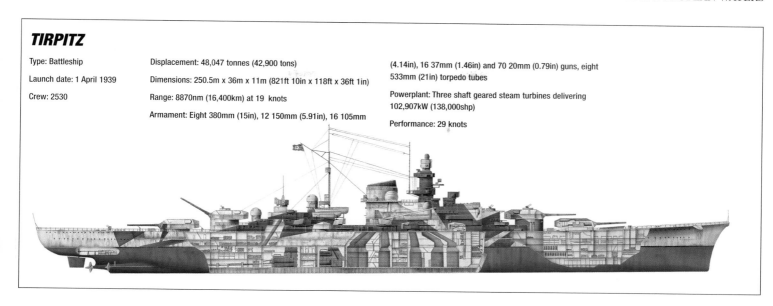

## TIRPITZ

Type: Battleship

Launch date: 1 April 1939

Crew: 2530

Displacement: 48,047 tonnes (42,900 tons)

Dimensions: 250.5m x 36m x 11m (821ft 10in x 118ft x 36ft 1in)

Range: 8870nm (16,400km) at 19 knots

Armament: Eight 380mm (15in), 12 150mm (5.91in), 16 105mm

(4.14in), 16 37mm (1.46in) and 70 20mm (0.79in) guns, eight 533mm (21in) torpedo tubes

Powerplant: Three shaft geared steam turbines delivering 102,907kW (138,000shp)

Performance: 29 knots

when relief reached the defenders following the Allied landings in North Africa and the Eighth Army's decisive victory over the Axis forces at El Alamein in October and November 1942.

## CHANNEL DASH

In home waters, at the beginning of 1942, against the depressing backdrop of Allied reverses in the Far East and North Africa, Admiral Sir John Tovey, the C-in-C Home Fleet, had two main anxieties. The first was the German Brest Squadron, of the *Scharnhorst*, *Gneisenau* and *Prinz Eugen;* the second arose through the movement of the new and very powerful battleship *Tirpitz* to join the Trondheim Squadron in mid-January, clearly to form the nucleus of a powerful battle group for operations against the Allied Arctic and North Atlantic convoys. On 12 January, following a further attack on the warships at Brest by RAF Bomber Command, Adolf Hitler decided that the vessels must be moved if they were to avoid further damage. Since there was little

Channel Dash. The German Brest Squadron proceeding at speed through the English Channel on 12 February, 1942. The operation was a profound embarrassment for the British.

likelihood that they might break out into the Atlantic unscathed, only two options remained open. The first was to return them to Germany by means of a high-speed dash through the English Channel; the second was to decommission them.

Faced with such a choice, Vice-Admiral Ciliax, commanding the Brest Squadron, produced an outline plan for a breakout operation, codenamed Cerberus. (In Greek mythology, Cerberus was the three-headed dog that guarded the gates of hell). The ships would leave Brest at night to avoid detection for as long as possible, and would pass through the Straits of Dover in daylight, placing them in a better position to fight off torpedo attacks by surface vessels and aircraft. Also, they would have full advantage of the strong air umbrella provided by the *Luftwaffe*.

Ten days later, the *Prinz Eugen* was torpedoed and put out of action by the submarine HMS *Trident* (under Cdr Sladen) while in passage from the Elbe to Norway with the *Admiral Scheer*. She was transferred to the Baltic Training Squadron, and in 1944 was used in support of the German Army against the advancing Soviets. In 1945, she was taken over as war booty by the Americans, participated as a target ship in the US atomic bomb trials at Bikini Atoll in June 1946, and having survived that experience was finally sunk at Kwajalein in 1947. The *Gneisenau* was hit by Bomber Command in Kiel harbour a fortnight after Cerberus and never went to sea again; her gun turrets were removed for coastal defence and she was sunk as a blockship at Gdynia, where she was seized by the Soviets and broken up between 1947 and 1951. Only the

### TALE OF INCOMPETENCE

The subsequent dash through the English Channel by the three German warships, which began on 12 February, was an undisputed success for the Germans. For the British, it was a woeful tale of incompetence, bad planning and humiliation, and not even the courage of the Royal Navy and RAF, both of which made determined and sometimes suicidal attacks on the enemy vessels, could compensate. The sequel to the operation was not a happy one for the enemy, however.

The heavy cruiser *Admiral Scheer*. The *Scheer* was a very successful commerce raider, and was a constant threat to Allied convoys until transferred to the Baltic in late 1944.

*Scharnhorst* re-emerged to threaten Allied shipping on the high seas.

## OPERATION CHARIOT

In March 1942, the Royal Navy participated in the biggest combined operation mounted so far by the British in World War II. Called Operation Chariot, it was born out of desperation. Behind it all lay the presence, in Norway, of the most

powerful German naval force so far assembled: the *Admiral Scheer*, *Lützow* and four destroyers at Narvik, and the *Tirpitz*, *Hipper* and six destroyers at Trondheim. Of these, the principal threat was the *Tirpitz*, capable of wreaking awesome havoc on the Allied convoys should she be let loose in the North Atlantic. One way of discouraging such a sortie was to make it impossible for the battleship to dock in western France. That meant putting out of action the facilities at St Nazaire, which featured the only dry dock capable of handling her. Known as the Normandie lock

through its association with the famous French passenger liner – or, more correctly, the Forme Ecluse – it was over 335m (1100ft) in length. (It was towards this haven that the *Bismarck* would have made had she not been sunk in 1941.)

The principal objective of the plan to raid St Nazaire was to ram and destroy the lock gates of the Forme Ecluse using the old ex-American destroyer HMS *Campbeltown*, her bows filled with explosives. The destruction of the smaller South Lock gates and their installations, pumping machinery for the outer dock, and any

The port of Dieppe, scene of the disastrous raid of August 1942. Many lessons were learned from the abortive attack, and were put to good use in the Normandy invasion two years later.

port'. It involved a frontal seaborne assault on the beaches of the small peacetime holiday resort by 4961 Canadian troops, supported by a tank battalion, while gun batteries on the headlands east and west of the town were to be silenced by 1057 British Commandos. As a prelude to the operation, the assault area was extensively photographed from the air and minesweepers cleared a way through the German minefield in mid-Channel ahead of the main force, which sailed from Portsmouth, Newhaven and Shoreham on the evening of 18 August. The naval forces supporting the operation totalled 237 craft of all types, including landing craft. Thirty-eight small craft of the Coastal Forces were also committed.

Too much has been written about the desperate gallantry of the Canadian infantry, tankmen and Commandos in the hours that followed the assault to bear repetition here. Suffice to say that the Canadians lost 215 officers and 3164 men and the Commandos 24 officers and 223 men killed, wounded or prisoners – 68 per cent of the attacking force. The naval forces offshore did what they could to lend fire support, but since none of the warships mounted guns of more than 102mm (4in) calibre the degree of help from this quarter was limited. Only about 1000 men were brought away in the assault craft that moved inshore to evacuate them at 1100 – an operation as desperate in its way as the fighting on land. Without doubt, the most important lesson learned at Dieppe was the absolute need for massive fire support from both sea and air in amphibious

U-boats or shipping present, were to be subsidiary objectives. The attack, which took place on 28 March, was brilliantly successful, and the lock gates were destroyed when the *Campbeltown* exploded, but the cost was high. Of the 62 naval officers and 291 ratings who had sailed from England, 34 officers and 151 ratings were killed or missing, and of the total of 44 officers and 224 other ranks of No. 2 Commando, 34 officers and 178 other ranks did not return. In fact, it was not until much later that the true casualty figures were established: 170 men killed or missing out of 621

committed. It was, however, an acceptable price to pay for the denial to the enemy of a major and threatening naval facility.

## DIEPPE

On 19 August 1942, the British launched Operation Jubilee, an ill-fated amphibious assault on Dieppe. The aim of the plan was, in the words of Winston Churchill, to carry out 'a reconnaissance in force to test the enemy defences on a strongly defended sector of coast, and to discover what resistance would have to be met in the endeavour to seize a

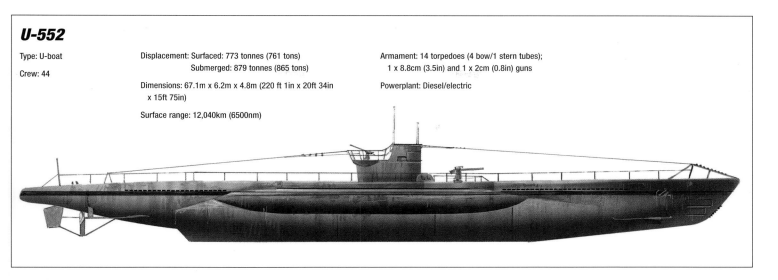

## U-552

**Type:** U-boat

**Crew:** 44

**Displacement:** Surfaced: 773 tonnes (761 tons)
Submerged: 879 tonnes (865 tons)

**Dimensions:** 67.1m x 6.2m x 4.8m (220 ft 1in x 20ft 34in x 15ft 75in)

**Surface range:** 12,040km (6500nm)

**Armament:** 14 torpedoes (4 bow/1 stern tubes); 1 x 8.8cm (3.5in) and 1 x 2cm (0.8in) guns

**Powerplant:** Diesel/electric

---

operations. Another lesson was the need to devise special equipment to overcome defensive obstacles, the realization of which resulted in a formidable array of specially equipped tanks being available to the forces that went ashore in Normandy two years later. For all three Services, the overall lesson of Dieppe was how not to do things – a lesson better learned in 1942 than in 1944.

### CONVOY BATTLES

The Atlantic battles of 1942 began with the dispatch, early in January, of 12 Type VII-C U-boats to operate in the area of the Newfoundland Bank. Between them, from 8 January to 12 February, they sank 21 ships. It was the beginning of the German submariners' second 'happy time', and the operations in Canadian waters were timed to coincide with the start of Admiral Dönitz's offensive against American mercantile traffic in the western Atlantic – Operation *Paukenschlag* (Drumbeat). Only five submarines were involved in this initial deployment, yet in operations from 11 January to 7 February 1942

Despite displaying prominent American flags, a US merchantman is torpedoed and sunk. Such acts persuaded the US government to join the anti-U-boat campaign.

they sank 26 ships, all of which were sailing independently, and damaged several more. A second wave of five Type IX U-boats, operating off the US east coast between 21 January and 6 March, sank a further 19 vessels, while off Canada another eight Type VII craft sank nine more, together with the destroyer HMS *Belmont*.

For some time, the United States Navy had been actively participating in Atlantic convoy protection work, and this was stepped up considerably following a meeting between Winston Churchill and President Roosevelt off Argentia, Newfoundland, on 10 August 1941. From 17 September, the US Navy's Task Force 4 assumed responsibility for escorting the fast convoys between Newfoundland and Iceland, while the slower convoys were escorted by the Canadian Newfoundland Escort Force as far as longitude 22° West, the so-called Mid-Ocean Meeting Point, where the Royal Navy took over. The growing

American participation, the increase in overall Allied escort strength, and the availability of more long-range maritime aircraft – together with the contribution of Ultra – meant that the war in the Atlantic was being won by the beginning of December 1941. In November, the U-boats sank only 13 ships, and in December the Allied shipping losses from all causes in the Atlantic amounted to just 10 vessels. Eight U-boats were destroyed in the latter month, five of them by warships escorting the Gibraltar convoy HG76. It was in passage with this convoy that the escort carrier *Audacity* was sunk by *U-751*, but not before her Martlet fighters had shot down four Fw 200 Kondor maritime reconnaissance aircraft.

### CONVOY SYSTEM

The high shipping losses suffered off the east coast of America between January and April 1942 gave the British Admiralty cause for concern,

> In November, the U-boats sank only 13 ships, and in December the Allied shipping losses from all causes in the Atlantic amounted to just 10 vessels.

**Oil tankers were a favourite target for U-boat commanders. Unless their crews could get away quickly, they stood little change of survival in a blazing sea.**

for some of the vessels were British and many were tankers, which were in short supply. It must also be said that the German successes during this period were attributable not so much to the skill and daring of their submariners, although they possessed both qualities in plenty, but to mistakes in strategy made by the Americans. They failed to institute an immediate convoy system, despite the British urging for them to do so. As a result, targets sailing independently, close to a coastline that was still often lit at night, were easy to sight, track

and sink. The Americans advanced a number of reasons for not implementing a convoy system on British lines – including the lack of sufficient escorts and the danger of concentrating targets – but there was a human factor involved as well. Admiral Ernest King, the C-in-C United States Fleet, believed that offensive tactics by patrol groups would produce better results. Apart from that, he was by no means an admirer of the British, and the idea of adopting a convoy system and naval control of shipping on the British pattern ran contrary to his nature.

It was not until May 1942 that the Americans established a system of convoy on their east coast routes, and

the result was immediately apparent: the U-boats were forced to switch their main area of operations to the Gulf of Mexico and the Caribbean, and it was only there that they continued to register successes for the next three months or so, until the convoy system was extended to cover these sectors too. It was at about this time that anti-submarine aircraft began to make their mark. During their 'happy time' off the US coast, the U-boat crews had practically nothing to fear from shore-based aircraft, as no experienced American ASW squadrons were available. And when Dönitz switched the weight of the U-boat offensive back to the North Atlantic convoy in July 1942, most of the submarine operations took place

**An Atlantic convoy setting sail. The convoy system worked well, but the Americans ignored it for a time, with the result that U-boats created havoc among American east coast shipping.**

in the 'air gap' outside the range of aircraft operating from Newfoundland, Iceland and Northern Ireland. To add to the Allies' problems, the Germans had introduced a new and more complex form of Enigma cypher in February 1942, which was solely for use with U-boats at sea, except for those in the Arctic and Mediterranean. Called Triton by the Germans, this new cypher defeated the experts at Bletchley Park for 10 months and deprived the Allies of their special knowledge of U-boat operations.

## LONG-RANGE AIRCRAFT

The one area in which Ultra was still useful was the Bay of Biscay, for Bletchley was able to decrypt the

Hydra cypher used by patrol vessels escorting the U-boats in and out. It was the custom of the submarines to traverse the bay submerged by day, and to recharge their batteries on the surface at night, when there was minimal risk from the patrolling aircraft of Coastal Command's No. 19 Group. On 6 July, however, the cover of darkness was suddenly stripped away when *U-502* was attacked and sunk by a Wellington of No. 172 Squadron, equipped with a searchlight. Following more 'Leigh Light' attacks, the German U-boat Command changed its tactics; submarines were now directed to pass through the Bay at night submerged and to surface to recharge their batteries in daylight, when aircraft

could be detected visually in time for the boat to dive.

The Germans had good reason to be satisfied with the results obtained by their U-boats in the first half of 1942; in all waters they had sunk 585 merchantmen, totalling more than 3,048,140 tonnes (3,000,000 tons).

They had commissioned over 100 new boats and lost 21, only six of which had been sunk in the western Atlantic. From July to December 1942, many convoys were attacked in the 'air gap'. The situation might have been

> Codenamed Metox, the receiver gave warning of the approach of an aircraft using ASV MkII from about 56km (30nm), which gave the U-boat ample time to evade.

alleviated by the provision of more very long range (VLR) aircraft to Coastal Command. (At this time, No. 120 Squadron, operating from Northern Ireland with detachments to Iceland, was the Command's only VLR unit, and it had only five Liberators.) For some reason, the 32 Liberators allocated to Coastal Command between July and September 1942 were not modified to VLR standard, but instead were given to Nos. 59 and 224 Squadrons, in southwest England, to strengthen the Bay patrols.

As for ASV (Air to Surface Vessel) radar, the Mk II set had been used by Coastal Command since the end of 1940, but it had its drawbacks. Its range was limited to about 22km (12nm) on an operational target – a fully surfaced submarine – and then only when the boat was lying beam-on to an aircraft flying at 600m (2000ft) or more. The main disadvantages of the equipment were a strong back echo, excessive sea returns, bulky aerials and a rather high optimum search height. Nevertheless, ASV Mk II was a proven success, and the number of U-boat sightings initially quadrupled after aircraft fitted with this equipment began operating at night to catch the enemy submarines on the surface.

In the summer of 1941, the first ASV Mk II sets were supplied to the

Americans, who were not yet at war, and these were installed in one PBY-5 Catalina each of Navy Patrol Squadrons VP-71, VP-72 and VP-73, and in two PBM-1 Mariners of VP-74. Additional aircraft were equipped in September. The squadrons all belonged to Patrol Wing 7, which became the first unit in the US Navy to be supplied with radar-equipped aircraft. The Catalinas and Mariners operated from Norfolk, Virginia, Quonset Point and advanced bases in Newfoundland and Iceland during the last months of America's 'neutrality patrol' prior to the attack on Pearl Harbor. Thereafter, Patrol Wing 7 joined the war against the U-boat.

In the spring of 1942, British ASV operations suffered a setback when a

Lockheed Hudson fitted with ASV Mk II fell into enemy hands in Tunisia. Within a matter of months, the Germans had produced a search receiver for installation in their U-boat fleet. Codenamed Metox, the receiver gave warning of the approach of an aircraft using ASV Mk II from about 56km (30nm), which gave the U-boat ample time to evade. As a consequence, the number of U-boat sightings dropped dramatically in the latter half of 1942 as the tactical initiative was restored to the submarines.

## DIRECTION FINDING

One measure that did give the Allies a considerable advantage in the Atlantic battles of 1942, however, was the large-scale introduction of shipborne HF/DF (High Frequency Direction Finding) equipment, known as 'Huff-Duff' to those who used it. The

*Torpedo los!* **The view through a U-boat commander's periscope. This shot was taken during a training exercise in the Baltic. In combat, attacks were usually carried out at night.**

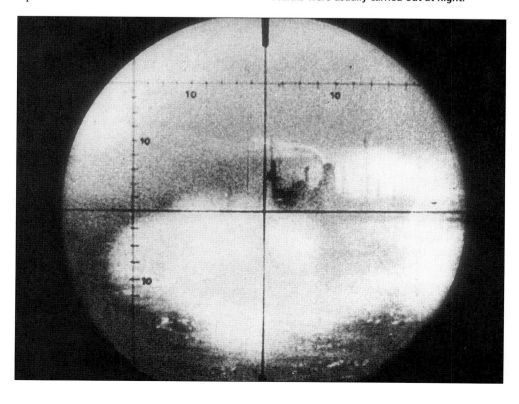

**Left: Merchant seamen are about to be rescued. One ship in each convoy was usually designated as a rescue vessel, but it was not always possible to stop when submarines were in the vicinity.**

The failure of the Americans to implement a convoy system in the early days of the U-boat offensive was a mistake. Here, a torpedoed merchantman sinks off the Florida coast.

wolfpack tactics employed by the U-boats required them to make radio reports to their shore stations when they made or lost contact with a convoy, and a single HF/DF ship could provide reliable detection of a U-boat making a transmission. Each HF/DF report enabled the escort commander to send an escorting aircraft if he had one, or anti-submarine ships to search for and attack the U-boat. The submarines needed their surface speed to keep up with or overtake a convoy, and even if the searching escorts failed to find and attack the U-boat, they could

probably force it to submerge until the convoy was out of sight. By the end of January 1942, 25 escorts had been fitted with HF/DF, and the

number increased steadily throughout the year. Next to centimetric radar, HF/DF was probably the most important element in winning the

## THE BREAKING OF THE CODES

In December 1942, in desperation, the Admiralty turned to Bletchley for help. It was not slow in coming. In that very month, by an astonishing coincidence, documents from a U-boat sunk off Port Said enabled the experts at last to break into the Triton cypher. The decrypts revealed that Admiral Dönitz now had over 100 U-boats deployed; 50 were in the Atlantic, and 37 of them were operating in the 'air gap' to the south of Greenland. The timely breaking of Triton, together with terrible weather conditions which hampered the U-boats as much as the convoys in the early weeks of 1943, meant that the Admiralty could once again adopt evasive routing. This undoubtedly saved many ships in January. As an added bonus, the Germans' own cypher-breaking service, the B-Dienst, temporarily lost its ability to read the British Convoy Cypher, which robbed the U-boats of vital intelligence.

Battle of the Atlantic. In combination with radar, it eventually made submarine attacks on convoys too hazardous to be attempted.

## MERCHANT SHIPPING LOSSES

In 1942, though, despite the growing number of Allied surface and air escorts, and despite the introduction of new equipment, merchant shipping losses mounted to unprecedented levels, and in November they reached an all-time record of 711,232 tonnes (700,000 tons). The Germans were now suffering severe reverses in Russia and North Africa, and the Atlantic seemed the one area in which they could inflict terrible damage on the Allies. With Allied shipping under immense strain, the outlook was bleak, and the optimism of 12 months earlier had vanished. When the figures for 1942 were added up, they reached the appalling total of 1664 merchantmen – nearly 8,128,375 tonnes (8,000,000 tons) – lost on the high seas. Unless this rate of loss could be reduced, there seemed no prospect that the construction of new merchant tonnage could outstrip sinkings, and the gloomy economic news was that Britain's imports had fallen to two-thirds of the 1939 total.

As a result, sinkings dropped dramatically during this period, although from 3 to 12 January the U-boats scored a notable success by sinking seven out of nine tankers in Convoy TM1, running from Trinidad to Gibraltar. Then, in February, the B-Dienst restored its ability to read the Convoy Cypher, and the U-boats attacked in groups of unprecedented size. Between 2 and 9 February, 20 boats of the Pfei and Haudegen groups fell on the slow convoy SC118 between Newfoundland and Iceland and sank 13 of its 63 ships. Later in the month, 16 U-boats were directed to attack the outward convoy ON166,

sinking 14 of its 40 ships, while other convoys were attacked in the Central by U-boats replenishing from *Milchkuh* supply submarines near the Azores. Allied losses for February amounted to 63 ships totalling 365,776 tonnes (360,000 tons), and worse was to come. In March, Bletchley lost its grip on Triton for a fortnight, with the result that this month became the worst ever for convoy sinkings.

It began with an attack on the slow convoy SC121, which lost 13 ships between 7 and 11 March. Then, from the 16th to the 20th, Convoys SC122 (60 ships) and HX229 (40 ships), both outbound from New York, were attacked by 40 U-boats. The HX

An escorting warship carries out a depth-charge attack. By 1943, the Allies had developed a formidable array of anti-submarine weapons and submarine detection devices.

convoy lost 21 merchantmen totalling 143,262 tonnes (141,000 tons); SC122 lost nine. In all theatres of war, in that terrible month, the boats sank 108 ships totalling 637,061 tonnes (627,000 tons). Losses were so severe, in fact, that the naval staff later recorded that the enemy had come 'very near to disrupting communications between the New World and the Old'. Compounding the tragedy was the fact that the two convoys from New York had been re-routed from the northern to the

**Admiral Sir John Tovey (right) meets Commodore J.C.K. Dowding, commodore of the ill-fated convoy PQ17. Later, Dowding was Principal Sea Transport Officer for the D-Day landings.**

southern route to avoid the *Raubgraf* U-boat group, which was shadowing another convoy, ON170.

But the tide was about to turn. In March, as the Atlantic battles raged, representatives of the British, American and Canadian navies met in the Atlantic Convoy Conference in Washington. It was agreed that the US Navy should assume responsibility for the tanker convoys running between Britain and the West Indies, leaving the North Atlantic entirely to the British and Canadians. The Royal Canadian Navy, directed by a new North West Atlantic Command HQ

at Halifax, would be entirely responsible for the North Atlantic convoys as far as 47° West, where the Royal Navy would take over. March also saw the formation of the first Support Groups, which would provide rapid reinforcement for convoys under threat.

## ARCTIC CONVOYS

By the end of 1941, merchant convoys to Russia carrying armaments and supplies had become well established: some 55 merchant ships had been dispatched in eight separate convoys up to the end of December. Murmansk was now the destination port, the passage to Archangel having been closed by ice. All the convoys so far had been unmolested by the enemy.

It was a traffic that the Germans could not afford to ignore, and on 25 December the German Navy C-in-C, Admiral Raeder, ordered the deployment of the U-boat group Ulan (*U-134, U-454* and *U-584*) to the passage south of Bear Island to lie in wait for the convoys. Their first success came on 2 January 1942, when *U-134* (under Kapt Lt Schendel) sank the British freighter *Waziristan* of convoy PQ7A, and on 17 January *U-454* (under Kapt Lt Hacklander) sank the destroyer *Matabele*, escorting convoy PQ8, as well as damaging the freighter *Harmatris*. On 21 February, a new but not unexpected threat to the Arctic convoys developed when the pocket battleship *Admiral Scheer* and the heavy cruiser *Prinz Eugen* were transferred from the Elbe to Norway, accompanied by the destroyers *Z25, Friedrich Ihn* and *Hermann Schoemann*. The warships were shadowed by RAF reconnaissance aircraft during their northward passage, and on 27 February the *Prinz Eugen* was damaged by the submarine *Trident* and forced to return home.

Before the end of the month, however, an even bigger threat materialized when the new battleship *Tirpitz* slipped out of the Baltic and arrived at Trondheim, bearing the flag of Admiral Ciliax. On 6 March, the *Tirpitz*, accompanied by three destroyers, set out to intercept convoys PQ12 and QP8, the first bound for Murmansk, the second on its way home. PQ12 had been detected by a Fw 200 the day before 130km (70nm) south of Jan Mayen Island, and the submarines *U-134, U-377, U-403* and *U-584* were also deployed to intercept it. The movements of the *Tirpitz* and her escorts, meanwhile, had been reported by the submarine *Seawolf*. As a result, units of the Home Fleet, comprising the battleships *King George*

The cruiser HMS *Kenya* in heavy seas. This 'Fiji' class warship served with the Home Fleet until 1943, when she joined the Eastern Fleet in the Indian Ocean. She was scrapped in 1962.

V, *Duke of York* and *Renown*, the carrier *Victorious*, the cruiser *Kenya* and 12 destroyers, placed themselves between the threat and the convoys, which passed one another off Bear Island at noon on 7 March. Ciliax detached some of his destroyers to search for the convoys and they sank one straggling Russian freighter; apart from that, no contact was made and the German commander turned southwards again.

The difficult and dangerous routes that had to be followed by Allied Arctic convoys to Russia. The winter route was the more perilous, as it brought merchant ships closer to German air and naval bases in Norway.

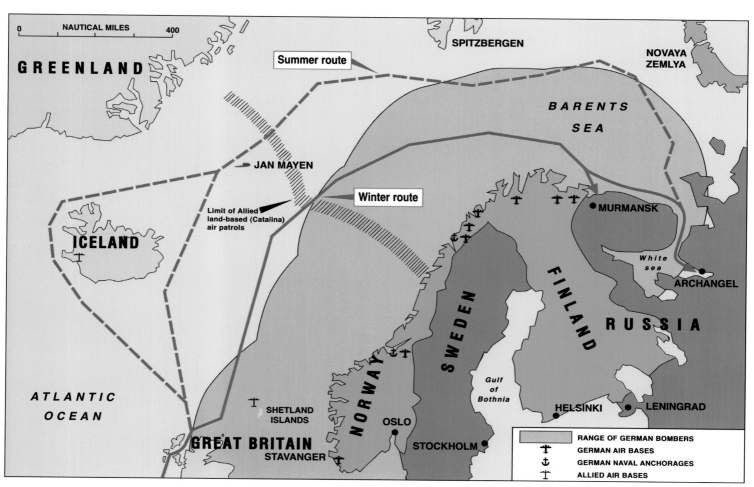

Thanks to Ultra decrypts, Admiral Tovey knew of the Germans' intentions and ordered his forces towards the Lofoten Islands in an attempt to cut them off. At daybreak on the 9th, a reconnaissance Albacore from the *Victorious* spotted the *Tirpitz*, and 12 torpedo-carrying Albacores took off soon afterwards to attack the warship. The attack, unfortunately, was carried out in line astern, which gave the *Tirpitz* ample room to avoid all the torpedoes, although one passed within 10m (30ft) of her. Two Albacores were shot down. The failure of this attack was a bitter pill for the Royal Navy to swallow, but it did have one result: on Hitler's orders, the *Tirpitz* never put to sea when carrier-based aircraft were known to be in the vicinity.

## MOUNTING LOSSES

On 20 March 1942, German naval strength in Norway was further

One of the 24 ships of convoy PQ17 sunk by enemy air and submarine attack. Ordering the convoy to scatter was a serious blunder, leaving the vessels isolated and vulnerable.

augmented with the arrival at Trondheim of the heavy cruiser *Admiral Hipper*, accompanied by the destroyers *Z24*, *Z26* and *Z30* and the torpedo-boats *T15*, *T16* and *T17*. The enemy now had a formidable striking force of aircraft, warships and submarines in the theatre, and convoy losses inevitably began to mount. Between 27 and 31 March, PQ13 became split up due to bad weather; two of its ships were sunk by the Ju 88s III/KG 30, operating from Banak, three by *U-376*, *U-435*, *U-436*, and one by the destroyer *Z26*, which was herself sunk by the cruiser *Trinidad*. The cruiser was then hit by one of her own torpedoes, and disabled; the *U-585* closed in to attack her, but was sunk by the destroyer *Fury*. The remaining 13 ships of PQ13 reached Murmansk, but two were sunk by air attack on 3 April.

Convoy PQ14, sailing on 8–21 April, found that the ice, not the Germans, was the main enemy; it ran into ice floes in thick fog and 16 of its 24 vessels had to return to Iceland. One was sunk by *U-403*. PQ15, sailing on 26 April to 7 May, was a large

convoy of 50 ships under heavy Anglo-American escort. Two of its vessels were sunk by air attack and one damaged. (This ship, the *Jutland*, was later sunk by *U-251*.) QP11, a homeward-bound convoy, was attacked by destroyers and U-boats; *U-456* hit the escorting cruiser *Edinburgh* with two torpedoes, and she was finished off later by other British warships after sustaining further damage from a destroyer's torpedo. Two British destroyers, the *Forester* and *Foresight*, were badly damaged in an engagement with the German destroyers *Z24* and *Z25;* the battleship *King George V* rammed and sank the destroyer *Punjabi* in a snowstorm and was herself damaged by the latter's exploding depth charges. To add to a catalogue of woe, the Polish submarine *Jastrzab*, a long way from her position on the flank of the convoy, was sunk by the Norwegian-manned destroyer *St Albans* and the minesweeper *Seagull*.

## THE TRAGEDY OF PQ17

Convoy PQ16, sailing on 25–30 May, was attacked by formations of Ju 88s

Thanks to Ultra decrypts, Admiral Tovey knew of the Germans' intentions and ordered his forces towards the Lofoten Islands in an attempt to cut them off.

and He 111s. Seven of its 35 ships were sunk with the loss of 43,898 tonnes (43,205 tons) of war stores, including 147 tanks, 77 aircraft and 770 vehicles. Then came the disaster of PQ17, which led to a complete revision of the Arctic convoy system. The 36 freighters of PQ17 sailed from Iceland on 27 June 1942, protected by a close support force and a cover group of four cruisers and three destroyers. Additional long-range support was provided by a cover force from the Home Fleet, consisting of the battleships HMS *Duke of York* and USS *Washington* (the latter attached to Admiral Tovey's command), the carrier *Victorious*, two cruisers and 14 destroyers.

As soon as they learned of PQ17's departure, the German Navy initiated Operation *Rösselsprung* (Knight's Move), its aim the total destruction of the convoy. In the afternoon of 2 July, Force I under Admiral Schniewind, comprising the battleship *Tirpitz* and the cruiser *Admiral Hipper*, with four destroyers and two torpedo boats, set out from Trondheim. The next day, Vizeadmiral Kummetz's Force II, comprising the heavy cruisers *Lützow* and *Admiral Scheer*, with five destroyers, sailed from Narvik and headed north to join Force I at Altenfjord. There they waited, the German commanders unwilling to risk their ships until they had more information about the strength of the enemy's covering forces.

Attacks by torpedo aircraft on the convoy began on 4 July, and in the evening the Admiralty received a false report that a Soviet submarine had sighted the German warships heading on an interception course. This, in addition to reports that the convoy was being continually shadowed by enemy aircraft, led to one of the most tragic decisions of the war: to withdraw the escorting cruisers and destroyers and to scatter the convoy, the merchantmen making their way individually to the Soviet ports. It was the signal for packs of enemy aircraft and U-boats to fall on the hapless transports and pick them off one by one. The slaughter began on 5 July and went on for five days, right up to the moment when the surviving ships entered Archangel. The convoy's losses were 24 ships out of 36, totalling 146,287 tonnes (143,977 tons). The losses in equipment were

astronomical: 3350 vehicles, 430 tanks, 210 aircraft and 100,910 tonnes (99,316 tons) of other war equipment. German losses, in more than 200 sorties flown by the *Luftwaffe*, were just five aircraft.

The next eastbound convoy was PQ18, its departure delayed until September because all the available aircraft carriers were engaged in escorting the desperately needed Pedestal convoy through to Malta. And, after the PQ17 fiasco, the dispatch of another convoy to Russia without a carrier escort could not be considered. When PQ18, 46 ships strong, finally sailed from Iceland on 9 September, its escort included the carrier HMS *Avenger*, a 'utility' vessel converted from a merchant ship in the United States. The Royal Navy's first such escort carrier, *Audacity* – a captured and converted German merchant vessel, the *Hannover* – had proved her worth on the UK-Gibraltar run, her Martlet fighters destroying

**Convoy PQ17 in Icelandic waters prior to sailing for north Russia. Most of the ships seen here were at the bottom of the ocean within days.**

**HMS *Archer* was one of the invaluable escort carriers that played a huge part in winning the Battle of the Atlantic. Formerly the merchant ship *Mormacland*, she could carry 15 aircraft.**

several enemy aircraft before she fell victim to a torpedo salvo from *U-751* on 21 December 1941. The *Avenger* was the second of her class; the first, HMS *Archer*, had been in service for some time, and two more, the *Biter* and *Dasher*, were due to be commissioned in the coming months.

## ESCORT CARRIERS

The *Avenger* carried Nos. 802 and 883 Squadrons, each with six Sea Hurricanes, together with three Swordfish of 'A' Flight 825 Squadron. Six more Hurricanes were carried in crates, as reserves. The fighters were in action almost from the moment the

convoy left Icelandic waters. On 12 September, a Blohm und Voss Bv 138 flying boat appeared to the south, shadowing the convoy, and the Hurricanes were flown off to shoot it down. They failed, and while they were chasing it six Ju 88s of KG30 dive-bombed the convoy. No ships were lost and the attackers were beaten off by AA fire, but soon afterwards 40 torpedo-carrying He 111s of KG26 appeared and attacked the convoy's starboard column while the Hurricanes were still over the horizon chasing the Bv 138. In exactly eight minutes, eight freighters were hit and sunk. All the German aircraft returned to base, but six of them were so badly damaged that they had to be written off.

The next day, KG26 was ordered to concentrate its attacks on the aircraft

carrier, which had not been located on the 12th because she had stationed herself some distance from the convoy in order to be in a better tactical position. This time, the carrier was sighted to the north of the convoy, and the German air commander ordered his formation to split up prior to making its attack when it was bounced by the Hurricanes. The Germans lost five Heinkels, and of the remaining 17 nine were damaged beyond repair. Subsequent attacks, on the 13th and on the 14th, were broken up by the *Avenger*'s Sea Hurricanes. In all, the fighters and the AA from the escort – mainly the latter, which because of the fighters' efforts was able to concentrate on individual aircraft – accounted for 20 Heinkels

> Admiral Tovey was concerned that large convoys would be in danger of becoming split up. He therefore recommended that the next convoy should be divided in two.

and Junkers (the British claimed 41 at the time). Four Hurricanes were shot down, three of them by friendly fire.

As PQ18 neared the end of its journey, it was attacked by U-boats on consecutive days (15–16 September), losing three more freighters. However, *U-457* and *U-589* were sunk by escorting destroyers, the latter after it had been located by Swordfish aircraft of 825 Squadron. On the 18th, as the convoy entered the Kola Inlet, it was subjected to further air attacks, this time by Heinkel He 115 floatplanes. Two more merchantmen were sunk, but two He 115s were destroyed by a Hurricane catapulted from the freighter *Empire Morn*. This was a Merchant Service Fighter Unit aircraft, piloted by Flying Officer A.H.

Burr, who landed at an airfield near Archangel after the engagement. There was no doubt that the carrier fighters had averted a disaster on the scale of PQ17; nevertheless, PQ18 had suffered the loss of 13 ships, and six more (including the destroyer *Somali* and the minesweeper *Leda*) were sunk by U-boats out of a homeward-bound convoy, QP14.

Although the Russian convoys were now shielded from air attack by the onset of the Arctic night, the winter brought with it extremely bad weather, and Admiral Tovey was concerned that large convoys would be in danger of becoming split up. He therefore recommended that the next convoy, PQ19, should be divided in two and its designation changed to

**The first really modern fighter to serve with the Fleet Air Arm was the Hawker Sea Hurricane, a naval adaptation of the fighter that rose to fame in the Battle of Britain.**

JW51 for security reasons. The First Sea Lord, Admiral Sir Dudley Pound, agreed, albeit reluctantly, and on 15 December 1942 the 16 merchant ships of JW51A left Loch Ewe, escorted by seven destroyers and five small A/S vessels. JW51B, of 14 ships with an escort of six destroyers and five small A/S vessels, sailed a week later. Both were covered by the cruisers *Sheffield* (under Capt A.W. Clarke, flying the flag of Rear-Admiral Bob Burnett) and *Jamaica* (under Capt J.L. Storey), with more distant cover provided by the new battleship

*Anson* and the cruiser *Cumberland*. JW51A was not detected by the enemy and reached the Kola Inlet without incident on Christmas Day, accompanied by Burnett's cruisers. On 27 December, having refuelled, Burnett took his warships to sea again to cover JW51B, one of whose ships had become detached in a storm and was proceeding independently, accompanied by an A/S trawler. Unknown to Burnett, the convoy had already been sighted on 24 December by a German reconnaissance aircraft and *U-354* (Kapt Lt Herbschleb). The German Admiralty at once initiated Operation *Regenbogen* (Rainbow), its object the convoy's destruction.

## BATTLE OF THE BARENTS SEA

On 30 December, Vizeadmiral Oskar Kummetz took his flagship, the

*Admiral Hipper* (under Kapt H. Hartmann), the *Lützow* (under Kapt R. Stange) and six destroyers out of Altenfjord. His tactical options were limited: he was under orders not to risk a night engagement against escorts that might make torpedo attacks on his ships; he was only to engage a force weaker than his own by day; and, furthermore, the *Lützow* was afterwards to make a sortie into the Atlantic, which meant that she would need to conserve fuel and ammunition, not to mention to avoid damage.

At 0830 on 31 December, the *Hipper* and her destroyers passed 32km (20 miles) astern of the convoy, while the *Lützow* and her escorts were 80km (50 miles) to the south and closing. Burnett's two cruisers were about 48km (30 miles) to the north. The

approaching enemy force was sighted by the corvette *Hyderabad*, which, mistaking the German destroyers for expected Soviet escorts, made no report. Ten minutes later, the German vessels were also detected by the destroyer *Obdurate*. Her captain, Lt Cdr C.E. Sclater, reported them to the escort commander, Lt Cdr R. St V. Sherbrooke, in the flotilla leader HMS *Onslow*, but did not identify them. Sherbrooke ordered Sclater to investigate and *Obdurate* closed to within 6km (4 miles) of the enemy, turning away when they opened fire.

Leaving the destroyer *Achates* and three smaller escorts to protect the

Admiral of the Fleet Sir Dudley Pound, First Sea Lord, who was reluctant to authorize the sailing of Arctic convoys in the summer months, when there was little or no darkness.

convoy with a smoke screen, Sherbrooke headed to join *Obdurate* at full speed, accompanied by the *Obedient* and *Orwell* and transmitting an enemy report to Rear-Admiral Burnett. At 0941, the *Scheer* opened fire on the *Achates* and was at once engaged by the *Onslow* and *Orwell*, Sherbrooke sending the other two destroyers to assist in protecting the convoy.

At 1020, the Hipper found *Onslow*'s range and set her on fire, putting half her armament out of action and holing her engine room. Sherbrooke, badly wounded, was obliged to turn over command to Lt Cdr D.C. Kinloch in the *Obedient*, who refused to leave the bridge until assured that his orders had been received. At the same time, the *Hipper* disappeared into a snow squall. Some minutes

later, at 1045, she encountered the little minesweeper *Bramble*, which was armed with only one 102mm (4in) gun, and quickly destroyed her with the loss of her captain, Commander H.T. Rust, and all his crew.

As soon as the *Hipper* disappeared, Lt Cdr Kinloch instructed all the destroyers to rejoin the convoy, which was now threatened by the *Lützow*, only 3.2km (2 miles) away. Stange, however, decided to stand off while the weather cleared, thus allowing a golden opportunity to wipe out the merchantmen to slip through his fingers. At 1100, while Kinloch manoeuvred his destroyers between the convoy and the *Lützow* group, still making smoke, the *Hipper* suddenly reappeared to the north and opened fire on the *Achates*, inflicting

**The German heavy cruiser *Lützow*, formerly the *Deutschland*, was a sister ship of the *Admiral Scheer* and the *Admiral Graf Spee*. She was blown up and scuttled in the Baltic in 1945.**

many casualties and killing her captain, Lt Cdr Johns; she sank early in the afternoon. The *Hipper* then turned her fire on the *Obedient*; the destroyer suffered only light damage but her radio was put out of action, so that Kinloch was compelled to turn over command to the *Obdurate*'s captain.

At 1130, as Hartmann drew away to avoid the destroyers' torpedo attacks, the *Hipper* was suddenly straddled by 24 15.2cm (6in) shells from the *Sheffield* and *Jamaica*, closing from the north. Burnett had been able to follow the action by means of *Sheffield*'s radar, but the radar picture

The destroyer HMS *Achates* was sunk in the Barents Sea by the *Admiral Hipper* on 31 December, 1942. One of the Royal Navy's older destroyers, she had been launched in 1929.

was confused and it was not until he obtained a positive sighting that Burnett felt able to engage the German cruiser. Three shells hit the *Hipper*, reducing her speed to 28 knots. Faced with this new threat, Kummetz ordered Hartmann and the destroyer captains to retire to the west. As they did so, the *Sheffield*'s guns turned on the destroyer *Friedrich Eckoldt* and quickly reduced her to a blazing wreck, but the other destroyer, the *Richard Beitzen*, followed the Hipper into a snow squall and got away.

Operation Torch, closely followed by the disaster at Stalingrad, was the beginning of the end for the Axis powers. The war in North Africa ended in May 1943, with a massive surrender of German and Italian forces.

## BEGINNING OF THE END

At about 1145, the *Lützow* also opened fire on the convoy from a range of 16,450m (18,000yds), then she too withdrew as the British destroyers began an attack. There was a further brief engagement between Burnett's cruisers and the enemy force at 1230, in which neither side suffered damage; the Germans continued to retire to the west and contact was lost at 1400. Three days later, JW51B reached the Kola Inlet without further harm. That it did so was due in no small measure to the tactical skill, leadership and courage of Captain Sherbrooke, who survived his injuries to receive the Victoria Cross. This

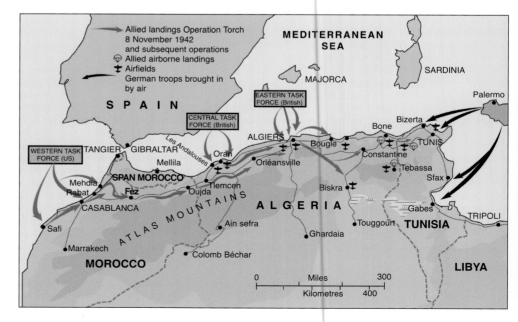

## OPERATION TORCH

**Although the final decision to go ahead was not taken until October, the Admiralty immediately took steps to assemble the necessary merchant vessels and escorts, and to plan the convoys that would carry the invasion force. Convoys to Russia and North Africa were temporarily halted to provide the necessary resources, and in August Admiral Sir Andrew Cunningham was appointed Allied Naval Commander Expeditionary Force for Operation Torch.**

action, which became known as the Battle of the Barents Sea, had an important postscript. The *Lützow*, her sortie into the Atlantic cancelled, never sailed again against the Allied convoys; she was transferred to the Fleet Training Squadron in the Baltic, where, after action against the Soviets, she was bombed and badly damaged at Swinemünde in April 1945, being blown up and scuttled a few weeks later. The *Admiral Hipper*, too, had made her last sortie; also transferred to the Baltic, she was bombed in Kiel in May 1945 and scuttled, being broken up in 1948–49. It may be said, with justification, that the Battle of the Barents Sea marked the beginning of the end of Germany's challenge on the oceans.

The United States entered the war in December 1941, giving Winston Churchill reason to 'sleep the sleep of the saved and the thankful', though not producing any overnight miracles. The Allied leaders quickly decided that the defeat of Germany was to be their first priority, but in the meantime the Americans were much too preoccupied with halting Japanese conquest in the Pacific to channel much in the way of immediate resources into the European theatre. The Americans advocated a cross-Channel assault in 1942; the British knew it would never work, and the subsequent tragedy of Dieppe proved them right. The British and Americans alike lacked the merchant ships, landing craft and trained men

to carry out such a venture, and Dieppe underlined the severity of the shortcomings. Any large-scale invasion of enemy territory in 1942, therefore, would have to be in an area where defences were weak and opposition likely to be minimal. On 25 July, the Allied leaders agreed that French North Africa was the logical objective, the landing of an expeditionary force to be timed to coincide with an offensive by the Eighth Army from Egypt.

### INVASION NORTH AFRICA

The operational plan envisaged two assaults in the Mediterranean, at Algiers and Oran, and one on the coast of Morocco near Casablanca. The Anglo-American convoys bound for Algeria would sail from Britain and would be covered and supported by naval forces commanded by Vice-Admiral Sir Harold Burrough (Algiers) and Commodore T.H. Troubridge (Oran). The task of

**Part of the mighty invasion force that assembled in early November 1942 for the invasion of North Africa. In some areas, the invasion was fiercely resisted by Vichy French forces.**

Vice-Admiral Sir Neville Syfret's Force H, reinforced by units of the Home Fleet, was to ensure that the Italian Navy was kept at bay during the operation. The naval force for Morocco, which would be all American, would sail direct from the United States under the command of Vice-Admiral H.K. Hewitt, USN.

After a number of delays, D-Day for Torch was set for 8 November 1942, H-Hour being 0100 at Algiers and Oran and 0400 in Morocco. The 240 merchantmen needed to transport the forces from Britain were gradually assembled in various ports,

**Warships off the North African coast put up a flak barrage to ward off enemy night bombers. The *Luftwaffe* succeeded in sinking a number of Allied ships, although its effort was piecemeal.**

mainly in the Clyde and Loch Ewe, while 160 warships were called in from other duties. Early in October, a series of advance convoys carrying various stores began to sail for Gibraltar; these were followed, between 22 October and 1 November, by four big assault convoys carrying the troops. All the convoys were routed well to the west of Ireland, keeping well out into the Atlantic before turning east towards Gibraltar. Although they were sighted by U-boats, no ships were lost; the enemy submarines, in fact, were heavily engaged in attacking the homeward-bound convoy SL125 off the African coast. The convoy lost 13 of its 37 merchantmen, and there is little doubt that their sacrifice enabled the Gibraltar-bound convoys to reach

their destination unmolested. (Indeed, it was suggested long after the war that SL125 was deliberately sacrificed in the interests of Torch, but there is no evidence to substantiate this.)

Inside the Mediterranean, the invasion force divided into its various components, each being guided to its respective assault area by marker submarines. At Algiers, the Eastern Task Force met with only slight resistance, and by daylight the troops were well established ashore with two local airfields captured. The destroyers *Broke* and *Malcolm* were assigned the task of penetrating the heavily defended harbour to land troops and also to prevent the French from scuttling their ships. The *Malcolm* was badly damaged and had

to break off the attack, and although the *Broke* smashed through the boom and got inside the harbour to land her troops, she came under heavy fire from shore batteries and French warships and suffered heavy damage, the next day.

At Oran, where the assault force was considerably larger, it encountered much stiffer opposition. An attempt by two sloops, the *Walney* and *Hartland*, to penetrate the harbour here was frustrated by heavy fire and both ships were sunk. Several French warships put to sea in an attempt to interfere with the invasion shipping, and in confused fighting the destroyers *Epervier*, *Tornade*, *Tramontane* and *Typhon*, a minesweeper and six submarines were sunk. The submarine *Fresnel* made an unsuccessful attack on the cruiser *Southampton* and escaped to Toulon,

where she was joined by two submarines from Algiers, the *Caiman* and *Marsouin*. At Casablanca, the French also put to sea to try to intercept the American invasion force, losing a cruiser and six destroyers; the unfinished battleship *Jean Bart* was severely damaged by bombardment and air attack.

## THE END IN AFRICA

There was a powerful French squadron at Dakar, from which the Americans had been expecting possible trouble, but it did not put to sea. Resistance at Algiers ceased at 1900 on 7 September, but at Oran the French continued to resist stubbornly until noon on 10 November, when British armoured vehicles penetrated the town. By this time, the American assault forces were firmly consolidated ashore and were making ready to

**Allied forces going ashore in Algeria during Operation Torch, November 1942. The landings effectively sealed the fate of the Axis forces in North Africa.**

attack Casablanca, but a ceasefire was declared by Admiral Darlan, the French C-in-C. The fighting had cost the Vichy French forces 462 dead, with more than 1000 wounded. German aircraft made sporadic appearances between 8 and 14 November, sinking two troop transports, a landing ship, two freighters and the gunboat *Ibis*; the aircraft carrier *Argus* was hit by bombs and the monitor *Roberts* severely damaged. The invasion of North Africa effectively sealed the fate of the Axis armies. After more than two years of bitter fighting, resistance in the theatre finally came to an end on 13 May 1943, when the last Axis troops in Tunisia surrendered.

# World War II
## The Switch to the Offensive 1943

**By the end of March 1943, Coastal Command's slowly growing force of VLR Liberators and Boeing Fortresses, together with carrier aircraft, were closing the Greenland gap and forcing U-boat shadowers to submerge. Improved anti-submarine tactics and weapons began to make themselves felt. Shipborne HF/DF maximized its exploitation of U-boat transmissions, often helping convoys to steer clear of danger and assisting air and surface escorts to seek out and kill the enemy. Above all, centimetric radar, now installed in surface escorts, and in aircraft as ASV Mk III, was turning them into deadly U-boat killers.**

In the three months to the end of May 1943, the Allies sank 56 U-boats, so that for the first time there was a net decrease in their operational number. The number lost in the period January to May was 96, of which 52 were sunk by aircraft. Signs of flagging morale now became apparent in the Triton decrypts, together with references to the U-boat crews' growing fear of air attack and the speed with which the escorts and Support Groups reacted to sightings.

**Grumman Hellcat fighters prepare to launch from the flight deck of a US aircraft carrier. The sturdy F6F Hellcat gave the Americans naval air superiority in the Pacific war.**

A U-boat sinking in the Atlantic after coming under air attack. By 1943, shore- and carrier-based air power was playing a leading part in defeating the German submarine fleet.

order from Dönitz insisting that U-boats traversed the Bay of Biscay on the surface by day – an order prompted by the erroneous belief that they would be able to shoot it out with Allied aircraft. The maritime crews took every advantage of the order, and in the 94 days that it remained in force – from 1 May to 2 August 1943 – they sank 28 U-boats in the Bay. But the success was not without its cost; 57 aircraft failed to return.

## DISTANT WATERS

From the end of July 1943, Bletchley and its American counterpart were able to break the Triton cypher until almost the end of the war, with only very rare delays. Its recovery was ably demonstrated when, with its assistance, American escort carriers and Coastal Command between them sank almost the entire fleet of *Milchkuh* supply submarines (only 10 were ever built). This reduced the U-boat campaign in distant waters to negligible proportions, and greatly diminished the effectiveness of the boats operating in the Central Atlantic. The success of the Allied achievement in the summer of 1943 may be judged by the fact that not one North Atlantic convoy was attacked in June, and in the Central Atlantic U-boats were suffering from the attentions of US carrier aircraft.

The lack of activity now enabled the Admiralty to move from defence to offence, and on 20 June the 2nd Escort Group under Captain F.J. Walker was ordered into the Bay to hunt U-boats in conjunction with aircraft. The *Milchkuh* tanker submarine *U-119* was rammed and sunk by the sloop *Starling*, while *U-449* was depth-charged and sunk by *Wild Goose*, *Woodpecker*, *Kite* and *Wren*. Other escort and support groups also participated in these operations, relieving one another at intervals of

By 19 April, Admiral Dönitz was conceding that Allied reaction – in particular, maritime air – was frustrating the U-boat 'pack attack' concept. On 25 May, he withdrew his submarines to the Central Atlantic, outside the radius of Allied land-based air cover and an area where convoys were less well defended. In this area, the U-boats had already scored considerable success in April; on the 30th of that month a single submarine, *U-515*, made three attacks on Convoy TS37 between Takoradi and Sierra Leone and sank seven of its 18 ships, totalling 43,949 tonnes (43,255 tons). During this series of battles, each side became aware that the other was learning of the movements and whereabouts of the opposing forces; the Allies, now convinced that the Convoy Cypher had been compromised, immediately brought a new one into force. Adding to the Germans' problems was an

> The maritime crews took every advantage of the order, and in the 94 days that it remained in force – from 1 May to 2 August 1943 – they sank 28 U-boats in the Bay.

five to eight days and sinking two more U-boats to bring the June total in the Bay to a somewhat disappointing four. Only 17 were sunk in all waters during the month.

## U-BOATS FRUSTRATED

In September 1943, Admiral Dönitz ordered group operations against the Atlantic convoys to resume, the U-boats now being equipped with search receiver equipment, eight 20mm (0.78in) anti-aircraft guns and a new acoustic homing torpedo, the T5 *Zaunkonig* (Wren). Twenty submarines passed through the Bay of Biscay to operate against Convoys ON202 and ONS18 on the eastern side of the North Atlantic. The Admiralty was advised of the movement by Ultra and a Liberator of No. 10 Squadron RCAF

sank *U-341* in the southern part of the patrol line on 19 September. However, grid-reference problems meant that the position of the first attack wave was miscalculated by 160km (100 miles), and the U-boats were able to achieve a measure of surprise. In a five-day battle, they sank three escorts and six merchantmen, losing three of their own number, but the U-boats were frustrated by the rapid reaction of Support Group B3 under Commander M.J. Evans, with 18 destroyers, corvettes and frigates, and by the VLR Liberators that were constantly over the convoys when the weather permitted. German claims to have sunk 12 escorts with 24 T5 firings resulted in the effectiveness of the new torpedo being greatly overestimated; in fact, many of the

The crew of the sloop HMS *Starling* searching for signs of U-boat wreckage after an attack. *Starling* was a successful hunter-killer vessel, one of 29 ships of the modified 'Black Swan' class.

torpedoes failed to explode or detonated in the ships' wash.

Other operations against the Atlantic convoys culminated in a disaster for the U-boats. In an attack on Convoys ON206 and ONS20 between 15 and 18 October, the submarines sank only one merchantman and lost six of their number, three to aircraft. In all, Dönitz lost 25 U-boats in the Atlantic during September and October 1943, and they achieved nothing more than the sinking of nine merchant ships out of the 2468 convoyed across the ocean.

A German U-boat entering its submarine pen after returning from a war patrol. U-boat pens on the French coast could not be penetrated by conventional bombs.

Preparatory movements for the invasion of Sicily – codenamed Husky – began on 16 June with the transatlantic passage of two American troop convoys to Oran and Algiers.

More escort carriers were now available for operations in the Atlantic. HMS *Tracker*, for example, was now working in conjunction with Captain Walker's 2nd Escort Group, and it was Walker who devised simple but effective tactics to make the U-boats' lives even more difficult. Once

search aircraft from the carrier had made contact with a submarine and directed Walker's ships on to it, he would position a 'directing ship' astern of the enemy to maintain

ASDIC contact. Meanwhile, two other escorts, not using their ASDIC, would creep up on either side of the submarine and release depth-charge patterns on the command of the

many battles were fought in Iberia and the southwestern approaches. But here, too, frustrated by Ultra-directed air patrols, support groups and evasive routing, they achieved little and suffered heavy losses.

## SICILY

Preparatory movements for the invasion of Sicily – codenamed Husky – began on 16 June with the transatlantic passage of two American troop convoys to Oran and Algiers.

The *U-664* (Lt Graef) under air attack by aircraft from the escort carrier USS *Card* on 9 August 1943. She had attempted to torpedo the carrier a few hours earlier.

Between 17 and 23 June, the British Force H, under Vice-Admiral Sir A.U. Willis, was transferred from Scapa Flow to Gibraltar, from where it sailed on to Oran; its assets comprised the battleships *Nelson*, *Rodney*, *Valiant* and *Warspite*, the carrier *Indomitable* and 18 destroyers. From Oran, the *Valiant*,

director vessel, giving the U-boat no time to take avoiding action.

Such vigorous action by air and surface forces, with evasive routing, compelled Dönitz to abandon his wolfpack tactics in November 1943 and to withdraw all but a few boats from the North Atlantic, where they continued for months to hunt for convoys with negligible success. The main U-boat forces were sent to operate against the Gibraltar convoys, where they had the advantage of air support, and in the ensuing months

### CAPTURE OF THE ITALIANS

The first half of 1943 saw a great deal of naval activity in the Mediterranean, as the Allies consolidated their position in North Africa and built up port facilities. British submarines were particularly active, sinking 30 enemy merchant ships and the submarine *U-303* during this period. The most important event following the Axis collapse in North Africa was the capture of the Italian islands of Pantelleria and Lampedusa in the Mediterranean narrows. This was achieved early in June after a fierce air and naval bombardment – Operation Corkscrew. The islands had been used as a base by Italian MTBs and submarines for attacks on the British Mediterranean convoys in 1942, and now that threat was removed.

*Warspite* and *Formidable*, together with the cruisers *Aurora* and *Penelope* and six destroyers, moved on to Alexandria, which they reached on 5 July. In the meantime, the battleships *Howe* and *King George V* had also arrived at Gibraltar, having been relieved of Home Fleet duties by the deployment to Scapa Flow of the US battleships *Alabama* and *South Dakota*.

The operational plan for Husky envisaged landings by both British and American forces. The British Eighth Army was to target five sectors of the east coast of Sicily stretching from just south of Syracuse to a point west of Cape Passero, while the US Seventh Army was to land on three sectors on the south coast. The initial objectives were to capture the ports

of Augusta and Syracuse, essential for subsequent resupply operations, and a clutch of airfields in the southwest corner of the island, for use by the Allied tactical air forces. The naval forces earmarked for the British assaults were to be commanded by Admiral Sir Bertram Ramsay, architect of the Dunkirk evacuation, while Vice-Admiral H.K. Hewitt USN was responsible for the American sectors.

In the British force, the troops earmarked for the three northern sectors were to sail directly from the Middle East, while the rest were to be transported from North Africa, Malta and Britain. In all, some 115,000 British Empire and 66,000 American soldiers were involved. D-Day for Husky was fixed at 10 July, and H-

**An Allied warship provides fire support for the amphibious landings on Sicily. All did not go well with the invasion, some troops being put ashore in the wrong place.**

Hour at 0245, about three hours before dawn. The operation featured a number of innovations, not the least of which was that the troops allocated to one of the British sectors were to travel all the way from North Africa or Malta in their landing ships and craft, without recourse to troop transports. A second was the appointment of a Beach Officer to each sector to control boat traffic, to maintain communications with the shipping offshore and generally to maintain order. The lessons of Dunkirk and Dieppe had been well learned.

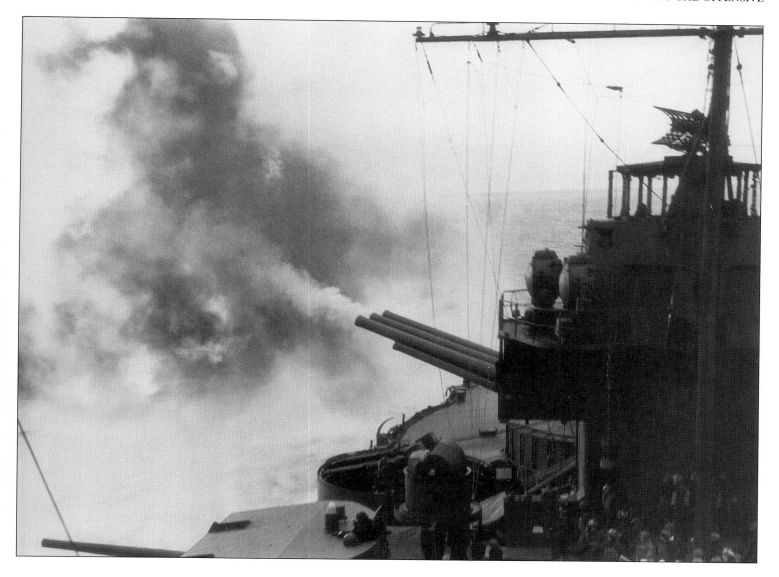

The battleship USS *Pennsylvania* prior to the Allied landing at Salerno. *Pennsylvania*, which escaped with only light damage at Pearl Harbor, was flagship of the US Fleet for many years.

The fact that the exploits of the American submariners remained a backwater of history until long after the war was due partly to inter-service rivalries, but in the main to the need to preserve one of the war's most closely guarded secrets: the fact that the Allies, because of high-grade Ultra intelligence, had access to the enemy's naval codes and therefore knew a great deal about the movements of his maritime traffic. In addition, US submarines played a key part in Operation Starvation from March to August 1945, in which thousands of mines were laid around the Japanese home islands.

The best and most prolific of the US ocean-going boats was the 'Gato' class of over 300 boats, construction of which was the largest warship project undertaken by the US Navy. These boats, more than any others, were to wreak havoc on Japan's mercantile commerce in the Pacific war. The exploits of one of them, the USS *Drum*, were typical. During her first offensive patrol in April 1942, *Drum* (under Lt Cdr Rice) sank the seaplane carrier *Mizuho* and two merchant ships. Later in the year, she carried out vital reconnaissance work prior to the American landings on Guadalcanal. In October 1942, she sank three more ships off the east coast of Japan, and in December she torpedoed the Japanese carrier *Ryuho*. She sank a

further two ships in April 1943, another in September, one in November, and three in October 1944, with another damaged.

## LONG ADVANCE
The long and costly American advance from Guadalcanal through the Solomon Islands towards the Japanese naval base at Rabaul began on 21 February 1943, when US forces made an unopposed landing on the Russell Islands, 48km (30 miles) northwest of Guadalcanal. It was the

start of a steady leapfrogging process, in which the occupation of each island or island group was followed by the establishment of bases and airfields.

On 18 April 1943, the Americans pulled off a spectacular coup when 16 Lockheed P-38 Lightnings of the 339th Fighter Squadron, Thirteenth Air Force, were despatched from Henderson Field, Guadalcanal, on a 700km (435-mile) flight to intercept a Mitsubishi G4M Betty carrying Admiral Isoroku Yamamoto on a tour of Japanese based in the Bougainville area. Thanks to their possession of the Imperial Japanese Navy codes, the Americans knew Yamamoto's exact itinerary. The Betty was shot down and all on board were killed. The death of Yamamoto was to have

a profound effect on the future conduct of the Japanese naval war.

In May 1943, US forces landed on Attu island in the Aleutians, where a Japanese garrison had been established. They captured it after three weeks of bitter fighting that saw heavy casualties on both sides, the 2500 Japanese defenders being virtually annihilated. Air support was provided by the escort carrier USS *Nassau* and, for the first time in the Pacific, air-ground operations were conducted by a Support Air Commander aboard the battleship USS *Pennsylvania*, which formed part of the naval bombardment force. Later, during the landing on Kiska by US and Canadian forces in August, air liaison parties were established ashore.

Pressure vortices swirl from the propeller tips of a Grumman F6F Hellcat fighter prior to take-off. The Hellcat destroyed more Japanese aircraft than any other type in the Pacific war.

## REMARKABLE ABILITY

Escort carriers were to play an immensely important part in the Pacific campaign, but it was the 27,433-tonne (27,000-ton) 'Essex' class, a new and improved version of the 'Yorktown' class of the 1930s, that became the standard US fleet carrier of the war and formed the core of the fast carrier task forces. These ships showed a remarkable ability to survive severe damage: although many were hit, none was sunk. Four of the 10 vessels built, including *Yorktown* and *Hornet*, were renamed for carriers that

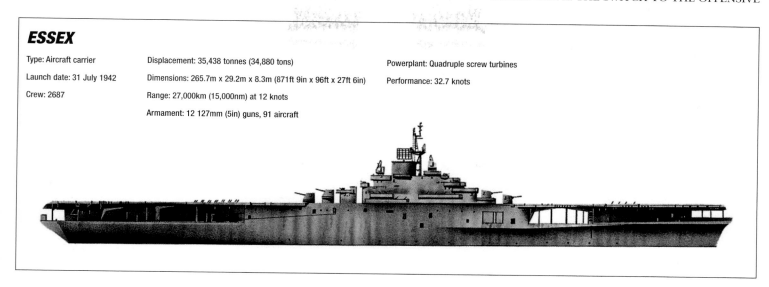

## ESSEX

Type: Aircraft carrier

Launch date: 31 July 1942

Crew: 2687

Displacement: 35,438 tonnes (34,880 tons)

Dimensions: 265.7m x 29.2m x 8.3m (871ft 9in x 96ft x 27ft 6in)

Range: 27,000km (15,000nm) at 12 knots

Armament: 12 127mm (5in) guns, 91 aircraft

Powerplant: Quadruple screw turbines

Performance: 32.7 knots

had been lost earlier. The 'Essex' class was supported by the smaller, 10,160-tonne (10,000-ton) 'Independence' class, whose nine ships had originally been laid down as light cruisers and re-ordered as carriers in 1942 under the War Emergency Program. Construction was rushed, the first ship being completed within a year. As conversions, the 'Independence' class was very successful.

Operations by US naval task forces had begun very cautiously in 1942, when aircraft from the USS *Enterprise* launched strikes on Wake Island, which had been captured by the Japanese in December 1941, and on Marcus Island. In August 1943, Task Force 15 (Rear-Admiral C.A. Pownall), built around the carriers *Essex*, the new 'Yorktown' and 'Independence', launched nine strike groups in a day-long attack on Japanese installations on Marcus Island. These were the first by the 'Essex' and 'Independence' class carriers, and marked the first combat operation of a new fleet fighter, the Grumman F6F Hellcat.

In September, the US Navy mounted a series of strikes against Tarawa and Makin in the Gilbert Islands, where US forces were landing. These operations were followed, in October, by another raid on Wake Island, when aircraft of Task Force 14

**The Betty was shot down and all on board were killed. The death of Yamamoto was to have a profound effect on the future conduct of the Japanese naval war.**

under Rear-Admiral A.E. Montgomery hit Japanese installations. The task force, comprising six new carriers, seven cruisers and 24 destroyers, was the largest carrier task force so far assembled. In November, carrier task forces delivered two air attacks on the enemy naval base at Rabaul, sinking one destroyer and damaging a number of other warships.

These operations were carried out in support of the US occupation of the Gilbert Islands in November 1943. On 18 November, six heavy and five light carriers of Task Force 50, under Rear-Admiral C.A. Pownall, opened the campaign to capture the islands with a two-day attack on airfields and defensive installations. Covering the landing of US Marines and Army troops on Tarawa, Makin and Abemawa Atolls, the Force also supported operations ashore. Eight escort carriers, operating with the attack forces, covered the approach of assault shipping, flew anti-submarine

and combat air patrols in the area, and were on call for close support missions. After the islands had been secured, one carrier group remained in the area for another week as a protective measure until naval aircraft were established on Tarawa airstrip. One escort carrier, the USS *Liscome Bay*, was lost to submarine attack on 24 November, and the light carrier USS *Independence* was damaged by air attack.

By mid-1943, the US Navy had substantial battleship force in the Pacific, used mostly in the pre-invasion bombardment role. US landings on New Georgia in June and July, for example, were supported by the *Massachusetts*, *Indiana*, *North Carolina* and two older vessels, the *Maryland* and *Colorado*. But the aircraft carrier and its air groups continued to be the primary weapon in the Pacific, as indeed it did in the Indian Ocean from 1944, following the strengthening of British naval resources there.

# World War II
## The End in the Atlantic 1945

As the mid-Atlantic struggle between the escorts and the U-boat packs continued in 1943, the battle flared up in Arctic waters once more. In September 1943, the *Tirpitz* and the *Scharnhorst* made one sortie to bombard installations on the island of Spitzbergen before scurrying back to their Norwegian lair, and in December the *Scharnhorst* put to sea once more. After an interval of several months, when no convoys passed through to Russia because of the dangers involved, they had resumed in November, when Convoy RA54A sailed from Archangel to the UK without incident. Two more outward-bound convoys, JW54A and JW54B, also made the journey from Loche Ewe to Russia unmolested.

The next two convoys, however, were both reported by the *Luftwaffe*. Admiral Dönitz issued orders that they were to be attacked not only by the 24 U-boats based on Bergen and Trondheim, but also by available surface units, the largest of which was the *Scharnhorst*. The convoys were JW55B, outward bound from Loch Ewe with 19 ships, and RA55A, homeward bound from

The German Navy's Commander Battleships, Vice-Admiral Ciliax, inspecting the crew of the *Scharnhorst*, accompanied by Captain Hoffman (right) and executive officers.

Kola. The former sailed on 20 December 1943, the latter three days later. Each was escorted by 10 destroyers and a number of smaller vessels.

At 1400 on Christmas Day, the *Scharnhorst* – under Kapt F. Hintze and flying the flag of Admiral Bey – sailed from Norway accompanied by the destroyers *Z29*, *Z30*, *Z33*, *Z34* and *Z38*. The mission was to intercept JW55B, which had been located by air reconnaissance on 22 December. The convoy had already been attacked by Ju 88s and by U-boats of the Eisenbart Group, but without success. On 26 December, Admiral Bey ordered his destroyers to form a patrol line to search for the convoy in heavy seas. He knew that a British cruiser covering force comprising the *Belfast*, *Norfolk* and *Sheffield* was operating in the Barents Sea; what he did not know was that there was also a distant covering force commanded by the C-in-C Home Fleet, Admiral Sir Bruce Fraser, and comprising the battleship *Duke of York*, the cruiser *Jamaica* and four destroyers, which had sailed from Iceland.

### SIGNALLING ERROR

Fraser, aware that JW55B had been located by enemy aircraft, was

> Before they were able to get into position, the battlecruiser retired to the northeast, her gunfire having put one of *Norfolk's* turrets and all her radar out of action.

convinced that the *Scharnhorst* would make a sortie against it, and detached four destroyers from Convoy RA55A, which he did not consider to be under immediate threat, to reinforce JW55B's close escort. His hope was that this strengthened destroyer force would not only be sufficient to drive off the *Scharnhorst*, but might perhaps damage her enough for the *Duke of York* to come up and finish her off. At this point, Fraser's ships were 320km (200 miles) southwest of North Cape and the cruiser force, under Admiral Burnett, 240km (150 miles) to the east.

Admiral Bey's five destroyers, meanwhile, had not only failed to locate the convoy; they had also, because of a signalling error, lost touch with the flagship and were subsequently ordered to return to base. As a result, they took no part in the coming events. At 0840 on the 26th, the cruisers *Norfolk* and *Belfast*

obtained radar contact with the *Scharnhorst* at 32,000m (35,000yds), and at 0921 the *Sheffield* glimpsed her in the stormy darkness at 11,880m (13,000yds). A few minutes later, all three destroyers opened fire on the battlecruiser and obtained three hits, one of which put her port 15.2cm (6in) fire-control system out of action. The *Scharnhorst* replied with a few harmless 27.9cm (11in) salvoes, then Bey turned away to the southeast while Burnett placed his cruisers between the threat and the convoy, screened by four destroyers from the escort.

At 1221, the three cruisers again sighted the *Scharnhorst* and opened fire with full broadsides at 10,000m (11,000yds), while the destroyers fanned out to attack with torpedoes. Before they were able to get into position, the battlecruiser retired to the northeast, her gunfire having put one of *Norfolk's* turrets and all her

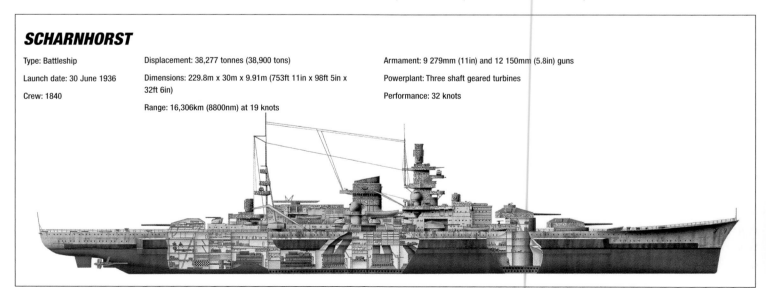

## SCHARNHORST

| | | |
|---|---|---|
| Type: Battleship | Displacement: 38,277 tonnes (38,900 tons) | Armament: 9 279mm (11in) and 12 150mm (5.8in) guns |
| Launch date: 30 June 1936 | Dimensions: 229.8m x 30m x 9.91m (753ft 11in x 98ft 5in x 32ft 6in) | Powerplant: Three shaft geared turbines |
| Crew: 1840 | | Performance: 32 knots |
| | Range: 16,306km (8800nm) at 19 knots | |

**The view from the bridge of the cruiser HMS *Belfast*. In 1971 this famous warship became a floating museum piece, and is today preserved on the River Thames.**

radar out of action; *Sheffield* also suffered some splinter damage. But the *Scharnhorst* had taken punishment too, including a hit abreast 'A' turret and one on her quarterdeck.

At 1617, the *Duke of York*, now 32km (20 miles) away to the north northeast, obtained a radar echo from the *Scharnhorst*. At 1650, Fraser ordered *Belfast* to illuminate her with starshell, and the *Duke of York* opened

fire with her 356mm (14in) armament immediately afterwards. Admiral Bey was now trapped between Burnett's cruisers to the north and Fraser's warships to the south, and he had no choice but to fight it out. Once *Scharnhorst*'s gunners had recovered from their surprise, their fire was accurate, although they failed to register a serious hit on her. The *Duke of York*'s gunnery was excellent; she scored 31 straddles out of 52 broadsides, with enough hits to put the battlecruiser's 'A' and 'B' turrets out of action and to rupture some steam pipes, which reduced her speed

so that Bey had no chance of outrunning his adversaries, even if the opportunity had arisen.

At 1824, the third of *Scharnhorst*'s turrets was put out of action, and Fraser, realizing that the *Duke of York*'s 35.6cm (14in) shells were unlikely to pierce the enemy's armour when fired at short range with a flat trajectory, turned away to let the destroyers finish the job. Two of them, the *Savage* and *Saumarez*, approached from the northwest under heavy fire, firing starshell, while *Scorpion* and *Stord* attacked from the southeast, launching their torpedoes at 1849.

> By 1930, the battlecruiser was a blazing wreck, her hull glowing red-hot in the Arctic night, and the destroyers closed in to finish her off with torpedoes.

As Hintze turned his ship to port to engage them, one of *Scorpion*'s torpedoes struck home, closely followed by three more from the first two destroyers. As the small ships retired under cover of smoke, the *Duke of York* and the cruisers closed in to batter the enemy warship with merciless fire. As Lieutenant B.B. Ramsden, an officer of Royal Marines on HMS *Jamaica*, later wrote, the *Scharnhorst*

> must have been a hell on earth. The 14-inch [35.6cm] from the flagship were hitting or rocketing off from a ricochet on the sea. Great flashes rent the night, and the sound of gunfire was continuous, and yet she replied,

but only occasionally now with what armament she had left.

### BLAZING WRECK

By 1930, the battlecruiser was a blazing wreck, her hull glowing red-hot in the Arctic night, and the destroyers closed in to finish her off with torpedoes. At 1945, she blew up, and only 36 of her crew of 1968 officers and men were rescued from the freezing seas. Like their comrades of the *Bismarck* two-and-a-half years earlier, they had fought their ship gallantly to the end. Now, treated with great kindness by the destroyer men who pulled them from the oil-soaked water, they were transferred to the *Duke of York* for the voyage to England, and captivity.

So ended the Battle of North Cape, and with it the last attempt by a German capital ship to challenge the supremacy of the Royal Navy. But

there was still the *Tirpitz* to be reckoned with. She had been damaged by X-craft (midget submarines) during a gallant attack on 18 September 1943, but it could be only a matter of months before she was made seaworthy again, and her continued presence in Norwegian waters constituted a permanent menace. In a bid to knock her out once and for all, the C-in-C Home Fleet planned a massive Fleet Air Arm strike against her. To simulate her anchorage in Altenfjord, a dummy range was built on Loch Eriboll, in Caithness, and during March 1944 this was the scene of intense activity as aircraft from the *Victorious* and *Furious* rehearsed the attack plan.

The strike was to be carried out by the 8th and 52nd TBR (Torpedo

The battleship *Duke of York* firing her main armament. She joined the Pacific Fleet in 1945, too late to take part in hostilities, and was laid up in reserve in 1951. She was scrapped in 1958.

Bomber Reconnaissance) Wings, operating the Fairey Barracuda, a type that had first seen action during the Salerno landings eight months earlier. In addition to their TBR Wings, *Victorious* and *Furious* each carried a fighter squadron equipped with American-built Vought Corsair fighters, and one each equipped with Seafires. More fighter cover was to be provided by Hellcats from the escort carrier HMS *Emperor* and Martlet Vs from HMS *Pursuer* and *Searcher*, while anti-submarine patrols were to be flown Swordfish from HMS *Fencer*. The carrier group was to be covered by warships of the Home Fleet, consisting of the battleships *Duke of York* and *Anson*, the cruisers *Belfast*, *Jamaica*, *Royalist* and *Sheffield* and 14 destroyers. The strike was timed to coincide with the passage of a Russian convoy, JW58.

On 30 March 1944, with the convoy well on its way, the Home Fleet units sailed from Scapa Flow in two forces, the first comprising the two battleships, *Victorious*, one cruiser and five destroyers; and the second, *Furious*, the four escort carriers and three cruisers. The actual attack on the *Tirpitz*, codenamed Operation Tungsten, was to be conducted by Vice-Admiral Sir Henry Moore, second-in-command of the Home Fleet, flying his flag in the *Anson*. The forces assembled in the afternoon of 2 April and proceeded to the flying-off position, 193km (120 miles) northwest of Kaafjord, reaching it during the early hours of the following morning. At 0430, 21 Barracudas of No. 8 TBR Wing, escorted by 21 Corsairs and 20 Hellcats, took off from the *Victorious* and set course for the target. Some

The destroyer *Saumarez* in northern waters, 1944. She was named after Admiral James Saumarez, a notable eighteenth-century British naval commander.

80km (50 miles) from their objective, the Barracudas, which had been flying low over the sea to avoid radar detection, went up to 2440m (8000ft) and began their final approach, preceded by the fighters, which went in at low level to suppress flak. The Germans were taken by surprise and the *Tirpitz*, lying virtually naked under the beginnings of a smoke screen, was hit by nine armour-piercing or semi-armour-piercing bombs. An hour later, a second attack was made by 19 Barracudas of No. 52 TBR Wing, escorted by 39 fighters, and the performance was repeated. By this time, the smoke screen was fully

A British midget submarine, or X-craft. These small, uncomfortable boats were used with success against the *Tirpitz*, and also against Japanese warships at Singapore in 1945.

developed, but it hindered the German gunners far more than it did the Barracuda crews, who had no difficulty in locating their target. In all, the battleship was hit by 14 bombs, 122 of her crew being killed and 316 wounded. The bombs failed to penetrate her heavy armour, but they caused extensive damage to her superstructure and fire-control systems and put her out of action for three months. The British lost two Barracudas and a Hellcat.

Convoy JW58 – with 49 ships, the largest convoy so far to sail on the Arctic route – accompanied by the cruiser *Diadem*, the escort carriers *Tracker* and *Activity*, 20 destroyers, five sloops and five corvettes, had meanwhile made steady progress. On 29 March, Captain F.J. Walker's 2nd Support Group scored an early success when it sank *U-961*, en route to the Atlantic. During the next three days, Martlet fighters from the escort carriers shot down three Fw 200, two Ju 88 and one Bv 138 reconnaissance aircraft. Three U-boat groups, *Thor*, *Blitz* and *Hammer*, with 12 boats between them and assisted by five more bound for the Atlantic, made repeated attacks on the convoy, but without success; *U-355* was sunk by the destroyer *Beagle* following a rocket attack by one of *Tracker*'s Avengers, *U-360* was destroyed by the Keppel, and *U-288* was sunk by aircraft from the two carriers, all between 1 and 3 April.

The *Tirpitz* photographed in Narvikfjord by a reconnaissance Spitfire in 1942. The protective anti-torpedo nets are clearly visible. Despite such precautions, the X-craft got through to attack her.

## OPERATION OVERLORD

In June 1944, the news of the war at sea had given place to an event for which the peoples of the free world and the occupied territories alike had been waiting: the Allied invasion of Europe. The naval preparations for the invasion – Operation Overlord – were breathtaking in their extent and remarkable for their forward planning. An outline plan for an invasion in 1943, called Roundup, was drawn up in 1941; and another one, Sledgehammer, was drafted in 1942, its aim being to seize and hold a bridgehead in France to take some pressure off the Soviets, who seemed in danger of collapse. In June that year, with the Allies suffering one reverse after another, the Admiralty appointed Admiral Sir Bertram Ramsay to be Naval Commander Expeditionary Force; two years later, with the invasions of North Africa and Sicily behind him, he was vastly experienced in the techniques of seaborne assault, and well aware of the naval firepower requirement that accompanied it.

Fleet Air Arm crews after an attack on the *Tirpitz* in 1944. The bombs carried by the naval aircraft were not sufficiently powerful to inflict serious damage on the battleship.

Further attempts to attack the *Tirpitz* in May were frustrated by bad weather, the naval aircraft instead turning their attention to enemy convoys off the Norwegian coast and scoring some successes. It was not until 17 July 1944 that another raid was carried out, this time by aircraft from the *Formidable*, *Furious* and *Indefatigable* under the command of Rear-Admiral R.R. McGrigor. However, on this occasion the enemy had plenty of warning. The smoke screen obscured the warship, the AA defences were fully alerted, and the raid was unsuccessful.

### SUCCESS!

The next attack, carried out on 22 August, was a disaster; the incoming aircraft were detected a long way from the target and were intercepted by Messerschmitt 109s of JG5, which shot down 11, mostly Barracudas. The escort carrier *Nabob* was torpedoed off North Cape by *U-534* and damaged beyond repair; *U-534* was herself sunk by aircraft from the escort carrier *Vindex* three days later. Two minor bomb hits were obtained on the *Tirpitz* in an attack on 24 August, the Barracuda crews bombing blind through the smoke; a further attack, on the 29th, was unsuccessful. Including a mission that had to be aborted because of the weather on

20 August, the Fleet Air Arm flew 247 sorties in this series of attacks. As for the *Tirpitz*, she was moved south to Tromso for repairs; and it was there, on 12 November 1944, that she was finally destroyed by 6.1-tonne (6-ton) Tallboy bombs dropped by the Lancasters of Nos. 9 and 617 Squadrons, RAF.

### NEPTUNE

By 10 April 1944, Ramsay had completed his final plan for the naval participation in the forthcoming invasion, codenamed Neptune. In a document that ran to over 700 foolscap pages, he stressed that the primary objective must be, in his own words, 'to secure a lodgement on the continent from which further offensive operations can be developed'. To achieve it, he assigned the available naval forces to convoy escort, minesweeping, fire support for the invasion forces, and a multitude of other tasks that were likely to arise.

Two large amphibious task forces were assigned to the assault: an Eastern Task Force under Rear-Admiral Sir Philip Vian, and a Western Task Force under Rear-Admiral A.G. Kirk, USN. The Eastern

Norwegian personnel inspecting the upturned hulk of the *Tirpitz* after the war. Cutting up the battleship was a gruesome business, as bodies were still entombed in the hull.

> Further attempts to attack the *Tirpitz* in May were frustrated by bad weather, the naval aircraft instead turning their attention to enemy convoys off the Norwegian coast.

Task Force was to land three divisions of the British Second Army on three beaches, codenamed Gold, Juno and Sword, on a 48km (30-mile) front west of the River Orne, while the Western Task Force was to land the US First Army on two beaches, Omaha and Utah, on a similar front to the west of the British assault area. Utah beach lay at the base of the Cotentin peninsula, and the early capture of Cherbourg depended on the speed at which it could be secured and the beachhead exploited.

Immediately behind the assault forces were to come two follow-on forces, one British and the other American, which would relieve the assault troops and open the way for a steady flow of reinforcements and supplies that would be necessary to defeat any German counter-offensive. To implement Neptune, Admiral Ramsay had a formidable array of 1213 warships at his disposal, 79 per cent of them British or Canadian, 16

Landing craft undergoing exercises in British coastal waters before the invasion of Normandy. Some LCAs were fitted with flame-throwers to support troops during landing operations.

Admiral Ramsay had 1213 warships at his disposal, 79 per cent of them British or Canadian, 16 per cent American and four per cent supplied by other Allied navies.

per cent American and four per cent supplied by other Allied navies. Of these, 107 were battleships, monitors and cruisers, representing the bombardment force; these assembled

**Jeeps being unloaded in Normandy. The naval aspect of the D-Day landings, Operation Neptune, was a masterpiece of planning and organization. Its mastermind was Admiral Sir Bertram Ramsay of Dunkirk evacuation fame.**

mainly in the Clyde and at Belfast, while the 286 destroyers, sloops, frigates and corvettes assigned to escort duty assembled at the south coast ports from which the invasion force would sail. The remainder of the force comprised all kinds of naval craft, down to the midget submarines that would approach the beaches well in advance of the assault force and act as pathfinders. Then there were the

combined operations craft, no fewer than 4126 of them, including big headquarters ships especially fitted out for the role; large merchant vessels converted to Landing Ships Infantry (LSIs), carrying Landing Craft Assault (LCAs); Landing Ships Tank (LSTs); Landing Craft Tank (LCTs); AA defence vessels; rocket-firing craft; smoke-laying craft; obstacle clearance craft; and repair and maintenance vessels. About three-quarters of the total were of American build.

In addition, hundreds of merchant ships were requisitioned to undertake such duties as channel marking; salvage and cable laying; replenishing the warships; providing harbour facilities; and towing the special constructions that were vital to the success of the invasion. Foremost among these were the two artificial harbours, known as Mulberries, and five craft shelters called Gooseberries. The creation of artificial harbours and breakwaters would involve the deliberate scuttling of 55 merchant vessels and some obsolete warships, while 160 tugs would be needed to tow the sections of the Mulberry across the Channel. About 400 units, totalling 1,524,070 tonnes (1,500,000 tons), made up the two Mulberries; the two concrete caissons that formed part of the breakwaters alone weighed 6096 tonnes (6000 tons). The Mulberries, with their miles of floating piers (called Whale units), were truly remarkable feats of engineering; when assembled, the British one – the larger of the two – would provide a sheltered anchorage for seven deep-laden ships of large tonnage, 20 coasters, 400 tugs and auxiliary vessels and 1000 small craft.

## FIRE SUPPORT

In the planning of Neptune, much attention was paid to accurate fire support procedures by the heavy bombardment ships. Each of the five assault forces was allocated a group of fire support warships, their initial targets being the 23 German gun batteries that commanded the assault beaches. An elaborate spotting system was devised, which included observation both from the air and from the surface. The lessons of Dieppe, and the subsequent Allied landings in Sicily and Italy, had been fully absorbed.

The Germans knew that the invasion was coming, but they did not know when and where the blow would fall. In the spring of 1944, however, they launched a series of air and sea attacks on the British coast in the hope of disrupting the build-up of invasion shipping. On 23/24 April, as part of the so-called 'little Blitz' on Britain (Operation *Steinbock*), the *Luftwaffe* flew 100 sorties against Portsmouth; and two nights later, 130 aircraft bombed the Poole and Swanage areas. Bombing accuracy was

**Planning for D-Day. British military personnel and civilian experts study German dispositions on the River Orne, where key objectives were to be seized by the 6th Airborne Division.**

very poor, a reflection of the low quality of the crews that were now reaching the *Luftwaffe*'s operational unit: in one raid on Bristol, no bombs hit the city, the majority falling on Weston-Super-Mare, 32km (20 miles) away. On 15 May, the enemy bombers flew 106 sorties, of which 60 were directed at the Portsmouth area; and towards the end of these operations, during the last week of the month, fast fighter-bombers made a series of attacks on the south coast harbours, which by now were crammed with shipping. The damage caused was negligible, and *Steinbock* cost the Germans more than 300 aircraft between January and the end of May 1944, effectively spelling the end of the German bomber force in the west.

The early months of 1944 also saw an increase in German naval activity in the Channel area, the S-boat flotillas having been reinforced. On the night of 5/6 January, seven S-boats of the

5th Flotilla (under Kapt Lt Karl Müller) attacked Convoy WP457 off the southwest coast of England. The boats fired a total of 23 torpedoes, swamping the escort, which was led by the destroyer HMS *Mackay*, and sinking three freighters and the naval trawler *Wallasea*. The escorts proved more effective on 16/17 January, successfully driving off seven S-boats of the 5th Flotilla that tried to

HMS *Ashanti* was one of the famous 'Tribal' class destroyers that gave invaluable service to the Royal Navy during some of the darkest and most dangerous times of World War II.

intercept a convoy off Lizard Head; the enemy fired 11 torpedoes, but all missed. On the last day of January, however, six boats of the 5th Flotilla attacked Convoy CW243 off Beachy Head, sinking two freighters and the

## COASTAL FORCES

The value of the British coastal radar defences in combating the S-boat threat was again demonstrated on two nights in March, when the 5th and 9th Flotillas set out to attack shipping off the Lizard and Weymouth on the 16th/17th and 20th/21st. The boats' radar detection equipment alerted the crews that they were being tracked, and the sorties were abandoned. The British coastal forces were also in action on the night of 20/21 March, when five MTBs attacked the German convoy Hecht, comprising the tanker *Rekum* escorted by the 18th Vorpostenboote Flotilla. The MTBs were beaten off, but the tanker was sunk by the Dover guns.

The cruiser *Bellona* was one of the warships assigned to protect the Channel area against S-boat attacks. She went on to serve with the Royal New Zealand Navy 1947–56.

naval trawler *Pine.* A few days later, on 5 February, there was a sharp engagement between the British destroyers *Brissenden, Talybont, Tanatside* and *Wensleydale* and the German minesweepers *M156* and *M206,* escorted by the destroyer *T29,* off the coast of northern Brittany. The *M156* was badly damaged and limped into L'Abervach, where she was destroyed later by air attack.

## INTENSE ACTIONS

Some of the most intense actions during this period were fought in the North Sea, where S-boats were carrying out minelaying operations off Grimsby and Great Yarmouth. In the Channel itself, a combination of radar

and rapid reaction by the escort forces were gradually getting the better of the S-boat forays towards the south coast. There were, nevertheless, some frenetic actions in the Straits of Dover during March, beginning on the night of the 14th/15th, when British MTBs attacked two groups of the German 36th Minesweeping Flotilla off Gravelines and sank the enemy leader, *M3630,* with a torpedo. Return fire was heavy and the British lost one boat, MTB 417. On the following night, 10 S-boats of the 5th and 9th Flotillas (under Kapt von Mirbach and Kapt Klug) attempted to attack Convoy WP492 off Land's End, escorted by the corvettes *Azalea* and *Primrose.* The German force was detected by air reconnaissance and other British warships in the area – the cruiser *Bellona,* the 'Tribal' class destroyers *Ashanti* and *Tartar,* the 'Hunt' class destroyers *Brissenden* and

*Melbreak,* two minesweepers and some MTBs – diverted to intercept. Faced with this formidable weight of firepower, the Germans had little choice but to disengage, but not before *S143* had been damaged.

The real breakthrough in this phase of the naval war in the Channel came in April, when the British

> In the Channel itself, a combination of radar and rapid reaction by the escort forces were gradually getting the better of S-boat forays towards the south coast.

adopted new tactics. These involved the use of the cruisers *Bellona* and *Black Prince* in the role of command ships, their radar enabling them to direct destroyers of the newly formed 10th Flotilla on to enemy targets and then maintain a constant plot of the action, and their long-range guns enabling them to engage the enemy force while illuminating it constantly with star shell while the destroyers closed in. The tactics worked well, and on 26 April they resulted in the sinking of the 'Elbing' class destroyer *T28*, two more destroyers – *T24* and *T27* – being badly damaged and forced to seek shelter in Morlaix. They broke out on the night of 28/29

**A United States convoy prior to the invasion of Normandy. The landings were supported by seven battleships, two monitors, 23 cruisers, 105 destroyers and 1073 smaller naval craft.**

April and were intercepted off Brieux by the 'Tribal' class destroyers *Haida* and *Athebaskan*. The Germans fired 12 torpedoes at their pursuers and

The boat crews moored their Filbert floats and laid a smoke screen, at the same time broadcasting recorded sounds of large vessels dropping anchor over loudspeakers.

*Athebaskan* was hit, sinking at 0442, but *T27* was further damaged by shells from the *Haida* and ran aground, to be finished off later by MTBs.

On the previous night (27/28 April), the S-boats achieved their greatest victory since 1940, and it happened more or less by accident.

On that night, nine boats of the 5th and 9th Flotillas (*S100, S130, S136, S138, S140, S142, S143, S145* and *S150*) sailed from Cherbourg to attack a convoy that was reported to be off Selsey Bill. Instead, they encountered a convoy of landing craft – eight US LSTs, escorted by the corvette *Azalea*, heading from Brixham and Plymouth for Slapton Sands in South Devon, where they were to take part in Exercise Tiger, a dress rehearsal for the American landing on Utah Beach.

The assault wave goes in on Omaha Beach. Most of the American casualties on D-Day were hurt on this strip of coast, where the invaders were pinned down on the beach for hours.

the Royal Navy – harbour defence vessels and motor launches – performed a vital task in the Pas de Calais. While RAF Lancasters orbited overhead, dropping bundles of Window, the naval craft operated a device called Moonshine, which picked up enemy radar pulses, amplified them and re-transmitted them, giving a 'solid' radar impression of a large concentration of ships forging slowly ahead. The boats also towed Filberts – barrage balloons 8.8m (29ft) long and fitted with radar reflectors, each one producing a radar echo similar to that of a 10,160-tonne (10,000-ton) ship. Near the enemy coast, the boat crews moored their Filbert floats and laid a smoke screen, at the same time broadcasting recorded sounds of large vessels dropping anchor over powerful loudspeakers. The whole object of this joint RAF/RN exercise was to lead the enemy to believe that the invasion was taking place in the narrowest stretch of the Channel, and it succeeded admirably.

By 0500 on 6 June, the LSIs had reached their lowering positions, some 11–12km (7–8 miles) off the Normandy coast, and the assault battalions embarked in their landing craft – no mean feat in itself, for a heavy swell was running and the craft were tossed up and down like corks. Nevertheless, the operation was accomplished with remarkably few mishaps. Visibility was poor as the assault craft and their supporting tank-landing craft began their run-in to the beaches, with the coastline obscured by haze and smoke from the tactical air bombardment that had been in progress for some time. A

The convoy should also have been escorted by the destroyer HMS *Saladin*, but she had been damaged in a collision with a landing craft in Plymouth harbour and no replacement had been assigned.

The S-boats fell upon the convoy as it entered Lyme Bay. In the torpedo attack that followed, *LST507* and *LST531* were sunk and another, *LST289*, was damaged. The loss of life was severe: 441 soldiers and 197 seamen. The attackers were pursued

by the destroyers *Onslow*, *Obedient*, *Ursa*, *Piorun* and *Blyskawica*, but escaped unharmed. The incident was kept a closely guarded secret for a long time after the war, and even today there is controversy over the actual loss of life, some sources putting it as high as 749.

## OVERLORD
In the early hours of 6 June 1944, as the invasion armada headed towards the Normandy coast, small ships of

The *Schnorchel* (Snorkel) apparatus enabled a U-boat to recharge its batteries while remaining below the surface, and was extremely difficult to detect by airborne radar.

fearful blanket of noise lay over the scene as the warships of the naval task forces hurled their broadsides at the enemy's positions. The entire force of Allied warships committed to Overlord totalled seven battleships, 23 cruisers, three monitors, 105 destroyers and 1073 smaller vessels; included among the latter were over 100 British and Canadian minesweepers, their vital task to clear the approaches to the landing areas, and 27 buoy-layers to mark the cleared lanes.

## ANTI-SUBMARINE GROUPS

One major concern of the Allied Naval Command during Overlord was to prevent interference by U-boats, in particular those equipped with the new *Schnorchel* device, which enabled them to stay submerged without the need to surface to recharge their systems. At the start of Overlord, however, there was such a large concentration of Allied air squadrons west of the Channel entrance, making radar searches by day and night, that it was impossible for U-boats without *Schnorchel* to come anywhere near the invasion area. All those that tried were heavily attacked by aircraft and either sunk or damaged so that they had to return to base or were recalled by the Commander U-boats. The *Schnorchel* boats were able to evade the air

attacks, but they then had to face very strong naval anti-submarine groups concentrated in the Channel entrance, and only a very few were able, after a fortnight or so, to enter the 'funnel', where they achieved minimal success. In fact, 10 Support Groups of destroyers, sloops and frigates formed a screen at either end of the Channel; six covered the Western Approaches and the Bay of Biscay, supported by the escort carriers *Activity*, *Tracker* and *Vindex*.

For some time, the Germans had been holding anti-invasion groups of U-boats at readiness in French and Norwegian harbours. When Overlord began, the Biscay group, together with all available S-boats and four destroyers from Le Havre (the *T28*, *Falcke*, *Möwe* and *Jaguar*), was ordered to proceed to the scene of the landings. The destroyers sank the Norwegian destroyer *Svenner* on the first day of the invasion, but they were attacked constantly from the air and were soon forced to run for shelter. The S-boats sank a number of landing craft, but in the main their attacks were beaten off.

On 6 June, 17 U-boats put to sea from Brest, 14 from St Nazaire, four from La Pallice and one from Lorient. They were soon in trouble; the next day, aircraft of No. 19 Group Coastal Command sank *U-955* and *U-970* in the Bay of Biscay, and four of the Brest boats (*U-963*, *U-989*, *U-256* and *U-415*) were all damaged and forced to return to base. On 8 June, a Liberator of No. 224 Squadron sank *U-629* and *U-373* in rapid succession; and on 9 June, *U-740* was also destroyed. A sortie from Brest by the German destroyers *Z24*, *Z32*, *ZH1* and

The *Neger* (Negro) one-man torpedo was used with limited success against Allied invasion vessels after D-Day, but its crews suffered terrible losses and the unit was eventually disbanded.

*T24* on the night of 8/9 June was intercepted by the British 10th Destroyer Flotilla; *ZH1* was sunk by torpedoes from HMS *Ashanti*, and *Z32* by gunfire from the Canadian destroyer *Haida*. Another Canadian destroyer, the *Huron*, was beached and blown up, while HMS *Tartar* was severely damaged.

Only nine U-boats of the Biscay group were *Schnorchel*-equipped, and eight of these attempted to infiltrate the Channel area from 7 June. Between that date and 11 June, three made abortive torpedo attacks, and *U-821* was destroyed by an aircraft. It was not until 15 June that they enjoyed some success: *U-621* sank the tank landing ship *LST280*; *U-767*, the frigate *Mourne*; and *U-764* the frigate *Blackwood*, which was taken in tow, but proved to be a total loss. On 18 June, *U-767* was sunk by destroyers of the

14th Support Group, and *U-441* by a Wellington of the No. 304 (Polish) Squadron.

A second group of *Schnorchel*-equipped submarines penetrated the invasion area during the second half of June. These suffered an early loss when *U-971* was sunk in the western part of the Channel by the destroyers *Haida* and *Eskimo* on the night of 22nd/23rd. Two nights later, the destroyers *Affleck* and *Balfour* sank *U-1191*, while *U-269* was destroyed by the *Bickerton*; the destroyer *Goodson* was

255

**Escort carriers like HMS *Attacker* were usually based on Greenock on the River Clyde, Scotland, and attached to escort groups. *Attacker* had been a merchant ship before her conversion.**

torpedoed and damaged by *U-984*. On 27/29 June, *U-988* torpedoed the corvette *Pink*, which was a total loss, and sank two ships of 9596 tonnes (9444 tons) before she was sent to the bottom by the 3rd Support Group. The biggest German success came that same day, 29 June, when *U-984* attacked Convoy EMC17 and torpedoed four ships totalling 29,251 tonnes (28,790 tons), three of which were sunk and the fourth beached. This attack showed what a *Schnorchel* boat could achieve under favourable circumstances, and it must be said that the U-boat operations in June 1944 had been dogged by technical failures; often, their torpedoes had detonated prematurely, or their motors had failed to work properly.

### GALLANT SORTIES

On 26 June, after a heavy bombardment by naval forces, Cherbourg fell to the Americans, and another vital port was lost to the enemy. Ultra now began to detect a steady movement of enemy submarines away from France to Norway; this transfer was accomplished with surprisingly few losses, because the U-boats could travel submerged and search aircraft were unable to locate the *Schnorchel*-heads in the sea clutter when they were raised above the surface at night for recharging the batteries. The S-boats continued to make gallant sorties against the cross-Channel supply routes during July, but the back of their offensive had been broken; the majority of their missions were disrupted by British Coastal Forces craft, joined now by American PT boats and destroyers.

On the night of 5/6 July, the Germans brought a new weapon into action: the *Neger* (Negro) one-man torpedo, 26 of which were deployed against the invasion area from Villers-sur-Mer. On this occasion, they sank the minesweepers *Cat* and *Magic*, and later in the month they sank the destroyer *Isis* and the minesweeper *Pylades*, and disabled the Polish-manned cruiser *Dragon* so severely that she had to be scuttled as part of a Gooseberry Harbour breakwater. *Neger* operations ceased in mid-August, their operating unit having suffered dreadful losses. Some success was achieved during this period by Small Battle Unit Flotilla 211, which used *Linsen* (Lens) explosive boats to sink the destroyer *Quorn* and the anti-submarine trawler *Gairsay* on the night of 2/3 August.

### OPERATION DRAGOON

On 15 August 1944, with the breakout from Normandy in progress, the Allies launched Operation Dragoon, the invasion of the French Riviera between St Raphael and Frejus. Dragoon was mainly an American and Free French operation, although the Royal Navy made a significant contribution to the escort carrier task force, TF88, which had once again been mustered to provide the necessary air cover. Commanded jointly by Rear-Admiral Sir Thomas

June 1944 had been dogged by technical failures; often, their torpedoes had detonated prematurely, or their motors had failed to work properly.

Troubridge and Rear-Admiral C.T. Durgin, USN, it comprised the British carriers *Attacker*, *Emperor*, *Khedive*, *Pursuer*, *Searcher*, *Hunter* and *Stalker* and the American carriers *Tulagi* and *Kasaan Bay*. Only feeble resistance was encountered and the Allies swept rapidly inland, the carrier aircraft being used mainly for strafing and reconnaissance. The Royal Navy also provided warships for escort and fire support; these included the battleship *Ramillies*, 11 cruisers, 27 destroyers and two gunboats.

In September, the seven Royal Navy carriers that had taken part in Dragoon sailed for the Aegean, where their aircraft flew in support of the Allied forces engaged in recapturing Crete and the other German-occupied islands. The fighters wrought massive destruction among the fleets of small craft, packed with enemy troops. The *Searcher* and *Pursuer* joined the Home Fleet at the end of the month, but the other five remained in the area until the beginning of November, by which time all the major islands had been re-occupied. It was the last wartime offensive operation mounted by carriers in the Mediterranean theatre.

## COSTLY LANDING

By the end of August 1944, the Allied naval forces had secured the Channel area. For at least part of the bombardment force that had covered the Normandy landings, however, there was still work to be done. In the first week of November 1944, a bombardment force led by HMS *Warspite* and the monitors *Roberts* and *Erebus* shelled the island of Walcheren, in the Scheldt estuary, in support of a hard-fought and costly landing there by Canadian forces and the Royal

**The escort carrier HMS *Searcher* on patrol in the North Atlantic. She was returned to merchant service in the USA after the war. She was scrapped in Taiwan in 1976.**

257

**Royal Navy personnel on board a captured Type XXIII U-boat, 1945. The Type XXIII was designed for operations in coastal waters, but it came too late to see operational service.**

Marine Special Service Brigade. On 8 November, the German commander and his 29,000-strong garrison surrendered, and the way was now open to the vital port of Antwerp, desperately needed to resupply the Allied armies advancing through northwest Europe.

During the winter of 1944–45, the *Schnorchel* U-boats launched their final offensive against Allied shipping in the Atlantic and in British home waters. Such was the weight of air and sea power ranged against them, however, that their freedom of

movement was severely restricted and they had to remain more or less stationary, waiting for targets to come their way. Early in 1945, the British air and surface anti-submarine forces literally swamped the sea areas around the British Isles, inflicting such heavy losses on the U-boats that they were forced out of the coastal waters. Between 15 November 1944 and 27 January 1945, the U-boats sank 31 ships, including some naval escort vessels, but they also lost 12 of their number. At the end of January, the new Type XXIII boats became operational, and in the following five-week period they sank 16 ships and damaged several others; but 10 more U-boats fell victim to the anti-submarine forces.

The surviving S-boats, concentrated now in Holland, continued to make forays into the North Sea and English Channel. The last was on 22 March, when boats of the 2nd and 5th Flotillas set out from Ijmuiden and Den Helder to attack shipping between the Thames Estuary and the Scheldt. The attack came to nothing, and the S-boats were driven off by the destroyer HMS *Mackay*.

The U-boats fought on to the end, and on 5 April they suddenly returned to British coastal waters. In a desperate, last-ditch offensive lasting a month, they sank eight ships, but 15 submarines were destroyed. Indeed, they continued right to the end: on 7 May 1945, the day before Germany capitulated, *U-2336* (Lt Klusmeyer)

The German Navy's last surviving warships, including the heavy cruiser *Admiral Hipper*, were used to cover the German evacuation from East Prussia. *Hipper* was scuttled on 3 May 1945.

sank the freighter *Avondale Park* in the Firth of Forth. But it was RAF Coastal Command that had the last word. That afternoon, a Catalina of No. 210 Squadron sank *U-320* in the North Sea west of Bergen.

## BALTIC STORM

There remained the Baltic. It was here, with the opening salvoes of the battleship *Schleswig-Holstein*, that the naval war in European waters had begun, and it was here, five-and-a-half years later, that it ended, not in a blazing twilight-of-the-gods battle, but in misery and desperation for millions of people.

In January 1945, Admiral Oscar Kummetz, former commander of the German heavy cruiser squadron in Arctic waters and now in charge of the German Naval High Command East, had the task of planning what was to become the greatest naval evacuation in history. With the Soviet armies advancing inexorably through East Prussia, Kummetz and his staff were tasked with evacuating huge numbers of German troops and civilians from Kurland and the Gulf of Danzig. They assembled a number of large passenger ships that had been employed as accommodation vessels at Pillau, Gotehafen and Danzig. The principal vessels were the *Cap Arkona* (28,003 tonnes/27,561 tons), *Robert Ley* (27,644 tonnes/27,288 tons), *Wilhelm Gustloff* (25,892 tonnes/25,484 tons), *Hamburg* (22,472 tonnes/22,117 tons), *Hansa* (21,470 tonnes/21,131 tons) and *Deutschland* (21,384 tonnes/21,046 tons).

On 30 January 1945, the evacuation fleet suffered its first major disaster. Early that morning, the 25,893-tonne

### FLIGHT IN THE WINTER

On 25 January 1945, the first evacuation ships sailed from Pillau, carrying 7100 refugees to safety in the west. By 28 January, 62,000 refugees had been evacuated. Also evacuated, on the light cruiser *Emden*, was the sarcophagus of President Paul von Hindenburg and that of his wife, which had been buried at the Tannenberg Memorial in East Prussia; the monument itself was blown up. The coffins of Hindenburg and his wife were taken to Marbug an der Lahn in Hesse, where they were hidden in an abandoned salt mine. They were discovered by US troops on 27 April 1945 and reinterred in the Elisabeth Church, Marburg.

(25,484-ton) passenger liner *Wilhelm Gustloff* left Gotenhafen, accompanied by another liner, the *Hansa*, and two torpedo boats. The ship was subsequently sighted by the Soviet submarine *S-13* (Captain Third Class Marinesko), on patrol in the area of the Stolpe Bank. The *Gustloff* was torpedoed 32km (20 miles) offshore, somewhere between Neustadt (present day Wladyslawowo) in West Prussia and Leba. Three torpedoes hit the liner, which sank within 70 minutes in 46m (150ft) of water. At the time of the attack, there were 7956 registered refugees on board the *Gustloff*, but it is estimated that about 2000 more joined the vessel at the last minute before she sailed, and several hundred refugees from Reval came on board while she was at sea. Together with the crew, the total number must

have been well over 10,000, of which only 1239 were saved by torpedo boats and minesweepers. The heavy cruiser *Admiral Hipper*, which was evacuating 1500 wounded soldiers, also came up to help with the rescue effort, but had to withdraw to the west because of the submarine threat.

On the following day, the *L-3* (under Captain Third Class Konovalov) made two abortive attempts to sink the fully laden *Cap Arkona*, but on 10 February *S-13*, still cruising in the area of the Stolpe Bank, sank the 14,895-tonne (14,660-ton) liner *General Steuben* with one torpedo. Escort vessels managed to pluck only 300 passengers from the freezing water, the survivors of more than 3000.

Despite the shipping losses caused by Soviet air attack, submarines and mines, the German transports evacuated huge numbers of people to the west. On 23 March, for example, the *Deutschland* sailed from Gotenhafen with 11,145 people on board, and five days later she took off another 11,295, while the liner *Potsdam* rescued more than 9000 in one uplift.

Gotenhafen fell to the Soviets on 28 March and Danzig two days later. On the night of 4/5 April, 8000 troops and about 30,000 refugees were evacuated from the Oxhöfter bridgehead and brought to Hela in 25 naval trawlers, 27 ferry barges, five heavy auxiliary gunboats and five other vessels in an operation dubbed *Walpurgisnacht*. These and subsequent operations were covered by the heavy cruiser *Lützow*, accompanied by a number of destroyers and torpedo boats, until 8 April, when the *Lützow*

and two of the destroyers had to be withdrawn because of shortage of fuel and ammunition.

Between 21 March and 10 April 1945, 157,270 wounded were evacuated from the Hela Peninsula, the narrow spit of land jutting out into the Bay of Danzig on its western extremity. In April, 264,887 refugees were taken by an armada of small craft from the ports that still remained unoccupied in the Gulf of Danzig, Pillau, Kahlberg, Schiewenhorst and Oxhöft. On 24/25 April, the last night of the evacuation of Pillau, naval ferry barges lifted off 19,200 troops and refugees, bringing the total evacuated from this one place since 21 January to nearly 500,000.

On 16 April, a convoy of eight ships leaving Hela came under heavy air attack, and the repair ship *Boelcke* was sunk. During the night, the submarine *L-3* (under Captain Third Class Konovalov) torpedoed and sank the 5314-tonne (5230-ton) transport *Goya*. Only 165 of the 6385 people on

board were rescued. On this day, the dwindling assets of the *Kriegsmarine* suffered yet another blow when 18 Lancasters of No. 617 Squadron RAF flew to Swinemünde to attack the heavy cruiser *Lützow*. Fifteen aircraft bombed the target with 5443kg (12,000lb) 'Tallboy' or 454kg (1000lb) bombs; the effects of one near-miss by a Tallboy tore a large hole in the bottom of the *Lützow* and she sank in shallow water as her crew tried to beach her.

## THE DEATH OF HITLER

On 30 April, with Soviet troops in the heart of Berlin, Adolf Hitler committed suicide. On the following day, the Soviet Second Shock Army, having pushed across the lower Oder, reached the ancient Hanseatic town of Stralsund in western Pomerania, while the Nineteenth Army advanced on Swinemünde. On 2 May, the old battleship *Schlesien*, fighting to the last, was sent to the Greifswalder Bodden – the coastal waters of the southern Baltic off Peenemünde between

**Surrendered German Navy personnel queue to have their details taken at Wilhelmshaven, May 1945. The sheer volume of prisoners presented the Allies with huge logistical problems.**

Rügen and Usedom Islands – to protect the Wolgast Bridge, across which refugees and troops were streaming over the Peene river. As she approached her station, she struck a mine and was towed back to Swinemünde, where she was beached. Two days later, she was blown up, together with the adjacent *Lützow*.

## CAP ARKONA TRAGEDY

On 3 May, the southern Baltic was the scene of a terrible tragedy when RAF Typhoon fighter-bombers attacked the passenger linker *Cap Arkona* and the freighter *Thielbeck*, assuming them to be laden with German troops being evacuated to Norway. Both ships were sunk with the loss of more than 7000 lives. The tragedy was that they were laden not with German troops but with former concentration-camp

inmates. Elsewhere, the desperate last-minute evacuations continued. Between 1 and 8 May, small craft and naval ferry barges of the 13th Landing Flotilla uplifted around 150,000 refugees and troops from the landing stages of the lower Vistula to Hela. From there, the transports *Sachsenwald* and *Weserstrom* and the torpedo boats *T36* and *T108* evacuated the first 8850 on 3 May. Following the surrender of German forces in northwest Germany and Denmark, the freighters *Linz*, *Ceuta*, *Pompeji* and the auxiliary cruiser *Hansa*, which were outside territorial waters at the time, proceeded to Hela on 5 May with the destroyers *Hans Lody*, *Friedrich Ihn*, *Theodore Riedel* and the torpedo boats *T17*, *T19*, *T23*, *T28* and *T35*. These vessels, together with a number of minesweepers and

*Under the watchful eyes of the Royal Navy, German naval personnel sweep Kiel harbour for mines, which remained a danger to shipping in European waters long after the war was over.*

training ships, embarked 45,000 refugees and sailed for Copenhagen, beating off attacks by Soviet torpedo-boats operating out of Kolberg on the way.

Arriving at Copenhagen on 6 May, the fast warships were unloaded in the roads in order to achieve a rapid turnaround. On 7 May, the destroyers *Karl Galster*, *Friedrich Ihn*, *Hans Lody*, *Theodore Riedel* and *Z25*, together with the torpedo boats *T17*, *T19*, *T23* and *T28*, were joined by the destroyers *Z38* and *Z39* and the torpedo boat *T33* from Swinemünde, and put into Hela. From there, they took off 20,000 soldiers and

refugees, who were disembarked at Glücksburg on 9 May, the day after the surrender of all German forces came into effect. A further 5730 refugees were taken off by the freighters *Weserberg* and *Paloma*, and 1500 by the small steamer *Rugard*, which evaded attempts by three Soviet torpedo boats to capture her on 8 May.

In all, between 25 January and 8 May 1945, 1,420,000 refugees were evacuated by sea from the Gulf of Danzig and Pomerania. This is the recorded figure; to it must be added some 600,000 more, evacuated over shorter distances a step ahead of the advancing Soviets.

It was not quite the end. On 8 May, 65 small craft of the German Navy set out from Libau, heading west and carrying 14,400 troops and refugees; 61 similar craft set out from Windau, carrying 11,300 troops. The next day,

some of the slower craft were intercepted by Soviet warships, but only 300 persons went into captivity to join the 200,000 left behind in Kurland.

## AFTERMATH

On 6 May 1945, a British naval force passed through the German mine barrages off the Skagerrak and arrived at Copenhagen on 9 May, where the cruisers *Prinz Eugen* and *Nürnberg* – the only major units of the *Kriegsmarine* still afloat – were surrendered by Vice-Admiral Wilhelm Meendsen-Bohlken, the last commander of the German surface fleet. Command of all German naval units was now assumed by Vice-Admiral Reginald Vesey-Holt, the newly appointed Flag Officer Denmark. The takeover operation was covered by a task force under

US sailors on harbour patrol take a look at a German destroyer. German destroyers were generally large, powerful vessels and were better armed than their British counterparts.

Vice-Admiral Rhoderick McGrigor; it comprised the escort carriers *Searcher* and *Trumpeter,* the cruiser *Norfolk* and the destroyers *Carysfort, Zambesi, Obedient, Opportune* and *Orwell.*

Later in the month, the *Prinz Eugen* and *Nürnberg* were escorted to Wilhelmshaven by British destroyers, where they remained to await disposal. The *Nürnberg* was ceded to the Soviet Union, and in January 1946 she sailed to Libau, where she was handed over to the Soviets. Renamed the *Admiral Makarov*, she served with the Baltic Fleet until at least 1953, being scrapped sometime in the following years.

An altogether grimmer fate awaited the *Prinz Eugen*, although before finally meeting it she showed a remarkable capacity for survival. Ceded to the United States, she sailed in 1946 for Boston with a mixed crew of Americans and Germans. In March, she passed through the Panama Canal to San Diego, where the last German crew members left the ship. In May, she sailed for Bikini in the Marshall Islands, where she was to act as a target vessel in America's first post-war atomic bomb tests. At 0900 on 1 July 1946, an atomic bomb dropped by a B-29 bomber detonated at just over 150m (500ft) above the fleet of target ships. *Prinz Eugen*, moored 1090m (1194yds) away from the point of the explosion, survived the test undamaged.

On 25 July 1946, she was subjected to an underwater atomic test at a range of 1819m (1990yds). Again, she survived with no apparent structural damage, but she was heavily contaminated by radioactivity. Towed to Kwajalein Atoll, she was decommissioned on 29 August 1946 and plans were made to use her as a naval torpedo and gunnery target. On 21 December that year, she took on a 35° list to starboard as a result of minor damage sustained to her stern. Salvage crews could not be brought in, but she was towed to Enubuj Reef, where she capsized the next day.

The US government refused to allow her to be scrapped because of the danger that her radioactive steel might enter the world market. She lies there still, with the exception of her 12.2-tonne (12-ton) port propeller, which was removed in 1978 at the request of former crew members and now stands as a memorial near Kiel.

## FATE OF OTHER WARSHIPS

Of the other major warships that had fought in the Baltic, the *Admiral Scheer*,

A captured German U-boat being used as a target by an American submarine. Note the torpedo track in the water. Captured German warships were used in various weapons trials.

capsized by RAF 'Tallboy' bombs at Kiel on 9 April 1945, was partially scrapped and the remains buried under rubble when the basin was filled in to make a new quay after the war. Her sister ship, the *Lützow*, also crippled by 'Tallboys', lay where she was beached at Swinemünde until the 1960s, when she was broken up. The hulk of the battlecruiser *Gneisenau* remained where she had been sunk as a blockship in Gdynia harbour until 1947, when work began on breaking her up. The heavy cruiser *Admiral Hipper*, heavily damaged by RAF bombing while in dry dock at Kiel in April 1945, was scuttled by explosive charges on 2 May. Refloated in 1946, she was towed to Heikendorf Bay, where she was broken up in 1948–49.

The fate of the light cruiser *Nürnberg* has already been described. Of the others, *Leipzig*, patched up and thrown into the last Baltic battle, served as an accommodation ship for the German Minesweeping Administration after the war. On 20 July 1946, she was sunk in the North Sea, laden with poison gas shells. The light cruiser *Köln*, which

had been used as a training ship in the Baltic, was heavily damaged by the RAF during a refit at Wilhelmshaven on 3 March 1945, settling on the bottom with her superstructure above water. She was scrapped in 1946.

The *Emden*, whose last duty had been to bear the coffins of Field Marshal Hindenburg and his wife from the Tannenberg Memorial, was heavily damaged by RAF bombing at Kiel, and scuttled at Heikendorf Bay on 3 May 1945. The wreck was broken up on the spot in 1949.

The aircraft carrier *Graf Zeppelin*, partly complete and scuttled by the Germans at Stettin in January 1945, was raided by the Soviets in 1946. On 7 April 1947, she was taken under tow to Leningrad, her flight deck laden with war booty. Later, she was towed out into the Baltic and used as a floating target for Soviet warships and aircraft in August 1947. The location of her wreck was unknown until 2006, when it was discovered in the southern Baltic.

# World War II
## The Pacific Theatre 1944–1945

For the United States Navy, operations in the Pacific began in earnest on 29 January 1944. Six heavy and six light aircraft carriers, operating in four groups of Task Force 58, opened the campaign to capture the Marshall Islands with heavy air attacks on Maleolap, Kwajalein and Wotje. By the end of the first day, the Japanese air forces in the area had been eliminated. Eight escort carriers also arrived in the area early in the morning of D-Day, their aircraft flying top cover and anti-submarine for the invasion fleet and providing air support for the landings. To neutralize Wake Island during the Marshalls operation, two squadrons of Consolidated PB2Y Coronados made the first of four night bombing attacks on that objective, the missions involving a round trip of 3218km (2000 miles).

On 17 February, the first strike on Truk was carried out by the Truk Striking Force, built around three fast carrier groups. In two days, the carriers launched 1250 combat sorties against this key naval base, sinking 37 war and merchant ships and inflicting heavy damage on base installations. In this operation, the first night-bombing attack in the history of US naval aviation was carried out by 12 radar-equipped TBF-1C Avengers of VT-10 from the USS *Enterprise*. Japanese aircraft made several night attacks on the task force and the USS *Intrepid* was hit by a torpedo. A week later, two carrier groups of Task Force 58 attacked targets on Saipan,

Allied warships beating off a Japanese air attack in the Pacific. The biggest threat to the Allied naval task forces came from the kamikaze suicide pilots, active from October 1944.

## INTREPID

**Type:** Aircraft carrier

**Launch date:** 26 April 1943

**Crew:** 2600

**Displacement:** 24,585 tonnes (27,100 tons)

**Dimensions:** 265.8m x 45m x 10.8m (872ft x 147ft 6in x 34ft 2in)

**Range:** 37,000km (20,000nm) at 15 knots

**Armament:** 4 twin 127mm (5in) 38-calibre guns; 4 single 127mm

(5in) 38-calibre guns; 8 quadruple 40mm (1.57in) 56-calibre
guns; 46 single 20mm (0.79in) 78-calibre guns; 90–100 aircraft

**Powerplant:** 4 geared steam turbines

**Performance:** 33 knots

Tinian, Rota and Guam for the dual purpose of reducing enemy air strength in the Marianas and gathering photographic intelligence for the forthcoming invasion. Japanese aircraft attempted to attack the carriers as they approached their flying-off positions; 67 were shot down and 101 destroyed on the ground.

On 30 March, in an operation designed to eliminate opposition to Allied landings at Hollandia and to gather intelligence, 11 carriers of Task Force 58 launched a series of attacks on Palau, Yap, Ulithi and Woleai atolls in the western Carolines. Palau harbour was mined by Torpedo Squadrons 2, 8 and 16, the first such mission by carrier aircraft and the first large-scale mining operation of the Pacific war. The attacks accounted for 157 enemy aircraft destroyed, 28 ships of 109,733 tonnes (108,000 tons) sunk, and the denial of Palau harbour for an estimated six weeks.

### EASTERN FLEET

In the Indian Ocean, the Royal Navy's Eastern Fleet had been steadily gathering its strength, and in January 1944, the British naval presence in the Indian Ocean was strengthened by the arrival at Colombo of the battleships *Queen Elizabeth* and *Valiant*, the battlecruiser *Renown*, the carriers

*Illustrious* and *Unicorn*, two cruisers and seven destroyers, the whole force having made a fast passage through the Mediterranean after leaving Scapa Flow and the Clyde a month earlier. A little later, the fleet was further strengthened by the arrival of the French battleship *Richelieu*.

In April 1944, the principal units of the Eastern Fleet made rendezvous with the American carrier *Saratoga*, loaned to the Royal Navy at Admiral Somerville's request to enable him to mount a big strike against Japanese targets in Sumatra. Operation Cockpit took place on 19 April, when *Illustrious* and *Saratoga* launched 83 aircraft in an attack on Sabang harbour and neighbouring airfields in the Netherlands East Indies. Two Japanese fighters were sunk and severe damage caused to the harbour installations; 25 aircraft were destroyed on the ground and three out of four G4M bombers attempting to attack the carriers were shot down. Only one aircraft, a Hellcat, was lost. A second operation, against the Japanese aviation fuel dump at Soerabaja, Java, was less successful.

A Japanese fuel dump ablaze at Aitape, New Guinea, after a successful attack by US Navy dive-bombers. The Japanese forces were starved of fuel, due to American air and submarine activity.

After this attack, the *Saratoga*, having been ordered to return to the United States for a refit, left the main force and sailed for Pearl Harbor.

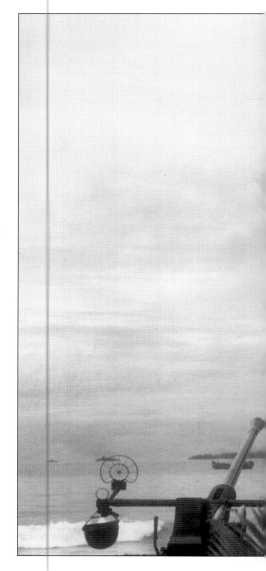

Back in the Pacific, in April, aircraft from five heavy and seven light carriers of Task Force 58 attacked airfields in the Hollandia area of New Guinea, covering Allied landings there. Thirty enemy aircraft were destroyed in the air and 103 on the ground. Later, Allied forces found 340 wrecked enemy aircraft on the Hollandia airfields. The relentless attacks continued into June, and on the 11th seven heavy and three light carriers of Task Force 58 began the campaign to occupy the Marianas with a late-afternoon fighter sweep that destroyed one-third of the defending air force. During the next three days, the carrier aircraft carried out intensive bombing and strafing attacks on shore installations and shipping, preparing the way for an amphibious assault on Saipan that took place on 15 June.

The action that became known as the Battle of the Philippine Sea began on 19 June, when Japanese carrier aircraft from the *Taiho*, *Zuikaku* and *Shokaku* (601st Air Group), *Hiyo*, *Junyo* and *Ryuho* (62nd Air Group) and *Chitose*, *Chiyoda* and *Zuiho* (653rd Air Group), together with shore-based aircraft, launched a day-long attack on Task Force 58. The enemy aircraft were detected by radar at a range of 240km (150 miles), and the carrier fighters were waiting for them. The great air battle that followed was a one-sided massacre that would go down in history as the 'Marianas Turkey Shoot'. American combat air patrols and anti-aircraft fire destroyed 325 enemy aircraft, including 220 of the 328 launched by Japanese aircraft carriers. American losses were 16 Hellcats in combat, and seven other aircraft shot down by Japanese fighters or ground fire. Many of the aircraft were destroyed by the gunfire of US battleships, deployed in a battle line 24km (13nm) to the east of the American carriers.

## LEYTE GULF
In October 1944, the reconquest of the Philippines began with the American landings at Leyte. On

# In three weeks of action, the Task Force claimed 600 enemy aircraft and destroyed and sank 330,215 tonnes (325,000 tons) of shipping.

learning of the invasion, the C-in-C Japanese Combined Fleet, Admiral Toyoda, ordered Vice-Admiral Kurita's Centre Force to sail from Brunei in Borneo on 22 October with the battleships *Yamato, Musashi, Nagato, Kongo* and *Haruna*, two cruisers and 15 destroyers. This was followed by Vice-Admiral Nishimura's Southern Force, with the battleships *Fuso, Yamashiro*, one cruiser and four destroyers.

On 24 October, the Centre Force was attacked by four waves of American aircraft from the Fast Carrier Force. During these attacks,

**A photograph taken from the USS *Lexington* during an attack on Saipan. The warship in the foreground is a 'South Dakota' class battleship, with an 'Essex' class aircraft carrier beyond.**

the *Musashi* was hit by 10 bombs and six torpedoes and sank in about eight hours, with the loss of 1039 of her crew. The *Yamato* was also hit by two bombs, but these had little effect on her. Japanese air attacks resulted in the loss of the light carrier USS *Princeton*. In the Southern Force, the *Fuso* was sunk by gunfire and torpedoes in Surigao Strait. This force was then engaged by the battleships *West Virginia, California, Tennessee, Maryland* and *Mississippi*, as well as US and Australian cruisers. Vice-Admiral Nishimura's flagship, the *Yamashiro*, was sunk, hit by numerous shells and three torpedoes; her commander went down with her.

The Japanese were to suffer still more losses. At dawn on 25 October, Task Force 34 was formed from the

US battleships *Iowa, New Jersey, Washington, Alabama, Massachusetts* and *Indiana*, four cruisers and 10 destroyers with the objective of destroying a diversionary force, approaching from the north under Vice-Admiral Ozawa. Instead, Admiral Halsey, flying his flag on *New Jersey*, took his ships south to hunt down what remained of Kurita's force, leaving carrier aircraft to deal with Ozawa. This tactic proved successful, and the carriers *Chitose, Zuikaku, Zuiho* and *Chiyoda*, as well as a destroyer, were all sunk.

## KAMIKAZES

The year 1945 opened with the invasion of Luzon, the largest of the Philippine islands, on 3 January. During the invasion and occupation of Luzon by Southwest Pacific Forces, which were supported by seven heavy and four light carriers of Task Force 38 and 17 escort carriers of Task Group 77.4, Kamikaze aircraft again provided serious opposition, sinking the *Ommaney Bay* and damaging the *Manila Bay, Savo Island, Kadashan Bay* and *Salamaua*. Task Force 38,

operating in bad weather, carried out attacks on Luzon, Formosa and the Ryukus, destroying more than 100 enemy aircraft and sinking 40,642 tonnes (40,000 tons) of shipping in the first week of operations. The task force then made a high-speed run through Luzon Strait for operations in the South China Sea, where strike aircraft sank a further 151,391 tonnes

**Survivors of the American light aircraft carrier USS *Princeton*, sunk by fire and explosions after being hit by aircraft bombs at the Battle of Leyte Gulf, 24 October 1944.**

(149,000 tons) of shipping before moving north to the Hong Kong area and concluding with operations against Formosa and Okinawa. In three weeks of action, the Task Force claimed 600 enemy aircraft destroyed and sank 330,215 tonnes (325,000 tons) of shipping. Two carriers, the *Ticonderoga* and *Langley*, were damaged by air attack.

## FIRST OF THE KAMIKAZES

**The Battle of Leyte Gulf spelled ruin for the Imperial Japanese Navy. Its carriers were gone, and although it still had surface warships, most were confined to harbour through lack of fuel. Losses at sea continued, too. On 21 November, the battleship *Kongo* was torpedoed and sunk by the US submarine *Sealion* northwest of Keelung. Even so, the Allies had a clear indication of the assault on the last Pacific islands before Japan itself, for the Battle of Leyte witnessed the first planned attacks by Japanese Kamikaze (Divine Wind) suicide pilots. In October 1944, four 'special attack' units were operational in the Philippines, each equipped with 12 Zeros armed with a pair of 227kg (500lb) bombs. The suicide pilots' primary targets were the aircraft carriers, and off Leyte they sank the escort carrier *St Lo* and damaged the *Sangamon*, *Suwannee*, *Santee*, *White Plains*, *Kalinin Bay* and *Kitkun Bay*. Further Kamikaze attacks damaged the carriers *Intrepid*, *Franklin* and *Belleau Wood*; the *Intrepid* was hit again in November, and the *Lexington*, *Essex* and *Cabot* were also damaged.**

## OIL REFINERIES

On 24 January 1945, British strike aircraft from the carriers HMS *Illustrious*, HMS *Victorious*, HMS *Indomitable* and HMS *Indefatigable* carried out a heavy attack on Japanese oil refineries at Palembang, Sumatra, while en route from Ceylon to the Pacific. A second strike was made five

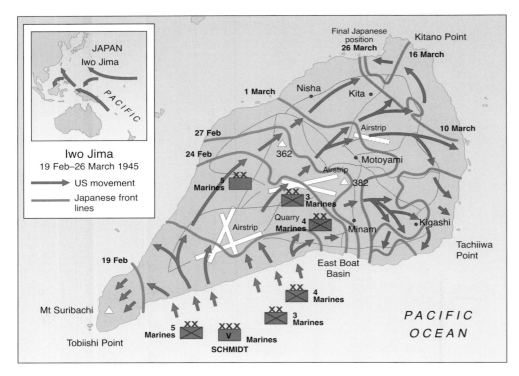

**Iwo Jima**
19 Feb–26 March 1945

→ US movement
— Japanese front lines

A map showing the American invasion and conquest of the island of Iwo Jima. Both sides suffered terrible casualties before the island was secured.

Damage crews struggle to put out the blaze after the aircraft carrier USS *Saratoga* was hit by four Kamikazes in rapid succession on 21 February 1945. She survived, only to be sunk in the US atomic bomb tests at Bikini in July 1946.

648 enemy aircraft and sunk 30,480 tonnes (30,000 tons) of merchant shipping. Kamikazes were again in evidence during the Iwo Jima operations, sinking the escort carrier *Bismarck Sea* and seriously damaging the *Saratoga* in a dusk attack on 21 February.

Between 18 and 22 March, 10 heavy and six light carriers launched heavy neutralization air strikes on the Japanese island of Kyushu prior to the US landings on Okinawa. Air attacks accounted for 482 enemy aircraft and another 46 were destroyed by ships' gunfire. On 21 March, 16 Mitsubishi G4M2 aircraft of the 721st Kokutai, each carrying a *Yokusaka Ohka* (Cherry Blossom) rocket-powered piloted suicide bomb on a mission against TF 58, were intercepted and forced to release their weapons short of the target. This was the *Ohka*'s

days later. During the two attacks, Fleet Air Arm Corsairs and Hellcats destroyed 30 enemy aircraft in air combat; many more were destroyed on the ground. On 19 March 1945, the British Pacific Fleet, having assembled in Sydney, arrived at Ulithi Atoll in the Caroline Islands. There, as Task Force 57, it formed part of the US Fifth Fleet. As well as the four British aircraft carriers, TF 57 consisted of the battleships *King George V* and *Howe*, the cruisers *Swiftsure*, *Gambia* (RNZN), *Black Prince*, *Euryalus*, *Argonaut* and 11 destroyers.

Meanwhile, on 16 February, 11 heavy and five light carriers of Task Force 58 launched a two-day series of heavy attacks on airfields in the Tokyo

area in a covering operation for the US landings on Iwo Jima, which began on 19 February. The Task Force then moved south to support the landings before returning for a strike on Tokyo on 25 February. After attacking Okinawa and the Ryukus on 1 March, the Task Force returned to Ulithi Atoll, by which time it had destroyed

The might of American naval power is epitomised by this line of aircraft carriers belonging to Task Force 38, the fast striking force that brought destruction to one Japanese-occupied island after another.

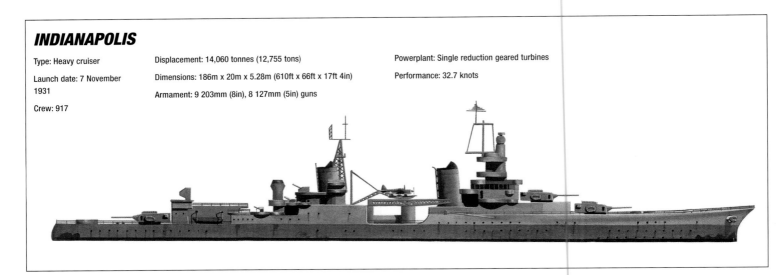

## INDIANAPOLIS

Type: Heavy cruiser

Launch date: 7 November 1931

Crew: 917

Displacement: 14,060 tonnes (12,755 tons)

Dimensions: 186m x 20m x 5.28m (610ft x 66ft x 17ft 4in)

Armament: 9 203mm (8in), 8 127mm (5in) guns

Powerplant: Single reduction geared turbines

Performance: 32.7 knots

first operation, and it revealed the missile's biggest drawback: the vulnerability of its carrier aircraft. The weapon's first success came on 1 April, when one hit and damaged the battleship *West Virginia*. The first Allied ship to be sunk by an Ohka was the USS *Mannert L. Abele*, lost off Okinawa on 12 April.

On 26 March, the four aircraft carriers and escorting warships of the British Pacific Fleet (Task Force 57) began operations south of Okinawa, their aircraft neutralizing airfields on Sakishima Gunto and Formosa and intercepting air raids heading for the Okinawa assault area. On 1 April, the Japanese appeared over the fleet in

strength; first high-level bombers, and then the Kamikazes. Most of the latter were shot down by the combat air patrol before they came within striking distance, but one managed to break through and hit the *Indefatigable* at the base of her island. If she had been an American carrier, with less armoured deck protection, the aircraft would have torn through and exploded in the hangar below. As it was, there was a delay of about 45 minutes while the wreckage was shovelled over the side, and then the *Indefatigable* carried on almost as if nothing had happened. All four British carriers were hit in Kamikaze attacks, but thanks to their armoured flight decks, which significantly reduced damage, all remained operational, a fact that effectively silenced some senior American officers who had criticised the relatively slow speed of the British carriers, a penalty imposed by their heavier armour protection.

### OKINAWA DAMAGE

During operations in March, Kamikaze attacks also damaged the

**Damage to the bridge of the destroyer USS *Bowers* after the ship was hit by a Kamikaze during the battle for Okinawa, April 1945. The US Navy suffered serious losses in these attacks.**

US carriers *Enterprise, Intrepid, Yorktown, Franklin* and *Wasp*. Ten US battleships lent their weight to the Fire Support Group during the

Okinawa invasion; they were the USS *Texas* and *Maryland* (Group 1, with one cruiser and four destroyers); *Arkansas* and *Colorado* (Group 2, with

two cruisers and five destroyers); *Tennessee* and *Nevada* (Group 3, with two cruisers and six destroyers); *Idaho* and *West Virginia* (Group 4, with three cruisers and six destroyers); and *New Mexico* and *New York* (Group 5, with two cruisers and seven destroyers). In addition, the battleships *New Jersey, Wisconsin, Missouri, Massachusetts* and *Indiana* participated in softening-up bombardments prior to the invasion, while the British battleships *King George V* and *Howe* joined naval aircraft in bombarding enemy airfields in the Sakishima Gunto island group southwest of Okinawa.

The *Indianapolis* (Fleet Flagship of Admiral Pruance, commanding the US Fifth Fleet), *West Virginia, Nevada* and *Maryland* were all damaged during the intense series of Kamikaze attacks that accompanied the preliminary bombardment of Okinawa and the landing phase itself, which took place between 1 and 5 April 1945.

## SUICIDE AT SEA

On 6 April, a Japanese task force under Vice-Admiral Ito sailed from Tokuyama, on Japan's Inland Sea, on what amounted to a suicide mission. At its heart was the mighty battleship *Yamato*, flying the flag of Rear-Admiral Ariaga. The battleship was accompanied by the cruiser *Yahagi* (Capt Hara, with the Commander of the 2nd Destroyer Flotilla, Rear-Admiral Komura, on board); and eight destroyers. The battle group's destination was Okinawa, and its objective was to inflict as much damage as possible on the US invasion fleet. It would be a one-way mission; a critical shortage of fuel ensured that there could be no return to port.

The assault on Okinawa. The Japanese threw everything they had into a desperate attempt to shatter the Allied invasion fleet, using Kamikazes on a massive scale.

273

It was unfortunate for the Japanese that their progress was reported by the crew of a B-29 bomber and then by two US submarines. Early on 7 April, the warships were sighted by reconnaissance aircraft, and at 1000 hours the American carriers off Okinawa launched a strike of 280 aircraft. In the first attack, the cruiser *Yahagi* and the destroyer *Hamakaze* were sunk; the battleship was hit by two bombs and a torpedo.

A second strike of 100 aircraft was launched at 1400. Its first victims were the destroyers *Isozake*, *Asashimo* and *Kasumi*. Then, after taking nine more torpedo and three bomb hits, the *Yamato* began to flood uncontrollably and develop a serious list. Finally, after the order to abandon ship had been given, she rolled over and blew up in a tremendous explosion, probably caused when internal fires reached her magazines. The loss of life was enormous: 3665 Japanese sailors perished, 2498 of them on the *Yamato* herself. Of the 386 American aircraft that took part in the attacks, only 10 failed to return.

The Kamikaze attacks that took place in April and May caused the US Navy the heaviest losses it had sustained in any campaign. Twenty-eight ships were sunk and 131 damaged, with 4900 men killed and missing. *Kaiten* one-man suicide torpedoes were also deployed during the Okinawa campaign; the Japanese submarine *I-8* was modified to carry four *Kaiten* in place of her aircraft hangar, but she was sunk by the destroyers USS *Morrison* and *Stockton* on 30 March 1945 while attempting to attack American ships involved in the Okinawa landings. *Kaiten* were used again at intervals during the following weeks, but met with little success.

Early in June, the US Fast Carrier Task Force, now designated TF38 under Admiral Halsey and operating to the east of Okinawa, was hit by a typhoon, and almost all the ships sustained varying degrees of damage, as did those of the vital Logistic Support Force. The most seriously

**The aircraft carrier HMS *Implacable* was one of four British fleet carriers to serve in the closing months of the Pacific War. Their armoured flight decks protected them when attacked.**

damaged vessel was the cruiser USS *Pittsburgh*, which had 35m (115ft) of her bows torn away. After three months of continuous operations, the Fast Carrier Task Force sailed for Leyte for repair and replenishment before returning to the combat zone for operations against the Japanese Home Islands.

## STRIKE ON JAPAN

Towards the end of June, the fleet carrier HMS *Implacable* joined the British Pacific Fleet at Manus anchorage, in the Admiralty Islands. The carrier had arrived in the Pacific three weeks earlier, and on 12 June, accompanied by the escort carrier *Ruler*, the cruisers *Swiftsure*, *Newfoundland*, *Uganda*, *Achilles* and five destroyers, she carried out a two-day series of strikes against the badly battered Japanese base at Truk. Now, fully worked up to operational standards, she replaced the *Indomitable*, which departed for a refit. The *Illustrious* had already been withdrawn from the task force in April, suffering from an accumulation of technical troubles that were the consequence of four years of combat operations. The fleet, under Vice-Admirals Rawlings and Vian and now designated Task Force 37, sailed from Manus on 9 July to join the US Task Force 38 under Admiral J.S. McCain in Japanese waters.

On 14 July, the Task Force launched over 1300 aircraft in attacks on targets in northern Honshu and southern Hokkaido. The attacks were repeated on 15 July, and for the first time American battleships – the *South Dakota*, *Indiana* and *Massachusetts* – shelled targets on the Japanese main islands. The British task force arrived on 17 July with the carriers *Formidable*, *Victorious* and *Implacable*, supported by the battleship *King George V*, seven cruisers and 15 destroyers, and lent its weight to the onslaught.

Towards the end of July, operations were delayed for nine days because of bad weather and the dropping of the first atomic bomb on the Japanese city of Hiroshima on 6 August. On the 9th, the day that a second atomic bomb obliterated Nagasaki, the attacks were resumed by a powerful British task force comprising the carriers *Victorious*, *Indefatigable*, *Formidable* and *Implacable*, the battleships *Duke of York* (flagship of Admiral Sir Bruce Fraser, C-in-C British Pacific Fleet), *King George V*, six cruisers and 17 destroyers.

This time, the main target was a concentration of shipping in Onagawa Wan. Shortly after sunrise, a strike of four Corsairs was flown off by the *Formidable*. Over Onagawa, the pilots sighted five enemy destroyers and escorts anchored around the fringes of the bay. While two of the fighter-bombers strafed enemy anti-aircraft positions and a third provided top cover, the leader – Canadian-born Lieutenant Robert Hampton Gray,

The Japanese surrender delegation photographed on board the battleship USS *Missouri* in Tokyo Bay on 15 September 1945. Starved of natural resources, Japan never had any real hope of defeating the United States.

who had won the DSC for his part in the *Tirpitz* strikes the year before – dived towards the escort sloop *Amakusa*. His aircraft was hit and was quickly enveloped in flames, but he pressed home his attack and his 454kg (1000lb) bomb sank the enemy vessel. Gray was awarded a posthumous Victoria Cross, the last to be won in World War II.

On 15 August, Fleet Admiral Chester Nimitz, C-in-C, Pacific Fleet, issued orders that all hostilities against the Empire of Japan were to cease. On 2 September, representatives of the Japanese government and armed forces signed the instrument of surrender in Tokyo Bay aboard the fleet flagship USS *Missouri*, bringing to an end the costliest war in the history of mankind.

# The Cold War Era

## 1945–present

**At the end of World War II, it was abundantly clear to the world's navies that the aircraft carrier, with its long-range striking power and its own air defence, would be the capital ship of the future. The war had shown that the battleship, bereft of air cover, was a vulnerable target to air attack, especially when stand-off missiles were used against it. The sinking of the Italian battleship *Roma* in September 1943 was a case in point.**

The immediate post-war years witnessed the reduction of the world's existing capital ships with almost unseemly haste. Of the US Navy's old reconstructed dreadnoughts, the USS *Nevada*, *Pennsylvania*, *New York* and *Arkansas* were expended as target ships in the American nuclear tests at Bikini Atoll in the Pacific. The *Arkansas* was sunk in the second test on 25 July 1946; the *Nevada*, *Pennsylvania* and *New York* all survived, to be decommissioned in 1946 and sunk as targets by aircraft and gunfire off Hawaii and Kwajalein in July 1948. Of the two 'New Mexico' class battleships, *Idaho* was decommissioned and broken up in the following year. *Mississippi* served on for some years after the war as a training and experimental gunnery ship before being deactivated and broken up in 1956. *Tennessee* and *California* were both decommissioned in 1957 and broken up in 1959, as were *Colorado*, *Maryland* and *West Virginia*. *North Carolina* had a better fate; in 1961, she was transferred to the care of the state, after which she was named and preserved as a memorial at Wilmington. There was no

The Russian aircraft carrier *Kiev* made its appearance in 1976, complete with its complement of Yakovlev Yak-38 VSTOL strike fighters. It was followed by two more in the same class, *Minsk* and *Novorossiysk*.

## NORTH CAROLINA

Type: Battleship

Launch date: 13 June 1940

Crew: 1880

Displacement: 47,518 tonnes (46,770 tons)

Dimensions: 222m x 33m x 10m (728ft 9in x 108ft 3in x 32ft 10in)

Range: 32,334km (17,450nm) at 12 knots

Armament: 9 400mm (16in) and 20 127mm (5in) guns

Powerplant: Quadruple screw turbines

Performance: 28 knots

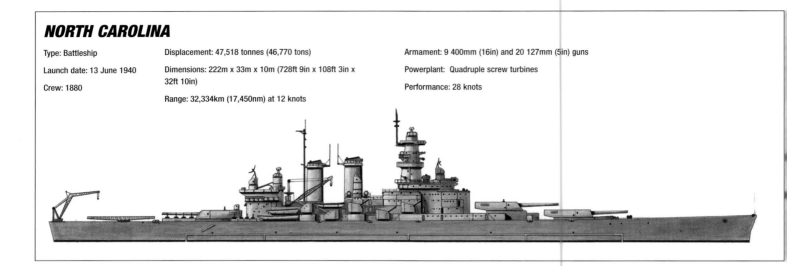

such happy outcome for the USS *Washington*, which was broken up in 1961. The *Alabama* was also preserved at Mobile by the state whose name she bore, and *Massachusetts* became a memorial at Fall River, but *South Dakota* went to the breaker's yard in 1962 and *Indiana* followed her a year later. Now only the four powerful 'Iowa' class remained. Their careers, however, were far from over, and they were to be given the chance to see active service again in various conflicts around the world.

All but the *Missouri* had been deactivated in 1948–49. The *Missouri*, the ship on which Japan's surrender was accepted by General Douglas MacArthur on behalf of the Allies, served with the Atlantic Fleet until 1950. She suffered a mishap in January of that year when she went aground in Thimble Shoal, Chesapeake Bay. She was refloated a fortnight later and deployed to Korean waters for bombardment duty. In 1951–52, she served once again with the Atlantic Fleet before returning to Korea for another tour of duty. She was then decommissioned in 1955.

### BREAKER'S YARD

The Royal Navy was quick to dispose of its battleships once hostilities were over. The *Nelson* and *Rodney* both went

> The Royal Navy was quick to dispose of its battleships once hostilities were over. The *Nelson* and *Rodney* both went to the breaker's yard in 1948.

to the breaker's yard in 1948. Of the 'King George V' class, the *Anson* returned from Far Eastern waters in 1946 to be placed in reserve, and was eventually broken up in 1957; the *Duke of York*, having deployed to the Pacific too late to take part in the final battles against the Japanese, was also laid up in reserve in 1951 and broken up in 1958. The *Howe*, veteran of battles from the Atlantic to Okinawa, suffered a similar fate, as did the *King George V*, the class leader having been decommissioned in September 1949.

Of the old 'Queen Elizabeth' class, HMS *Warspite*, as though protesting her fate, ran aground and was wrecked in Mounts Bay, Cornwall, while under tow to the breaker's yard in April 1947. Her sisters, the *Valiant* and *Queen Elizabeth*, were both broken up in 1948.

The 'Lion' class of 1938–39 – enlarged 'King George V' types with 406mm (16in) guns, which were to have been named *Conqueror*, *Lion*,

*Thunderer* and *Temeraire* – was never built. Only one British battleship was laid down during the war, in 1941; she was HMS *Vanguard*, also an enlarged 'King George V' type of 45,215 tonnes (44,500 tons). Launched in 1944, she was commissioned too late to see service in World War II. Her four twin turrets mounted 380mm (15in) guns originally used in the light battlecruisers *Courageous* and *Glorious* before their conversion to aircraft carriers; she also carried 16 133mm (5.25in) guns and a very heavy AA armament of 71 40mm (1.6in) Bofors guns. She carried a complement of 1600.

### LAST BATTLESHIP

In 1947, *Vanguard* made a royal tour to South Africa and in 1949 served

HMS *Vanguard* was the last of the Royal Navy's battleships. Completed too late to see service in World War II, she was placed on the Reserve in 1956 and broken up at Faslane in 1960.

briefly in the Mediterranean before being placed on the reserve in 1946. She was decommissioned and sent to the breaker's yard at Faslane in 1960, the last battleship to serve in the Royal Navy. At one point in her short career, in 1953, *Vanguard* exercised with the American battleships *Iowa* and *Wisconsin* in the Atlantic. It was the last time that an Anglo-American battleship force put to sea together.

France continued to operate her two battleships, the *Richelieu* and the *Jean Bart*, for some years after the war. The former was used for fire support duty during the French operations in Indo-China in 1945–46; she was placed in reserve in 1956 and broken up in 1960. The *Jean Bart*, damaged at Casablanca by gunfire from the USS *Massachusetts* and air attack in November 1942, was towed to Cherbourg after the war and completed at Brest. In 1956, she operated in support of ground forces and in an anti-aircraft role during the Anglo-French operations in the Suez Canal Zone. From 1961, she was used as a gunnery training ship, being broken up in 1970.

Of the Italian battleships that had surrendered to the Allies in 1943, two (the *Littorio* and *Vittorio Veneto*) were interned until February 1946, when they were returned to Italy. Both were stricken in 1948 and broken up in 1960. The *Andrea Doria*, after internment at Malta, was briefly used as a training ship by the Italian Co-Belligerent Navy in 1944 before being inactivated. Reactivated in 1949, she was once again used for training until 1956, when she was stricken. She was broken up at La Spezia in 1961, where the *Caio Duilio*, also interned at Malta and subsequently used for training, had been broken up in 1957. Italy's other battleship, the *Giulio Cesare*, was transferred to the Soviet Union under peace-treaty terms in 1948 and renamed *Novorossiysk*. Assigned to the Black Sea Fleet, she blew up and sank in Sevastopol harbour on 4 November 1955.

## SOVIET BATTLESHIPS

The Soviets had laid down four new battleships in 1937. These were the *Sovietski Soyuz*, *Sovietskaya Bielorossia*, *Sovietskaya Rossia*, and *Sovietskaya*

*Ukraina*. Difficulties in obtaining construction materials seriously delayed the building programme, and two were abandoned in 1940. The *Sovietski Soyuz* was ready for launching when the German invasion of June 1941 brought a halt to further work on her, and she was broken up on the slip in 1948–50. The *Sovietskaya Ukraina* was 75 per cent complete when she was captured by the Germans at Nikolayev; they destroyed the ship to prevent her being launched after their retreat from the Crimea, and she was broken up between 1944 and 1947.

The Soviet Navy consequently had only three indigenous battleships in commission during World War II, all belonging to the 'Gangut' class of 1908 dreadnoughts. One of these, the *Marat* (formerly the *Petropavlovsk*) was severely damaged on 23 September 1941 during an attack on Kronstadt harbour by Ju 87 Stuka dive-bombers,

The battleship *Littorio* was named after Lictor, an official of ancient Rome who bore the *fasces*, the bundle of sticks adopted by the Fascists as their symbol.

# GANGUT

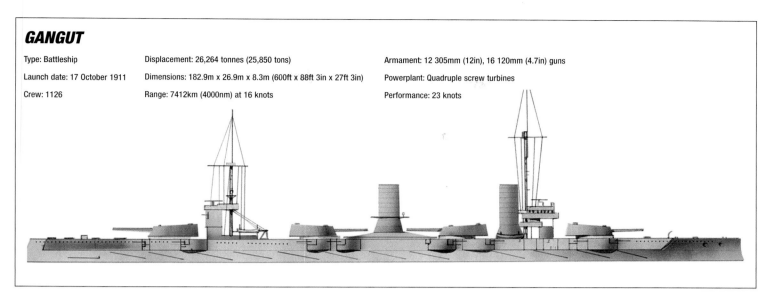

| | | |
|---|---|---|
| Type: Battleship | Displacement: 26,264 tonnes (25,850 tons) | Armament: 12 305mm (12in), 16 120mm (4.7in) guns |
| Launch date: 17 October 1911 | Dimensions: 182.9m x 26.9m x 8.3m (600ft x 88ft 3in x 27ft 3in) | Powerplant: Quadruple screw turbines |
| Crew: 1126 | Range: 7412km (4000nm) at 16 knots | Performance: 23 knots |

her bow and 'A' turret being destroyed and resting on the bottom. Refloated in 1943, she became a training ship, renamed *Volkhov*, and was broken up in 1953.

The second battleship, the *Oktabrskaya Revolutsia*, was the original *Gangut*, having been renamed in 1925. She was used for bombardment duty during the brief winter war with Finland in 1939–40, and later for the defence of Leningrad. During the air attack on Kronstadt on 23 September 1941, she was hit by six bombs and severely damaged; and on 4 April 1942, she was hit by another four bombs. She was broken up at Kronstadt in 1956–59.

That left the *Sevastopol*, which was named the *Parizhskaya Kommuna* from 1921 to 1943, when she reverted to her original nomenclature. Serving with the Black Sea Fleet, she was used in the defence of Sevastopol in 1941–42. Damaged by German air attack in September 1942, she was not repaired until 1946, being broken up in 1957.

In May 1944, the British battleship *Royal Sovereign* was loaned to the Soviet Navy and renamed *Archangel*. In service with the Arctic Fleet, she went aground and was damaged in the Barents Sea in 1947. In February 1949, she was returned to Great Britain and broken up. The Soviets also planned to build two 39,036-tonne (38,420-ton) battlecruisers, the *Moskva* and *Stalingrad*, during the war, but construction only began afterwards and was abandoned following a change of policy. The *Moskva* was broken up on the stocks in 1954 and the *Stalingrad*, launched in 1953 when 60 per cent complete, was used for weapons trials before being grounded off the Crimea in 1954, to end her days as a target ship.

## WAR IN KOREA

Combat requirements in Korea were quite different from those of the Pacific island-hopping campaign of World War II. Only the amphibious landing at Inchon, 10 weeks after the start of the conflict, followed the familiar pattern. Mainly as a result of conditions imposed by the United Nations, which confined the battle area to the Korean peninsula, air operations in support of ground forces were limited in their scope. This was a normal enough experience for carrier air, but the need to sustain

## TIME OF TRANSITION

**The outbreak of the Korean War in June 1950 caught the armed forces of the United States in the middle of a period of transition. The establishment of the Department of Defence in 1949 had required major readjustments within the services, and they were still in the process of becoming acclimatized. Successive cuts in the military budget and the promise of more to come had reduced the size of all services, and the reorganization of existing forces to keep them within prescribed limits was in progress. New weapons and equipment had not been completely integrated, and tactical doctrine and new techniques for their most effective deployment were still being evolved. This was particularly apparent in naval aviation, where the introduction of jet aircraft had created a composite force in which carrier air groups were equipped with either jet or piston-engined types that had wide differences in performance characteristics, maintenance and support requirements, and tactical application.**

operations for extended periods over a large land mass was a new experience. Carrier-based aircraft also flew deep support missions; attacked enemy supply lines; roamed over enemy territory seeking targets of opportunity; bombed bridges; interdicted highways and railroads; attacked refineries, railway yards and hydroelectric plants; and escorted land-based bombers. All these tasks were carried out effectively, but were new experiences for units trained to interdict enemy communications on the sea lanes and to provide defence against attack by enemy naval forces.

General Douglas MacArthur, Commander-in-Chief of the Allied forces in Korea, surveys the progress of the Inchon landings from the amphibious force flagship *Mount McKinley*.

> In comparison to the forces engaged in World War II, Korea was a small war. At no time were more than four large carriers in action at the same time.

In comparison to the forces engaged in World War II, Korea was a small war. At no time were more than four large carriers in action at the same time. Yet in the three years of the Korean War, in terms of combined effort, combat sorties flown by Navy and Marine Corps aircraft rose from less than 10 per cent in World War II to more than 30 per cent in Korea.

There was another, and perhaps a greater difference between the two wars. Although the support of the forces in Korea required major attention from the planners and of the units assigned to logistic supply, the action in Korea was only a part of the total activity of the period.

**FIRST STRIKES**
The first two carriers to see action in the Korean War were the USS *Valley Forge* and the British HMS *Triumph*, the latter having been in

action earlier against communist terrorists in Malaya. Together, these two craft formed the nucleus of Task Force 77. The North Korean Air Force's airfields were early targets for the naval aircraft, and on 18 and 19 July they were heavily attacked by aircraft of Task Force 77, which claimed the destruction of 32 enemy aircraft on the ground and a further 13 damaged. The naval aircraft also hit railroads and factories at

Hungham, Hamhung, Numpyong and Wonsan, where particularly heavy damage was inflicted on the oil refinery by Skyraiders and Corsair. During the remainder of the month, TF 77 struck deep behind enemy lines and flew close support missions as required, the carriers moving around the peninsula from the Sea of Japan to the Yellow Sea.

The naval close support missions in these early stages were not particularly

**Inchon was difficult for an amphibious landing. At low tide the inner harbour was a mud flat with a narrow channel. For the landing craft to catch the high tide timing had to be perfect.**

successful for a variety of reasons, not least the fact that Air Force and Navy were using two types of map. Naval pilots also found difficulty in establishing contact with the airborne controllers, so that in many cases they were reduced to flying around seeking

British aircraft carriers participated in the Korean War from the beginning. Here, a Fairey Firefly fighter-bomber from HMS *Theseus* rejoins formation after attacking Chinnampo docks.

targets of opportunity, with no guidance from anyone. The British element of TF 77, meanwhile, was experiencing growing problems with the serviceability and suitability of its aircraft, particularly the Seafires, which had a very restricted endurance and were prone to deck-landing accidents because of their narrow-track undercarriage. In the end, they were assigned to CAP duties over the fleet, leaving the American aircraft to concentrate on ground attack operations.

## 2ND INFANTRY DIVISION

The last day of July saw the arrival in Korea of the 2nd Infantry Division, the first ground troops to reach Korea from the continental United States. They were followed on 2 August by the 1st Provisional Marine Brigade,

US Marines scrambling down nets to board their landing craft. In both World War II and Korea the marines had the most difficult and dangerous task of all, and their casualties were high.

The North Korean assault across the 38th Parallel and the Allied withdrawal into the Pusan perimeter. Only air power saved Allied ground forces from destruction in the first weeks.

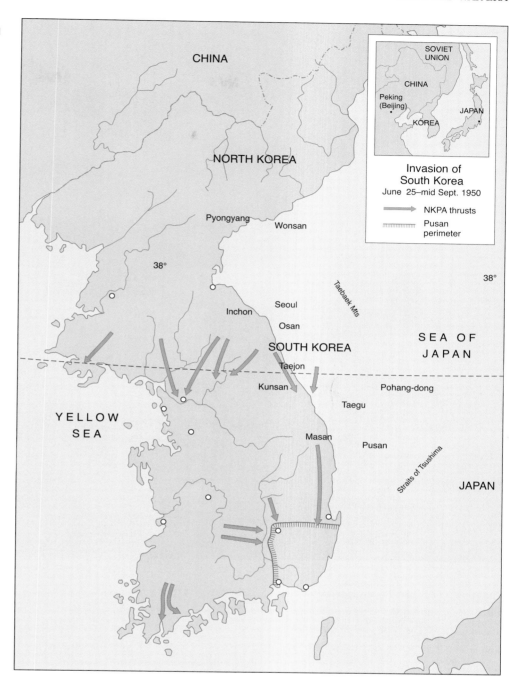

Invasion of
South Korea
June 25–mid Sept. 1950

→ NKPA thrusts

⊓⊓⊓⊓ Pusan
perimeter

also from the United States. The 5th Regimental Combat Team was also deployed to Korea from Hawaii and attached to the 24th Infantry Division. With the Marines came air support: first of all Marine Air Group 33, which arrived at Kobe, Japan, on 31 July and proceeded to Itami to begin working up. MAG 33 was the vanguard of the 1st Marine Air Wing, which was the air component of the 1st Marine Division. The Group's two tactical support squadrons, VMF-214 and VMF-323, both equipped with F4U-4B Corsairs, were immediately tasked with the support of the 1st Provisional Marine Brigade, and on 3 August VMF-214 (the 'Blacksheep') deployed aboard the escort carrier USS *Sicily*, which had transported them to the theatre, to begin operations. Two days later, VMF 323 (the 'Deathrattlers') also deployed to the escort carrier USS *Badoeng Strait*, and the two carriers – designated Task Element 96.8 – stationed themselves off the south coast of Korea to begin offensive operations. The remainder of the Marine Air Group, with no possibility of deployment to Korea for the time being, was placed under the temporary control of the Fifth Air Force in Japan; VMF(N)-513, equipped with F4U-5N Corsair night-fighters, was attached to the 8th FBW at Itazuke and began night intruder operations over Korea as directed by Fifth AF, while Marine Observation Squadron VMO-6 remained at Itami. The first Marine air strike of the Korean War was flown by VMF 214 on 3 August, the Corsairs attacking supply dumps, bridges and railways at Chinju and Sinban-ni. By the end of the first week of the month, the

Marine pilots were flying an average of 45 sorties a day.

Prior to the landing at Inchon in September 1950, designed to cut the invading North Korean armies in two, the carriers of Task Force 77 – the USS *Boxer*, USS *Leyte*, USS *Philippine Sea*, and USS *Valley Forge* – were directed to concentrate 50 per cent of their strike missions against the local defences at Wonsan. On 8 October, additional striking power was added to TF 77 in the shape of HMS *Theseus*,

which relieved HMS *Triumph* in Korean waters. She had been in port in the UK when she was alerted for Korean duty in late August; the two squadrons of her 17th Carrier Air Group, No. 807 with Hawker Sea Furies and No. 810 with Fairey Fireflies, immediately embarked on a period of intensive training that lasted six weeks, both in the UK and while the carrier was en route to the Far East. *Theseus* went on active duty in the Yellow Sea on 9 October,

285

**The Vought F4U Corsair was the workhorse of the US Navy and Marine Corps ground-attack squadrons during the early months of the Korean War, until it was replaced by jet types.**

launching her first sorties that same day. Four other British light fleet carriers – HMS *Glory*, HMS *Ocean*, HMS *Theseus* and the Australian-manned HMAS *Sydney* – operated in rotation in Korean waters for the duration of hostilities.

## RETURN OF THE BATTLESHIPS

The war in Korea also saw the return to action of some of the US Navy's battleships. The *Missouri* was followed by the USS *Wisconsin*, which was damaged by a shell from North

Korean shore batteries on 15 March 1952. Returning to the Atlantic Fleet, she was badly damaged in a collision with the destroyer USS *Eaton* and was repaired with the bow section of another 'Iowa' class vessel, the *Kentucky*. The latter had been laid down in 1944, and scheduled to commission in September 1946, but work on her was suspended when she was 69 per cent complete. She was launched in January 1950, simply to clear the slipway, and in 1954 she went aground in James River during a hurricane. She was broken up in 1958 after being used as a target. The *Wisconsin* was also decommissioned in 1958. The other battleships called up for Korean war service, *Iowa* and *New*

*Jersey*, came through their tours of duty off Korea unscathed. Both warships subsequently served with the Atlantic Fleet before being decommissioned in 1957–58.

Although the contribution made by the British light fleet carriers to the Korean War was relatively small compared with that of their larger and more numerous American counter-parts, it was nevertheless significant, and it was to provide valuable experience when, three years later, the Royal Navy became involved in

**The battleship USS *Missouri* on bombardment duty off the Korean coast. The 'Mighty Mo', which was also deployed on active service during the Gulf War of 1991, is now a floating museum.**

286

## NAUTILUS

Type: Battleship

Launch date: 21 January 1954

Crew: 105

Displacement: surfaced: 4157 tonnes (4091 tons);
submerged: 4104 tonnes (4040 tons)

Dimensions: 97m x 8.4m x 6.6m (323ft 7in x 27ft 8in x 21ft 9in)

Range: Unlimited

Armament: 6 533mm (21in) torpedo tubes

Powerplant: Twin screws, 1 S2W reactor, turbines

Performance: surfaced: 20 knots; submerged: 23 knots

### NUCLEAR-POWERED SUBMARINE

The world's first nuclear-powered submarine was the American *Nautilus*, launched on 21 January 1954. Apart from her revolutionary propulsion system, she was of a conventional design. Early trials established new records, including nearly 2250km (1213nm) submerged in 90 hours at 20 knots – at that time, the longest period spent underwater by a US submarine, as well as being the fastest speed submerged. She was also the first submarine to pass under the Arctic ice pack. There were, in fact, two prototype nuclear attack submarines; the other vessel, the USS *Seawolf*, was launched in July 1955 and was the last US submarine to feature a traditional conning tower, as distinct from the fin of later nuclear submarines. *Nautilus* was the more successful of the two; *Seawolf* was designed around the S2G nuclear reactor, intended as a backup to the S2W, but it had many operational problems and was replaced by an S2W in 1959. *Nautilus* was preserved as a museum exhibit in 1982.

another 'limited' conflict. In the summer of 1956, President Nasser of Egypt nationalized the Anglo-French Suez Canal Company and seized British and French assets in the Canal Zone. As a 'precautionary measure', a preliminary to possible armed intervention, units of the French fleet, including the carriers *Arromanches* and *Lafayette*, were assembled at Toulon, while three British aircraft carriers – HMS *Bulwark*, HMS *Theseus* and HMS *Ocean* – were despatched to join HMS *Eagle* in the Mediterranean. A further carrier, HMS *Albion*, also sailed for the Mediterranean following completion

of a refit. Both *Ocean* and *Theseus* had been used as training carriers since their tour of duty in Korean waters. Both were now assigned new roles as helicopter carriers. The other carriers were armed with strike squadrons, equipped variously with Hawker Sea Hawks, de Havilland Venoms and Westland Wyverns. At first light on 1 November 1956, the Fleet Air Arm's strike squadrons joined RAF squadrons from Cyprus in the task of eliminating the Egyptian Air Force, which was equipped with modern MiG-15 jet fighters and Ilyushin Il-28 jet bombers. The two French light

carriers, with their complements of piston-engined Corsairs and Skyraiders, were to cover the air and seaborne landings later on, once the Egyptian Air Force had been neutralized. In the meantime, their task was to seek out and disable any Egyptian warships that might pose a threat to the inbound troop convoys.

On 6 November, with the Egyptian Air Force rendered ineffective, British and French airborne forces landed on their respective objectives. In their wake, waves of helicopters carrying men of No. 45 Royal Marine Commando lifted off from the carriers *Ocean* and *Theseus* and headed for Port Said. It was the first helicopter assault in history, and a fitting climax to an operation that had proved yet again – despite the unfortunate political outcome – that the aircraft carrier was a vital component in projecting naval power across the world.

### NUCLEAR SUBMARINES
Yet the aircraft carrier, like the battleship before it, was becoming increasingly vulnerable to attack from the air and under the sea, and it needed powerful defensive measure to support it. In the 1950s, the Americans and Russians both began to explore the concept of the nuclear-

powered ballistic missile submarine, a vessel capable of remaining submerged for lengthy periods, making use of the polar ice-cap and various oceanic features to remain undetected. Armed with nuclear-tipped rockets, it would be the ultimate deterrent.

Although the Americans were the first to make the nuclear-powered submarine breakthrough, with an early class of boat based on the prototype *Nautilus*, what the US Navy really wanted was to merge the new technologies of ballistic missiles, smaller thermonuclear weapons, and inertial guidance systems into a single weapon system. They succeeded with the deployment, in 1960, of the first Fleet Ballistic Missile (FBM) submarine, armed with the Polaris A1 missile.

The Soviets' first nuclear submarine design was the 'November'

class, 14 units of which were produced from 1958 to 1963 at Severodvinsk. This was designed for the anti-ship rather than the anti-submarine role. Armed with nuclear torpedoes, the task of these boats was to attack carrier battle groups. They were very noisy underwater and were prone to reactor leaks, which did not endear them to their crews. They were involved in a number of accidents.

## BLUE-WATER NAVY

The decade that followed the rise to power of Nikita Khrushchev following the death of Stalin in 1953 witnessed a huge leap forward in Soviet weapons technology. This became apparent in the development of a 'blue water' navy in the early 1960s. During the Stalin regime, the Soviet Navy's main role was to defend against a seaborne invasion and to intercept the

transportation of US troops and supplies before they could reach Europe, but the means to achieve these tasks were limited. Adding to the Soviets' defensive problems were America's aircraft carriers, which had the ability to strike at targets in the Soviet Union from positions far out at sea. This meant that a Soviet forward deployment involving ocean-going submarines, long-range surface-to-surface missiles and long-range aircraft became mandatory.

The 1960s witnessed a marked development in Soviet maritime activities involving new construction and an increasingly bold fleet policy. Previously, in accordance with Soviet military doctrine, the Navy was little

**The USS *Seawolf* nuclear attack submarine was intended to succeed the 'Los Angeles' class, but the end of the Cold War resulted in the original order for 29 boats being reduced to three in 1995.**

more than an extension of the Red Army, and naval strategy was consequently based on the defence of the homeland. The sight of Soviet warships on the high seas was extremely rare, except for occasional transfers of units between the Baltic and Northern Fleets. These transfers were always carried out in great haste and gave the impression that the Soviets felt somewhat uncomfortable outside the waters of their own fleet areas.

Things began to change in 1961. In July, the first significant Soviet out-of-area exercise took place, with eight surface combatant units, associated support vessels and four submarines exercising in the Norwegian Sea. This was followed, in 1962, by the first transfer between the Black Sea and Northern Fleets, and an exercise in July included four surface units plus support ships and more than 20 submarines, operating within an exercise area that extended from the Iceland–Faeroes Gap to Norway's

**An American warship closes with a Russian freighter bound for Cuba in October 1962. The Cuban missile crisis brought the world to the brink of nuclear war.**

> The sight of Soviet warships on the high seas was extremely rare, except for occasional transfers of units between the Baltic and Northern Fleets.

North Cape. Soviet maritime aircraft also took part in strength.

### MISSILE CRISIS

The inability of the Soviet Union to match the United States in terms of sea power became apparent in late 1962. In October, the Americans imposed a blockade of Cuba following the infiltration of Soviet strategic and tactical missiles, as well as Il-28 jet bombers, into the island. Lacking the means to break the quarantine, and unwilling to risk all-out nuclear war, Premier Khrushchev was compelled to back down and order the removal of the missiles and bombers.

The Cuban crisis taught the Soviets a stern lesson in the importance of sea power, and future Soviet naval policies were amended accordingly. A pattern of bi-annual exercises was established in 1963; in March and

April, seven surface units plus support vessels exercised near the Lofotens, and in August a similar force conducted exercises in the Iceland–Faeroes Gap. Part of this group circumnavigated the British Isles before returning to the Baltic. Inter-fleet transfers between the Northern, Baltic and Black Sea Fleets continued and intensified. The exercises of 1964 saw the introduction of the latest missile-carrying warships; fleet strengths were increased and the scope and type of exercises between the North Cape and the Faeroes Gap revealed more imagination and expertise. The Soviet Mediterranean Squadron was also established on a continuing basis, although small numbers of submarines had been in the Mediterranean since 1958, and there was a transfer of ships to Cuba.

In fact, the Soviet Navy's challenge

to NATO on the high seas was only just beginning. In 1968, a small exercise in the Iceland–Faeroes Gap in May and surveillance of a NATO exercise off the Lofoten Islands prefaced the largest Soviet out-of-area exercise ever held. Exercise *Sever* (North), which was held in the Norwegian Sea, was a multi-phased, multi-area operation involving a very large number of surface units, submarines and aircraft. Later, from October to December, a small force patrolled an area off northeast Scotland and a single vessel patrolled north of the Faeroes in August. In the Mediterranean, force levels were maintained and deployments

lengthened. In September, the 5th Eskadra received a major addition in the shape of the new helicopter carrier *Moskva*, classified by the Russians as an anti-submarine cruiser. Completed in 1967, the *Moskva* was a hybrid helicopter carrier and missile cruiser, designed to counter western nuclear ballistic missile submarines in seas close to the Soviet homeland. A sister ship, the *Leningrad*, was completed in 1968. Each vessel carried an air group of 14 Kamov Ka-25 'Hormone' helicopters.

The spring exercise of 1969 began in the Iceland–Faeroes Gap during March and involved a large number of ships. During this period, the first

A Nimrod maritime patrol aircraft of the Royal Air Force keeps a watchful eye on a Soviet 'Moskva' class anti-submarine warfare ship in the Mediterranean.

large-scale relief of Mediterranean forces by the Northern Fleet took place, and an ASW exercise was conducted in the Norwegian Sea. Other exercises took place in the North Sea and in the area of Jan Mayen Island.

## NEW TYPES

The extension of Soviet naval power into the South Atlantic, Mediterranean and Indian Ocean in little more than a decade was, of

The design of the Soviet cruiser *Sverdlov* was inspired by the design of pre-World War II Italian warships. Seventeen units were built, mostly in the early 1950s.

course, made possible only by the deployment of new types of surface warships and submarines. New, large anti-submarine warfare ships that were deployed in the second half of the 1960s were as essential a part of the new strategy as were the ocean-going submarines that came off the ways during the same period. Between 1962 and 1974, the Soviets produced 38 cruisers, 10 destroyers, two helicopter carriers and 60 ocean-going escorts, and construction of their first aircraft carrier was well advanced.

In 1965, the dozen or so 'Sverdlov' class light cruisers and 'Kynda' class guided-missile cruisers were joined by the first of a new class, the *Kresta I*, a guided-missile cruiser that carried

SSN-3 Shaddock anti-ship and SAN-1 Goa anti-aircraft missiles. The cruiser was also the first to have a helicopter pad and hangar. Since the Shaddock had a range of well over 482km (300 miles), it needed mid-course guidance provided by the helicopter. A follow-on cruiser, *Kresta II*, was built in 1868 and was deployed in 1970. It had a more sophisticated missile armament than its predecessor, comprising twin quadruple launchers for the SSN-10 and two twin launchers for the SAN-3 Goblet, a naval version of the SA-6 Gainful. The next Soviet large anti-submarine warfare ship, the *Kara*, was first seen in 1973. This 10,160-tonne (10,000-ton) guided missile cruiser was armed with three separate missile systems, comprising eight tubes for the SSN-10 short-range anti-ship missile, two twin launchers for the SAN-3 Goblet, and two twin launchers for the SAN-4 anti-aircraft weapons. All four of the news cruiser classes

carried a helicopter, torpedo tubes, and many guns (ranging in calibre from 30mm/1.2in to 76mm/2.9in), as well as multi-barrel anti-submarine rocket launchers.

The early post-war 'Skory' class destroyer and the 'Kotlin' and 'Krupny' classes of the 1950s were joined in 1962 by the first of the 'Kashin' class, the first large gas turbine ships. Some of the 'Krupny' class were converted to 'Kanin' class with the addition of a helicopter pad, more torpedo tubes and extra guns; and eight 'Kotlin' class destroyers were converted to Kotlin SAM anti-air vessels with the addition of a twin launcher for the SAN-1 Goa anti-aircraft missile. Finally, in 1971, came the 'Krivak' class guided missile destroyer, the most heavily armed destroyer afloat. Its gas turbine propulsion gave it speed, and its armament of four tubes for SSN-10 missiles, two SAN-4 launchers,

# Over the next 15 years, the Soviets produced a dozen more submarine types, including the diesel-electric Foxtrot and Romeo attack boats.

four 76mm AA guns and eight torpedo tubes made this ship a very formidable opponent.

## SUBMARINE PROGRAMME

The USSR's submarine building programme was even more spectacular than its production of new cruisers and destroyers. Prior to 1958, the Soviet Navy's ocean-going submarine fleet consisted of some 150 'Whisky' class and 57 'Zulu' class diesel-electric boats, and the remainder were coastal types. Then, in 1958, the first units of the 'Hotel' class nuclear-powered ballistic missile submarine (SSBN) and the 'November' class nuclear-powered

attack submarine (SSN) appeared, ushering the Soviet fleet into the nuclear age. Over the next 15 years, the Soviets produced a dozen more submarine types, including the diesel-electric Foxtrot and Romeo attack boats. Built in the periods 1958–68 (45 units) and 1971–74 (17 units), the extremely popular 'Foxtrot' class remained in production at a slow rate for export, the last unit being launched in 1984. The class proved to be the most successful of the post-war Soviet conventional submarine designs, 62 serving with the Soviet Navy. Three Soviet Navy Fleet Areas operated Foxtrot, and the Mediterranean and Indian Ocean

Squadrons regularly had these boats deployed to them. The first foreign recipient of the type was India, which received eight new boats between 1968 and 1976. India was followed by Libya, with six units received between 1976 and 1983, and Cuba, three boats being handed over between 1979 and 1984. All Soviet Foxtrots were withdrawn by the late 1980s.

Between 1958 and 1963, two new types of nuclear-powered submarine, the Echo and Golf, entered service. The five 'Echo' class SSNs were originally built at Komomolsk in the Soviet Far East in 1960–62 as 'Echo I' class missile submarines (SSGNs). Armed with six tubes for the SS-N-3C 'Shaddock' strategic cruise missile, they lacked the fire control and guidance radars of the later 'Echo II' class, 29 of which were built. As the

On the foredeck of this Russian Krivak frigate are its quadruple SS-N-14 'Silex' anti-submarine rocket launchers. The 'Krivak' class carried a huge array of electronic and sensor equipment.

Designed in the mid-1950s, the Soviet 'Golf' class were diesel-electric missile submarines. The first boats were commissioned in 1958 and the last in 1962. Seen here is a Golf II.

Soviet ballistic missile submarine force was built up, the need for these 'stop-gap' missile boats diminished, and they were converted to anti-ship attack SSNs between 1969 and 1974.

Some 23 'Golf I' class ballistic missile submarines were completed between 1958 and 1962, and entered service at a rate of six to seven a year. The ballistic missiles were housed vertically in the rear section of the extended fin, which produced a great deal of resistance underwater and reduced speed, as well as generating high noise levels. However, the boats could be driven by a creep motor, giving quiet operation and very long endurance. Thirteen Golf I boats were modified to Golf II standard starting in 1965, using the SS-N-5 ballistic missile. The 'Juliet' class was, in effect, a diesel-electric verion of the Golf, armed with the SS-N-3 missile.

## MODERN SUBMARINES

Next came the 'Charlie I' class, the first Soviet nuclear-powered guided missile submarines capable of launching surface-to-surface cruise missiles without having to surface first. The Charlie Is were all built at Gorky between 1967 and 1972; 10 were still in commission in the late 1990s, all based in the Pacific. One was leased to India in January 1988, and another sank off Petropavlovsk in June 1983, and was later salvaged. The Charlie I carried the SS-N-15 nuclear-tipped anti-submarine missile, which had a range of 37km (20nm). The 'Charlie II' class, built between 1972 and 1980 at Gorki, was an improved Charlie I with a 9m (29ft 6in) insertion in the hull forward of the fin to house the electronics and launch systems necessary for targeting and firing the SS-N-15 and SS-N-16 weapons. In both 'Charlie' classes, the submarine had to return to base once the missiles had been expended, to be reloaded. The six Charlie II boats are also armed with the SS-N-9 Siren anti-ship missile, which cruises at 0.9 Mach and has a range of 110km (60nm) and can be fitted with either a nuclear

## SOVIET NUCLEAR SUBMARINES

The first really modern Soviet nuclear submarines began to appear during the six years between 1967 and 1973. The first was the 'Yankee' class of 1967. During the Cold War period, three or four Yankee boats were on station at any one time off the eastern seaboard of the United States, with a further unit either on transit to or from a patrol area. The forward-deployed Yankees were assigned the wartime role of destroying time-sensitive area targets such as SAC bomber alert bases and carriers/SSBNs in port, and of disrupting the American higher command echelons as much as possible to ease the task of follow up ICBM strikes. As they progressively retired from their SSBN role, some Yankees were converted to carry cruise or anti-ship missiles as SSNs.

(250kT) or conventional warhead. The 'Charlie II' class vessels were all based with the Northern Fleet, making occasional deployments to the Mediterranean.

Until the early 1970s, the United States led the world in highly sophisticated and effective nuclear missile submarines. Then the Soviets deployed a new class of ballistic missile submarine, the Delta I, or 'Murena' class SSBN, which was a major improvement on the earlier 'Yankee' class and which was armed with missiles that could out-range American's Poseidon. The first Delta was laid down at Severodvinsk in 1969, launched in 1971 and completed in the following year. The Delta II and Delta III were improved versions. The 'Delta III' or 'Kalmar' class SSBN, completed between 1976 and 1982, had some visible differences from the earlier 'Delta II' class from which it evolved. The most noticeable was that the missile casing was higher to accommodate the SS-N-18 missiles, which are longer than the SS-N-8s of the Delta II. The last of the 'Delta' class was the Delta IV, construction of which was first ordered in December 1975. The first of eight boats was launched and commissioned in 1984 at Severodvinsk.

The Soviet 'Juliet' class submarines were diesel-electric boats, deployed in the 1950s to give the USSR the means of launching a nuclear attack on the eastern seaboard of the United States.

## FROM VIETNAM TO THE FALKLANDS

The United States' involvement in the Vietnam War during the 1960s saw the US Navy's aircraft carriers in action again, their aircraft operating intensively and at considerable cost. As in Korea, the carrier force was designated Task Force 77. Its operations began on 5 August 1964, when strike aircraft from the carriers *Ticonderoga* and *Constellation* attacked naval bases and oil-storage facilities in response to an attack by North Vietnamese torpedo boats on US warships in the Gulf of Tonkin. Two of the 64 strike aircraft involved, an A-1 Skyraider and an A-4 Skyhawk, were shot down by AAA fire, one pilot being killed and the other (Lt Everett Alvarez) becoming the first US pilot to enter captivity in North Vietnam. He was to endure nearly nine years

A Russian 'Charlie II' class nuclear attack submarine travelling at speed. These submarines were intended to attack high-value surface targets, such as aircraft carriers, with missiles.

> Lt Everett Alvarez became the first US pilot to enter captivity in North Vietnam. He was to endure nearly nine years of brutality before his release.

of brutality before his release. For the next six months, the operations of Task Force 77 consisted of standing by for retaliatory strikes against North Vietnam with various bomb loads and missiles. Photographic reconnaissance flights were also made over South Vietnam and Laos to detect concentrations of Viet Cong and the infiltration of North Vietnamese troops along the Ho Chi Minh trail. Strikes by small groups of carrier aircraft were made on trucks and material storage areas in South Vietnam wherever they were found.

### FLAMING DART

The routine bombing of North Vietnam did not begin until 7 February 1965, when the campaign was launched in response to a heavy Viet Cong mortar attack on Pleiku air base. It was originally given the codename Flaming Dart. Task Force 77's commander, Rear-Admiral H.L. Miller, who was embarked in the USS *Ranger*, received orders to assemble TF 77 and to prepare for retaliatory strikes on North Vietnam. Two other carriers, the USS *Coral Sea* and USS *Hancock*, then en route to the Philippines, were turned around and joined *Ranger* in the early afternoon of 7 February. Between them, the three carriers launched 83 strike aircraft at North Vietnamese barracks and port facilities, causing significant damage. One A-4 was lost

The USS *Ticonderoga* on station off Vietnam.
She saw active service in World War II and was
reconstructed in 1955–57, being fitted with
an angled flight deck.

and eight damaged.

On 11 February, the three carriers
of TF 77 launched 99 strike aircraft
against selected targets in Flaming
Dart II, and on this occasion three
F-8 Crusaders from the USS *Coral Sea*
failed to return. Two of the pilots were
recovered. By this time, the Americans
were becoming uncomfortably
aware that the accuracy and fighting
intensity of North Vietnamese AAA
fighter was much greater than had
been anticipated.

**ROLLING THUNDER**
From March 1965, TF 77 participated

in Operation Rolling Thunder, the
ongoing bombing campaign against
North Vietnam. A geographic point in
the Gulf of Tonkin was selected as the
focus of operations for TF 77 and
given the codename Yankee Station.
Attacks involving up to 70 aircraft
from the *Hancock* and *Coral Sea*
were made against radar stations,
communications and supply dumps.
On 29 March, the task force suffered a
serious loss during an attack on radar
facilities at Bach Long Vi, when three
out of six aircraft in the first strike
wave were shot down. Luckily, two of
the pilots, all squadron commanders,
were rescued.

In April 1965, pilots of Task Force
77 were assigned a second task, flying
close support missions against the Viet
Cong in South Vietnam. Initial

operations, flown by aircraft from the
USS *Midway* and USS *Coral Sea*, plus
Marine Corps F-8E Crusaders flying
from the USS *Oriskany*, was so
successful that the US land forces
commander, General Westmoreland,
requested the assignment of one
carrier at all times to close support
work. As a result, 'Dixie Station' was
established about 160km (100 miles)
southeast of Cam Ranh Bay. By this
time, North Vietnam's air defences
had received a major boost with the
deployment of the first SA-2
'Guideline' surface-to-air missile
batteries. Because of the fear that
air attacks might kill Soviet
technicians, authority to attack the
sites was not forthcoming for several
weeks. Finally, on 12 August 1965, an
anti-SAM campaign called Operation

Iron Hand was implemented, using Shrike anti-radar missiles. The SA-2s were mobile and difficult to track down, and it was not until 17 October 1965 that a flight of Iron Hand A-4Es, led by an A-6 Intruder from the USS *Independence*, destroyed the first operational and occupied SAM site near Kep airfield, northeast of Hanoi. By this time, encounters between US Navy and Marine Corps pilots and North Vietnamese MiG-17 jet fighters were becoming frequent; the US Navy's first MiG kills came in June 1965, when two were shot down by Sparrow AAMs launched by F-4 Phantoms of VF-21 from the USS *Midway*.

One of the last air strikes of 1965 was a big one, involving 100 aircraft from the *Enterprise*, *Kitty Hawk* and *Ticonderoga* against a thermal power plant near Hanoi, the first industrial target authorized by the Joint Chiefs of Staff. The target was severely damaged and two A-4s were lost.

## BOMBING PAUSE

Starting on Christmas Day 1965, there was a 37-day bombing pause, during which attempts were made, unsuccessfully, to bring the North Vietnamese government to the peace table. Rolling Thunder operations were resumed on 31 January 1966, the emphasis now switching to interdiction in an attempt to shut off the flow of men and materials to South Vietnam. In a SAM-dominated environment, low-level operations also became the order of the day. In March, TF 77 flew 6500 sorties, 11 aircraft being lost. April was a bad month, with 21 aircraft lost.

In June 1966, the focus of the air

**Aircraft carriers and escort vessels of the US Navy's Task Force 77 in the Gulf of Tonkin, Vietnam. American aircrews had to penetrate the heaviest anti-aircraft defences in the world.**

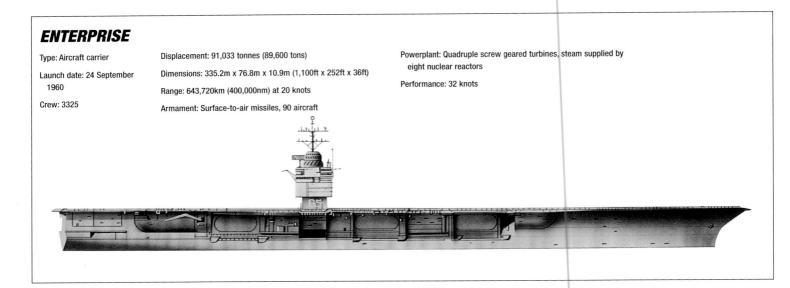

## ENTERPRISE

Type: Aircraft carrier

Launch date: 24 September 1960

Crew: 3325

Displacement: 91,033 tonnes (89,600 tons)

Dimensions: 335.2m x 76.8m x 10.9m (1,100ft x 252ft x 36ft)

Range: 643,720km (400,000nm) at 20 knots

Armament: Surface-to-air missiles, 90 aircraft

Powerplant: Quadruple screw geared turbines, steam supplied by eight nuclear reactors

Performance: 32 knots

> By the end of 1966, Task Force 77 had mounted more than 30,000 attack sorties against North Vietnam, with 20,000 more against targets in South Vietnam.

attacks switched to the North Vietnamese petroleum, oil and lubricants (POL) storage and distribution system. The campaign, however, came too late. By this time, the North Vietnamese, anticipating that their POL facilities would come under attack, had dispersed them very thoroughly.

Nevertheless, there was no doubt that the interdiction campaign was beginning to cause Hanoi some serious problems. By the end of 1966, Task Force 77 had mounted more than 30,000 attack sorties against North Vietnam, with 20,000 more against targets in South Vietnam. More than 120 aircraft had been lost on combat missions, with 89 airmen having been killed, captured or reported missing.

In 1967, minelaying was added to TF 77's operational tasks, and mines were laid by A-6 Intruders from the carriers *Enterprise* and *Kitty Hawk* in

the mouths of five North Vietnamese rivers. The mining of the deep water ports, however, was not authorized because of the risk of damage to third-party shipping, particularly that belonging to the Soviets, whose tankers were regular visitors. For the same reason, no blockade was ever imposed on the principal port of Haiphong, which would have severed Hanoi's main source of supply. Instead, the Americans attempted to isolate Haiphong by means of a sustained bombing attack on the roads and railways radiating from the port, with their associated bridges and other weak points.

In March 1967, the US Navy deployed a new weapon in Vietnam, the Walleye TV-guided air-to-surface glide bomb. After some preliminary attacks on barracks and bridges, It was used on 19 May against the Hanoi Thermal Power Plant, the attack being made by two F-4

Skyhawks from the *Bon Homme Richard* with F-8 Crusaders acting as flak suppressors. On the way back from the target, the latter became engaged with 10 MiG-17s, shooting down four of the enemy jet fighters. The use of Walleye marked the first occasion on which so-called smart bombs were employed.

### FORMIDABLE DEFENCES

During the year, 12 carriers took part in operations as part of Task Force 77: the *Bon Homme Richard, Constellation, Coral Sea, Enterprise, Hancock, Forrestal, Hancock, Intrepid, Kitty Hawk, Oriskany, Ranger* and *Ticonderoga*. Their aircrews had achieved much, despite bombing restrictions, bad weather and the formidable enemy defences, destroying 30 SAM sites, 187 AAA batteries, 955 bridges (with a further 1586 damaged), 734 motor vehicles, 410 locomotives and 3185 watercraft. Fourteen MiGs had been destroyed in the air and 32 on the ground. US Navy combat losses were 33 aircraft, with around one-third of their crews rescued.

In January 1968, TF 77 flew 811

**The deck of an aircraft carrier was a dangerous and difficult working environment, as this photograph shows. It took tight discipline and good teamwork to prevent serious accidents.**

attack sorties in support of the US Marines at Khe San, and in February almost 1500 sorties were flown in support of this besieged Marine base. Another 1600 attack sorties were flown in March, the TF 77 pilots often dropping their ordnance within 100m (328ft) of the Marines' forward positions. In the north, much of the interdiction work was carried out by the Grumman A-6 Intruder, whose ability to deliver a wide variety of ordnance with pinpoint accuracy at night and in all weather conditions was outstanding.

During the whole of the Vietnam conflict, the US Navy employed 17 attack carriers, 10 from the Pacific Fleet and seven from the Atlantic:

**British shipping assembling off Ascension Island, en route to the Falkland Islands in April 1982. The Americans, who used Ascension as a base, gave the British unstinting support for the operation.**

## THE FALKLANDS CAMPAIGN

**Less than a decade after the US withdrawal from Vietnam, the Royal Navy found itself embroiled in a war for which it had never planned. Following the Argentine invasion of the Falkland Islands and South Georgia on 2 April 1982, the UK Government initiated Operation Corporate, the plan to recapture these territories. What followed was an incredible mixture of innovation, improvisation and, to no small extent, luck. Within days, a hastily assembled task force was on its way to the south Atlantic, nearly 13,000km (8000 miles) from the British Isles, while stores, equipment and stocks of fuel were built up at Ascension Island, at roughly mid-point in the Atlantic.**

indeed, every carrier in its inventory with the exception of the USS *John F. Kennedy*. Between them, these vessels made 73 combat deployments up to August 1973. The Navy's losses amounted to 530 fixed-wing aircraft, most of them carrier-based, and 13 helicopters. A total of 317 Navy airmen lost their lives.

The Vietnam War also brought

about a new lease of life for the battleship USS *New Jersey*. On 6 April 1967, she began her second reactivation refit for active service as a fire support ship. During this deployment, she spent 120 days on the 'gun line', firing 5688 406mm (16in) rounds and 14,891 125mm (5in) rounds at various targets. Her main armament had a maximum

range of 38km (23.6 miles), which meant that she was able to lend her fire support to US forces deep inland.

## WAR IN THE FALKLANDS

On 20 April 1982, a Royal Air Force Victor K2 aircraft made a radar search

of 388,500 square kilometres (150,000 square miles) of ocean in the South Georgia area before returning to Ascension Island after a flight lasting 14 hours 45 minutes. This was the longest reconnaissance mission carried out up to that time, and was an essential preliminary to the reoccupation of South Georgia. Five days later, as part of this operation, the Argentine submarine *Santa Fe* was attacked and disabled by Lynx, Wasp and Wessex helicopters using machine-gun fire and an AS-12 missile launched by a Wasp from the patrol vessel HMS *Endurance*. The submarine was based at Grytviken.

The Argentine Navy's principal assets were its sole aircraft carrier, the *Veinticinco de Mayo* (formerly the British light fleet carrier HMS *Venerable* and Royal Netherlands Navy *Karel Doorman*) and the cruiser *General Belgrano* (formerly USS

**The Argentine cruiser *General Belgrano* sinking after being torpedoed by the British nuclear submarine HMS *Conqueror*. Formerly the USS *Phoenix*, she was bought by Argentina in 1951.**

*Phoenix*). As the British Task Force approached the Falkland Islands, an attempt was made by these vessels to intercept it, but the Argentine carrier failed to launch her eight heavily laden Douglas A-4 Skyhawk jets because of unfavourable conditions.

On 1 May 1982, following a night attack on Port Stanley airfield by a lone Vulcan bomber operating out of Ascension Island, the airfield and the airstrip at Goose Green were attacked by 12 British Aerospace Sea Harriers of No. 800 Squadron from HMS *Hermes*, armed with 453kg (1000lb) bombs. In this, the first-ever combat operation by a V/STOL aircraft, one Sea Harrier was damaged. Later in the day, the Argentine Air Force launched

During the whole of the Vietnam conflict, the US Navy employed 17 attack carriers, 10 from the Pacific Fleet and seven from the Atlantic.

The Type 21 frigate HMS *Antelope* on fire
and sinking in San Carlos water after being
hit by Argentine bombs on 23 May 1982.

The Type 21 frigate HMS *Antelope* on fire
and sinking in San Carlos water after being
hit by Argentine bombs on 23 May 1982.

40 sorties against the British warships
off the Falklands. A Dassault Mirage
III was shot down by a Sea Harrier of
No. 801 Squadron, HMS *Invincible*; a
second, damaged, was destroyed in
error by Argentine AAA over the
islands. An IAI Dagger (Israeli-built
Mirage 5) was shot down by a Sea
Harrier of No. 800 Squadron, and
one of six Canberras of Grupo 2
was destroyed by a Sea Harrier of
No. 801 Squadron. All Sea Harrier
kills were achieved with the
Sidewinder AIM-9L AAM.

On 2 May, the cruiser *General
Belgrano*, judged to be a threat to the
Task Force, was sunk with heavy loss of
life by two Mk 8 torpedoes launched
by the nuclear hunter-killer
submarine HMS *Conqueror*. It was
an event that sparked off much
controversy, as the cruiser was sailing
away from the exclusion zone
imposed by the British around the
Falkland Islands at the time. On the
following day, the Argentine patrol
craft *Comodoro Somellera* and *Alferez
Sobral* were attacked by Lynx
helicopters from the destroyers HMS
*Coventry* and HMS *Glasgow*. The
former was sunk by Sea Skua missiles,
the second badly damaged.

On 4 May, three Sea Harriers of
No. 800 Squadron attacked Goose
Green; one was shot down by AAA
and the pilot killed. Later, the Type
42 destroyer HMS *Sheffield*, on radar
picket duty west of the Falklands, was
hit and disabled by an Exocet ASM
launched by a Dassault Super
Etendard of the 2 Escuadrilla de Caza
y Ataque; the warship was abandoned
and later sunk.

Following further air attacks, and
raids by the Special Air Service and
Special Boat Service, ships of the

British amphibious landing force
entered San Carlos Water on 20 May,
under cover of a diversionary SAS
attack at Goose Green, and began
unloading. It was the signal for two
days of intense combat operations to
begin. Sea Harriers flew combat
patrols, while six RAF Harrier GR.3s
(which had arrived earlier on the MV
*Atlantic Conveyor*, together with eight
more Sea Harriers) carried out attacks
in support of the troops ashore. One
GR.3 was shot down, and the injured
pilot taken prisoner. Argentine attacks
on the landing force vessels began
with a single run by an Aermacchi
MB.339 of the 1st Naval Attack
Escuadrilla, which hit the Leander-
class frigate HMS *Argonaut* with 30mm
(1.2in) cannon shells and rockets.
This was followed by an attack by six

Daggers of Grupo 6, one of which was
shot down by a Sea Cat SAM.

## SEVERE DAMAGE

The 'County' class guided missile
destroyer HMS *Antrim* was hit by a
bomb, which failed to explode, while
the Type 22 frigate HMS *Broadsword*
was damaged by 30mm (1.2in) shells.
Two Pucara ground attack aircraft of
Grupo 3 were engaged by three Sea
Harriers of No. 801 Squadron, and
one was shot down. The next force to
attack comprised four Skyhawks of
Grupo 4 and two of Grupo 5; one of
the former was shot down by a No.
800 Squadron Sea Harrier. Next came
four Daggers of Grupo 6, one of
which was also shot down by a No. 800
Squadron pilot. Meanwhile, Skyhawks
attacking ships in Falkland Sound hit

HMS *Argonaut* with two 453kg (1000lb) bombs, causing severe damage; soon afterwards, the surviving Daggers of Grupo 6 bombed the Type 21 frigate HMS *Ardent*, which also sustained heavy damage. The frigate was again hit by Skyhawks of Grupo 5. Elsewhere, over West Falkland, three Daggers were destroyed by two Sea Harriers of No. 801 Squadron. In the meantime, HMS *Ardent* was attacked yet again, this time by three Skyhawks of the 3rd Naval Fighter and Attack Escuadrilla, causing yet more damage with 227kg (500lb) Snakeye retarded bombs. These aircraft were engaged by Sea Harriers of No. 800 Squadron, which destroyed one with an AIM-9L and another with 30mm (1.2in) cannon fire. The third, hit by small arms fire

> The Argentineans had lost 12 aircraft, nine destroyed by Sea Harriers, but the cost to the Task Force in ships lost and damaged was giving cause for serious concern.

from *Ardent*, came down off Port Stanley, the pilot ejecting. HMS *Ardent* sank that night, having been hit by seven bombs and an eighth that failed to explode. During the two days of fighting, the Argentineans had lost 12 aircraft, nine destroyed by Sea Harriers, but the cost to the task force in ships lost and damaged was giving cause for serious concern.

On 22 May, two Sea Harriers of No. 800 Squadron attacked and disabled

the Argentine Coast Guard patrol vessel *Rio Iguazu* in Choiseul Sound, and four Harrier GR.3s of No. 1 Squadron RAF attacked Goose Green. To the north of the Falklands, a Boeing 707 reconnaissance aircraft of Grupo 1 was engaged by Sea Dart SAMs launched at extreme range by the Type 82 destroyer HMS *Bristol* and the Type 42 destroyer HMS *Cardiff*, but escaped.

The next day, 23 May, was another

British Aerospace Harrier GR.3 strike fighters on board the conveyor ship *Atlantic Conveyor*. Fortunately, the Harriers were offloaded before the merchant vessel was sunk by Exocet missiles.

bad one for the Royal Navy. It began well enough, when Sea Harriers destroyed three Puma and one Agusta 109 helicopters on the ground. Then, however, the Type 21 frigate HMS *Antelope* was attacked in San Carlos Water by Skyhawks and hit by two bombs that failed to explode. The ship blew up later while a bomb

disposal team was working on board. One of the Skyhawks was shot down by a Sea Wolf SAM, another crashed on landing at base. During the day, Rapier SAM crews claimed the destruction of three Argentine aircraft and a Dagger was destroyed by a Sea Harrier of No. 800 Squadron. One of the squadron's Sea Harriers crashed into the sea after taking off from HMS *Hermes*, the pilot losing his life.

On 24 May, Sea Harriers of No. 800 Squadron and Harrier GR.3s of No. 1 Squadron attacked Port Stanley airfield, but failed to crater the

runway. Warships off Pebble Island were attacked by Daggers of Grupo 6, one of which was shot down by the Sea Harrier CAP. Vessels at San Carlos were also attacked by Daggers and Skyhawks; one of the latter crashed into the sea. Three ships were hit by bombs, but none exploded.

### ATLANTIC CONVEYOR

The fighting continued with almost unabated intensity, and the Task Force continued to suffer. Three Skyhawks were shot down by ground fire on the morning of 25 May, but in the afternoon six Skyhawks of Grupo 5 attacked warships off Pebble Island, sinking the Type 42 destroyer HMS *Coventry* with three bomb hits. The container ship MV *Atlantic Conveyor*, northeast of the Falklands, was hit by an Exocet launched by a Super Etendard and had to be abandoned. The ship was burnt out and lost, together with the stores she carried, which included 10 transport helicopters.

On 27 May, Harrier GR.3s attacked Argentine positions in the Goose Green area; one was shot down, the pilot ejecting. Two Skyhawks of Grupo 5 successfully bombed a stores dump at Ajax Bay; one aircraft was shot down by 40mm (1.6in) Bofors fire, the pilot bailing out. The next day, British paratroops advancing on Goose Green were subjected to attacks by Pucara aircraft, which shot down an army Scout helicopter. One Pucara was shot down by a Blowpipe SAM, a second by ground fire, and a third crashed into high ground in cloud. An Aermacchi 339 was also destroyed by a Blowpipe. Argentine positions at Goose Green were attacked by No. 1 Squadron's Harriers, using cluster bombs and rockets. The Argentine garrison surrendered the next day, after fierce fighting.

On 29 May, air operations were

hampered by bad weather. To the northeast of the Falklands, the tanker *British Wye*, bringing fuel for the task force, was nonetheless attacked by a C-130 aircraft of Grupo 1, modified as a bomber. The aircraft released eight bombs, but only one struck the tanker, and that failed to explode. On the following day, Argentine Navy Super Etendards made an Exocet attack against the main body of the task force, but the missiles were deflected by chaff countermeasures. Two Skyhawks of Grupo 4 were shot down by Sea Dart ASMs fired by the Type 42 destroyer HMS *Exeter*.

By 5 June, Harriers and Sea Harriers were able to deploy from the carriers to an airstrip at Port San Carlos, enabling them to provide more effective support for the ground forces. Hercules aircraft of No. 38 Group RAF, which now had a flight refuelling capability enabling them to reach the Falklands from Ascension Island, were also able to make low-level supply drops to the task force at sea. On 7 June, the Sea Dart SAM once again proved its effectiveness when one fired by HMS *Exeter* destroyed a reconnaissance Learjet flying at 12,190m (40,000ft).

## SAN CARLOS AND FITZROY

Although the Argentine forces were clearly losing the battle for the Falklands, they were still able to inflict substantial damage on the task force. On 8 June, Skyhawks of Grupo 5 and Daggers of Grupo 6 launched heavy attacks on vessels at San Carlos and Fitzroy, hitting the logistics ships *Sir Tristram* and *Sir Galahad* and causing heavy loss of life, particularly on the latter vessel. Another attack just before dusk was intercepted by Sea Harriers, which shot down three out of four Skyhawks with Sidewinders. It was the Argentineans' final fling; on 9 June, the British advance on Port Stanley got under way, supported by Royal Navy Sea King and Wessex helicopters and a solitary RAF Chinook, the others having gone down in the *Atlantic Conveyor*. By 13 June, forward air controllers were in position on the hills around Port Stanley, enabling No. 1 Squadron to use its laser-guided bombs to good effect against the Argentine forward positions. A Canberra of Grupo 2,

Fighting fires on the logistics ship RFA *Sir Galahad* after she was hit by bombs at Bluff Cove. The attack killed 48 men of the 1st Welsh Guards, as well as other personnel.

The ability of the Soviets to deploy so many warships and supporting units at one time and with speed alarmed NATO planners.

bombing Mount Kent from 12,190m (40,000ft), was shot down by a Sea Dart launched by HMS *Exeter*. On 14 June, Argentine positions at Port Stanley were attacked by Scout helicopters launching SS-11 anti-tank missiles against bunkers. These were

the last offensive operations of the conflict; the Argentine garrison at Port Stanley surrendered later that day.

### THE LAST YEARS OF THE COLD WAR

The performance of the British forces, and in particular that of the Royal Navy, had been watched with interest by observers of both power blocs. From the naval standpoint, one

aspect that was immediately apparent was the high degree of cooperation that existed between the Royal and United States Navies; the Americans had lost no time in redeploying naval forces to compensate for the gaps left by the deployment of RN warships to the South Atlantic. Many lessons were learned, too, not the least of which was that determined attacks pressed home with 'iron bombs' could inflict terrible damage on surface forces, and that there was consequently a pressing need for warships to carry close-in warfare air defence systems to counter attacking aircraft that broke through the SAM defences and combat air patrols, as well as sea-skimming anti-ship missiles like the French-made Exocet. Although it was used with some success in the

**A British Aerospace Sea Wolf short-range rapid-reaction missile being launched from a Type 22 frigate. Later versions of the Sea Wolf could be launched vertically.**

## ALFA

Type: Attack submarine

Launch date: 1970

Crew: 31

Displacement: surfaced: 2845 tonnes (2800 tons);
submerged: 3739 tonnes (3680 tons)

Dimensions: 81m x 9.5m x 8m (265ft 9in x 31ft 2in x 26ft 3in)

Range: Unlimited

Armament: 6 533mm (21in) torpedo tubes; conventional or
nuclear torpedoes; 36 mines

Powerplant: Liquid-metal reactor, two steam turbines

Performance: surfaced: 20 knots, submerged: 42 knots

Falklands campaign, the British Aerospace Sea Wolf short-range rapid-reaction missile, deployed on the Type 22 frigates HMS *Brilliant* and HMS *Broadsword*, revealed some shortcomings that resulted in urgent further development, leading to the vertical launch Sea Wolf and a lightweight version.

As a last-ditch defence against sea-skimming missiles, the US Navy had already deployed a rapid-fire minigun system called Phalanx on its warships. After the Falklands experience, this was installed in some of the Royal Navy's warships. Phalanx, which is extremely quick-reacting, can lay down 20mm (0.78in) shells in the path of an attacking missile or aircraft at the rate of 4500 rounds per minute.

### SURPRISES

The rapid development of the Soviet Navy into a true ocean-going fleet in the 1960s had surprised NATO commanders, but in the 1970s there were more surprises in store. In April 1975, the Soviets conducted the largest maritime exercise ever witnessed, with more than 200 ships and submarines and large numbers of aircraft participating in a centrally controlled worldwide operation.

The exercise areas included the Norwegian Sea, the North and Central Atlantic, the Baltic and Mediterranean Seas and the Indian and Pacific Oceans. Submarine activity in the Atlantic was concentrated in the gap between Iceland and Jan Mayen Island and off the west coast of Ireland. All phases and methods of modern naval warfare were practised, including the deployment of strategic nuclear submarines. The exercise was also significant in that it included the participation of merchant shipping in a convoy role, and a simulated convoy off North Cape was the subject of intensive air attacks.

The maritime event of 1976 was the emergence of the Soviet capital ship *Kiev* from the Black Sea in July. This ship, designated by NATO as a missile-equipped anti-submarine warfare carrier, deployed into the Atlantic after a moderate amount of exercise and training in the Mediterranean. While in the Mediterranean, the Soviets took the opportunity to demonstrate their new Yak-38 Forger V/STOL strike aircraft, as well as Hormone ASW helicopters. The *Kiev* entered the Soviet Northern Fleet area early in August. Two more 'Kiev' class vessels, the *Minsk* and *Novorossiysk*, were

deployed in subsequent years. A fourth ship, the much-modified *Baku* (later renamed *Admiral Gorshkov*), was commissioned in 1987; this vessel was later sold to the Indian Navy as the INS *Vikramaditya*.

The pattern of Soviet naval exercises continued on an annual basis, and new warships continued to make their appearance. In the spring exercise of 1984, the Northern Fleet conducted a large-scale deployment to the Norwegian Sea; this was the largest exercise of its type yet seen, with two aggressor groups, mainly of 'Krivak' class ships simulating NATO forces, deploying from the Northern and Baltic Fleets. Defending units included a large task force, at the heart of which was a new 25,402-tonne (25,000-ton) cruiser, the *Kirov*.

### DISQUIETING TREND

The ability of the Soviets to deploy so many warships and supporting units at one time and with speed alarmed NATO planners. The lesson was clear: if the Soviet Navy could achieve similar surprise at the outset of a real conflict, it would be able to secure the northern part of the Norwegian Sea and thus prevent the deployment of NATO reinforcements to northern Norway in the event of a Soviet

The 'Akula' class Russian nuclear attack submarine was a follow-on to the 'Victor' class. These craft were the quietest ever built when they were first deployed in the late 1980s.

offensive. A further factor that was of major concern to the Supreme Allied Commander Atlantic (SACLANT) was not so much the current Soviet naval force levels, but the fact that the NATO nations were no longer numerically equal to their potential enemy in shipbuilding terms.

Another trend, even more disquieting, was the closing of the quality gap that SACLANT once enjoyed over the Warsaw Pact. This was due partly to the transfer of huge amounts of Western military technology that was freely available to the Warsaw Pact countries, but also to the huge resources that the Soviet Union had devoted to improving the capability of its naval forces. Each successive naval platform had far greater capability in terms of improved weapons, electronics and

an increased durability for sustained operations. By the mid-1980s, almost every unit in the Soviet maritime inventory was armed with a missile of some sort, including very effective sea-skimming anti-ship weapons.

Development of the Soviet submarine fleet in the 1980s was also impressive. In 1985, 10 submarine classes were under construction and two conversion programmes were underway. In fact, some of the submarine designs were not as impressive as NATO analysts believed them to be. One of them was the second Soviet titanium-hulled submarine design, the Project 705 Lira, known in the West as Alfa, which

came to light in December 1971, when the first unit was commissioned. Five more followed in 1972–82. A single reactor and turbine plant drove the boat at a phenomenal 42 knots under water. When British and American submariners first encountered Alfa, they were astounded, but what neither they nor the Western naval intelligence services realized at the time was that there was a serious flaw in the lead-bismuth system of Alfa's 40,000hp reactor cooling system. The plant was very unreliable, and the cost led to the Lira/Alfa being nicknamed the 'Golden Fish'. In addition, the design was not stressed for deep diving, as

During the last two decades of the Cold War era, naval strategy was dominated by the carrier battle group and the increasing use of 'smart' weapons.

was assumed in the West – with the result that NATO navies allocated massive research and development funding to the development of deep-running torpedoes.

## BATTLE GROUPS

The 'Oscar' class was a different story. The underwater equivalent of a 'Kirov' class cruiser, the first 'Oscar I' class cruise missile submarine (SSGN) was laid down at Severodvinsk in 1978 and launched in the spring of 1980, starting sea trials later that year. The second was completed in 1982, and a third of the class – which became the first 'Oscar II' – completed in 1985, followed by a fourth, fifth and sixth at intervals of a year. The primary task of the 'Oscar' class was to attack NATO carrier battle groups with a variety of submarine-launched cruise missiles, including the SS-N-19 Shipwreck; this has a range of 445km (240nm) at Mach 1.6. The biggest surprise of all was the massive 'Typhoon' class, displacing 27,357 tonnes (26,925 tons)

submerged. This was the largest class of submarine ever built, capable of hitting strategic targets anywhere in the world with its Makayev SS-N-20 Sturgeon three-stage solid fuel missiles, each of which had 10 200kT nuclear warheads and a range of 8300km (4500nm). The launch tubes are positioned forward in the bow section, leaving space abaft the fin for two nuclear reactors. The fin was capable of breaking through ice up to 3m (9ft 10in) thick, and the submarine's diving depth is in the order of 300m (1000ft). Six Typhoons were commissioned between 1980 and 1989; all were based in the Northern Fleet at Litsa Guba. Newer still was the 'Akula' class, the quietest Soviet submarine ever built, armed with torpedoes and anti-ship missiles, which completed its operational trials in 1985.

No one could have foreseen, then, that in less than a decade the Soviet Navy and the Soviet Union itself would be in a state of disintegration, its most advanced warships mouldering in their harbours.

## PUNITIVE STRIKE

During the last two decades of the Cold War era, naval strategy was dominated by the carrier battle group and the increasing use of 'smart' weapons. In April 1986, the US Sixth Fleet in the Mediterranean became involved in a brief 'shooting war' when, in response to Libya's growing involvement with international terrorism, its aircraft joined USAF F-111s in attacks on selected Libyan targets. Grumman A-6 Intruders and Vought A-7 Corsairs from the carriers USS *America*, USS *Saratoga* and USS *Coral Sea*, on station in the Gulf of Sirte, attacked a military barracks near Benghazi and the airfield at Benina. Throughout the operation, top cover was provided by Grumman F-14 Tomcats and F/A-18 Hornets, directed by Grumman E-2C Hawkeye command and early warning aircraft.

In 1991, the Soviets received a

**The McDonnell Douglas F/A-18 Hornet has been the principal strike aircraft of the US Navy since the mid-1980s. The latest version is the Super-Hornet, which is more powerful.**

**The Type 42 destroyer HMS *Gloucester*
accompanied by a Fleet Replenishment Ship and
an American 'Spruance' class destroyer during
the Gulf War of 1991.**

sharp reminder that Western naval
technology had not lagged behind. In
Operation Desert Storm Coalition

naval forces went into action in
support of a United Nations
resolution to remove invading Iraqi
forces from Kuwait by force. US Naval
Air support in the Gulf was provided
by the carriers USS *Independence* and
USS *Dwight D. Eisenhower* (both of
which were withdrawn before the UN

deadline expired), the USS *Midway*,
USS *Ranger* and USS *Theodore Roosevelt*.
The carriers' air groups comprised
squadrons of F-14s, F/A-18s, A-6Es
and SA-3s, supported by E-2C
Hawkeyes, EA-6B Prowlers and SH-3H
Sea Kings. The *John F. Kennedy* also
had two squadrons of A-7E Corsair IIs.

## CRUISE MISSILES IN ACTION

Of all the 'smart' weapons used in the 1991 Gulf War, the most remarkable was the General Dynamics BGM-109 Tomahawk cruise missile. Incredibly accurate, launched from warships in the Gulf, the cruise missiles were used to attack high-value targets such as command and control centres at the outset of the campaign. The air assault phase of Desert Storm began on the night of 16/17 January 1991, the attacks being directed against command and control centres, ministries, barracks and individual targets in the Iraqi capital of Baghdad. Outside the capital, airfields and air defence radars and SAM/AAA sites were attacked, as were NBC and conventional armament plants, oil refineries, and 'Scud' missile launching sites. All types of strike aircraft were used in these operations, supported by tankers, surveillance and countermeasures aircraft.

The US Marine Corps deployed squadrons of F/A-18 Hornets and AV-8B Harrier IIs to the Gulf.

## FIRST COMBAT

The first anti-surface vessel combat of the war took place on 24 January 1991, when Lynx helicopters from the British Type 42 destroyer HMS *Cardiff* detected three Iraqi naval vessels and called up US Navy A-6E Intruder strike aircraft. The Intruders sank a patrol boat and landing craft, and a minesweeper was scuttled to avoid capture. Three Iraqi Mirage F.1EQ aircraft, armed with Exocet sea-skimming missiles, were detected by the radar picket ships HMS *Gloucester* and HMS *Cardiff*. The formation was intercepted by two Royal Saudi Air Force F-15Cs, one of which shot down two Mirages. The third turned back. On 29 January, 17 Iraqi small craft, detected by an SH-60B helicopter off the island of Maradin, were attacked by Lynx helicopters from the frigate HMS *Brazen* and the destroyers HMS *Gloucester* and HMS *Cardiff*. Using Sea Skua missiles, the Lynx sank four vessels; 12 more were damaged in attacks by A-6Es and and AH-1 Cobras.

The next day, a Lynx helicopter from HMS *Gloucester* hit an Iraqi T43 class mine warfare vessel with Sea Skuas, leaving the ship dead in the water and burning. The Lynx also disabled an ex-Kuwait navy TNC-45 fast attack craft armed with Exocets, and damaged another Type 43. Four out of eight Iraqi fast patrol boats were sunk outside Kuwait harbour by A-6Es and F/A-18s, while RAF Jaguars and USN A-6Es attacked and sank three 'Polochny' class tank landing craft. On the 31st, a Lynx engaged an 'Osa' class missile boat near Bubiyan Island, again using Sea Skuas. The craft returned fire before exploding.

The Sea Skua proved its worth in the Gulf War, as did the well-tried Sea Dart. On 25 February, the day the ground offensive to liberate Kuwait began, the Iraqis launched two Silkworm anti-ship missiles at the USS *Missouri* in the Gulf. The battleship was accompanied by two 'goalkeeper' warships, the USS *Jarrett* and HMS *Gloucester*. A Sea Dart fired by the latter destroyed one Silkworm; the other Silkworm flew into the cloud of debris and crashed into the sea.

## MODERNIZATION PROGRAMME

The USS *Missouri*, along with the other three 'Iowa' class battleships, had undergone a major modernization programme in the 1980s, starting with the USS *New Jersey*, which was recommissioned in 1982. She began her operational deployment with the Pacific Fleet in March 1983. By the end of that year,

*Missouri* and *Wisconsin*, however, remained active, and both were deployed in support of Coalition operations in the Gulf in 1991. From her station in the Red Sea, *Wisconsin* fired dozens of BGM-109 cruise missiles during the opening phase of Desert Storm, while *Missouri* sailed into the Gulf to join other coalition warships shelling Iraqi positions in Kuwait. Initially, the warships fired from a range of 30km (18.6 miles), but once the threat from Iraqi Silkworm anti-ship missiles was removed by air attack, they closed in to 20km (12.4 miles), at which range their gunnery was immensely effective.

## DEFINITE PATTERN

The naval operations that took place in the latter years of the twentieth century, in support of United Nations-authorized actions in the Balkans, Afghanistan, Iraq and elsewhere, set a definite pattern for those that are likely to occur in the twenty-first. Sea warfare will never be the same again. The titanic mid-ocean battles that were a scenario of the Cold War will never be enacted. Instead, future naval battles will be fought along coastlines against developing countries or regional powers that present a threat to the international community. Carrier task forces, operating in conjunction with amphibious forces, will remain the key factor, while at the other end of the scale the nuclear missile submarine will remain an insurance against any dictator who might try to hold the world to ransom by threatening the use of weapons of mass destruction.

> Sea warfare will never be the same again. The titanic mid-ocean battles that were a scenario of the Cold War will never be enacted.

she had served as part of the task forces deployed off the Nicaraguan coasts in response to a crisis, and off the Lebanon coast, where she used her formidable armament to bombard Syrian anti-aircraft positions that had fired on US Navy reconnaissance aircraft supporting US Marine Corps units operating ashore.

As part of the modernization

The battleship USS *New Jersey* saw combat in World War II and ended her active service in the Gulf War. The holder of 19 battle and campaign stars, she was decommissioned in 1991.

programme, the 'Iowas' received new fire control and multi-functional radar systems; Tomahawk and Harpoon cruise missiles; and upgraded communications equipment, including WSC-3 SATCOM. In 1989, an explosion in one of *Iowa*'s 406mm (16in) gun turrets killed 47 officers and men; plans to repair the turret were deferred when it was decided that *Iowa* and *New Jersey* would be mothballed in 1991. In fact, *Iowa* was paid off in October 1990 and *New Jersey* in February 1991.

# Index